Oracle Insights:
Tales of the Oak Table

MOGENS NØRGAARD,
JAMES MORLE, DAVE ENSOR, TIM GORMAN,
KYLE HAILEY, ANJO KOLK, JONATHAN LEWIS, CONNOR MCDONALD,
CARY MILLSAP, DAVID RUTHVEN, GAJA KRISHNA VAIDYANATHA

Apress®

Oracle Insights: Tales of the Oak Table

ISBN (pbk): 1-59059-387-1

Printed and bound in the United States of America 10 9 8 7 6 5 4 3 2 1

Trademarked names may appear in this book. Rather than use a trademark symbol with every occurrence of a trademarked name, we use the names only in an editorial fashion and to the benefit of the trademark owner, with no intention of infringement of the trademark.

Lead Editor: Tony Davis
Technical Reviewers: Richard Foote, Julian Dyke
Additional Material: Mario Broodbakker
Editorial Board: Steve Anglin, Dan Appleman, Ewan Buckingham, Gary Cornell, Tony Davis, Jason Gilmore, Chris Mills, Steve Rycroft, Dominic Shakeshaft, Jim Sumser, Karen Watterson, Gavin Wray, John Zukowski
Project Manager: Sofia Marchant
Copy Edit Manager: Nicole LeClerc
Production Manager: Kari Brooks
Production Editor: Janet Vail
Compositor: Diana Van Winkle
Proofreader: Katie Stence
Indexer: Kevin Broccoli
Cover Designer: Kurt Krames
Manufacturing Manager: Tom Debolski

Distributed to the book trade in the United States by Springer-Verlag New York, Inc., 175 Fifth Avenue, New York, NY 10010 and outside the United States by Springer-Verlag GmbH & Co. KG, Tiergartenstr. 17, 69112 Heidelberg, Germany.

In the United States: phone 1-800-SPRINGER, e-mail orders@springer-ny.com, or visit http://www.springer-ny.com. Outside the United States: fax +49 6221 345229, e-mail orders@springer.de, or visit http://www.springer.de.

For information on translations, please contact Apress directly at 2560 Ninth Street, Suite 219, Berkeley, CA 94710. Phone 510-549-5930, fax 510-549-5939, e-mail info@apress.com, or visit http://www.apress.com.

Contents at a Glance

Contents at a Glance

Contents

Foreword

OVER THE PAST fifteen years I have worked for Oracle Corporation, and with many customers who were keen to find the limitations of the (then) current Oracle database on the latest and greatest hardware platforms of the day.

These customers have demanded ever increasing database performance at what seems a continually reducing price. In these fifteen years I have seen CPU designs, operating systems, and programming languages develop, become popular, become a standard of the day, and then fall out of favor and eventually become relegated to obscurity. The only constant, from my somewhat narrow perspective, has been the Oracle database and its continual evolution and adoption to new hardware and software architectures and configurations.

I have worked with many of the contributors to this book, who have either spent time in their careers at Oracle or have been highly qualified users and customers of the Oracle database. Each of the contributors can recount the number of bottlenecks they have uncovered in applications, databases, or operating systems, in the course of developing, rolling out, and managing leading-edge Oracle database implementations. These experiences form the basis of many war stories which I'm sure will be repeatedly be debugged and debugged again all over the globe.

On reading each contributor's story, you may start to see various patterns (or anti-patterns, as it were) emerging. Once you recognize these patterns, you can use them to avoid problems when building large systems. These are as follows:

- **Getting the application design wrong**
  It cannot be emphasized enough—if you do the basic things right in application design then your performance problems will be relatively minor issues. This is as true today as it was in the 1970s. Bad application design, and the resulting bad applications, starts from the data model onwards. Bad table designs yield bad index designs, which yield bad access paths. This can be compounded by suboptimal SQL, and very quickly a system consumes orders of magnitude more resources than anticipated and never scales to high throughput. This can be further compounded by poor use of database sessions, cursors, and application interfaces.

  Getting the application design right will make more difference to the overall performance than any other part of the system. If it is badly designed and implemented, the application will place unpredictable stresses on all system components or destabilize the entire software stack.

- **Not understanding the technology**

  In too many cases system architecture is done on a white board, with lots of cryptic acronyms and with little comprehension of how and why things actually work. In this way, many system architectures reach an upper ceiling for performance that is way short of the business requirements.

  I have often referred to these types of issues as *brick walls* that prevent a system from scaling. The term "brick wall" is very descriptive because if you ever run into one, you most certainly come to a halt (rapidly!) as well as feeling quite bruised and battered afterwards. These brick walls could range from basic errors, such as poor capacity planning, to core design limitations of any of the major software components.

  This classic example of a brick wall observed in database projects could be described as a "hardware wall." Consider when system architects specify disk storage by capacity and not bandwidth. As disks get larger by the day, there is great temptation to buy a few large disks resulting in little I/O connectivity bandwidth. As disks have got larger, their performance has not kept up with the rapid advances in CPU power. When I/O bandwidth is critical to performance, it is important to engineer it into the solution and make sure that CPU, I/O connectivity, and disk spindles are all up to the job.

  "Software" walls are more interesting to discover and require a more complete knowledge of the system architecture when deriving a solution. They are also much more expensive to fix in the long run. Some classic examples of software walls include

  - Building serialization points into an application

  - Running a suboptimal number of connections to the database

  - Failure to use share cursors correctly

  - Using single row operations when bulk operations would be optimal

  In summary, system architects hit brick walls to performance when they have not fully understood the technology they are using, or when they have not implemented it correctly. This applies to new techniques and features also. Remember, new features are not a replacement for good analysis and design. It still surprises me that the IT industry allows so many errors to be made quite simply by poor design, poor understanding of the technology, and poor implementation.

  If system architects were held to the same standards as today's bridge builders, aeronautical designers, and naval architects, where human life is at stake and designers are accountable for failures, I suspect we would see

fewer problems in production of today's systems. These engineers understand the limitations of the materials they use, they apply factors of safety in
design, and they understand the concepts of balanced design where there
can be no weak link.

- **Insufficient or irrelevant testing**
  Today's commercial systems are extremely complicated and today's projects
  really do not allow enough time for testing (the combinations and permuta-
  tions make it impossible).

  This is an industry problem that we will probably have to live with forever.
  The important thing is to make the testing count—by testing at scale and
  stressing the most important components of the system. This means fully
  scaled tests with realistic workloads. Workload simulation is not simple or
  cheap, but just because it is not easy does not mean it should be neglected.

  Testing is also an ongoing process. Components are always being
  upgraded and enhanced, so the testing process cannot stop after the first
  cycle. Likewise the testing process must be continually enhanced after
  implementation when true production workloads are fully understood.

  In the last 15 years I have seen the Oracle database grow up; from dealing with user populations of just a few dozen, to potentially infinite numbers (via the Internet), from database sizes of a few megabytes to tens of
  terabytes. I foresee no change in this rate of progress. There will be higher
  throughput requirements, on ever bigger databases, that need to be constantly available, as well as being able to accept new business-generated
  application challenges.

  The authors of this book have all spent considerable amounts of their
  career making the Oracle database scale to the next set of business challenges. The reader would be smart to learn from their mistakes as well the
  things they did get right (by luck or good judgment). I have always maintained there is no replacement for experience in this game, but learning
  from other people's experiences can certainly fast track your own ability to
  face the next big challenge.

  Good luck in all your efforts. I look forward to hearing about them!

  —Andrew Holdsworth
  Director of Real World Performance
  Oracle Corporation

About the Authors

Mogens Nørgaard is technical director at Miracle A/S (http://www.miracleas.dk), a database knowledge center and consulting/training/support company based in Denmark, and is the co-founder and "father figure" of the OakTable network. He is a renowned speaker at Oracle conferences all over the world and organizes some highly respected events through Miracle A/S. These include the annual Master Class (2001: Cary Millsap; 2002: Jonathan Lewis; 2003: Steve Adams; 2004: Tom Kyte; 2005: Tim Gorman), and also the Miracle Database Forum, which is a three-day conference for database people. He is the co-founder of the Danish Oracle User Group (OUGKD), the BAARF Party, Miracle Breweries A/S (http://www.MiracleBreweries.dk), and was voted "Educator of the year" in *Oracle Magazine*'s Editor's Choice Awards, 2003. He can be reached at mno@MiracleAS.dk.

I would like to extend my deepest gratitude and love to my rather small family, the fantastic, unmatched Miracle staff, the formidable knowledge sharing and friendship of the OakTable members—and not the least my incredible neighbors and friends in Måløv, Denmark. Thank you, friends. You make it all worth it.

Dave Ensor spent over 35 years in IT, almost all of it in a hands-on role as a programmer, a designer, or a researcher into the performance characteristics of specific pieces of software. He worked with Oracle databases for fifteen years in all three of these roles, also building a worldwide reputation for his ability to present technical material with both clarity and humor. Dave is co-author of the books *Oracle Design* and *Oracle8 Design Tips* and is an Honorary Oracle9i Certified Master. He holds undergraduate degrees in both Mathematics (1965) and English Law (2003).

Dave is now a volunteer worker with the Citizens Advice movement in the UK, interviewing and advising clients in addition to managing a small PC network. Much of his limited spare time is dedicated to motorcycling.

My chapter is dedicated to the many, many Oracle staff members who took time out to share their knowledge and insights with me. As a result of their work I came to understand what Sir Isaac Newton meant when he attributed his success to "standing on the shoulders of giants."

Tim Gorman began his IT career in 1984 as a C programmer on UNIX and VMS systems, working on medical and financial systems as an application developer, systems programmer, and systems administrator. He joined Oracle Corporation in 1990 and became an independent consultant in 1998 (http://www.EvDBT.com). Mr. Gorman is co-author of *Essential Oracle8i Data Warehousing* (2000) and *Oracle8 Data Warehousing* (1998) from John Wiley & Sons. He specializes in performance tuning applications, databases, and systems, as well as data warehouse design and implementation, backup and recovery, architecture and infrastructure, database administration, and light comic relief.

Love and gratitude to my beautiful wife Jarmila, my son Peter, and my daughter Marika.

Kyle Hailey worked for Oracle on and off since 1990. He started in UNIX support, ported Oracle version 6 onto Digital UNIX machines, worked in Oracle France on performance and support problems for some of the largest European customers and benchmarks, and worked in Oracle's kernel development group on performance issues. In between stints at Oracle, he worked at a dot-com and at Quest software developing performance monitoring tools. Currently he works in the Enterprise Manager group at Oracle. His personal tuning web site, including documentation and tools, can be found at http://oraperf.sourceforge.net.

Anjo Kolk is currently the Chief Oracle Technologist with Veritas Software Application Performance Management (APM) Products. Prior to that, he worked at Oracle Corporation for over sixteen years, mostly in the areas of RDBMS Performance and Oracle Parallel Server. During those 16 years he lived and worked in the Netherlands, Ireland, Japan, and the USA. During his time in the Oracle Server Performance Group, he worked with many different ISV's (Baan, SAP, Amdocs and so on) and with many large customers (such as NTT Docomo, and other Telco's) all over the world, helping to improve the performance of their systems and implementations.

While working on these performance issues he developed a tuning methodology called YAPP (Yet Another Performance Profiling method) whereby Oracle systems are tuned based on response times. He has taught many Oracle internals classes all over the world, is author of the well known and often cited "Oracle7 Wait Events and Enqueues" whitepaper as well as the http://www.oraperf.com website, and is a founding member of the OakTable network.

Dedicated to my father, my wife Astrid, and our kids Michael and Shaun.

Jonathan Lewis has been involved in database work for more than nineteen years, specializing in Oracle for the last sixteen years, working at consultant level for the last twelve years. Jonathan is currently a director of the UK Oracle User Group, and is well known for his many presentations at the UKOUG conferences and SIGs. He is also renowned for his tutorials and seminars about the Oracle database engine, which he has held in various countries around the world.

Jonathan is author of the acclaimed book *Practical Oracle 8i* (Addison-Wesley, ISBN: 0201715848), writes regularly for the UK user group magazine, and occasionally for other publications, including *OTN* and *DBAZine*. He also finds time occasionally to publish Oracle-related material on his website http://www.jlcomp.demon.co.uk.

Connor McDonald has been working with Oracle since the early 1990s. His involvement with the Oracle database started with versions 6.0.36 and 7.0.12. Over the last twelve years he has worked with systems in Australia, the United Kingdom, Southeast Asia, Western Europe, and the United States. Connor is a well-known personality both on the Oracle speaker circuit and also hosts a hints and tips website (http://www.oracledba.co.uk) to share his passion for Oracle. His most recent consulting assignment is also his most challenging one—the imminent arrival of a first child.

Thanks to my wife Gillian for her unending patience and tolerance, and to my mother Barbara—a budding novelist who is still bitter that I got published first.

Cary Millsap is the principal author of *Optimizing Oracle Performance*, and the lead designer and developer of the Hotsos PD101 course. Prior to co-founding Hotsos in 1999, he served for ten years at Oracle Corporation as one of the company's leading system performance experts. At Oracle, he also founded and served as vice president of the 80-person System Performance Group. He has educated thousands of Oracle consultants, support analysts, developers, and customers in the optimal use of Oracle technology through commitment to writing, teaching, and speaking at public events.

Thanks to all the usual suspects who have made it possible for me to prepare this work: Jeff Holt, Juan Loaiza, Anjo Kolk, Mogens Nørgaard, Virag Saksena, Dave Ensor, Willis Ranney, Gary Goodman, James Morle, Jared Still, Steve Adams, Gaja Krishna Vaidyanatha, Kirti Deshpande, Karen Morton, Richard Foote, and Julian Dyke. Thanks also to my wife Mindy, our boys Alexander and Nikolas, and my parents Van and Shirle.

James Morle has fifteen years' experience in professional computing and has been personally responsible for the architecture and implementation of some of the world's largest and most complex business systems, including a 3-node Oracle Parallel Server configuration that services 3,000 online users. James is a highly regarded member of the Oracle community, and is the author of the critically acclaimed book, *Scaling Oracle8i* (Addison-Wesley, ISBN: 0201325748). He is the co-founder of Scale Abilities (http://www.scaleabilities.com), a specialist consulting and training company focusing on aspects of system engineering related to building very large and complex computer systems. You can reach him at James.Morle@scaleabilities.co.uk.

To my wife, my children and my friends: Thank you for all your love, understanding, and support that keep me going.

David Ruthven has over twenty years' experience in IT, and has held both technical and management roles in systems programming, technical support, and sustaining engineering. David started his career developing text retrieval systems but since then has worked with Ingres and Sybase databases before joining Oracle in 1989. David's passion is to help customers develop successful applications through old fashioned software engineering techniques and the appropriate use of highly advanced software such as the Oracle database.

Dedicated to my wife Helen, and our daughters Gillian and Rebecca.

Gaja Krishna Vaidyanatha has more than twelve years of industry technical expertise experience working with Oracle systems. In recent years, he has worked in a product management role providing strategic and technical direction to application performance and storage management solutions for companies like Veritas Corporation, Oracle Corporation, and Quest Software. He worked as a consultant, specializing in Oracle Systems Performance Management and Storage Management. Gaja is the primary author of *Oracle Performance Tuning 101* published by Oracle Press. His key areas of interests include application performance and storage architectures for Oracle-based systems. He holds a master's degree in computer science from Bowling Green State University, Ohio. He has presented many papers at various regional, national, and international Oracle conferences and has served as faculty of the IOUG-A Master Class University. He can be reached at gajav@yahoo.com.

Thanks to all of my co-authors in this project. I have learned a lot from each of you and will continue every day forward. Tony Davis, you're da man ... thank you for believing in CTD and its mass appeal. Also, a job done well by Richard Foote and Julian Dyke in reviewing this and every other chapter in this book for technical accuracy and relevance. Brilliant work guys! Many thanks to my parents for the unflinching support they continue to give me and for the constant source of strength that they provide on a perennial basis. Thank you to all my friends who have supported me in the past year, which has been difficult in every imaginable way. Last but not the least, my heart and my gratitude goes out to my son Abhimanyu—your zest and thirst for learning is unparalleled. I derive inspiration from that every single day.

About the Technical Reviewer

Richard Foote has worked in the IT industry for nearly twenty years, a thought that Richard reflects on with a combination of both pride and growing horror. After immigrating to Australia from England in 1982, Richard obtained a degree in computing studies in 1986. In 1985 while still studying, he got his first IT position as a humble Cobol programmer in the Australian Public Service. What was to be only a temporary move evolved into a mini career in various public service IT departments, working mainly in IBM shops, first with hierarchical IMS and then with relational DB2. Roles included programming, project management, data modeling, database design, finally specializing in application tuning and technical training. In 1997, he joined Oracle, as a DBA specialist and trainer. In his first year he learned and taught many of the common "myths" surrounding Oracle that were popular at the time. After discovering for himself that these myths were actually wrong, Richard began his search for the technical truth and his quest to expose and dispel myths that surround the Oracle database. During his time at Oracle, Richard became regarded as one of the top DBA specialists and instructors in Australasia and won many internal awards. In 1999, he won the best paper award (along with Marcel Kratochvil) at Australia's OpenWorld for the ground breaking "Good DBA Bad DBA," which highlighted many bad DBA practices and uniquely combined a technical presentation with "theatre," rarely attempted before. In 2002, Richard left Oracle to become an independent consultant. He's currently president of the Australian Capital Territory Oracle User Group where he presents regularly. He can also be found regularly contributing to Oracle-related newsgroups and forums, where he still exposes myths whenever they appear. His other great passion is the music of David Bowie; Oracle is not the only thing that has a "Space Oddity." He is happily married with two beautiful children and lives in sunny Canberra, Australia.

Introduction: Oracle and the OakTable

by Mogens Nørgaard

WHO WOULD HAVE thought that a casual remark one evening in 2002 would lead to a press label, a certain degree of notoriety, and a string of invitations to talk and present around the World, and, of course, this book?

But that is what has happened. So let me dedicate this introduction to the history and members of the OakTable network.

Two things happened while I was still working for Oracle and managing Premium Services in Denmark: we invited certain Oracle "names" to visit Denmark, either to present a technical seminar (like Cary Millsap from Oracle's System Performance Group presenting his "VLDB" seminar) or to just discuss issues and problems with my people in Premium Services.

The Master Classes, Part I

I quit Oracle in 2000 and started up Miracle A/S. It wasn't long after that we ran our first Miracle Master Class, in January 2001, with Cary Millsap (who had by then started Hotsos). We invited a number of friends and acquaintances to the class, and they all stayed in my house in Måløv just outside Copenhagen.

That turned out to be really nice, although not too spacey. Several of the people invited had known each other for ten or more years, had perhaps even reviewed books for each other, but had never met. At some point the tradition of each guest bringing a bottle of whisky to the table was born.

When 17 guests are staying in the house, it requires some discipline, especially in the mornings. We had some initial experiences with Cary and Anjo that indicated we needed strict rules.

We (Anette Jensen and I) have two bathrooms in the house, called Water Park One and Water Park Two. In addition, we have my neighbor Peter's bathroom, called Water Park Three, at our disposal. Fifteen minutes are then allocated to each guest.

Each morning I get up and start waking up the guests in the right order. The combined result of late nights and jetlag can clearly be seen on some of the members' faces when they are woken up early in the morning. It can also be rather harsh for them to brave ice and cold at 6 in the morning in order to visit Peter (known as Naboo, a name James Morle invented for him) and Water Park Three.

Cary has gotten rather good at staying within the 15-minute limit (down from an average of 42 minutes). Anjo is a different story, and needs special treatment and understanding in the mornings.

During Oracle World in Copenhagen 2002 we also had to force a special guest, Dave Herrington, CEO of DARC Corp, to sleep in the garage (which doubles as Miracle's HQ), because of his incredible noise levels when snoring. People were falling out of their beds and getting injured, and we needed all available hands for the activities at the OakTable stand in the exhibition hall.

It was also during Oracle World in Copenhagen that another special guest, Susan Dorn, CEO of Ringmaster, proved that she was a very good shooter with my air rifle. I shall refrain from discussing the targets we used, except perhaps hint that some of them were in form of pictures, while others looked more like cans.

Anette Jensen deserves a special mentioning here. Having 20 (mostly men) staying in the house for several days can be a challenge for most, and Anette is handling it rather well, with a minimum of nervous breakdowns or fits. She's slowly undermining the grand tradition of bringing a bottle of whiskey by convincing (forcing, really) some of the members to bring red wine and chocolate instead.

The Name and the Table

At the Master Class in January 2002 I asked one evening if we shouldn't give this gathering a name. I had a couple of suggestions that were quickly shot down by the Americans (for good reasons), and then Anjo suggested that we name it the OakTable network, since we were always gathered around my solid oak table in my kitchen.

Two minutes later `http://www.OakTable.net` was a reality.

The table itself was discovered by an ex-wife of mine (while we were still married, of course) in a rather fancy store. Fortunately, it was on sale, so it was only expensive, not terribly expensive. It did become terribly expensive when I had to buy it a second time during the divorce process.

But the table has stood the test of time; it has been dragged around, and even transported to the Oracle World exhibition hall in Copenhagen in 2002 and to the Database Forum 2003. It takes between four and six men to carry it. There are pictures of selected oak tables on the web site, including mine, Cary Millsap's (which he built himself—most impressive), and Lex de Haan's.

Recently, Lex has started producing Mini or Mobile Oak Tables (MOT's), made out of real oak, and even branded underneath with the work "Oak." These tables measure about 15×10 centimeters and can easily be carried around for conferences. I have one permanently in my car, which obstructs my view to the speedometer.

Lex is incredibly good with wood, and he has even produced a special side table (made out of oak, of course) for Water Park One, with the universally acknowledged measurements 42 × 42 × 42 centimeters.

The Master Classes, Part II

So, the Miracle Master Class 2001 was with Cary, who presented the first version of the "Hotsos Performance Diagnosis 101" class there, and spent several late evenings with Anjo understanding the internals of Oracle latching and much more.

The Master Class 2002 was with Jonathan Lewis presenting his "Optimising Oracle" seminar, and we had to repeat that one because of the sheer interest in it. That was also the year when we had invited Klaus Andersen to speak during the Gala Dinner. He used to run the Oracle Education business in Oracle Corp., but had just become the new Managing Director of Microsoft Denmark. That proved quite interesting . . .

In 2003 it was Steve Adams (perhaps the most knowledgeable person in the world when it comes to Oracle internals), and in 2004 it was Tom Kyte, the master of http://askTom.rracle.com. As I'm writing this, it has already been decided that the Master Class 2005 will be delivered by Tim Gorman.

Three whole days of presenting to 50–80 people, including peers from the OakTable, is a tough challenge for most speakers. After his Master Class, Tom Kyte declared that he never wanted to see a database again. But it's also tough on the OakTable members. They're often sleeping on the floor in sleeping bags, staying up late talking and working on their laptops, and then they have to get up early in order to catch the bus for the venue.

The Database Forum

Each fall, usually in October, we also host the Miracle Database Forum, and the OakTable members are again invited. Usually they'll stay a day or two in the house before the conference, then we'll all go to the conference venue, and perhaps they'll stay a day or two in the house afterwards.

The venue is a real water park called Lalandia (http://www.lalandia.dk), except in 2002 when we had to use another venue in a Danish town called Middelfart (which, believe it or not, is close to another town called Strib). We also have a

Danish town called Tune, which I would love to use as a setting for one of our events, but I have yet to locate a building near it that can accommodate more than three people. It's a very small town.

A special case of the Database Forum was when we ran it in Sydney with great help and assistance from Steve Adams. Steve opened his house to all of us, found some very nice tables, and made us feel very much at home. His wife and kids actually moved out of the house in order to provide enough room for us!

The meeting around the Oak Table twice a year has led to many things. Many ideas are fostered, tested, discarded, or matured there. The networking is probably the most important component.

The Network

In and of itself, the OakTable network is just a bunch of people who would like to talk to and be in contact with like-minded people, i.e. people with a scientific approach (and enquiring mind) regarding Oracle's database technology.

If a current member suggests a potential new member, he or she is allowed into the network (or not) by the so-called Junta, which consists of Anjo Kolk, Cary Millsap, James Morle, Jonathan Lewis, me, and Steve Adams.

James runs the website along with his wife Elaine, and although it doesn't get updated with new content very often, it is useful at least for providing the links, names, and such. We also use it for the Challenge questions and answers.

The Challenge is something we occasionally run during conferences. Ask us anything (technical) about Oracle, and if we can't find the answer (whether it be yes, no, or a solution) within 24 hours, the person who asked the question gets a T-shirt stating that he or she beat the OakTable.

The Challenge, though, is not used as much as we'd like, probably because it looks as if we want to be challenged with questions to which we cannot find answers. The opposite is actually true—the purpose is to answer questions from anybody, regardless how "simple" or "easy" they might seem.

The Politics

How often have you heard the phrase "Oracle says that ... " or "Oracle Support promised ... " Well, most of the times it isn't Oracle as a corporation that "says" something, but an individual who has an opinion or an idea. I know, because I spent ten years working for Oracle Support, and it is indeed a strange feeling to hear one's own words later repeated as the words of Oracle Corporation (or at least Oracle Denmark).

It is the same with the OakTable. We don't act as a single body, but as individuals. Some (technical) views might be shared, but that's just lucky coincidence. There are no guidelines regarding the individual member's conduct or attitudes, except that ideas should be shared and guessing should be eliminated by constantly pushing boundaries.

Sometimes, though, some members of upper management within Oracle Corp. can get frustrated by private opinions expressed by members of the OakTable, and then we see (more or less subtle) attempts at controlling, limiting, or curtailing the Oracle-employed members.

That is, of course, unfortunate, but there's really not much to do about it. Sharing ideas openly between peers and striving for scientific methods is what the OakTable network is all about. On those aims there can and will be no compromise.

The Members

I recently read the book *Operation Certain Death*, about an operation in Sierre Leone by the British Special Forces. I want to make perfectly clear that in no way can the physical abilities of the OakTable members be compared to those of the Special Forces. In fact, not at all.

But somewhere in the book the author makes the observation that the Special Forces soldiers are all totally convinced of the maxim that anything can be done with two elastic bands and a piece of rope, if you think long and hard enough about it. In other words, never, ever give up.

That struck me as something I also have observed with the OakTable members: they all believe that there's always one more option, always one more way of looking at things. It might take a chat with another member, maybe even a Chinese parliament, but the idea of giving up on a problem really is not acceptable, unless you're ordered to.

So imagine bringing a bunch of people with that attitude (and a tremendous respect for each other) together for even just a few days. It's never boring, and you very rarely see them waiting on an idle wait event, as we put it.

Imagine standing on the cold, gray cement in the exhibition hall at Oracle World in Copenhagen, realizing that we hadn't paid for carpeting or anything, just 6×6 meters of cement floor. Well, it turned out the Intel guys had some spare super-quality Astro Turf carpet, but needed beer. It was Gary Goodman who brokered that deal within half an hour.

Then Johannes Djernes saw the BMC guys bringing all their advanced exhibition stuff in, placed in two crates that each measured 2.5×1×1 meters. Two cases of beers later we had borrowed the empty crates. Then Johannes went out and bought various bits and pieces, and within a few hours we had the tallest tower (five meters high) in the whole exhibition area. It was possibly also the ugliest, but people noticed it.

During the same event, James Morle fought like a lion to establish the World's Biggest Laptop RAC Cluster, using a NetApp filer, a Linux boot CD, and the laptops of anybody who happened to pass by. It was a huge success, but without the *Never Give Up* attitude of James and of others like Michael Möller and Morten Egan, it would never have happened.

One of the more memorable events was when a bus driver in Måløv decided that he would harass Anette Jensen, who was simply trying to park her car outside the house. He blocked her way so that she was stuck between another parked car and his bus, and refused to move (for whatever reasons—the only clue we have is that he had many tattoos).

Most of us were in the house and didn't know about this development, but Connor McDonald came racing in and alerted us, and about 10 seconds later the bus driver was confronted by 15 old, bitter, and twisted men who hadn't had too much sleep, and didn't really care what his problem was. They just stood there and watched him. He got out of the way fast. He didn't even know that Cary and Gary are black belts, that Jonathan and Julian Dyke both have solid military backgrounds. It was probably enough for him just to see the expression on Pete Sharman's face.

New members of the OakTable are still being added, with some of the latest additions being Connie Green (one of the true "fathers" of Statspack) and Tuomas Pystynen (who was one of the first members of the Kernel Testing Group, and later the RMAN group). At the time of writing, the number of members is approaching 50, and I have no doubt we will continue to add members with the enquiring, scientific, never-give-up attitude that is the hallmark of this extraordinary group of humans.

This is my salute to the brightest bunch of people I have ever worked with. Respect!

The Books

In the appendix to this book, you can read how James Morle came up with the idea of the BAARF Party while having a Larsen cognac. Well, that same evening we had dinner with Tony Davis from Apress, and that's when James came up with this idea of a press label called OakTable Press. Tony thought that was a splendid idea, and a few days later it was a reality.

The idea was to let OakTable members either write books or at least review books before they were published under this label. At least two OakTable members must review and OK a book before it can be published.

Sometimes it can be hard to meet the requirements. When David Kurtz (see Appendix for more information about David) wanted to write a book about People-Soft on Oracle, it was hard to find reviewers within the OakTable network who knew enough about both topics. But Wolfgang Breitling stepped forward and, with a little encouragement, so did I.

Connor McDonald's book, *Mastering Oracle PL/SQL*, became the first OakTable Press book, and hopefully many more will follow.

This Book

The present book—which I still refer to by its working title, TOTOT: Tales Of The OakTable, must have been a nightmare for Tony Davis (Tony is English, so he doesn't say horrible things about us, but he did at one stage quietly remark that he was now officially off the Apress production staff Christmas card list). Unusual in its concept and contents, he must have used a fair amount of convincing inside Apress. Getting so many individuals to contribute the various chapters must also have been, err, interesting. Thank you, Tony.

The idea of having a bunch of OakTable members contribute to the same book, with a chapter each, was appealing for three reasons:

- It would represent a wide spectrum of experience and knowledge.

- It would be a reasonable amount of work per participant.

- It would allow the OakTable network to share a lot of our stories (hopefully useful) with the readers.

I think we have achieved all of that, although it was much more work than most of us expected at first.

Many of the chapters take the form of a story, detailing a certain project with which the OakTable member was involved, the people they met, the challenges they faced, and the techniques, ideas, and software that they introduced in order to surmount those challenges. Some of the fundamental changes to the Oracle kernel, such as indexing certain x$ tables and sort segments, and having several library cache latches, have been made in response to the dire needs of the projects described in this book.

Some readers might be surprised to find that this book doesn't contain the usual "read all about the latest features of 10g" or "learn to use numerous new features and secret parameters in Oracle" party lines. In fact, some of the projects written about in the pages of this book happened ten whole years ago (or longer). What I hope you'll find, though, is that they contain "eternal truths" about software projects, use of databases, solid Oracle advice, and so on. Nothing you will learn here is based on theory. All of the material is solidly based on observation, prediction, experiment, and proof. The careful reader should be left with a very solid basis for acting quickly, convincingly, and correctly in most Oracle-related (or other database-related) situations, in his or her future.

There is a certain lack of "best practices" in the book. In the words of Cary Millsap, best practices set the bar at a certain level, and don't encourage people to raise it or question it, until the evidence becomes too vast to ignore.

Continuous study of worst practices, on the other hand, tends to push limits and boundaries, and questions conventional wisdom. This book is to a large degree dedicated to worst practices from which we can all learn.

Following is a chapter-by-chapter breakdown to give you a proper feel for what the book is about:

- **Chapter 1: "A Brief History of Oracle," by Dave Ensor.** In this chapter, Dave, the grand old man of performance optimization methodology in the Oracle world, gives a personal perspective on the key events that have shaped the way in which the Oracle database has developed, and the way in which it is used (and abused). It is packed with wisdom and insight but is also rather long. Life's like that sometimes.

- **Chapter 2: "You Probably Don't Tune Right," by Mogens Nørgaard.** Why does history repeat itself? Who will live, who will die? What is the true meaning of life? Why do Danish towns have such strange names? The answer to all these questions, apart from the last one, can be found here. In this chapter, Mogens yearns for a quiet, peaceful life where database systems are stable and predictable, patches are a thing of the past, and people don't all try to get on the fast lane of the highway during traffic jams. He argues that the only way to experience the first two is to build systems that are fully instrumented and tested, and that use response time-based performance optimization techniques. The only way to experience the third one is to move to Middelfart, in Denmark.

- **Chapter 3: "Waste Not, Want Not," by Connor McDonald.** Connor explains why most database performance problems are caused by unnecessary *waste*, by making the database perform more work than is necessary to achieve a task. This often arises when people try to build "generic" (e.g. "database-independent") applications. Once these design mistakes have been made they can't always be undone, but Connor shows that, with a bit of lateral thinking, you can successfully tune a database to acceptable levels even with one hand tied behind your back (and the other holding a stubby). [*Ed: "Stubby" is Australian for "a bottle of weak, flavorless lager" (allegedly).*]

- **Chapter 4: "Why I invented YAPP," by Anjo Kolk.** While stationed in Japan for Oracle Development, Anjo was trying to find a way to convince the Japanese developers on the project that it was a good idea to use *fewer* servers in the system. They said he was crazy, and perhaps there was some truth in that, but out of this was born the YAPP method, which was to revolutionize the way the Oracle world think about performance optimization.

- **Chapter 5: "Extended SQL Trace Data," by Cary Millsap.** On a dark and rainy Texan night in 1999, Jeff Holt and Cary were faced with a serious performance problem during a customer visit. They had heard rumors about an extended SQL trace facility in Oracle and decided to investigate. The rest is history. This is the story of how to turn a "simple," yet starkly overlooked, feature of Oracle into a global business, in the process forcing most competitors to change their ways. [*Ed: No box turtles were killed or injured during the making of this chapter.*]

- **Chapter 6: "Direct Memory Access," by Kyle Hailey.** One fateful day in 1994, Kyle met a man called Roger Sanders, and was sucked into the twilight world of Direct Memory Access. Some years later he emerged, battered and bruised (but with perfect hair), clutching his own fully operational SGA attach program. In this chapter he explains how and, more importantly, why.

- **Chapter 7: "Compulsive Tuning Disorder," by Gaja Vaidyanatha.** For the knock-down price of $39.99 (the cost of this book) the master Standup Database Comedian himself provides the first total therapy session for those people who don't know how or when to stop tuning. Includes psychological analysis, palliative treatment, and outlines your (long) path to redemption. All future sessions will be charged at market rates.

- **Chapter 8: "New Releases and Big Projects," by James Morle.** In 1993, James cut short his honeymoon to join a landmark project that would turn out to have widespread consequences for the customer and for several future members of the OakTable network. Armed only with endless determination and a winning smile, James fought against the dark forces of OPS and eventually prevailed. Peace was restored, happy customers wandered into the sunset clutching their rented toilet brushes. Aaahh ...

- **Chapter 9: "Testing and Risk Management," by David Ruthven.** Software quality and testing is something David knows about. As head of Oracle's European DDR group, which makes the decisions about what bugs to fix, or not, his acute observations and insights are more useful than ever in today's multi-component, multi-tier IT environments. David tackles his subject with a calm and measured approach, providing a refreshing antidote to the chaos and confusion around him.

- **Chapter 10: "Dreadful Design," by Jonathan Lewis.** According to Jonathan, an Oracle project is like a "duck faced with a 12-bore shotgun." If it's quick on its feet it might survive, with a just few grazes to show for it. In this chapter, however, Jonathan tells the heartbreaking tale of the duck that took every pellet. Not for the faint-hearted.

- **Chapter 11: "Bad CaRMa," by Tim Gorman.** Sometimes the cleverest people make the most fundamental mistakes. And when they do, the results can be horrifying. In this chapter, Tim describes a really bad case: a vision and design for an entire OE/CRM application housed in one table (named, appropriately enough, DATA). It stored data just fine, but retrieval was a problem that was never resolved. The company that tried to make the vision a reality paid with its life. . .

- **Appendix: "Join the BAARF Party (or Not)," by Mogens Nørgaard and James Morle.** The Battle Against Any Raid Five/Four/Free Party was founded in Birmingham because Mogens and James had had enough fruitless discussions about the inferior RAID-F technologies. This chapter is *definitely* the last word they'll ever mutter on the subject.

Although the style of the book (hopefully) will be seen as interesting, perhaps even entertaining, to read, the knowledge and experience documented here is not your "fast and funny tips and tricks" variety. The book demands a good deal from the reader, who in return will gain a deep understanding of the techniques and mindsets used by some of the best brains in the business.

Dear Reader,

It is with the utmost pleasure that I introduce the first writer, Dave Ensor. When I call him the former Jonathan Lewis; when I call him the oldest and bitterest man ever to set foot in the global Oracle community; when I accuse him of retiring for the sixth time; ... it's all because of my incredible respect for the man.

Dave's extremely deep understanding of the Oracle kernel, his world-class (and wonderfully twisted) brain, and his Monty Python-esque observations of his surroundings—it all combines into a light tower of the Oracle World.

Dave spent many years in Oracle, where he—among several other initiatives— created a group consisting of himself, Graham Wood (now the main architect of Oracle10g Manageability features) and an equally brilliant third person, whose name I have forgotten. The group offered several very useful utilities that could take snapshots of bstat/estat *reports, analyze trace files, and much, much more. They also created a product named Oracle Metrics whose aim was to collect every conceivable number, ratio, or counter available, store it all in a repository, and from that deduct the true meaning of Life, the Universal Installer, and Everything If-Then-Else. Compare that idea to AWR and ADDM in Oracle10g!*

So Dave and his merry men might be the true inventors of the Oracle World of Ratios that we finally are getting rid of now. But the really incredible thing about the group was this: Oracle employees could access a Forms 3.0 application (this was many years before the web) and order the products on tapes. A few days later the tapes arrived with the products on. It worked, and it rocked. So it's really only fair to say that Dave and Graham (and the third person) were the true inventors of the Internet. It wasn't, as most people are led to believe, former Vice President Al Gore.

After Oracle, Dave joined BMC for many years, and then retired. Again and again. The day Dave really, truly retires from the Oracle World, we will have lost one of the greatest thinkers we will ever have in our mist (sic).

—Mogens Nørgaard

CHAPTER 1

A Brief History of Oracle

By Dave Ensor

THERE ARE AT LEAST three good reasons why this chapter is not a complete history of either Oracle Corporation or even just their database software. Firstly this history is selective, and concentrates on the evolution of Oracle's database engine, especially aspects that are relevant to the issues raised in the remaining chapters. To that extent it can be viewed as a rather extended introduction. If at any point you are not enjoying the chapter and, like me, always want to get into the real subject matter of any book, then I would encourage you to skip to another chapter that looks more promising.

The second reason follows quite naturally from the first. My research for this chapter uncovered a number of interesting facts of which either I had not previously been aware or which I had forgotten. However, this chapter is written primarily from my own experiences and observations, just as each of the other chapters is based on the considerable experience of its individual author or authors. That is what Mogens Nørgaard (the Great Dane, micro brewer but macro beer consumer, part-time keeper of full-time goats, and owner of the physical instance of the Oak Table) asked for when he started recruiting authors for this venture, and that is what we all agreed to do.

Thirdly Oracle has a lot of history and it would simply not be possible to put it all into one chapter, or indeed one book unless it was a very large book. I started to hear interesting fragments of Oracle's early history while working for Oracle as a performance troubleshooter from 1987 to 1994. After joining Oracle I became interested in the way that the company was developing, and continued this interest from 1994 to 2003 during my time as an "Oracle expert" at BMC Software. It is worth noting in passing that the term "Oracle expert" can mean whatever you want it to mean, and I don't think that there was ever real consensus about what it meant to BMC Software. Despite this, or perhaps because of it, I enjoyed my nine years at BMC nearly as much as I enjoyed most of my time at Oracle. I spent my time at BMC trying to work out either what Oracle were about to do or what they had just done, and what Oracle's customers might as a result want that Oracle was not supplying. I was also encouraged to present the former at Oracle User Group meetings around the world and occasionally allowed to mention the latter at internal product planning meetings.

Working out what Oracle is about to do is essentially guesswork based on the marketing documentation that gives advance information for some future release, and on the very active Oracle rumor mill. Once the software has been released no guesswork is required, and many of the most authoritative rumors will be found to be less than completely accurate. As will at least some part of the advance documentation. What a particular release does (and does not do) can be established beyond reasonable doubt by installing it, firing it up, and running valid tests. The importance of carrying out well-designed tests is a recurrent theme in this book, and for good reason. Too many of the "facts" widely stated and accepted about Oracle are just plain wrong and most often this can readily be proved.

Of course if you do not have time to run and validate your own tests, then you have to rely on the opinions of others; just remember that these opinions may well have no objective basis. Shortly before the release of Oracle9i it was my "pleasure" to attend a presentation on Oracle9i New Features delivered by a self-professed Oracle expert. The audience were somewhat taken aback when the speaker introduced the topic by saying that he had no access to Oracle9i itself, nor had he seen or read any Oracle9i documentation, but that his presentation was based on research he had performed by reading magazine articles on the subject. One of the unwritten rules of membership of the OakTable is that the members have good solid proofs for their "opinions"; that particular "expert" is not a member.

Oracle documentation is not universally accurate, but it is a great place to start on almost any technical issue. For much of my time at BMC both my company laptop and my personal machine at home had their home web pages set to the index page of the latest Oracle database documentation set. It is entirely up to you whether or not that makes me a sad person, but what does make me sad is hearing an (alleged) "Oracle expert" answering complex questions about Oracle without either referring to the doc or running any tests.

But back to the history, and to the documentation. The way that a company sets out its doc, and the things that it chooses to disclose, along with the things that it tries to hide, can tell us a lot about how the company sees itself and wants us to see its products. This chapter is a history written by a technician. If you'd like a rather different take on Oracle history, then I recommend Mike Wilson's, *The Difference between God and Larry Ellison* (originally published by William Morrow, ISBN 068816353X, although in January 2004 Amazon.com were also listing a later edition published by HarperBusiness, ISBN 0060008768).

The key difference, according to the cover of the book, is that "God does not think that he is Larry Ellison." Mike Wilson is a journalist and I read the earlier edition with great interest and enjoyment. Unusually for anything written by a journalist, almost every reported fact about which I had prior knowledge seemed to me to be substantially correct. As I hinted above this, sadly, is not true of either Oracle's own documentation or of many of the books by "Oracle experts." Sources of information about Oracle often tell the reader more about what the author finds convenient to believe than they do about how Oracle really works. If you regard each book about Oracle as another version of the truth, then the books become rather like Oracle itself—there can be several versions in use at one and the same time, and it may be absurdly difficult to determine the best one for any given purpose. Of course with the software, once you have taken the trouble to determine which version will best meet your needs you may well find that you cannot have it. It may not yet have been released on your chosen hardware, or it may now be a superseded release (or, in some cases, both of these).

Before the Relational Model

In the early days of computing all bulk storage was serial, so that processing a file or (as IBM called it) a "data set" meant starting at the beginning and reading all the way through until either the program had found all the records it wanted or it had reached the end. The classic medium was the 2400-foot reel of half inch wide magnetic tape though the earliest equipment used either punched cards or paper tape (or both).

....

Media Madness I

At one point in the mid 1970s a multinational research organization had an operations center in Germany whose machine room contained 11 almost identical computers, each with either a card reader or paper tape reader as its input device and each with either a card punch or paper tape punch as its output device. Unfortunately each machine that had card input was equipped with paper tape output, and each machine that had paper tape input was blessed with card output.

Most commercial sites, however, did manage to decide on just one of the two paper media and to make reasonably consistent use of it though towards the end of the punched card era IBM had the brilliant notion of using different shaped cards on different product lines.

....

So far so good, but the requirement to process data serially with only a severely limited number of devices led programmers to create highly complex records. As an example, a typical payroll application in the late 1950s or early

1960s would have an employee file on magnetic tape and each tape record would contain the entire payroll data for that employee. When the time came to run the payroll at least two tape drives were needed: one carried last week's payroll master file, the other was used to write a new payroll master file. A third device, which might be a tape drive or might read one of the paper media, provided this week's payroll updates giving details such as hires and fires, hours worked per employee, absences, and so on.

NOTE *Rolling back was almost the only part of this kind of processing that was easy to arrange. Reversing out a run could be as simple as throwing away the new master tape, or more likely rewinding it back to the beginning and over-writing it.*

Sorting was a big feature of this kind of processing, but my overriding memory of those days is the extreme complexity of the record structures. A file containing all the updates for a payroll might have over 100 distinct record types with little in common other than the employee's payroll number and the effective date. The main payroll record would often contain any number of sub-records, and each sub-record might appear any number of times and itself contain repeating sub-records. Sub-fields were also common, so a time field might be defined as six characters long with HOUR, MINUTE, and SECOND each as two-character subfields.

The limitations of serial devices, such as magnetic tapes, were evident right from the earliest days of the computer industry, and both the computer suppliers and their customers could see the benefits of being able to get quick access to the required records and only the required records. Currently the standard solution for instant access to a permanent data store is to use rotating disks with a read/write head that moves across the disk surface to the required track. The time taken for the disk heads to move to the correct track is "seek latency" and the time taken for the correct sector to then appear under the head is "rotational latency." Throughout this book any reference to "disk" or to a "disk drive" can safely be taken to refer to a device that incurs both of these types of latency, which typically add about 10 msec (one hundredth of a second) to each disk read or write. At the high end of the market solid-state stores are available, offering much lower access latency at much higher cost.

Large and highly complex record structures were almost inevitable in a tape-based application. They were regarded as a necessary evil even though their complexity was a common cause of application bugs, many of which caused record corruptions that were not detected for several weeks or months by which time it was all but impossible to repair them. These large composite records were necessary to allow tape-based systems to function, but became a liability when disk drives started to become available in the mid 1960s.

For example, each process step in a payroll system uses only quite a small part of the total data held for each employee, and the same observation was even more true for order processing and accounting systems. Worse, effective access to a specific record on demand required the programmer to provide the record number within the data set or to have some form of index in which the program could look up a key such as an employee's payroll number. The reference to record numbers is entirely deliberate; the majority of early systems that gave random access required the use of fixed length records. Both disk space and memory space were limited, and the extreme maximum length of the composite record structures made it impossible to consider rendering them as fixed length. It was around this time that *normalization* entered the vocabulary of the designers of commercial applications, and it was found that abandoning composite records removed a major source of programming and design errors. Unfortunately the new data structures with parent/child record structures required careful navigation from one record type to another to acquire all of the data to perform some processing step such as printing a pay slip. Worse it was all too easy to perform a partial update either through program failure, or fatal hardware or software error.

Initial file indexing schemes only allowed one key per file, but application architects soon saw the advantages of being able to search quickly on any one of a range of keys. In the early days of indexed files this was often achieved by having a second file that contained only the secondary key and record number from the first file, and indexing this second file on the secondary key. Not only was the application programming team fully responsible for the navigation of the structure for retrieval, they were also responsible for ensuring that the second file was updated each time in sync with the first file. It should come as no surprise to readers that this was another source of much error.

Media Madness II

Many of the early attempts at random access stores took the form of drums rather than disks, and for some time both disks and drums had a fixed read/write head for each track. Recording densities were low and in the early 1970s device capacity was rarely much greater than 10MB. It was clear that security agencies would need an enormous number of such devices if they were to have instant access to all of their intelligence data.

One proposed solution was to hold the data on short lengths of tape in a large magazine, and provide a drum store with an index to the data. The index would tell a servo mechanism which piece of tape to fetch, and that length of tape would be wound onto a drum for "instant" access. Had the device ever worked then its latency would have been several seconds, but still much shorter than reading all the way through a conventional reel of tape to find the required record. The project name was Oracle and Larry Ellison was part of the project team reporting to Bob Miner, who later stated that he could not recollect ever having given Larry a direct instruction that was obeyed.

There were other difficulties, including the problem of ensuring that every program used exactly the same specification as all other specifications for each file that it accessed. This was traditionally addressed by the use of *copy books*, code templates that contained the definitions of the file records. Even when these were correctly used it was difficult to ensure that all the affected programs were recompiled each time a file definition was changed. In 1967 the author was one of a team of 50 programmers working on an online application that was sustaining between 10 and 20 file layout changes per day; code stability was a myth despite extensive catalogs and procedures.

Early RDBMS Implementations

The problems discussed previously are easy to identify with the luxury of over thirty years of perfect hindsight, but even in the late 1960s there were a number of people in the computer industry who could see that there had to be a better way both of cataloging data structures and of accessing data. The database industry was born, but initial commercial products did not change the file paradigm, but rather concentrated on making its use more manageable (often *much* more manageable). However, responsibility for navigating the data structures remained with the programmer, and in most environments the program was required to specify not only which data sets were to be accessed and in which order, but also which indexes should be used to achieve the accesses. Any search for records with specific values in named fields required the programmer to code a search loop, even if an index was available. A complex query stretching across several related files (such as an employee, his attendance records, and his appraisal results) required a complex set of nested loops.

In 1970 Dr Edgar F. Codd (more usually referred to as Ted Codd) was working at the IBM Research Laboratory in San Jose, California. A graduate in both Mathematics and Chemistry, he had started to look at applying the 19th Century discipline of Relational Calculus to the non-procedural expression of data queries. Although both set theory and vector theory were already important issues in academic mathematics, the application of Relational Calculus to sets of vectors had been all but ignored until Codd published his seminal paper "A Relational Model of Data for Large Shared Data Banks."

It was to be over ten years before any applications went live that depended on a relational database, and these first databases were small even when judged by the limited mass storage capabilities of the early 1980s. However, Codd's original paper had clearly argued that the advantages of his proposed approach would be of particular significance to "large shared data banks." By the time of his death in 2003 the relational model, albeit with some ingenious adaptations, was managing multi-terabyte databases with tens of thousands of simultaneous users. We should credit his original paper with having made its point.

From Theory to Practice

His 1970 paper was both a manifesto and a clear signpost to a new direction in database technology, one in which pointers were no longer the primary mechanism for linking records within a database. Codd demonstrated that pointers could be replaced by primary and foreign keys to support relationships between records, but his mathematical papers most definitely did not represent a design that could be implemented. The world, or at least the small part of it that read Codd's 1970 paper, had a theoretical proposal for a new type of database that should allow much simpler coding of information access requests but had no detailed specification for such an engine. The theories were interesting, but they were just theories.

The first significant project created to put these theories into practice was the System R project, begun at IBM's San Jose Research Laboratory in 1973. The historical notes that follow on System R are derived from an extract from the IBM Research Journal at http://www.research.ibm.com/resources/news/20030423_edgarpassaway.shtml (accessed 15 Jan 2004).

In a brief history of Oracle, System R is perhaps most significant for the initial specification of the Structured Query Language (SQL), though it is worth remembering that this was originally intended as a *Query* language, and that to this day there are no effective standards for much of the Data Definition Language (DDL). However, when comparing Oracle to IBM's DB2, particularly in its original mainframe guise, it is important to note that System R expected database queries (in other words the SQL statements) to be precompiled, optimized, and cataloged ready for execution. In System R, and in the later IBM products, *ad hoc* query composition and execution was provided but seems to have been intended only as a means of allowing rapid development and testing. Also System R provided online data definition; in other words it recognized the need to be able to change the database structure without having to switch off the database service to query users.

Ray Boyce, who worked on the SQL language, also worked with Ted Codd to define Boyce-Codd Normal Form (BCNF). The advantages of Third Normal Form (3NF) were already known to a number of data designers including some of those working with conventional indexed files, but BCNF improved on 3NF and should be regarded as the minimum level of normalization acceptable in an initial database design. Many of the disasters described later in this book feature inadequate or incompetent normalization as one of their harbingers of doom.

The System R papers were in the public domain; Larry Ellison saw an opportunity when he read them and persuaded his then boss (Bob Miner) and a coworker (Ed Oates) to join him in a company that would implement and market a SQL database engine. They formed the company now known as Oracle Corporation and agreed that Bob and Ed would write the code while Larry looked after the marketing. Between them they were able to release the first commercially available relational database product in 1979. Twenty-five years later memories seem to differ on the version numbering. Chris Ellis, who was my boss in Oracle for over six years and a founding member of Oracle UK, told me that he had tried to run Oracle Version 1 in 1978 or 1979 and that it had not really worked. More recently the received wisdom within Oracle Corporation has held that there was no Version 1, and that Larry called the initial release Version 2 so that the market would view the product as more mature and established than it really was.

IBM announced its first relational product, SQL/DS, in 1981 but the release date seems to have been closer to 1983. IBM announced their flagship relational product DB2 in 1983 but again followed industry tradition for almost all new software by announcing the product long before it was ready to ship. This gave rise to the proud claim that Larry was fond of making in the middle and late 1980s that his database was "plug compatible six years before IBM built the plug."

Of course Oracle also conforms to the accepted software industry standard and is happy to announce both new products and new versions of existing products well in advance of these developments being ready to ship. To compound the misery and confusion caused to their loyal customer base, the initial releases of these much delayed versions are routinely shipped with major "negative undocumented features," more widely referred to as "bugs" (more on this later).

The key similarity between Oracle and the two IBM products was that all three used the SQL language. SQL/DS, IBM's initial effort, was only ever released under the VM operating system, and is hardly mentioned any further in this chapter. For some reason IBM keep changing the name of their flagship mainframe operating system, but if my memory serves me correctly it was still called MVS when DB2 was finally released. In the mid and late 1980s only moderate care was needed to code SQL queries that would run under the versions of both Oracle and DB2 then in use, but this little-used compatibility hid massive differences in the software architectures. To be blunt about it, Bob Miner had taken a number of short cuts in order to get a product to market as quickly and as cheaply as possible. A number of key design decisions allowed Ellison's tiny startup to ship Oracle Version 2.3, a fully working RDBMS, in the early 1980s. Many of these ingenious short-cuts, such as simply not allowing precompilation of SQL statements, continue to influence the product over twenty years later, and in some cases their impact on performance can be extreme if they are not understood by designers. However, before we look at these features we need to discuss why relational databases were, and remain, so different from the traditional alternatives of file-based, hierarchical, or networked data managers.

The 12 Rules

By the mid 1980s buyers had a wide choice of relational database engines, at least in name. Some of the early efforts had fallen by the wayside, either because capital was not available to exploit their initial market penetration (Logica's Rapport, for instance) or because they were "born again" products that relied on an unsuccessful relational interface to an earlier networked database. With care such an interface could be quite compelling and IDMS-R, perhaps the most famous of the born-agains, was still available from Computer Associates at the time of writing. Come to that so was Ingres, Oracle's most serious competitor for much of the 1980s. Ingres was and still is clearly an RDBMS, but many of the other products sold as relational in the mid 1980s were in reality just older database technology with a new name. As a result prospective buyers found it difficult to determine whether or not the product was truly relational. This mattered a great deal to a number of people, including both Ted Codd and the sales and marketing departments of the truly relational vendors, albeit for rather different reasons.

In 1985 Codd published 12 rules to which any relational database should conform, and these are discussed in the upcoming sections. As you will see, no relational database (not even Oracle) has ever fully conformed to all 12 rules and it seems unlikely that any commercial product ever will. This does not mean that Oracle is not a relational database (though every release is less purely relational than its predecessor), but rather that Codd was at heart an academic and was expressing a series of theoretical goals. In the years immediately following the publication of the rules, RDBMS vendors and market analysts used to write papers explaining how well this database engine or that new release conformed to them.

In parallel with this harmless but fundamentally useless activity, Codd engaged in vigorous debate with other mathematicians and industry gurus about the correctness and necessity of the rules, and more rules appeared at intervals. The rules are rarely discussed by Oracle practitioners these days, which is perhaps a pity. They give useful insights into some of Oracle's features and properties and can also help us to understand some of the performance difficulties routinely encountered. The original 12 rules are discussed in turn under the names that Codd gave them. The rest of the words are mine, and open to debate.

Rule 1: The Information Rule

All data should be presented to the user in tables, which Codd called *relations* in his academic papers. Tables contain rows or *tuples*, but there is no implicit or explicit sequence in which these rows are either stored or retrieved. All the rows in any given table contain exactly the same columns, and every column has three important properties.

Firstly each column should be scalar, meaning that it can only contain one value at a time. Secondly the definition of the table may not apply any form of redefinition to a column so, for example, it cannot contain subfields. Lastly the column name must be unique within the table.

Clearly a traditional Oracle table will meet the information rule, and equally clearly Oracle's object extensions violate the information rule by allowing the declaration of column substructures such as repeating groups. It may be helpful to look at this the other way round. The complex abstract datatypes introduced in Oracle version 8 are only required when the data has not been fully normalized, and we have abundant experience that tells us that rigorous normalization reduces programming errors and improves application performance. This issue was discussed at (much) greater length by Dave Ensor (that's me) and Ian Stevenson in our book, *Oracle8 Design Tips*. As this book is now out of print and almost nobody uses the object extensions I suggest that you just take my word for the fact that they are a bad idea.

One down, eleven to go, and Codd's first rule is looking good in that at least some exceptions to the rule can be shown to make data structures less usable.

Rule 2: Guaranteed Access Rule

Each item of data should be accessible without ambiguity. In a purely relational database this can always be accomplished by giving the table name, primary key value, and column name. This rule cannot be met unless every table both has a primary key and the uniqueness of that key is rigorously enforced. Pointers were a key feature (pun intended) of earlier database management software and most master/detail navigation relied on them. In the relational model pointers simply do not meet the guaranteed access rule and are not part of the scheme.

Pointers can allow very fast navigation from one record to the next, or the previous, or to its parent, or to its first sibling. That's the good news. The bad news is that they can get corrupted. A "pointer integrity checker" is a key component of any database that relies on pointers and in the early 1970s I had great fun coding one in PDP-15 assembler for the MUMPS hierarchical database manager. Detecting such corruptions is not especially difficult but takes time for a database of any size. Repairing bad pointers is much more difficult. If the pointer-based relationships are not also supported by keys stored in each individual record (mandatory in a relational model), then in general it is impossible to be sure of the original value of a corrupted pointer. Designs for purely hierarchical databases tended to omit these key values on the grounds that they consumed storage to no immediately visible advantage.

Even after fifteen years of using Oracle, it still amazes me how often I find tables that either have no unique key, or where there is a key that should be unique but the constraint has been relaxed "in order to make the system work." This usually translates as "in order to make the application fail later and in rather less predictable ways than if the constraint was enabled."

The usual root cause of later pressure to remove unique key constraints is that the original analysis work was incomplete, inadequate, or over-simplified in order to control costs and meet deadlines. An all too common example is that an application is built without having any ability to cope with the arrival of erroneous data. For example, an application may erroneously assume that every key that makes its way into the database from the outside world during the life of the application will be a valid key. Sadly your own organization is not the only one in the world that ships out bad data from time to time. As data warehouse designers become quickly aware, there is usually an unlimited supply of bad data arriving and demanding to be entered into your shiny new application. If your primary key structure prevents this bad data from being recorded, then the problem is with your design, not the data (because the need to record bad data could reasonably have been predicted). To expand the well-known cliché, shit not only happens but it is frequently necessary to record accurately and in some detail that shit has happened.

In the absence of any columns that use the object extensions, Oracle's Index Organized Tables (IOT's) do meet the guaranteed access rule (a primary key is mandatory), but of course they violate the Information Rule because they have an implicit sequence (the rows are ordered on the primary key).

Two rules in, and we (or properly Ted Codd) have established simple data structures, have made it impossible to have duplicate records, and abolished the troublesome physical pointer. So far, so good.

Rule 3: Systematic Treatment of Null Values

One of the great bugbears of programming prior to relational databases was that there was no convenient way of marking a value to show that it was not there. This was a particular problem with numeric fields, where 0 was liable to be ambiguous and so various artificial conventions were used over the years, most famously by Waterloo University in Canada in their fast Fortran implementations.

....

WATFOR

WATFOR was the standard abbreviation for The University of Waterloo Fortran IV Compiler, described in a January 1967 paper to the CACM (Canadian Association for Computing Machinery) as "a student-friendly variant of Fortran." This compiler generated code for a pseudo machine that was implemented via an interpreter, and in that respect was analogous to Oracle's original PL/SQL implementation. However, it was also very fast, a major advantage to a computer science school with many students and a single mainframe computer that was perhaps a thousand times slower than a modern workstation.

To help students locate one of the most common programming errors, WATFOR implemented a flag for every program variable that allowed the interpreter to tell whether or not any value had ever been stored in that variable. An error was signaled if any program tried to use a variable that had no value.

This novel feature led to much debate and consideration about using additional flags to hold properties such as arithmetic underflow, which would not be equal to zero, but would have a lower magnitude than any number that was neither a zero nor an underflow. Such proposals usually flounder when the designer tries to define a completely rational result for all possible operations involving combinations of the pseudo-numbers and real numbers. More than a little like NULL, then.

....

Oracle enthusiastically implemented null values from the outset but made the tragic mistake of equating the empty string with the null value. This caused many bizarre errors and "negative features" in early systems, especially when handling free format text fields for SQL*Forms V2. Equating a string that contains no characters to a NULL string was convenient to those coding the Oracle engine, who as a result could rely on every NOT NULL value having a length greater than zero, but in reality it was no more sensible than equating the number 0 to a null value.

Other than the string anomaly, Oracle's treatment of NULL values was pretty much "systematic" unless you believed the bit in the manual where it told you that index entries were never created for NULL values. Even before bit-mapped indexes (which do index null values) there was a strange anomaly in the handling of unique concatenated keys. In order to avoid duplicate concatenated keys in a unique index on (say) (SURNAME, FIRSTNAME) Oracle will assert that one key value ('ENSOR', NULL) is equal to any other key value ('ENSOR', NULL). Under any other circumstance Oracle will assert that it cannot tell whether one NULL value is equal to another.

Rule 4: Dynamic On-Line Catalog

Codd required a relational database to provide access to its structure through the same tools that are used to access the data. Oracle's data dictionary does exactly this, and starting with Version 6 has not only given access to the entire structure but has also been the definitive store for the structure. In earlier versions the on-line data dictionary was an alterative representation of a number of internal control structures held in pre-defined database blocks and also in table and index headers (space management data has always been held in internal structures in addition to being presented in table form).

By implementing the X$ tables and associated V$ views in Version 6 Oracle went a stage further than required by this rule and gave access through the query language to an ever-widening range of control and performance data. This is, however, a two-edged sword because although the V$ views present a huge amount of useful information, queries against them (especially joins) are capable of using prodigious amounts of CPU and, to a lesser extent, memory. If the server is short of resources, or the Oracle server is deadlocked for some reason, then these information sources may have unacceptable response times or be simply unavailable.

Also anyone using the V$ views should continually remind themselves that these views are simply not subject to any form of query consistency. The values returned are the values as they were at the precise nanosecond that the query engine visited that particular metric or property. The results returned from long-running queries that join multiple V$ views may contain any number of internal inconsistencies, and we have seen quite knowledgeable DBA's wasting huge amounts of time trying to reconcile such data.

So far so good on the Dynamic On-Line Catalog, but there are a series of issues with the design of Oracle's on-line data dictionary that require almost unbelievably complex queries to meet quite simple reporting needs. As with all other cases that I have seen where highly complex queries are required to meet essentially simple information needs, the root cause is that the underlying tables are not adequately normalized. It is tempting to infer that Oracle's recruiters, when hiring database kernel developers, do not put database design skills at the top of the requirements list but concentrate instead on a candidate's ability to code complex logic in C. It is less clear why exactly the same design inabilities manifest themselves from time to time in Oracle's application products.

Rule 5: Comprehensive Data Sublanguage

The only language currently used to meet this rule is SQL (Structured Query Language) in all its many and varied forms; each dialect is, of course, claimed by its vendor to be completely standard. A number of the early relational database implementations used proprietary languages such as Ingres with QUEL and Digital Equipment whose imaginatively named relational database, Rdb, originally used the proprietary language Rdo (Relational Database Operator). By the mid 1980s both these companies were re-designing their database engines to support SQL and their proprietary languages were quietly dropped. These data sublanguages are declarative rather than procedural. There is no concept of being able to sequence operations, no looping constructs, and no branching. Not even the CASE statement counts as procedural branching because it simply declares what the result should be.

The designers of the infant Oracle made exactly the right choice by adopting SQL from System R as their data sublanguage rather than spending valuable time and money on the design and implementation of a language of their own (we'll look at PL/SQL later). However, Oracle's SQL implementation has an extraordinary number of non-standard embedded functions and extended features, and the full ANSI join syntax remained unsupported until Oracle9i. As a result most join queries in Oracle list all the tables in a comma separated list, and then separately list all of the join and filter conditions in a long ANDed list. The tidiest coders at least try to achieve some correlation between the orders of the two lists, but this standard Oracle approach is much less readable than the ANSI INNER JOIN, LEFT JOIN, and RIGHT JOIN constructs in which each additional table is immediately followed by its own join conditions.

A key feature of the query language is that the result set is always a table even if this table has only one column and possibly does not have any rows, as in

```
select count(*) from EMP where SAL = 0
```

In general we will not be able to tell before issuing a query how many rows will be returned, though when used in a query without a GROUP BY clause, the aggregate function COUNT(*) is a special case that is guaranteed to return one and only one row if it executes without error.

In the preceding example we can improve the resulting table by giving its only column a valid column name, as in

```
select count(*) ZERO_SAL_QTY from EMP where SAL = 0;
```

With valid names on the returned columns, relational database queries have a property that mathematicians call *closure*. When we perform a valid query (joining any number of tables), the result is always another table though the table will not have a name unless we use a table alias, as in the somewhat tortuous

```
select XX. ZERO_SAL_QTY
from (select count(*) ZERO_SAL_QTY from EMP where SAL = 0) XX;
```

Given this ability to provide any query result with both a valid table name and valid column names, we ought to be able to use a query anywhere and everywhere that we can use a table. Originally Oracle only supported this through the view mechanism, which defines a query in the data dictionary allowing it to be used as a table (albeit with some restrictions, see the next rule).

Current versions of Oracle do a better job of exploiting query closure, though for some reason buried in the Oracle psyche they like to refer to a query used in place of a table name as an "in-line view" when really it is just a query, pure and simple. Of course Oracle also refer to an expression-based index as a function-based index, a semantic error that requires them to use the bizarre term "in-line function" to describe an expression in a statement such as

```
create index BOX_VOLUME on BOXES ( HEIGHT * WIDTH * DEPTH );
```

Because there are no user-apparent pointers, the query language has to use data values such as keys in order to achieve a join.

Rule 6: View Updating Rule

Because any query can be cataloged as a view, and should therefore be interchangeable with a table, Codd stated that every data manipulation operation that could be performed on a table should also work against any view (and any query). This presents some interesting logical challenges, and over the years Oracle has gradually expanded its support for the updating of tables expressed as queries.

As far back as Version 5 Oracle allowed the updating of some views based on a single table, and there is now limited support for updating join queries though it is little used. In later versions there is also the INSTEAD OF trigger, which allows any view to be made updateable by providing procedural code to perform the update. Unlike table triggers, which can only supplement (or prevent) the action of a SQL statement, view triggers define the entire operation that will take place. It is, for example, entirely possible to code an INSTEAD OF INSERT trigger to do nothing other than to delete rows, which is "unlikely to be what the application programmer expected."

Rule 7: High-level Insert, Update, and Delete

This rule follows on from rules 5 and 6 to state that INSERT, UPDATE, and DELETE operations should be supported for any retrievable set of rows. The rule is only satisfied in Oracle for operations against tables and updateable views as in

```
update EMPS set JOB = 'Data Executive' where JOB = 'DBA' and SAL > 100000;
```
and
```
insert into EXECS select * from EMP where lower(JOB) like '%executive%';
delete from EMPS where lower(JOB) like '%executive%';
commit;
```

We have got so used to the set-oriented nature of these SQL operations that this rule now seems almost redundant. However, twenty years ago programmers working in procedural languages were used to dealing either with data files or with database management software that required them to code record by record loops for every database change that affected multiple records. Sadly many of their successors continue to this day to code such loops. The negative impacts on both performance and maintainability can be massive.

Rule 8: Physical Data Independence

This rule states that the user (the person coding the SQL statements) should not need to know anything at all about the physical mechanisms used to store and retrieve data. For query and update operations Oracle completely meets this requirement, allowing SQL to be written with no knowledge whatever of the underlying hardware or software. One of the great strengths of Oracle over the years has been the ease with which an application can be moved from one server technology to another without any code change whatever.

The other side of the coin, however, is that Oracle's DDL forces the mixing of both logical and physical specifications in every statement that creates a physical storage object. This need to quote space management along with storage location attributes, such as the tablespace name, has caused considerable difficulty over the years for developers who needed to build portable database creation scripts. During Cary Millsap's time at Oracle his group developed the best practice statement OFA (Oracle Flexible Architecture) that allowed customers to change the physical location of Oracle data files without necessarily having to recreate the database. In Oracle10g users are invited to use Oracle's own file system, which is claimed to insulate them from such problems. However, the history of IT is that you can always spot a pioneer by the arrows sticking out of his chest.

Rule 9: Logical Data Independence

Codd insisted that the users' view of the data should not have to change solely because of a change to the logical structure of the database (in other words, the table definitions). Again the term "user" is not (normally) the end user but rather the user composing the SQL.

Oracle can trivially achieve this requirement for read-only data provided only that the required view of the data can be achieved by a query against the new underlying tables. This technique has been used by Oracle to aid migrations from one version of the data dictionary to the next by providing the new data dictionary with views that mimic the information sources in the old dictionary. This is useful, but if the old and new underlying data structures are radically different, then such "compatibility views" may be extremely complex, with severe execution penalties. Worse, if the new structure does not present exactly the same attributes as the old structure, then creating views to mimic the old structure can be misleading.

However, using views to achieve Logical Data Independence can work, and the data dictionary is a good candidate for its use because its tables (and views) are protected from direct updating. To preserve the integrity of the dictionary they must only be changed through DDL statements or Oracle-supplied stored packages. However, attempts to use this approach in applications that require the issuing of DML have been less than successful, which is another good reason for taking great care over data design in the first place.

Poorly normalized data structures can make application SQL statements extremely difficult to write. More than one programming team faced with this issue has tried to create a set of Oracle views to present a more easily navigated table structure, and to thereby overcome their coding difficulties through Logical Data Independence. Sadly the complexity of the views means that this approach carries a cast-iron guarantee of poor performance.

Rule 10: Integrity Independence

The data definition language, and therefore the data dictionary, should support the declaration of constraints that operate to maintain database integrity during updating. Before Version 7 Oracle enforced only two such constraints: the unique index and the NOT NULL column constraint. Version 6 allowed the declaration of additional constraints, but these were not enforced until Version 7. Each new Oracle version usually has excellent backward compatibility with earlier versions so most SQL statements that worked under the previous version will still work. They may no longer be ideal, and parts of them may even be ignored, but they will usually work.

Sadly Oracle drastically changed the constraint syntax between Versions 6 and 7. Any user who had coded constraints as a documentation aid under Version 6, or to get ready for the brave new world, had created DDL statements that could not execute under Version 7. The moral of this story, if there is one, is that it is usually best to avoid use of any feature that is known not to be working. Not much of an insight, you might think, but both Oracle staff and the corporation's customer often demonstrate an astounding degree of optimism about the reliability and stability of brand new database features.

Until Version 7 introduced foreign key constraints and check constraints the entire job of ensuring data integrity lay with the application. Not only are applications justifiably famous for containing bugs, Oracle also provides DBA's with handy tools like SQL*Plus and (more recently) Enterprise Manager so that they can "repair" the database without having to go through the application. Declarative data integrity cannot guarantee that every value in every column of every table will always meet every data integrity rule, but it can prevent a large number of user and application errors. This is a major reason why both users and developers keep asking for constraints to be disabled.

The constraint mechanism is also strongest when applied to data structures normalized to Boyce-Codd Normal Form. As we have already discussed, relatively few database designs conform to BCNF, and this may be another of the reasons that Oracle's declarative constraints seem to be sorely under-exploited by application designers.

Rule 11: Distribution Independence

This rule adds another dimension to Rule 8 on Physical Data Independence. To exhibit Distribution Independence it must be possible for (different) parts of the database to be physically stored on different database servers. This was a major issue when the rule was first proposed in 1985; although a limited number of applications such as airline reservation systems were by then giving wide area networked access to central databases, this could realistically only be achieved with carefully hand-crafted software running on the largest (and most expensive) mainframe servers then available. In most enterprises the combination of project cost and the politics of data ownership mitigated against the use of a single central database.

Media Madness III

As computers developed, both desktop and server technologies developed along the same lines. Everything got smaller, faster, and cheaper. In 1967 I was working as a support programmer in the Educational Psychology department of a Canadian University when we took delivery of a Digital Equipment PDP-9, then regarded as a reasonably powerful minicomputer. Finding that its single user operating system gave my team less hands-on time than each of us needed, I created a multi-user operating system for the machine which then gave reasonable performance to 4 simultaneous users. Current data servers routinely support several thousand sessions, with many supporting hundreds of thousands of sessions.

The CPU ran at 1 MHz, or a few thousand times slower than a modern PC, and the machine had an effective 40KB of memory, around ten thousand times less than a modern PC. We were also blessed with an 8MB fixed head disk with a latency of 7 msec, compared with a latency of about 8 msec from the seek head disk in a standard office PC.

For reading a single record, our 1967 fixed-head disk was therefore slightly *faster* than its current seek-head equivalent though to be fair the current device will offer about 10,000 times as much storage. So thirty-five years of progress in mass storage devices have given us 5 orders of magnitude more data that we might need to acquire randomly from each device, 6 orders of magnitude more users asking for data, but a slightly slower device.

Although a great deal of nonsense is talked about both data caching and data placement by people who should know better (but not, of course, by members of the OakTable), Oracle performance can often be improved both by decreasing the I/O load and by spreading it more evenly across more devices. Unfortunately these goals are not necessarily achieved either by increasing the buffer cache hit ratio or by putting a table on a different drive from its indexes.

Many things have changed since 1985. High-end servers have become much more powerful, cost much less in real terms, and are now capable of achieving high levels of availability while running under operating systems previously classed as "minicomputer" environments. Current server hardware and operating systems can support several thousand simultaneous users without the use of extreme software techniques, and the Internet is now available to link almost any place of business to a central server. The increasing deployment of n-tier architectures spreads the load, and with appropriate application infrastructure there will be little or no response time penalty to the users resulting from the database now being global rather than national or regional. All of these developments should reduce the importance of achieving Distribution Independence because we can make a case for never needing it.

At first sight it is tempting to also claim that Oracle already provides Distribution Independence through the distributed database features first introduced for query only in Version 5, and then augmented in Version 7 to allow updating. However, nothing in Oracle's current two phase commit (2PC) or partitioned table support allows a single logical table to be automatically partitioned across multiple data base servers without compromising guaranteed access. You can achieve guaranteed access with replicated tables because primary key uniqueness can be maintained, but if the table is partitioned across servers, then application code will be required to prevent two rows with the same primary key being inserted into different (logical) partitions of the table on different nodes. It is also worth noting that Oracle's customer base has been "less than unanimous" in its adoption of distributed databases.

At the time of writing it is unclear how fully the world will adopt the Oracle vision of *grid computing* disclosed by the Oracle10g announcements. It may be more Larry's personal vision than Oracle's collective vision, but it will take major customer investment for it to be deployed and Oracle's recent track record is not good. First local tactical databases were the future, then client server was the future, then distributed databases were the future, then the network computer was the future, then the database appliance was the future, and then Java code in the database was the future. None of these brave new worlds delivered on the claims made at the time they were announced. The market quietly ignored most of them though many customers who should have known better spent a fortune failing to get client/server to perform (it is architecturally flawed, and mathematically certain to fail in almost every case). Strangely, each of these failed initiatives shared one special characteristic at the time it was announced—Oracle's competitive position would be strengthened if it took off.

If the future of enterprise computing is that each global enterprise will operate a single (logical) storage farm against which (all) their servers operate, then distribution independence would no longer be a legitimate requirement. This would be highly convenient as distribution independence has thus far eluded database implementers. Finally we should note that if each discrete enterprise in the world provisioned database service from its own (global) grid this would not remove the requirement for distributed database support—that would require a single global grid!

Rule 12: Nonsubversion Rule

Codd's final 1985 rule was then, and remains now, a thing of great beauty. There was to be no back door into the relational database; you had to use the set-oriented database language in order to make changes. Codd's justifications for this rule may have been quite academic but mine are extremely simple: if there is only one way of adding, changing, or removing data, then these operations will always be subject to the same rules. If there are multiple different ways of doing something, then they may not all have precisely the same effect; Oracle's direct path loader is a clear illustration of this. Not only does direct path loading bypass the enforcement of integrity constraints, it also takes a different approach both to allocating space within the table and to making index entries for the rows added.

What's Missing?

As mentioned earlier, Codd's 12 rules form a useful standpoint from which to analyze Oracle's relational database engine, or indeed any database product. However, the rules say nothing at all about the linked subjects of transactional integrity and isolation levels. This is an area in which later refinements to the Oracle architecture got things spectacularly right, so it is worth spending a little time reviewing why these areas are so important and how Oracle addressed them. The 12 rules also say nothing about privilege management and enforcement, an area in which Oracle has arguably been less successful.

Transactional Integrity

Let's say that some transaction needs to make two inserts and two updates. It might need to insert a record of a debit against one account, to update the account header with the new balance, insert a record of a credit against another account, and then update that account header as well. If we have any dreams at all of our data staying internally consistent, then either we need to perform all four of these operations or none of them. That's why database engines have a rule that inserts, updates and deletes don't take effect until we COMMIT the transaction, and if we encounter an error, then we need to ROLLBACK. If our program just stops without saying whether or not it really meant its updates, then the database engine will deem us to have asked for a ROLLBACK and any changes we've made since the last commit will be carefully undone (unless, of course, we are in SQL*Plus which performs a COMMIT on exit by default).

All of this was perfectly well known before the relational era, and by the early 1970s commit processing was an important part of the CICS package for hosting online transaction processing on IBM mainframe computers. Of course as soon as the rules say that a program has made a change to the data, but that this change has not really happened yet because it is not committed, then you require some scheme to define what answers others might get if they were to try to access the data while it is in the process of being updated. That's where isolation levels come in.

Before we get there, however, it is only fair to mention that early versions of Oracle were based on some regrettable design decisions as well as the inspired ones. One little understood piece of Oracle trivia is that before Version 6 the database engine did not recognize the SQL statements COMMIT and ROLLBACK. In Versions 4 and 5, the end of a transaction was implemented as a direct database call rather than as an SQL statement and prior to Version 4 (1984) Oracle did not support these operations. Only quite recently have Oracle started to use the SQL statements in preference to the direct calls in their own code. Do not despair if you ever find yourself looking through a sql_trace file and cannot find any SQL statements that end individual transactions. Assuming that the application was indeed issuing commits (or rollbacks) you will find lines in the form

```
XCTEND rlbk=0, rd_only=0
```

and these mark the transaction boundaries. The zeroes shown follow the C language norm for Boolean values, so the preceding example is a commit rather than a rollback, and the transaction committed was not read only.

Isolation Levels

We've just seen that database updating can involve making many changes to a database that might be best viewed as an indivisible set of operations, a so-called "atomic transaction." You should be starting to suspect that this might be easy to say, but not quite so easy to achieve in practice, but unless you've walked down this path before you may be surprised to learn there is no single agreed way of deciding what other users should see if they visit data that is being modified by another transaction.

The relevant ANSI standards specify four different levels of isolation, numbered from 0 to 3. In almost any other industry they would be numbered from 1 to 4, but the numbering is perhaps appropriate as isolation level 0 does not give any isolation whatever. It is informally called *dirty read*. During my time at Oracle many customers asked for (and in some cases demanded) the ability to issue dirty reads because they could see that there would be performance benefits. Oracle's unvarying response, to their eternal credit, was that if they provided a means to enable isolation level 0, then customers would use it inappropriately, would find themselves relying on dirty data that would be potentially inconsistent, and it would all end in tears.

Oracle's default locking model operates at isolation level 1, which means that no transaction will ever see an uncommitted change made by another transaction. Each query sees the data as it was at the time that the query started (rather than how it was at the time the transaction started) so by default Oracle does not have *repeatable reads*. However, the genius of Oracle's implementation of its default behavior is that by using rollback data the model operates without using any read locks. When I joined in 1987 Oracle's most popular sales and support mantra was "readers do not block writers and writers do not block readers." This is still true today, and it is still a valuable feature in any multi-user system.

Prior to Version 4 Oracle had neither transaction boundaries (discussed earlier) nor support for read consistency; it was up to the application to place any locks needed to prevent queries from returning inconsistent data, and to remove these locks when they were no longer required. It is difficult to enforce such a scheme on application programmers, and if enforced the scheme severely limits the ability of the application to allow multiple users to run update transactions at the same time.

It is also worth noting that from Version 6 onwards Oracle has supported isolation level 3 for transactions declared as read only. Once the declaration has been made, then however long the transaction lasts, it can see all of the data committed before the transaction started even if the rows are subsequently deleted. This establishes repeatable reads. The transaction will also be unable to see any rows committed to the database during the life of the transaction, and this avoids *phantom reads*. Again this is achieved without Oracle having to take any read locks as the database engine uses rollback data to present the required view of the data. Unfortunately if a query runs for too long, then the user may well get an ORA-01555 error. Life is like that.

From Oracle7 onwards `SERIALIZABLE=TRUE` can be set at database instance level. Enabling this option means that every query takes a table level share lock on every table that it references, and these locks are held until the end of the entire transaction. With more than one session, these table level locks can seriously impede inserts, updates and deletes by other sessions. Furthermore, if query users neither commit nor rollback until they disconnect, then updating by other users is effectively impossible. Hardly surprising, then, that this option was quietly dropped from the documentation after a short and unhappy career as a published feature. Despite not being mentioned anywhere the feature remains available for use by the brave and/or stupid and has not even suffered the indignity of being prefixed with an underscore. In Oracle9i R2 its "description" in `V$PARAMETER` is its name. Life can be like that.

As discussed previously, Oracle's default query behavior in a read/write transaction is that each query will show committed data as it was at the time that the query started to execute, plus any uncommitted changes already made by the session issuing the query. If other sessions are active, then during the life of a transaction the same query may give different results at different times as a result of the other sessions committing changes. The reads are not repeatable and phantom rows may appear. In a multi-user system, this in turn means that if the database were to be reset to some previous state and the intervening workload were to be re-run with the same transactions being executed in the same order, then you would not necessarily get the same end result. So if you want to design a replication or recovery mechanism that will actually work, then you must capture the order in which changes were actually made to the database, not the order in which the input transactions arrived. I once had the "pleasure" of explaining this at great length to a project manager who then blew over $10 million of someone else's money on a project whose replication mechanism relied on serializability. He did this, he confidently told me later, because what I had told him "could not possibly be true." Life is occasionally like that but it happens more often than you might realize. A Texas-based energy conglomerate, later to collapse, had the same problem in one of their Oracle-based applications though it did not (as far as I know) contribute to their downfall.

In summary, as early as Version 4 Oracle had achieved the minimum acceptable isolation level (hiding both uncommitted changes and committed changes made by others during query execution) without having to take any read locks, and could therefore allow a table to be updated while other sessions were executing queries against it. Exploiting this requires a design that does not rely on serialization, and but few designs do rely on this. Just as well, really.

Enforcing Serialization

The main text explains why it is undesirable to set Oracle in serializable mode at the instance level if there is a high probability that two users will require to reference the same table at the same time. The longer either transaction will take, the greater the impact of serializing. However, because serialization appeals to some designers because it can simplify recovery issues, Oracle users sometimes ask whether they can achieve it in just one part of an application while leaving the rest of the application unaffected.

The simple answer to this question is "No, you can't—the rest of the application is still liable to be affected." Some projects have relied on using select ... for update for all queries, but the absence of a table level lock means that other transactions can still add rows in parallel, and phantom reads are likely to be encountered.

Privileges

Data is valuable, and needs to be guarded against both unauthorized disclosure and (even more seriously) unauthorized modification. The more accessible the data server becomes, either physically or more likely through network links, the more seriously the issue needs to be taken. Oracle have claimed that

Oracle9iR2 is unbreakable but the history of applications running under Oracle databases has also been a history of inadequate data security. There are a variety of reasons for this, but there is necessarily a series of conflicts between good security, ease of access, and ease of management.

Oracle Version 4 had named user accounts that could be secured with passwords, but the passwords were held in clear text in the table SYSTEM.USERS, a feature that some felt to be less than totally secure. In Version 5 the password was held in an encrypted form though the encryption was less than secure and to the author's knowledge at least two people wrote successful decryption programs. By the time that Version 6 came around the passwords were more secure, and each subsequent version has added further security features. Oracle7 added the comprehensively misunderstood ROLE mechanism which is at its most effective when the designer has made the seriously flawed assumption that each individual end user must have their own personal database authentication: in other words, their own Oracle username and password.

This assumption has been a fundamental problem in Oracle's approach to security, and the reliance on data-based security rather than application-based security has been another. As we shall see later on this chapter, only smaller systems can reasonably allow each simultaneous end user to have their own Oracle session. The efficient architecture for dealing with thousands or tens of thousands of simultaneous end users is to implement session sharing through some form of web server and/or TP monitor. As soon as this is done the detailed enforcement of data security must pass from the database server to the application servers. Secondly there are many, many cases in which access to a particular data object should be restricted to applications that have been verified as processing that data in accordance with approved policy. As a simple example, a payroll clerk may well have the authority to update salaries through the production on-line application but is unlikely to be encouraged to use this authority while logged into SQL*Plus.

More recently Oracle has introduced the Virtual Private Database (VPD) feature. This allows blocks of procedural code called *security policies* to be assigned to tables and views, and invoked before any query is executed against that table. The security policy can interrogate the session environment and use this information to extend the WHERE clause to prevent the query from accessing rows that the session has no right to see. Despite its considerable sophistication, VPD fails to address architectures that employ session sharing.

A more intellectual weakness in Oracle security has been the failure to distinguish adequately between a named account such as PROD_USER or PAYROLL_MAINT and a schema such as PRODUCTION_DATA or PAYROLL_MASTER_DATA. The user may be expected to have access privileges to specified dictionary objects, but the schema is simply the collective name of some set of database objects that together form a logical database entity. Even the commonly used term "owner" is an unnecessary semantic overlay—a schema need be no more and no less than simply a schema.

Early Days, Key Decisions

Oracle Version 2 was implemented only on Digital Equipment's PDP-11 platform. The original model, the PDP-11/20, was designed in the late 1960s and spawned a long series of variants that enjoyed major commercial success. Although it was arguably the leading mini-computer of its era, the architecture was starting to show its age by the time that coding started on the Oracle database engine. One of the key limitations of all PDP-11's was their use of a 16-bit address space along with the prolific use of the high order bit of an address word to indicate indirection.

The net result of the addressing scheme was that once an executable had more than 32KB of code it needed to call overlays. These were reasonably well supported, but both calling them and returning control from them had significant performance overheads, so the baby Oracle database needed to run with an executable of less than 32KB. The hardware could support several times as much physical memory as a program could readily address, and a set of special registers allowed a program to address both a program space and a data space. Digital Equipment's early history of supplying computers for process control applications had led to the development of a multi-tasking operating system, RSX, which was particularly strong at inter-process communication.

Oracle arrived at an effective and elegant solution to their address space problems. Each application program would start a separate database engine process and these two processes would talk to each other using the inter-process messaging that was already available. The database processes would hold their control information in a shared area that became the Shared Global Area (SGA).

....

Names and Things, the Rules (Lack Of)

Oracle started life as a multi-user database, but around 1985 Version 4 was ported to the PC where (in the pre-Windows, pre-Linux era) it became, of necessity, a single user database. Realizing that there was no opportunity to share the SGA in this environment, somebody helpfully started referring to these memory structures as the System Global Area and the new name caught on without ever displacing the old name. Both names remain in common use today.

Since the launch of Oracle Version 6 there has been a similar issue with undo segments. The developers originally called them exactly that—undo was stored in the database in undo segments, and both these undo entries and the changes that they were capable of undoing were held in redo logs. Someone (I've never been able to find out whether it was Marketing or Documentation) argued that the undo segments should be called *rollback segments*. They won the battle but not the war. Oracle9i has brought us *Automatic Undo* as the replacement for rollback segments.

Version 6 also saw the birth of the SCN, which might be either a System Change Number or a System Commit Number. Clearly a session can make a potentially unlimited number of changes in a single transaction so it might just be important to know which of the two possible meanings you should assume in any particular context.

Then again there is Oracle's Multi-Threaded Server (MTS) feature, an interesting piece of software that I advise people not to run except under very specific and very rare circumstances. You may start to get the idea that this feature is not all that it seems when I tell you that it is not multi-threaded. Most people read the name and assume that it is multi-threaded, a truly understandable error.

Two names for the same thing, two things with the same name, things with totally misleading names. These things happen all the time with life in general, and with Oracle in particular. You should at least try to get used to them and not let them bother you. One approach is to regard them as interesting examples of techno-diversity, whatever that this.

So Oracle started right from the beginning with an architecture that relied on message passing between the applications and the database, and years later this "two task architecture" provided the basis for first SQL*Net and then Oracle Net, the latter being SQL*Net with a new name. This same architecture separated the user and database processes, and gave Oracle the ability to maintain its integrity by allowing the control structures in the SGA to be protected from user code.

 NOTE *Perhaps we had better make that "protected from code written by all but the most determined or best informed users." Over the years considerable effort has been expended by a large number of people to get access to the SGA and at least a few have succeeded, including some of my fellow authors. If you decide to map the SGA into one of your C or C++ programs, then I recommend that you make sure that your access is read only—it is deeply anti-social to alter the SGA while Oracle is running.*

You may recall that a key part of IBM's System R project had been the development of mechanisms for the precompilation of SQL statements so that they were ready for execution on demand. This approach was in line with the mainframe performance and integrity paradigms of doing everything possible to make sure that the application is ready to run, and that it runs in exactly the approved form and no other. The mechanisms required to ensure these goals cost a lot of time and money to develop, and also impeded ad hoc users.

In the mid 1980s, IBM was a world leader (if not the world leader) in the supply of feature-rich environments for the development and deployment of production databases and the applications that used them. Their flagship product was the hierarchical database manager and transaction processing monitor IMS, which was highly effective though daunting for application programmers and data administrators alike. Successful IMS database designs were closely aligned to the transaction processing needs of the application, often to the point of compromising the ability of the development team to code decision support reports. Ad hoc queries were effectively unthinkable, but there was a clear market demand for them among IBM's most important customers.

The solution, thought IBM, was to offer their mainframe customers two types of database engine: the hierarchical IMS for transaction processing and the relational database DB2 for decision support queries. In reality DB2 had inherited from System R an architecture aimed more at transaction processing than at ad hoc queries but, hey, this was marketing and the IMS software revenues had to be protected.

Enter, Stage Left, the PC

The need to be able to produce management reports was so badly met by hierarchical and networked databases that all kinds of desperate solutions were tried. One of the craziest was also from IBM, and involved building a computer so small that it would fit on a desk. The production systems would produce simple tabular statistics from time to time (the development teams could just about manage those if they were given enough budget) and then the important marketing executive (or his somewhat less well-paid secretary) would key the tabular data into a personal computer where one or the other of them could do whatever they liked with it.

We tend to forget now that the Wintel world was originally the property of IBM, and that they saw this low-value device as a way making their mainframe solutions more important, not less important. They "knew" that the PC would never be of any real use in its own right without a mainframe to supply the data.

Given the current web paradigm of PC's running browsers interacting with central databases through web servers and app servers you'd have to say that IBM Marketing got it right, at least in concept. However, Microsoft, not IBM, now control the PC market and it is the entire Internet or intranet, not just a single corporate mainframe, that makes the PC so powerful.

The company that was to become Oracle Corporation, on the other hand, had a very small development budget and needed to take the shortest possible path from where they were (little capital, no product, and therefore zero product revenue) to having a product generating revenue from the marketplace. One way of reducing the development load was to ignore all this inconvenient stuff about compiling and cataloging queries. Clearly the tables, their columns, and any indexes needed to be cataloged but with that done a suitably designed query engine has enough information to allow an application to present a query (or a DML statement) and request that it be "parsed." The statement has to pass two tests at this stage.

Firstly it has to make *syntactic* sense; in other words, it must read like a SQL statement with the right reserved words and grammatical constructs in the right places, so

```
get me ENAME out of EMP for everyone with SAL = 0
```

is syntactically invalid, and

```
select D.DNAME, E.ENAME
from EMP E, DEPT D
where E.DEPTNO = D.DEPTNO and SAL = 0
```

makes complete sense, at least as far as the syntax goes.

One of the convenient features of the SQL language was that a parser could tell whether a name should be a table name or a column name without having to look anything up in the catalog or dictionary. Assuming that it is being executed under an Oracle version prior to 7, when things got rather more complicated, we know in the preceding statement that SAL must be either a column or a pseudo-column, and that EMP and DEPT must be tables. Of course either EMP or DEPT might well be a synonym or a view, but provided it is a valid synonym or view then closure will eventually resolve it to a table.

Secondly the parser has to determine the *semantic* meaning of the terms that it has found in the statement. It does this using both the data dictionary and the construction of the references in the statement. For example in the preceding statement SAL is not a pseudo-column so it should be a column in either EMP or DEPT. If it appears in both, then Oracle will not resolve the ambiguity for us—it will simply give an error.

Once these two stages are complete the database engine knows what the query meant, but it does not yet have a plan for how it might go about executing it. Producing such a plan is usually called *optimization* though the term can be misleading. As those with any interest in Oracle performance know all too well, from time to time the optimizer comes up with an execution plan that is clearly less than optimal. Query optimization is a massive subject, but for the moment suffice it to say that Oracle Version 2 took a fairly simple heuristic approach using a series of rules, and the Rule Based Optimizer (RBO) was born.

The Rule Based Optimizer (RBO)

This section gives a short explanation of how (and why) the rule based optimizer worked. I use the past tense because as of Oracle10g RBO is officially no longer supported; we are told that it is no longer present in the code and it is up to you whether or not you believe this. Oracle's story is that it has been removed, it is bereft of life, it has gone to a better place, it has snuffed it, it is a dead parrot (sorry, did I write parrot, I meant optimizer). If you already know how RBO worked, then you might want to skip to the section "RBO, the Bottom Line."

RBO built a list of the tables that it needed to visit to execute a query. It already had a built-in list of the ways in which Oracle could access a table, and knew what data was necessary to make that type of access. The access list was held internally in a preference order that used to be documented. Even though different documents disclosed slightly different lists, the consistent message was that finding a row by being given its ROWID (pointer, the things that relational databases were supposed to get rid of) was best and doing a full table scan was worst. Having an entire unique key was next best, and so on.

So for each table in the FROM list the optimizer would check which access methods were possible, and would pick the table that had the "best" access method to be the driving table. It would then take that table out of the list, and work out which access methods were now possible against the remaining tables, and pick the best one. Once it knew how to access the second table it could decide how to join these two tables together, and proceed to the next table and do the whole thing over again. Any time that two or more tables draw for positions in the priority list then the one nearer the end of the FROM list would be used. Any time that more than one index on a table was at the same position in the ranking then the optimizer would use the first of these indexes that it encountered (often wrongly stated to be the first one to be created). The whole process was clearly not rocket science, but it was impressively quick in an era when processors were impressively slow by today's standards.

The decisions made for any given query were completely stable against everything other than object creation or deletion. Once the tables had been defined and their indexes had been specified then only some change to this structure (for example, adding a new index) could change the execution plan that would result from any given query. So far, so good, but even ignoring the fact that RBO never supported hash join the arbitrary choices that were sometimes made caused very real problems in the real world. Without going into detail, the main issues were that RBO had no concept of the selectivity of a non-unique index and also ranked fully satisfied keys more highly than partially satisfied keys. As a result it frequently picked the "wrong" index when accessing a table with several indexes, and also had a tendency to pick the "wrong" driving table for queries that needed to access what are now called *dimension tables*.

On the other hand highly normalized table structures rarely need many indexes. So provided that the data was normalized to at least BCNF and care was taken not to create unnecessary indexes then most queries in transaction processing would optimize to reasonably efficient execution plans. Decision support queries ran rather less well because this is the area where hash join can make a large impact. Overcoming RBO's habit of picking the "wrong" driving table required that the application programmers carefully coded their FROM lists in what was naturally the reverse order with the anticipated driving table last. That way, if the query that was the main focus of the query was ranked equally with a dimension table, then the main focus would be the driving table.

RBO, the Bottom Line

So here's a funny thing. This discontinued optimizer had at least three major advantages. It executed quickly, with a little help from the coder it gave efficient query plans for well-written transactional queries against well-normalized and well-indexed tables, and it was totally stable. Only the execution of DDL (for example creating a new index) could change a given statement's execution plan, whereas the cost based optimizer is at the mercy of the object's statistics. However, in Oracle's view there were good reasons why it had to go. Over many years it had not been updated to support new access methods such as hash joins, new object types such as Index Organized Tables, or new storage arrangements such as partitioned objects. And it had a terrible name for generating very bad query plans, though as we have seen this was often a reflection of poor database design.

What the World Wanted

The IT departments in most large enterprises were as poorly regarded twenty years ago as they are today. They spent their entire lives failing to deliver huge corporate flagship projects while departments all over the enterprise failed to meet their local goals because they had inadequate IT support. Many department or divisional managers believed that there was a simple solution, DIY (Do It Yourself for those who do not spend every weekend rebuilding your home, you lucky people). Proprietary minicomputers such as the PDP-11 with their incompatible operating systems were evolving into much more powerful machines such as the VAX-11/780, Digital Equipment's first true 32-bit architecture. Many manufacturers continued to develop proprietary operating systems though VAX/VMS was to emerge as by far the most successful of these. In parallel with this trend an ever increasing number of manufacturers were starting to offer UNIX servers to the commercial IT market.

Very few of these machines were networked in any modern sense, but they were capable of driving a limited number of character mode terminals. In the early days these terminals were linked through dedicated twisted pair connections but these were soon replaced by the beginnings of the modern office network. The application architecture (if it can be called that) was that each user ran their own session on the server with an application program that operated in a fully conversational mode.

In the interests of efficiency mainframe applications continued to demand block mode terminals, a much more demanding environment than character mode for programmers. Also in the interests of efficiency, mainframe applications continued to demand pseudo-conversational mode application dialogs. The secret of this mode is that whenever a response is sent to the user the application saves the whole of the context away in some special area of the server, and makes itself available to process a message from another user. All locks must be released each time the application wants to wait for user input, and all database contexts must be closed. In effect the program had to start again from the beginning for each user input. This was a very much more demanding environment for programmers than fully conversational character mode, where the program just paused in-line when it needed user input in much the same way as waiting for any other I/O operation.

Lastly (for the moment), in the interests of efficiency mainframe applications continued to use hierarchical or networked database managers such as IMS or IDMS to save overhead by requiring the programmers to code their own access to discrete data files. In any event the application program was entirely responsible for all data navigation, including decisions as to which index to use for any given query, in which order to navigate from one record to another, and for all of the loop control required to iterate through sets of records at each stage of the process. This was orders of magnitude more demanding for programmers than presenting a join in SQL and only having to cope with a single level of retrieval loop.

So what the world wanted was, in one word, *control*. In particular, divisional management wanted a cheap and effective way of meeting their tactical information processing needs. The market was offering servers that were cheap enough to be dedicated to a single tactical application along with simple low-cost terminals that could be linked up using a simple two wire connection (twisted pair). Applications could be written in fully conversational mode so that user errors were flagged as and when they were made, and by the mid 1980s high-productivity development tools were becoming available that offered huge savings on coding and testing. Oracle, along with Ingres and (later) Sybase and Informix, had arrived with products for which there was a "clear and present market need."

INSIGHT *So the original DB2, released years after Oracle Version 2, had an architecture designed for production jobs, ran only on mainframes, and was marketed as a decision support tool. Oracle was still using its low-cost start-up design that treated every query as though it was an ad hoc query, took an almost laughably simple approach to query optimization, ran on (relatively) low-cost hardware, and was being used for tactical production applications that took work away from IBM's mainframes. Both were based on IBM's System R, but at that time Oracle had the practical advantage of having just one product and no established revenue stream to protect. Strange old world, is it not?*

Evolution of Expectation of Ease

The few applications that were written to use Oracle Version 2 ran on relatively low-cost hardware but their creation required a programming team capable of writing in a procedural language. This was typically C or Fortran, though Pascal was used on at least one major project. I have also heard rumors about the use of a language called COBOL, whatever that was. Whatever the procedural language (but particularly if it was Fortran or COBOL, neither of which could handle memory pointers) the need for procedural code dramatically raised the cost of putting Oracle to use. This effect was much more severe in applications where some form of on-line user interface was required as even the simple character mode screens of the early 1980s were notoriously difficult devices to program effectively. Basic columnar reporting could be achieved in UFI (later SQL*Plus) with very little effort and Oracle also had the report production utility RPT.

A Shadow of Past Failure

The tool that became SQL*Plus in Version 5 was called UFI (User Friendly Interface) in earlier versions. Given that command line interfaces were state of the art at that time, the name may not have been as misleading in the early 1980s as it appears now. However, the original plans for replacing UFI were much more ambitious than anything achieved in SQL*Plus.

The command line user was to be given a powerful procedural tool for both ad hoc database manipulation and running packaged database scripts. In common with other DBMS vendors Oracle tried to create a procedural environment from scratch without fully considering any of the real needs of the users, the mathematical properties of the procedural language, or the difficulties of achieving adequate performance. The good news is that Oracle relatively quickly abandoned this effort.

Instead of becoming AFI (Advanced Friendly Interface) as originally intended, UFI evolved into the rather less exciting but more predictable SQL*Plus. By 1988, just three years after the launch of SQL*Plus, Oracle had PL/SQL. This procedural language owes its structure to the publicly funded ADA with a syntax extended to allow SQL statements to be embedded in procedural code in a deceptively straightforward way. Another major change was that PL/SQL ran in the database kernel rather than in a command line tool.

However, one tiny vestige of AFI remains in the Oracle product set to this day. AFI needed to allow the user to edit an ad hoc command of potentially any length, and the developers realized that the easiest way to do this was to pass the command buffer to the system editor. The AFI development platform was VAX/VMS and the standard text editor under VMS at that time was the venerable EDT. So the interface file was called `AFIEDT.BUF`.

Please accept my apologies if the name `AFIEDT.BUF` means nothing to you, but this book was originally intended for Oracle geeks and propeller-heads. All of these people are well-used to a file of this name appearing in every directory or folder from which they run SQL*Plus; because its name starts with the letter A it is invariably shown in any window before the file for which you are looking. If the UFI replacement had been called eXtended Friendly Interface, then this work file would presumably have been called `XFIEDT.BUF` and would have appeared near the end of any sorted list. We might all be much less aware of it.

....

It would be misleading to call RPT, and its support utility RPF, a report writing package in any sense that the term would be understood today. To my chagrin I became something of an expert not just at creating reports in RPT but also at troubleshooting them and I cannot deny that it could produce almost any fixed pitch, fixed character set report if the author tried hard enough. It could, however, take a long time and for any development team with C skills it was sometimes easier to code the report in C. RPT was definitely not the right tool for an end user who needed an ad hoc report. Their only hopes were SQL*Plus or the short-lived Easy*SQL, which arrived in the Version 4 timeframe (around 1985). The former required them to learn SQL and although the latter worked it had many limitations.

Oracle was being used predominantly for (smaller) on-line transaction processing (OLTP) systems and the company started to develop non-procedural tools to allow database tables to be queried and maintained from character mode displays with 24×80 screens. The initial efforts, Easy*SQL (again) and Fastforms, shipped with Version 4.1 though neither survived for very long. The big market breakthrough came in 1987 when reliable versions of SQL*Forms Version 2.1 became available along with Oracle Version 5.1.

Oracle's sales force now had a great business proposition to offer anyone with a budget anywhere in a large enterprise. The story went something like "If your corporate IT or MIS department cannot meet your needs for tactical applications then all you have to do is to buy the minicomputer of your choice. Oracle will run on (almost) any machine you buy, you'll need to buy a few character mode terminals and put in some wiring, and then you will be able to develop the application yourself using our high-productivity tools." In a number of territories, but especially the UK, Oracle had a killer strategy if the prospect expressed doubt about their ability to develop the required application; Oracle simply promised to do the job for them at a great price. Packaged applications already existed, but were not yet a major factor.

Whoever was to develop the application the customer was led to believe, with some justification, that they could forget all about the complexities of block mode terminals, the difficulty of getting themselves allocated a large enough share of a corporate mainframe computer, and the problems of getting high enough up the corporate IT development priority list. In short buying from Oracle was the easy route to taking control of effective service delivery for your niche within the enterprise. Despite competition from (in particular) Ingres, this "take control" message was a major market success. If you liked big commission checks this was a good time to be a member of the Oracle sales force; as one of the more successful sales reps from that era later put it, "We did not really have to do much selling, we just had to write down the orders."

As at least some of these tactical applications started to deliver results to their buyers, Oracle had reinforced the "expectation of ease" that had gained them these sales in the first place. Of course, the reality never quite met the expectation, and as we shall see much of the rest of Oracle's history has been their struggle to keep their technology ahead of the expectations of their customer base.

Even in 1987 there were a number of issues, though many of these caused Oracle themselves more problems than they caused the average customer. One was that although SQL*Forms was based on a simple paradigm that was easy for users to learn, it required a large number of keyboard controls, e.g., F9 for "I'd like to abandon any changes I've made to the data" or F10 for "I'd like to commit all my changes up to this point." Sometimes these controls used function keys and sometimes they used control sequences such as Ctrl+N for "next record." Each porting group had the right to pick which keys would execute which functions on their platform, and they asserted this independence by picking a different set of keystrokes for every platform. The average customer only had to learn one set of keystrokes, but on any given day an Oracle support analyst was liable to be asked a detailed question about any one of 50 keyboard mappings.

Another was that very few customers could install either Oracle or its tools unaided because the install scripts were, frankly, full of bugs. Fortunately the customers were running single tier architectures so all of the tools were installed on the same machine as the database. Unlike the keystroke problems, most of the

UNIX install script problems were common across all the UNIX ports so provided you knew how to fix the VAX/VMS install script, the C shell script, and the Bourne shell script then you were usually able to bluff your way through most installs.

The big problem, however, was scalability. For a variety of architectural reasons the Version 5 architecture could only support about 40 simultaneous sessions though for reasons that will be obvious to some readers the limit is often quoted as 42.

 NOTE *The cult book* The Hitchhiker's Guide to the Galaxy *by Douglas Adams introduced the interesting notion that the answer to "the ultimate question of life, the universe and everything" is 42. If you need to know more, then get hold of a copy of the book, or better still get hold of all five books in the misleadingly named* Hitchhiker's Guide *trilogy. These books are more amusing than this book, though not so informative about Oracle. And know this: while writing the books and the BBC radio series of the same name, Douglas Adams bought himself a MicroVAX 2, the most popular minicomputer for running Oracle Version 5, to use as a word processor.*

Users could throw as much CPU power or Oracle support consultants as they liked at the problem. Somewhere around 40 simultaneous users Oracle's throughput would degrade in a spectacular manner. The users had collided with what Andrew Holdsworth taught me to call a *software wall*, and the analogy is a good one. Colliding with a software wall is just like colliding with a concrete wall; it hurts and the best way of dealing with the problem is to avoid the collision.

Had it been the fashion in 1987 to connect to Oracle through a TP Monitor such as Tuxedo then this scalability restriction might not have been severe. However, SQL*Forms did not run under a TP Monitor. It ran in its own process and demanded a dedicated connection to the database for each simultaneously connected user whether or not they were active. Some applications forked additional connections to produce reports, so a really unfortunate customer could reach the scalability limit with as few as 20 on-line users. On the other hand, the Digital Equipment MicroVAX 2 was arguably the most popular Oracle platform of the era, and in its standard configuration would support perhaps 6 on-line SQL*Forms users. So for the average customer there was not much of a problem unless they foresaw growth. However, the applications that were likely to grow would need more powerful machines on which to run, and this would bring Oracle significant additional license revenue if only the software would scale. This was a severe commercial problem for the vendor as well as for the customers.

Not only did Version 5 have a critical limit on its scalability, a lack of instrumentation made it very difficult to find out what was going on inside the engine. Something had to be done. Something was done. It was called Version 6, and we shall look at it in more detail later. Right now it is only necessary to note that Version 6 immediately raised the scalability limit on the number of simultaneous users to around 120 and a series of sub-versions increased this to perhaps 250. The release of Version 7 increased the limit again, to perhaps 1,250.

When I performed an initial design review for the project described by James Morle in Chapter 8 of this book it was clear that they intended to support 3,000 simultaneous users and I realized that this was greater than 1,250. I've always been good at basic arithmetic. I suggested that they might want to consider using a TP Monitor to limit the number of Oracle sessions and the designer told me not to be silly—they needed the increased development speed that would come from being able to rely on having a dedicated Oracle session for each user. The expectation of ease was on its way to claiming one of its most expensive scalps.

Outriders Become Insiders

As news got around of the rapid and successful implementation of Oracle for departmental tactical applications there was a natural and inevitable conse-quence. Corporate IT divisions stopped saying that UNIX would never catch on outside the colleges and that relational databases were not suitable for prime time. They wanted in on the act. If they were completely wedded to the mainframe they achieved this not by buying Oracle, but instead by explaining to IBM that even if Big Blue thought that DB2 was for decision support this particular customer was going to use it for production applications. Whether IBM liked it or not.

Increasingly, however, the mainframe world was losing out to what had once been called minicomputers. VAX/VMS and UNIX servers were getting more power-ful though it was a long time before their disk drives approached mainframe qual-ity. The idea of one server per application or per logical database was also attractive to both end users and to those responsible for IT provisioning. The users liked it because at least if they were kept waiting it was their own load that was causing the problem. IT liked it because it eased the problems of mainframe scheduling which had become so severe that one of IBM's solutions was to offer PRiSM. This software solution partitioned a single mainframe and caused it to behave as if it were several smaller machines, each dedicated to a single application or set of applications. When the solution to scheduling your expensive mainframe is to tell it to pretend to be several smaller boxes then it is not a difficult conceptual leap to provision addi-tional applications by buying additional smaller boxes.

If the word on the street insists that it is easier to build and commission new applications on these smaller boxes than it is on the mainframe, then the cost sav-ing looks even more attractive. In parallel with these revelations in the corporate IT bunkers, previously happy tactical users were starting to learn unpleasant lessons. These server things that they had installed constantly needed all kinds of technical intervention. There were things called *backups* that were really difficult to understand and which seemed to have to be performed out of hours when the users should be at home with their families. Then there were new releases of the software that fixed things called *bugs*, but which arrived on stuff called *media* with an instruction to read a file called README.TXT but without a nice support person to install them.

The self-empowered divisional decision makers had made their point. They could get tactical applications up and running faster without any help whatever from Corporate IT. But if a central team was willing to take on the unpleasant production roles of keeping the application up and running, year in and year out, then it really would be rather foolish not to let them get on with it. In addition application requirements were becoming more demanding and the application horizon could no longer be confined to the department or the depot. To be effective Customer Relationship Management (CRM) needed access to all of the enterprise contacts with all of the customers and not just those made with local customers by local staff. Multiple Stock Management databases that held different specifications for the same stock codes caused severe problems in inter-divisional stock transfers. And so it went on. And on. And on.

Deployment of Oracle could no longer be handled as a local tactical solution; it needed to be a global strategic commitment. From Version 5 onwards Oracle's market success routinely created technical problems for the user community that Oracle had no real option but to solve. The company continued to provide real technical innovation in many of its solutions, but to suggest that the evolution of the database was either technically led or marketing led is to ignore commercial reality. Whatever Oracle themselves believe, the market was leading the company by the nose with the largest and most disgruntled customers in complete control when it came to setting the key development goals. Success can be like that.

Part of Oracle's collective genius was that they often managed to meet and exceed the customer expectations and demands with highly innovative solutions. In other words Oracle accepted the functional goals set by the customer base (and in a few cases by the competition) but took their own paths to achieving these goals.

The "Tipping Points"

The following sections discuss the key technical developments during Oracle's evolution from Version 4 thru to Version 10 (Oracle10g). I've called these "tipping points" because each of the features that I've selected for more detailed discussion meets either or both of the following characteristics. Most of the features were added by Oracle in response to (sometimes overwhelming) customer pressure, and many required major changes in customer practice or technique to allow them to be exploited effectively. As we work our way through these seven versions I'll try to give you a personal perspective on where Oracle were trying to head, what their driving forces were, and why Oracle took some of the more radical decisions.

The analysis is not completely chronological as some topics, such as Oracle's support for clustered hardware, are best looked at across a series of versions. If you want to skip straight to that story, then you'll find it under "Version 9: Real Application Clusters (RAC)." Similarly Oracle's porting efforts are discussed under "Version 4: Portability Across Platforms" but the discussion runs forward through other versions so that the complete porting discussion appears in one place.

Rather obviously, most of the features discussed as tipping points are genuinely useful. Features that have little or no benefit to the real world business of providing IT service find it difficult to qualify as tipping points. But there are exceptions, and as already mentioned Oracle's fifteen-year-long attempt to provide useful support for clustered hardware is discussed under "Version 9: Real Application Clusters." I hope that you'll read it, but if you would rather have a one word summary of the entire subject of Clustered Oracle, OPS, and RAC, then I can provide it here. "Turkey."

Version 4: Portability Across Platforms

Version 2.3 was a good product by the standards of its time, but it ran only on a PDP-11 and Oracle soon realized that this was rather market-limiting. Popular though the machine was, not every prospective customer either already operated them or was prepared to start doing so. There was also the revenue desire to be able to offer Oracle on more powerful machines where it could command a higher price. To get portability the kernel was rewritten in Whitesmith C in 1983 to produce Version 3. My information is that this version was less than fully functional but it did pave the way for Version 4. This time the developers adopted standard C, usually called K & R after Brian Kernigan and Dennis Ritchie, who first defined the language in the famous Blue Book.

The key benefit of the rewrite was that from Version 4 onwards the database engine was portable to any platform that supported C, provided that the operating system had a reasonably flexible file system and offered a shared memory region. It worked rather better if the platform also had a robust inter-process message facility, could instantiate processes on demand, and the hardware had an atomic "test and set" operation.

Test and Set

The Oracle kernel is, with good justification, rather fond of placing "pins" on database blocks and "latches" on internal memory structures.

The preferred method of ensuring that two processes do not simultaneously assume that they have exclusive control of the same memory block is to test whether the block is free, and if so to mark it as allocated, in a single hardware instruction that can never be interrupted. If two (or, more likely three) separate hardware instructions are required, then even with only a single CPU there is always a risk that in between the "test" and the "set" the process will find itself pended, and the next process that is allowed to run will allocate the resource to itself. This second process may then lose control to the first, which will assume that its test is still valid, and integrity is seriously compromised.

So even with only one CPU a reliable "test and set" operation is needed for safe Oracle operation. But starting with the Sequent Balance in the mid 1980s, Oracle has been routinely run on machines with many CPU's all accessing the same shared memory region and using proprietary mechanisms to ensure cache coherency across each of the CPU's. Operating in these environments without a totally reliable "test and set" is fundamentally unsound. Oracle's porting teams would implement the Lamport algorithm so that they could support the database kernel on platforms that did not feature the required hardware operation. This was completely reliable, but was reputed to have a significant CPU overhead.

The (sole) core development platform for Versions 3 thru 6 was VAX/VMS, an operating system that had (and still has) much to commend it but which also featured a few distinctly unfriendly characteristics. One of these was that both *process instantiation* and *image activation* took totally excessive amounts of CPU. On the other hand VMS allowed a process to call libraries that had more privilege than the calling process, and could run these libraries within the same process space as the caller. Oracle exploited this by permitting a "single task" architecture under VMS so that only one process was required in which both application and database kernel could run, with only the database kernel being able to see the SGA. On UNIX platforms the application and database kernel were always run in separate processes to protect the SGA so every call to and from the database incurred two process context switches. Fortunately this was the era of RISC processors and most of the UNIX platforms were capable of fast context switches; the VAX was a complex instruction set machine on which context switches were rather slower.

I have been unable to find out exactly how many platforms Oracle was ported to during the 1980s and early 1990s, but to those of us in support there seemed to be no machines of any size on the market anywhere in the world that did not have at least the claim of an Oracle port. The standard insult thrown at the UNIX porting group in those days by pre-sales support was "it takes you two weeks to get the database running on a new platform, and six months to release an eight page install doc that tells us nothing." In the Version 5 era Oracle were quite happy to issue (sell) porting kits to hardware manufacturers and to let them get on with their own porting effort. The business motivation was that this expanded Oracle's potential market without requiring scarce development effort to create the required OSD (Operating System Dependent) layer.

Some of these "external ports" suffered from bizarre omissions. Manufacturer porting groups were apparently empowered to make arbitrary decisions about what features to include and which to exclude. This freedom could be exercised even where the feature had no effect whatever on the OSD layer, and sometimes the omission would have a catastrophic effect on either or both Oracle functionality and Oracle performance. On one occasion I asked the lead programmer of a manufacturer porting team to explain the absence of a particular feature. He was able to give instantly the succinct, but deeply unsatisfactory, reply "we could not see the point of it so we commented it out." To be fair he did follow up this observation with "Is there a problem?" When I explained why the customer was suffering a 300% CPU overhead as a result of the absence of the feature, and he at least had the decency to say "Oh dear."

The extreme variety of ports served Oracle well in the Version 5 and Version 6 eras. Where overall IT service delivery in a major enterprise relied on 10 or 20 different operating systems from different manufacturers it was a major advantage for the Oracle salesman to be able to claim that their product would run unchanged on any or all of them. Subject only to the issues discussed previously of missing features in some ports, the claim was also substantially true. In my humble experience truth is not a universally consistent property of claims made by a sales force, so well done Oracle.

As the hardware manufacturers started to fall by the wayside and the majority of the proprietary operating systems withered on the vine, the number of Oracle ports declined and Oracle brought all of the porting back in house. That done, they set up cooperative programs with the key manufacturers to ensure that ports fitted comfortably onto their hosts and the manufacturers started to put new features into their operating systems (and occasionally their hardware) to help Oracle run better. Many customers were buying servers specifically to run an Oracle database, and it made huge business sense to ensure that the server was kind to the database software. So well done both Oracle and the hardware manufacturers. That said there have been instances over the years of particular manufacturers doggedly resisting a trivial change to their operating system that would have greatly benefited their Oracle customers.

It appears Sequent were the first hardware manufacturer to work cooperatively with Oracle to create a better database platform. As early as 1987 the two companies worked together to improve the performance of Version 5.1 on the Sequent Balance, an early SMP (Symmetric MultiProcessor) architecture. Around 1990 similar work was underway at nCube to make their MPP (Massively Parallel Processors) architecture more Oracle-friendly. These two companies were essentially self-selecting as development partners. At the time Larry Ellison held a sizeable percentage of Sequent's equity and nCube was then owned outright by Larry Ellison and Bob Miner. Sequent was eventually bought by IBM; nCube survived and now sells highly specialized VoD (Video on Demand) servers.

More recently IBM themselves have partnered with Oracle to improve their offering on UNIX platforms on which DB2 UDB was also available, but before leaving our porting discussion we need to look at Oracle's lack of success on other IBM-inspired platforms at either ends of the hardware spectrum.

Having been in Larry's words "plug compatible six years before IBM built the plug" it is hardly surprising that Oracle set their sights on the lucrative mainframe market. Oracle Version 5 was ported to both VM/CMS and MVS operating systems running on IBM mainframes (and compatibles) in anticipation of creating a major revenue stream of high-value licenses. In addition to performing the porting Oracle also hired support staff with IBM mainframe experience, including Jerry Baker as Support VP. Jerry's clearly and often stated view was that to get to critical mass on the mainframe platform Oracle needed to gain experience by running their business under Oracle on the mainframe. Oracle UK went halfway towards this by running their local applications on Oracle under VM/CMS but the real mainframe market was under MVS and Oracle's internal HQ applications continued to be run under VAX/VMS.

In any event Oracle's database server did not sit that comfortably under MVS and attracted a reputation of requiring much more than an informed edit of the install script to get it up and running. Although there were, and still are, a few customers for mainframe platforms, the bottom line is that Oracle is not a major force on the mainframe. On the other hand the traditional mainframe has long since ceased to be a growth area for IT revenues so perhaps the failure to win a significant mainframe market has not cost Oracle that much revenue in the long term. They have, however, spent a large pile of money not getting there.

The PC market was something else, and in 1986 Oracle Version 4.1.4 was available in a strong cardboard container open on one side and containing three ring-bound manuals and a set of floppy disks from which Oracle could be installed on almost any Intel PC with MS-DOS, 640KB of memory, and a hard disk. This packaging quickly became known as "The Cube," and was many people's introduction to Oracle. The software bundle included the development tools UFI, RPT, and Fastforms so this was a pretty cool product in a command line world with 24×80 screens, but fate was not kind to the Wintel port in the years that followed. Version 5 required (much) more than the then standard 640KB memory and required great care over memory configuration. Installing Oracle on the PC had become a battle, and one whose only return seemed to be that the customer could operate a complex multi-user database engine in single user mode. It was the emergence of Windows/NT 3.51 as a potentially viable server that brought Oracle back into PC ports to any serious extent though an OS/2 port was also available for a time.

The Wintel platform is now widely deployed as a server under Windows 2000 Professional and Windows XP Professional, and Oracle has the ports to match for all recent versions. However, although they are now almost trivial to install (provided that you have plenty of time) they still seem to demand more administration effort than (apparently) cheaper Microsoft equivalents.

At the time of writing the online Oracle Store is offering the Database Enterprise Edition for Microsoft Windows variants and for UNIX platforms from HP, IBM, and Sun (including Solaris x86) along with Linux on both Intel and IBM mainframe platforms. OpenVMS is still offered though only for Alpha processors so the VAX is no longer supported.

There is also a z/OS port—this is the latest version of Oracle under MVS as in the intervening years IBM have twice renamed their flagship mainframe operating system, firstly to OS/390 and from there to z/OS. Prior to being called MVS the same architecture had originally been known as MVT and then OS/VS2. In light of this we should be grateful that the Oracle database is still called the Oracle database after all this time, and that the version numbering has remained sequential. Having to refer to Oracle Version 8.1 as Oracle8i seems like a small price to pay in light of IBM's apparent compulsion to rename their key products.

Version 5: Subqueries, Tools, and SQL*Net

As we have already seen, Version 5 did not scale but it was useful enough to create real customer demand for scalability from the Oracle data server. As with each of these sections I've had to leave out many significant features, but three merit particular attention.

Subqueries

Oracle's SQL implementation has moved on a great deal since, but the key step in Version 5 was the implementation of *subqueries*, which were simply not recognized by the Version 4 parser. With both subqueries and views (which had been in Version 4) a SQL-savvy application developer could generally manage to extract the required data out of even quite a poor table design, and could code the cross-posting of data from one table to another as a true set operation.

Tools

Oracle's key proprietary application development tools from this era have already been discussed, but there were other important tools initiatives in Version 5. Right at the start Oracle had adopted the SQL language from System R, and in the Version 5 era they again copied IBM syntax where it suited them to do so. It is difficult to be sure whether these later decisions were simply convenient shortcuts or part of Oracle's planned assault on the mainframe market.

From Version 2 onwards Oracle had provided library calls to allow 3GL languages to execute SQL statements, but these libraries were less than convenient to call and justifiably unpopular with applications programmers. IBM, on the other hand, had developed a precompiler syntax that allowed SQL execution to be "embedded" in a 3GL program; the programmer still had some work to do, but the coding was much easier than using OCI (Oracle Call Interface). When Oracle built its precompilers it simply adopted the IBM syntax. Unfortunately IBM were primarily concerned with COBOL, Fortran IV, and their own proprietary PL/1 and had seen no real need to fully support pointers in their precompilers. As a result Oracle's call libraries continued to be the preferred interface for many C (and later C++) programmers. This was an extremely unfortunate decision on the part of these programmers as for several years Oracle performed no upgrades on the OCI libraries, and in particular it was Version 8 before they got the full benefit of the reductions in the number of message pairs sent across Oracle's messaging interface between the application and the database. As we shall see shortly, this could have a major impact on client/server performance.

SQL*Net

In Version 5 Oracle provided an explicit message transmission layer that took advantage of the two process architecture to allow two clever tricks. Firstly the application no longer needed to be on the same machine as the database, and did not even need to be operating under the same operating system or using the same character set. The two processes were connected by SQL*Net, which over time became available for a whole host of communications protocols, most of which have fallen out of use to be replaced by TCP/IP. In the late 1980s, however, it seemed like magic to have two cooperating processes running on different platforms and connected by the customer's choice of network technology.

The second trick was that the Oracle database engine could act as an application and use SQL*Net to execute queries against another database. A new dictionary object, the database link, was created to allow a data dictionary entry in one database to point to a table or view in another database. Oracle now had (query only) distributed database support, and extended this by providing SQL*Net gateways for other database engines. At least in theory, a SQL*Forms application connected to an Oracle database could retrieve and display data from DB2 on the corporate mainframe.

Later, in Version 7, Oracle added two phase commit (2PC) which allowed the database to support distributed updating. This in turn allowed Oracle to add both synchronous and asynchronous replication during Version 7 and the Advanced Queuing (AQ) option in Version 8. At the same time databases were becoming larger and more centralized, making distributed database support rather less important. The only lasting significance of these developments for most users is that they enabled the development of Snapshots and Materialized Views, about which more is said later.

Client/Server

The early on-line applications running against Oracle used predominantly character mode devices. Even if the users were sitting at workstations the chances were that they were running the Oracle application in a 24×80 text window somewhere on their screen. In the late 1980s PC's started to appear on corporate desk tops, by which I mean the literal tops of employees' desks or tables depending on their status.

As soon as the PC's became connected to the corporate network then a marked imbalance in utilization became apparent. The poor Oracle server, running both database engine and applications, was liable to be critically overloaded and the corporate PC's were laughably under loaded except during startup and shutdown, which for no apparent reason took forever. The obvious solution was to remove the application from the database server and run it instead on the desk top. Unfortunately this disastrous solution was only half right; it made a great deal of sense to move the application away from the database server, but for several reasons it made no sense whatever to run it on the desktop.

Although Oracle's two task architecture made it conceptually quite simple to substitute a network protocol such as TCP/IP for the inter-process calls used in earlier versions, the tool developers had always assumed that the two tasks would have an instant connection with the result that in Version 5 execution of a simple SQL query would require several message pairs to pass between the application and the server. The number of message pairs varied with several factors but an average of 6 or 7 per statement would be quite low. These message pairs ate large quantities of both elapsed and CPU time when passed through several layers of networking stack.

Each type of network had a message turnaround time which varied from a few milliseconds for 10 MHz Ethernet to about half a second for an X.25 wide area network. In 1990 it was entirely normal to see a client/server application running across a wide area network that made it impossible to complete a simple SQL query in less than 2 seconds. If the application issued 5 such queries in the transition from one screen field to another, then the response time for that field transition would never fall below 10 seconds. This was "rarely satisfactory to the users," and the problem was compounded by routine response from application developers that they simply could not reproduce the problem—this was not surprising as they were always linked to their development server by a local area network.

Not only did the messages take time to arrive, the protocol stacks often used more CPU than the application. So the customer benefits of client/server were that they now needed an even more powerful database server (which meant buying a more expensive Oracle license), they had to buy an Oracle tools license and SQL*Net license for every user, the users got longer response times, and remote users got much poorer service than local users. On the frequent occasions that there was a change to the application code then this change had to be replicated to PC's all over the enterprise. This alone caused client/server to fail in many enterprises, especially those with multiple applications and multiple database servers. Client/server was an attractive architecture. Not.

The failure of client/server propelled the IT industry into a rapid wave of both technological and architectural development. On the networking side we got faster networks with both lower latency and much more efficient protocol stacks. On the Oracle side the message counts were greatly reduced, and within a few years an Oracle application could execute a good proportion of its queries in a single message pair. Lastly, and most importantly, n-tier architectures started to become fashionable and we finally had a workable means of relieving the database server of the application load. Client/server was a bitch, but it was a bitch that had a litter of beautiful puppies. And it was SQL*Net that made client/server working possible under Oracle.

Version 6: First Steps Towards Scalability

To put this section in context we need to remind ourselves that in the late 1980s a number of tactical projects had proved to enterprises all over the world that Oracle could form the basis for rapid development of on-line applications. The databases were measured in megabytes (albeit some were hundreds of megabytes), and typically had less than 20 simultaneous users. Very few had more than 40 simultaneous users because Oracle simply did not scale that far.

Diagnosing performance problems was largely a matter of opinion because Oracle Version 5 externalized very few metrics about its operation. The utility ODS presented a single 24×80 screen of instance statistics, and would also show the contents of the lock pool provided that they would all fit on a single page. If Oracle's lock pool contained more than 23 locks, then ODS would usually crash, and in conversation the program was usually called "odious."

My recollection of that era is that there were few batch reporting systems running on Oracle databases that were refreshed from operational systems. Oracle's rule based optimizer was not industrial strength for Management Information or Decision Support queries but was adequate for operational queries against well-normalized schemas. In addition to its limit on the number of simultaneous sessions Oracle also suffered from not having precompiled queries, and in Versions 4 and 5 the database engine often used substantially more CPU time parsing SQL statements than it did actually running them. The shorter the statement execution time, the greater the percentage overhead of parsing the statement for each execution.

A truly Oracle-savvy developer working in (say) C could ensure that each query was only parsed once per user session, but many were reluctant to do so because of the possible memory requirements. Oracle's market success was also starting to attract interest from tools and applications vendors who saw real revenue opportunities if only their products would run against an Oracle database. The "database agnostic" application was born, and started to cause major performance problems because such applications made no concessions to the needs of any particular database product. A full discussion of this problem area is outside the scope of this chapter, but if you are desperate to learn more, then just buy me a glass of dry white wine some day. No, make that a bottle. Or perhaps a case.

We can see that Oracle's customers were starting to use Oracle for strategic applications that Version 5 was not realistically able to support. Several things had to be done. Several things were done. But it took a decade to get some of the solutions to fulfill their original promises.

True Row Level Locking

Oracle's true row level locking appeared in 1988 as part of the Version 6 launch. Initially an extra-cost option, it was (and still is) a major technical achievement. True row level locking, in which only the row is locked rather than some other unit of storage such as the block containing the row, took the database industry by surprise to such an extent that some industry pundits were (rather foolishly) prepared to state for the record that it was impossible. I had the extreme pleasure of demonstrating an early production version of Oracle Version 6 to one of these "experts" who sat silently through the demo and then, when we asked if he had any questions, just stood up and walked out.

Previous versions of Oracle had protected updates by taking table level locks, and this had been one of the major causes of Oracle's inability to scale the number of simultaneous users. Competitive products of the same era featured both table level and block level locking, but held all locks in a lock pool. When the lock pool was full then additional locks could only be acquired by "escalating" some of the existing locks. In simple terms some of the block level locks had to be merged into table level locks.

Oracle's novel solution was that row level locks did not require entries in the lock pool. Each transaction took a single transaction lock in the lock pool and the transaction ID was recorded in the header of each database block in which the transaction updated table rows or index entries. The individual rows that were modified by each transaction were tied back to the entry in the block header, and through that to the lock. So far so good, but the cleverest part was yet to come. When a transaction completed, its locks were invalidated by simply removing the transaction level lock in the lock pool. The lock-related entries in the individual database blocks were not immediately removed. This behavior followed the general rule that Oracle defers action where possible.

Avoiding Unnecessary Action

In the discussion on true row level locking we see that the lock related entries in database blocks are (normally) left in place when the transaction ends, and the task of "block cleanup" is left to some future operation. This is far from the only case in Oracle where most users would expect some action to take place, but Oracle simply does not bother to take the action because the developers are confident that correct operation does not require the missing action.

Thus if a transaction allocates space to a table or index and then rolls back the space will not be de-allocated. Future queries will get the correct result even if the additional table blocks are retained, and it is always possible that some future transaction will fill up the space. In any event rolling back the space allocation would require some form of block level locking to ensure that no overlapping transaction used any of the new space. The smart move really is not to even try to recover the space, and if the table is growing then the new space should get used pretty soon anyway.

Updates to the branch block structure of an Oracle B*tree index used to be treated in the same way. The branches were never trimmed, and this had the necessary consequence that even completely empty leaf blocks were left in the tree. Eventually Oracle got so fed up with the volume of alleged bugs that were reported as a result of their original go-faster decisions that they started to find ways of pruning the index structures under certain circumstances. From Oracle8i onwards "block cleanup" can also occur before commit if the blocks are still in the cache. Both of these changes are simple examples of Oracle developments that were purely customer driven.

True row level locking had two fundamental effects and a major hidden defect. The first, positive, effect was that it relieved one of the major limits on Oracle's ability to scale. The second effect (and this is the bad news) was that it rendered much of the operation of the database counter-intuitive to many administrators and application developers. Because the lock-related entries were left in place in the blocks at commit, they would be encountered by the next SQL query to visit the block which would then check whether or not the lock was still valid. If it was not, then it would be removed, and the resulting database activity was the result of many calls to support.

The hidden defect was that the initial implementation of row-level locking only supported exclusive locks. Share locks were only possible at table level, and this restriction remains to this day. If you want to stop other sessions from updating a particular row, then you have two choices, an exclusive lock on the row or a share lock on the table. The former prevents other users from sharing the stability of the row and the latter prevents any other user from updating any part of the table. Life can be like that sometimes.

 NOTE *This short section on true row level locking gives only a partial description of the implementation, and deliberately ignores several important changes that have been introduced in the algorithms over the fifteen-plus years since it was first released. The tortuous history of TM locks has been omitted, which may disappoint those who were forced to master this abstruse subject. More importantly the discussion does not cover the steps taken in more recent versions to allow database administrators to exercise some control over the timing of block clean-out, the process that (eventually) removes the lock-related entries in database blocks.*

Shared Code

We know that Oracle has only ever supported dynamic SQL, so every SQL statement must be both parsed and optimized before it can be run. Prior to Version 6 each session had to parse its own SQL statements, so if there were 40 sessions running the same application under the same Oracle username, then each statement would get parsed (a minimum of) 40 times.

From Version 6 onwards, the results of parsing and optimization have been held in the shared pool and have been available to all sessions. So although the applications still have to present their SQL statements for parsing, in many cases no parse is required. The session just picks up from the shared pool a pre-parsed version of the statement called a *parse block*; this look-up is called a *soft parse* in Oracle-speak.

This mechanism has been and continues to be very good news for both performance and scalability, but has caused Oracle development a great deal of trouble over the years in three major areas. Firstly a number of defensive mechanisms are required to ensure that parse blocks are not shared when it is inappropriate to do so, and that cached parse blocks are invalidated if the table definitions on which they depend are changed. If there is any defect whatever in these rules, then one or other of the following problems may occur. Blocks may not be shared when they should be, causing performance and memory overheads. Alternatively blocks may be shared when they should not be, causing potentially erroneous results. Neither is good, but the latter is much worse than the former. Both have been seen in bug reports.

Secondly the parse blocks, which include PL/SQL triggers and procedures from Version 7 onwards, vary enormously in length and Oracle did not pay enough initial attention to the memory management problems that would arise in the shared pool. Unbelievably this took almost ten years to fix.

Lastly the mechanism worked best for statements that used bind variables, for example,

```
select ENAME from EMP where EMPNO = :e
```

rather than,

```
select ENAME from EMP where EMPNO = 45
```

Although Oracle-savvy developers used bind variables, coders "trained" in the worlds of Java and Visual Basic found it more natural to build dynamic statements that contained the literal values for each specific transaction. These had to be re-parsed every time the literal values changed, which was typically for every execution of the statement. In Oracle8 the developers took the easy (but very effective) way out and allowed the database administrator to set a mode in which all literals are converted to bind variables. This is a clear example of a long-term trend in Oracle's technical approach. In Oracle's early days it was up to the customer base to work out how best to exploit the database engine. As time has gone by the number of customers has increased and the individual customers have got less skilled and more vocal; as a result Oracle Corporation now allocates a significant part of its development budget to saving customers from the results of their own technical errors. Of course if Oracle's solution works, then the previously offending code no longer represents an error. Life can be like that.

Logging and Read Consistency

Prior to Version 6 all of Oracle's logging was performed at database block level. This used a lot of storage when large numbers of small changes were made to large blocks, but it was both simple and reliable. However, block level locking was completely inadequate to support a database in which multiple simultaneous transactions might update the same block, but then some might commit and some might roll back. The logging could have been changed to row level, but in another inspired jump forward Oracle opted to log at field level.

The masterstroke, however, was to keep the rollback segments (the undo, as discussed earlier) within the database. They therefore became database blocks and changes to them were logged just like changes to table blocks and index blocks. So the redo log, written to a succession of serial files, could recover not only the changes to the data but also could recover the undo structures that were needed to back out uncommitted transactions.

As we have already seen, every query has a single read consistency point. The query has to view each data block as it was at the read consistency point but ignoring any uncommitted changes. The undo entries for each table and index block are maintained in a backward chain, and a query may have to visit a virtually unlimited number of undo entries in order to construct the read consistent image that it needs. As ever, if the query process reaches the end of the undo chain before moving the block far enough back in time, then the result is the dreaded ORA-01555 error.

The conclusion is that Oracle has a highly robust read consistency mechanism that has served the users well though under some loads the mechanism may use excessive resource or give errors without warning (or both). Also throughout the 1990s it was very difficult to accurately allocate and manage rollback segments; this issue has been addressed by the AUTOMATIC UNDO feature in more recent releases.

MTS

The feature that Oracle call their Multi-Threaded Server is not multi-threaded. This is a pretty strong indicator that it fails to provide everything that the naïve customer might expect from it. It is a recurring theme in this history that a traditional on-line Oracle application is written in the expectation that each simultaneous user will have their own database connection, and therefore their own Oracle server process. The immediate consequence of this architecture is that the total amount of virtual memory allocated on the database server (the "memory charge") can be very high indeed.

In the early days of Oracle's application products it was quite normal for each additional session to add between 5- and 7MB to the memory charge on the server. To avoid page file traffic with 100 simultaneous users the server would need an absolute minimum of 1GB of memory to house all the session memory, the operating system, and the SGA. In 1990 this was a very tall order—servers simply did not have that kind of memory. At the same time as the customers were starting to complain about the memory requirement, Sybase had emerged as Oracle's greatest competitive threat in the US Financial Services market. This was a strong market for on-line applications with high numbers of users, and at one time Sybase was claiming with an entirely straight face that each additional user added 16KB to the overall memory requirement on the server. Oracle needed a quick fix.

"Clearly," the argument went, if many Oracle sessions could share a small pool of server processes, then this would save the process memory allocated for each of the sessions. This was mathematically true, but the impact was insignificant. On some UNIX platforms the operating system allocated as little as 50KB to each process as it was created. Another 5- to 7MB was allocated by Oracle in the form of the Program Global Area and contained the context needed to manage the Oracle session. So MTS did not save very much memory, though it did add to the CPU load because each incoming message (database request) and outgoing message (database response) required additional handling. The more efficient the SQL statements were, the greater this overhead became as a percentage of overall load.

If the application contained long-running SQL statements, whether by accident or design, then MTS also exhibited a nasty effect called *thread-blocking*. Each database request was placed in a queue, and then handed to the first shared server process to become available. It held onto that server process until the call was complete, which could be a long time. If every server process was allocated a message to process that turned out to take a long time, then no more calls could be initiated until one of the existing calls had ended. The threads were all blocked.

....

MTS to the Rescue

We saw earlier that process creation on VAX/VMS has a long instruction path length. If an application frequently connects to, and disconnects from, a database running on a VMS-based server, then this operating system overhead can become highly significant. MTS represents an effective solution because no new process needs to be created for each database connection, and the savings on CPU may be much more than the additional cost of running MTS. My thanks to my friend and former colleague Graham Wood for alerting me to this (and much, much more that is contained in this book but not specifically acknowledged).

....

So MTS saves a small amount of memory, increases CPU consumption, and client sessions run the risk of being blocked by long-running statements. This does not sound like a good deal to me, but factions within Oracle insist to this day that MTS is the way forward for the smart customer. Employers are entitled to expect some loyalty from their staff, but surely there need to be limits!

Version Upgrades

Now here is a strange fact. Version 6 contained a whole series of radical improvements over Version 5 but demanded little or no change to best practice in application design and programming. What migration from Version 5 to Version 6 did demand was that the database be completely unloaded to serial files and reloaded from scratch—there was no migration utility and the process required careful planning and execution to avoid data loss. It also took an inordinate amount of time.

Planned upgrade outages of 48 or even 72 hours were not uncommon at the largest sites, CPUs being very much slower then than they are now. Oracle had trapped their largest customers between a rock and a hard place; they had to upgrade because they were suffering from Version 5's lack of scalability, but the same lack of throughput meant that they could ill afford the outage required to perform the upgrade. The protests and recriminations were long and loud, and since then Oracle has always provided migration in situ so the data store has been preserved. However, as we shall see, later version upgrades have made some radical changes to best practice.

Version 7: A More Active Database

Up to and including Version 6 every application running under Oracle was (almost) totally responsible for ensuring that the data was valid. In other words the application had to enforce data integrity. Oracle would guarantee key uniqueness and prevent some fields from being left null, but other than that it was up to the application developer. And using tools such as the ubiquitous SQL*Plus the application could be trivially bypassed by anyone with a knowledge of an Oracle username and password that gave insert, update, and delete access to the underlying tables.

Declarative Constraints

Originally planned to be released with Version 6, Oracle introduced declarative constraints with Version 7. They were both effective and efficient, and for the first time the schema for an Oracle database could start to defend itself against various types of application error.

PL/SQL

The PL/SQL language arrived with Version 6 but was little used throughout the life of that version, partly because it was riddled with bugs but mainly because there was no mechanism for storing PL/SQL code within the data dictionary. Those of us who experimented with the language at this stage noticed that it had several remarkable features.

On the positive side, PL/SQL stood alone amongst procedural languages in making it both easy and natural to embed SQL statements into program logic. On the negative side, at times it looked to the outsider as though there was a state of war between the separate Oracle development groups responsible for the SQL engine and the PL/SQL engine. The construction of the language allowed SQL statements to appear as normal language elements in a block of procedural code but the details of the implementation often led to either poor runtime performance or, worse, spurious fatal errors. These problems have markedly reduced over time, but the execution overhead of calling from one engine to the other still remains an issue.

In Version 7 PL/SQL was the only language supported by Oracle's implementation of both table level triggers and stored procedures. Java was added in Oracle8, but this appears to have been more in the nature of a fashion statement rather than the important increase in functionality claimed by Oracle marketing. Procedural coding inside a database engine is, or certainly should be, all about presenting an interface between the data and the application. The requirement is therefore for a language that makes it as easy as possible to interface with the database. Java may be good at managing windows on a graphical display (and I only said "may"), but that is not what database procedures are about, and Java conspicuously fails to make it easy to embed SQL statements.

Stored Code

Table level triggers and stored procedures both arrived with Version 7 and it took the Oracle community some time to realize that exploiting these features required radical changes in design approach. The features also arrived at much the same time as packaged applications started to move into widespread use and the package vendors wanted to maximize their market by creating database agnostic designs. Oracle's triggers and stored procedures, on the other hand, can only be exploited effectively in an Oracle-specific design so their use is confined to custom builds and applications packages that are intended only for the Oracle market.

The arrival of triggers and stored procedures presented application designers with the means to prevent rogue applications or users of SQL*Plus from circumventing the application rules, but their effective use requires an understanding of the key difference between a trigger and a callable procedure (or function).

Triggers work best for implementing data rules. Thus if it is a data rule that every change to an employee's salary must be entered both on the employee record and in the salary change log, then the best way of achieving this is through the use of triggers on the table that contains the employee's salary. It then becomes impossible for most users to change a salary without creating a log record, though with sufficient privilege a user can always either disable the trigger or delete the log entry after the trigger has made it.

Stored procedures, on the other hand, work best for implementing application or process rules, allowing these rules to be defined just once (in the database) rather than running the risk that they may exist in different forms in different programs. Thus the rule for calculating the maximum allowable discount on any given order is an application rule, and should be contained in a stored procedure. It is worth noting that several improvements were made to Oracle's security model at the same time as stored procedures were introduced, and it became possible for an administrator to give a user the privilege to execute a procedure that (say) created a new order record without giving that user any privilege to update the tables that were used by the procedure. In this way that user simply could not create orders by using SQL*Plus to directly inserting rows into the tables because they would not have the authority to do so.

Applications designed specifically for Oracle from Version 7 onwards had available to them both declarative constraints and stored code to help promote data integrity in the widest sense. These mechanisms not only made it possible for designers to be more effective in protecting data integrity, their use was also capable of improving performance by reducing the message traffic between the application process and the database process. Unfortunately this was a two-edged sword. Data servers were (and still are) more susceptible to overload than application servers, and care is needed to ensure that they are not burdened with processing that can equally well be performed elsewhere.

Cost Based Optimizer

Oracle's Cost Based Optimizer (CBO) was new in Version 7, and if you've been reading carefully thus far, then you will probably not be surprised to learn that it did not work very well. This is a recurring pattern with major new features. On the other hand it did get (much) better with time.

Of all the many problems with CBO, the most staggering was a basic design error. SQL statements require CPU and I/O in order to run, so the naïve expected Oracle's new optimizer to take account of both. It did not. It only took account of I/O and it was designed in an era in which Oracle was invariably CPU limited rather than being I/O limited. This was strange. Even more strange was the optimizer's blithe assumption that physical I/O was required every time the SQL engine needed to look at a database block, in other words, make a "block visit." Oracle has never made much of a secret about the fact that their database engine has a buffer cache, and it is surprising that the CBO team were apparently unaware of this. To this day CBO has a strong tendency to perform full table scans where an index lookup can be trivially proved to be faster in both CPU and elapsed time.

Despite its many bugs, and its predilection for full table scans, right from the start CBO had a number of attractive features. Provided that table and index statistics had been gathered, it knew how long the tables were, how long the indexes were, and most importantly how selective the indexes were.

RBO resolved a choice between two indexes by picking the one that it found first (though a multitude of other theories have been floated over the years) whereas CBO picked the index that was most selective. This is better. Similarly if RBO could not decide which table to use as the driving table, it would pick the last one in the FROM list whereas CBO would pick the one that it calculated as presenting the least number of rows to the next stage of the join. This is also better. Lastly CBO could take advantage of each of the new execution techniques that were being added to Oracle whereas RBO was not enhanced after Version 6.

Many project teams had expended vast tuning effort to allow their applications to give adequate performance under RBO and were unwilling to consider a migration to CBO. Running under Version 7 this was almost certainly the smart call, and even in the Version 8 timeframe it was defensible under some circumstances. By the time we got to Version 9.2 then CBO was definitely the way to go and it had only taken Oracle ten years to get it right.

Version 8: Partitioning and Object Support

Version 8 continued the evolution of stored code and cost based optimization, but it also brought new features that varied from being absolutely essential to large users (such as improved storage management) to being totally irrelevant to almost everybody (such as object support). We'll look next at the most important areas of this version.

LOBs

Traditionally Oracle had supported the datatypes LONG and LONG RAW to allow the storage and retrieval of unstructured data (or data whose structure was not declared to the SQL engine), but this data was stored in-line and subject to a number of restrictions. As the storing of data items such as document images became more widespread, the limitations on the LONG datatypes became a major issue with many customers and these were addressed by providing the new LOB datatypes. Unfortunately it took two more versions before Oracle offered automatic conversion between the two approaches.

Partitioning

Throughout the twenty-five-year life of the Oracle database product both schemas and tables have consistently got larger and larger. Early Oracle databases tended to have less than 200 storage objects (tables and indexes) and were a few megabytes in size. There is now nothing unusual about a database with 30,000 storage objects or a multi-terabyte table. However, just making Oracle capable of handling very large tables did not make them easy to handle, especially as both the index and the table were units of failure in a classic Oracle schema.

As a result of massive customer pressure, Oracle8 saw the introduction of table and index partitioning. Now a database table referred to by the application as a single entity could be held in as many separate chunks as the administrators or designers decided. Very large objects had become effectively unmanageable under Version 7, but were back under a measure of control.

Materialized Views

Oracle Corporation (and, to be fair, their competitors) have long been obsessed with the performance of their database product against industry benchmark tests. Arguably that was the motivation that drove the introduction of true row level locking, though as we have seen there was also massive customer pressure for better scalability at that time.

Materialized views, however, were simply the result of benchmark opportunism. According to the Transaction Processing Performance Council web site (http://www.tpc.org/tpcd/default.asp), the data warehousing benchmark specification TPC-D represented

a broad range of decision support (DS) applications that require complex, long running queries against large complex data structures

Somebody in Oracle realized that the fastest way to retrieve the results of a long running query was to have already executed the query and stored the results. Then the next time the query was issued all they would need to do was just go fetch the results.

The implementation details are complex, with queries being quite literally re-written by the SQL engine, but the exciting result for Oracle's customer base was that in Oracle8i they received a mechanism that allowed them not just to catalog a query (in other words, create a view) but to execute that view and store the results (in other words, materialize the view). Oracle's motivation was that they were able to run certain benchmark queries over a thousand times faster than SQL-Server. This was good for marketing. The "side effect" was that Oracle's customers received a product feature that could save them similar levels of disk and CPU time under the right circumstances, and in some cases could realize these savings without changing any application code. This was good for customers.

Function-Based Indexes

Up to and including Version 7, Oracle only allowed simple column values as index keys. Much of the time this was entirely adequate, but it required a complex design solution to meet a requirement such as an efficient case independent look-up on a customer name. A natural solution to this problem is to allow the index key to be an expression such as upper(CUST_NAME), but for many years Oracle claimed that this was too difficult. When they finally introduced expression-based indexes in Oracle8 the company somewhat bizarrely called the new feature *function-based*. This semantic error led the documentation team to describe the expression in

```
create index BOXES_VOLUME on BOXES (HEIGHT * WIDTH * DEPTH);
```

as an *in-line function*. Whatever the shortcomings in its name, the feature proved to be worth waiting for and its implementation turned out to be surprisingly complex. The use of these indexes in queries relies on the same query rewrite technology used to exploit materialized views.

Bit-mapped Indexes

Oracle adopted B*tree indexes right from the beginning, though for performance reasons the database engine never found it necessary to fully balance the trees as required by the classic description of a balanced B-tree. Although there were both competitive pressures and customer demands for other direct access methods, prior to Version 7 the B*tree was the only form of lookup that Oracle supported. Version 7 saw the introduction of a form of hash lookup, but the implementation could be fairly described as "somewhat half-hearted." It was used by some of the customers who had been clamoring most loudly for hashing, but has not gained wide acceptance.

By the 1990s Oracle was being used extensively for data warehouse applications in addition to its transaction processing applications, and the limitations of B*tree indexes were becoming critical. The greatest problem was the optimization of queries against fact tables where there were a large number of columns that might appear in query predicates, but where each query tended to use a different set of columns. A concatenated B*tree index is effective for any one such query, but the number of indexes required to support all likely queries becomes excessive if there are more than four such columns. Version 5 had featured very effective B*tree merge logic to allow several single column indexes to be merged to support equality predicates against all of their columns, but for reasons the author has been unable to discover this mechanism was at least one order of magnitude slower in Version 6 than it had been in Version 5.

Bit-mapped indexes hold a compressed bit map for each key value present in the table. Each bit map has an entry for each row in the table, and this makes bit map merges both straightforward and efficient. This type of index first appeared in Version 7.3 of Oracle, but is discussed under Oracle8 because there were some issues with the initial releases. With Oracle8 bit-mapped indexes became a major performance feature for data warehouses. The downside was that they were then, and remain, very expensive to update in real time.

Initiatives such as bit-mapped indexes and the separate star query transformation greatly improved Oracle's performance in many data warehouse applications, but Oracle9i brought another innovation, the *bit-map join index*. This type of index essentially allows an index built on one table to contain key columns that are in one of more other tables provided that the join condition to derive the value is declared. It should not come as a surprise that there are a number of restrictions on the construction of such an index, but these are outside the scope of this chapter.

> **INSIGHT** *This complex index type gives a good illustration of how Oracle allows its development to be largely customer-led, but nevertheless provides true technical innovation. Arguably this trend started with true row level locking, a major leap forward introduced when the market aspiration would almost certainly have been met (for a time) by block level locking and the risk of lock escalation.*
>
> *It is possible that some customer designed the bitmap join index and then asked Oracle to implement it, but it seems more likely that Oracle was faced with customers whose performance problem was that whichever table was the driving table for a join, too many rows were discarded after the join. The bitmap join index is an elegant solution to this problem. Brilliant.*

Version 9: Real Application Clusters (RAC)

Some new technology directions find real resonance with senior IT management and create misplaced expectations that no amount of negative practical experience seems able to completely remove. The miracle of hardware clustering is arguably at the top of this list. In the mid 1980s the Digital Equipment Corporation was failing to make the inroads into the mainframe market that company founder and chief executive Ken Olsen felt that his company deserved. His VAX CPU's were simply not powerful enough to compete with mainframe CPU's so Ken commissioned work on two different architectures, each of which would allow multiple CPU's to run in parallel.

The first initiative was to build machines with multiple CPU's operating against the same physical memory. Around the same time Sequent were also doing this with relatively slow Intel commodity processors, as were Pyramid with (I think) Motorola processors, but Digital's architecture was intended to use the fastest processors that they could build. The approach is known generically as *Symmetric Multi-Processing*, the symmetry being that any processor can undertake any function. There are several design issues that have to be solved to make this work, but the only one that merits consideration here is *cache coherency*. In order to allow a CPU to run faster than the memory which stores its data, the processor needs a memory cache. If processes are reliant on current values in shared memory, and some processes also modify these memory values, then the processor memory caches are liable to get out of date. If the caches are not kept "coherent," then Oracle cannot work properly even if there is only one active user session as the signaling between that task and the Oracle background processes will fail.

These problems have been solved with good engineering and SMP works. At the time of writing almost every server is marketed with support for multiple CPU's. Each architecture and operating system combination does have a scalability limit, especially for shared data services such as the Oracle kernel, and this can (only) be established by careful testing. So far so good, even if the hardware vendor will be perfectly happy to let you order a server with four times as many CPU's as can be fully exploited when running Oracle underneath your particular application load.

Olsen's second initiative to make a machine at least appear to be more powerful was to park several complete machines side by side, connect them together, give each machine access to the same pool of disks, and claim that the total power of the configuration was the sum of power of the individual parts. The group of interconnected machines (each with its own CPU's and memory) was a *cluster* and each individual machine was a *cluster node*. Although some signaling between nodes was always necessary, if the individual nodes were running unrelated processes, then the overall throughput of the whole could approach that of the sum of the parts.

If several clustered nodes were each running an Oracle instance but each instance had the same database open for both read and write, then all of the Oracle sessions in the cluster were strongly related to each other because they could both read and modify data that they all shared. The problem was still cache coherency, but now entire disk blocks were likely to have been altered in the cache of another cluster node, and the changed block would often require to be shipped between nodes. The lock pool in each node also had to be kept coordinated with the lock pool in the other nodes. The net result of all this is that a "shared instance" of Oracle will *always* run any given work load more slowly than an "exclusive instance." The most dramatic effect that I have personally verified for this slow-down was an incredible 50-fold increase in run time. Admittedly this was a long time ago using both software and hardware that has been long since desupported, but it makes a vital point. There is a real penalty for running shared instances.

Since releasing "Clustered Oracle" for Version 5 in 1985 Oracle has now spent almost twenty years continually redesigning and rewriting its cluster support for various platforms, claiming all the time that running Oracle on clustered hardware gives the customer both increased throughput and failure resilience. The reality is that with today's hardware and operating systems the customer is unlikely to need the former and even more unlikely to achieve the latter. Clustered nodes crash more often than unclustered machines, and the surviving nodes take a minimum of several seconds to handle node failure. This is called the "cluster transition time" and can freeze a cluster for several minutes, making nonsense of the idea that clusters are an easy route to non-stop computing.

Clustered Oracle became Oracle Parallel Server (OPS) in Version 6.2 though this numbering was short-lived, and OPS was folded back into Version 6.0 and carried forward to Versions 7 and 8. With the launch of Oracle9i cluster support was renamed Real Application Clusters (RAC). If the customer base can be persuaded to run their databases on clustered hardware, then the benefits to Oracle are clear.

License revenue is increased and competition is pretty much eliminated because the competitors' clustered solutions are even less attractive than Oracle's. But a magic bullet it is not.

On the other hand, in the twenty years since Ken Olsen commissioned Digital's first clusters the other "big idea" of the day, the SMP machine, has become proven and provides scalable technology up to a throughput level that is sufficient for almost every application. It is now extremely rare for SMP servers to suffer a total failure (other than from external causes), whereas service is still routinely lost at many sites as a result of either finger trouble or application bugs. Clusters do nothing to ameliorate these problems, and as hinted previously their hardware and software complexity introduces a number of additional failure points.

As a final note on Oracle clusters, Larry Ellison seems to have become fascinated by massively parallel computers (MPP's) in the mid 1980s leading to his buying nCube as mentioned earlier. From a database architect's point of view an MPP is little more than a "cluster on steroids"; it will have more processors than a clustered host, and possibly orders of magnitude more processors. The universal experience of MPP's has been that they are not effective hosts for multi-user shared databases (unless, of course, you know different).

Data Compression

Databases are getting big, very big. Disk storage is no longer very expensive, but multiple terabytes of data take time to back up and take time to scan. Given the widespread use of data compression techniques in most other facets of IT you might expect that a premier database engine like Oracle would feature data compression. You would be correct, though table compression arrived as late as Version 9.2. The original B*tree index compression was removed in the transition between Versions 5 and 6, and a new algorithm was supplied within the Oracle8 timeframe. Both table and B*tree index compression must be explicitly enabled for each object to which they are to apply.

Oracle has never supported the use of external compression on the "container files" that make up the database. The database internals make endless calculations to come up with database block numbers, often referred to as *Kernel Block Addresses*. These are used to allow Oracle to make direct access to the disk blocks that it requires, and are a major feature in promoting Oracle throughput. If file level or container level compression has taken place, then the database engine cannot calculate the offset within the container where it will find the required block.

However, the customers kept asking for index and table compression, so Oracle finally gave it to them. But only at block level. In a compressed table each database block is separately compressed, and therefore each table block has to bear the overhead of its own lookup table. In a compressed index repeated key values are held once at the start of each leaf block. Both approaches are compression, and they work. However, they do not seem to be exactly what the customers had in mind.

Flashback Query

Forget the sarcasm that you may have detected in other parts of this chapter. We now move into a subject that a senior and normally totally loyal member of Oracle support recently described to me as "complete farce." The marketing story is that if some naughty person deletes some rows from your database, or accidentally updates the wrong row, then you can come along a few hours (or days) later and use the rollback data to query the data as it was before the unwanted change. And using this data you can repair the error.

The feature works. The problem is that it cannot always deliver the benefits that Oracle leads the terminally naïve to expect. It can, of course, be argued that any company is entitled to give a rosy interpretation of what their products can achieve, but many of us feel that Oracle have just gone too far in promoting flashback.

There are two main issues that make it impossible for most users to exploit the feature in the ways confidently described by Oracle's marketing machine. The first is that flashback query relies on the availability of rollback data, and ever since 1984 when Oracle introduced the BI file long-running queries have been failing with the infamous ORA-01555 error "Snapshot too old." Oracle has a long history of letting the developers determine the error text with the result that "some of their error messages are not always informative to the average reader." This one is trying to tell you that the snapshot that you need for a valid query is older than the oldest one Oracle can create. In current on-line transaction processing applications it is entirely normal to start getting this error after a query has been running for just a few minutes. In the real world your chances of managing to query data several days after it has been changed or deleted are precisely zero unless you are prepared to keep terabytes of rollback data "just in case." Even then the ability to issue a flashback query is not guaranteed.

The second issue is more profound and has been the basis for sub-plots in more than one science fiction film about time travel. Once database changes have been committed they are visible to every user with the necessary privileges and the new values can be used as a basis for application and user decisions that are not so easy either to detect or to rollback even if they can be detected. For flashback query to offer a genuine ability to unravel an erroneous transaction Oracle would have to be able to report everything that has occurred based on each update. The database engine may be clever, but it isn't that clever (at least not yet).

Anything Else?

Although Oracle9i had a large number of detail improvements, consolidated in Oracle9i Release 2, there was very little other than RAC that belongs under the umbrella of "Tipping Points." The emergence of Enterprise Manager as a convenient and usable database tool does seem to qualify, and is briefly discussed under Version 10, below.

Version 10: Grid Computing and Manageability

The official story is that Oracle10g is all about "grid computing," but never in my meanderings through the industry have I encountered a harassed looking Oracle Administrator or IT Services Manager staring into their coffee and quietly whispering "I just wish that it was easier to run this software in a grid." On the other hand I have met literally hundreds of skilled professionals who find Oracle difficult to manage.

Manageability

As early as 1990 Oracle Corporation was aware that both the skills levels and man-hours required to perform effective administration of Oracle databases was a significant sales objection, and impacting corporate revenue. Many customers also made repeated complaints to Oracle about the difficulty of finding the "correct" settings for some Oracle configuration parameters (of which there were by then several hundred) and about the need to buy third-party tools to ease their difficulties in this area. Nonetheless it was not until 1996 that Oracle announced Oracle Enterprise Manager (OEM), their first graphical tool to help production database administrators. In later versions the name was shrunk by one word to become Enterprise Manager, but from the outset the tool had a justifiable reputation for being poorly conceived and even more poorly constructed. It was buggy, very slow, and had an architecture that made it both complex and expensive to install for more than one database server. The customers (including, according to reliable sources, Oracle's own internal IT department) continued to spend considerable sums of money buying Oracle management tools from third-party companies.

Over the years Oracle have got much smarter about the default values for most of the key parameters, but more importantly large parts of Enterprise Manager have been redesigned and rewritten. The versions shipped with Oracle9i finally made most administrative tasks easier and faster to perform from the GUI than from the SQL*Plus command line, but even with this version the user still needed a considerable amount of technical knowledge about Oracle in order to be effective.

Oracle Marketing are now telling the world that manageability is the key achievement within Oracle10g. At the time of writing it is too early to tell how well the latest release will meet the market's needs for a database engine that is simple to deploy, easy to keep running, and straightforward to diagnose when performance or availability issues arise. The initial signs are promising, and a single architect has taken responsibility for both the performance management goals to be met and the specification of the statistics being gathered by the engine in order to support Oracle's tool set to help meet them. Not only is there the ability to enable automatic collection of Oracle operating statistics into a repository, but there also is an automatic diagnostic function to review the statistics in this repository and make wide-ranging recommendations on how performance can be improved.

However, even if Oracle10g turns out to be completely self-managing (which I somehow doubt though it is clearly moving in the right direction), we might still be pardoned for feeling that it has taken Oracle altogether too long to meet the market's aspirations in this important area. The Tales of the Oak Table that make up the rest of this book contain abundant evidence to support this view.

The main thesis of the latter half of this chapter has been that Oracle's development priorities have been set by the customer base rather than by Oracle's own technical visionaries or market planners. It has taken nearly fifteen years for Oracle to squarely address the manageability issue, so could this be an exception? Some might even argue that it is an exception that proves the rule, but sadly the reality is that Oracle manageability was a desire rather than a demand. The largest customers might have resented the money they had to spend on database administrators, but they could afford to pay. They could not deliver the required service to their end users without features such as row-level locking, declarative constraints, triggers and stored customers, and table and index partitioning. Many of them at least believed that they needed to run Oracle on clustered hardware, though as we have seen they may have been mistaken about this.

The main beneficiaries of the manageability improvements in Oracle10g should have been the smaller customers, many of whom have no full-time DBA. Had the new workload repository and its analysis engine been part of Oracle's Standard Edition then perhaps we could justifiably refer to Oracle10g as Oracle10m, where *m* stands for "manageable."

Sadly, in April 2004 when this section was written, Oracle marketing had recently decided not only that these new features should be an extra-cost item, but also that Oracle's Enterprise Edition should be a prerequisite. In other words a low-end customer might have to triple their license and support fees to take advantage of them. Presumably Oracle sees no need to meet the needs of their smaller customers at reasonable cost, and also sees no market disadvantage in asking their high-end customers to pay rather more if they want to save time and money on database administration.

Product Quality

I've never tried pitching horseshoes against a stake with the objective of achieving a dead ringer, but I imagine that it is rather more difficult than it looks. This has certainly been true of most of the sports that I have tried. However, while living and working in North America I frequently came across the saying that "Close does not count except in Horseshoes." Not having played the sport in question I cannot be absolutely sure that "Close" does indeed count in that domain, but it certainly does not count in the database arena. Features either work or they do not work.

We work in the software industry so perhaps it is unreasonable for us to expect products to work as delivered. The problem is not new, but came to a head with the first production release of the eagerly awaited Oracle Version 6. Oracle Corporation tried to run a number of their key internal applications under release 6.0.21 with the result that they were unable to execute key business processes. The result was that a significant part of the database development team found themselves trying to rescue a bookkeeping application rather than working on their day jobs, but there were benefits. As a direct result of the problems they encountered Oracle got features like the original tkprof, and the "hidden" init.ora parameters that allow the database to survive various flavors of block corruption.

At least Oracle now supplies install scripts that usually work, but their track record for the overall operability of the initial release(s) of any version is not good. We have been told that it will all be different with Oracle10g—we shall see. A computing grid is a complex and challenging environment, and it seems more than likely that yet again the pioneers will wind up with arrows in their chests.

A Briefer Technical History of Oracle

So what are the highlights of the twenty-five years of Oracle's technical history from 1979 to 2004?

At the start in 1979 Version 2 (or perhaps Version 1) was the first commercially available relational database. You no longer needed to be in a research establishment to express your data manipulation operations in a set-oriented language and have them executed.

By 1983 this database engine had become portable with Version 3, and by 1984 Version 4 had given it both transactional integrity and the read consistency model that we still have today. During this period Oracle was also arguably the only supplier you needed other than a hardware and operating system vendor. They not only had a database engine but also shipped application development tools.

In its early days Oracle was used to support limited tactical operational systems, but during the 1990s the customer base widely adopted it for ever-larger strategic applications, and it also started to serve major data warehouses.

In 1988 Version 6 started the long haul towards providing a database engine that would scale with the users' needs and aspirations leading to the introduction of partitioning in Oracle8. In the meantime Version 7 did not primarily address scalability but rather put in place the features required to promote database integrity.

In each version since 6 the optimizer has improved, and new execution strategies have been introduced. Finally in 2004 Oracle10g promises us manageability, albeit at a price.

The Last Word

There is a lot missing from this short history; both distributed transactions and replication were omitted in their entirety to save space, as was a page or so on multiple extents. After some debate with the editor and my reviewers we also decided to go to press without covering either stand-by databases or backup and recovery. Much else may have been omitted because of my ignorance of particular issues or events, but I won't know that until someone tells me. Please do so. I am not impressed by Oracle's current family of development tools, but I am an Oracle database enthusiast.

I hope that my enthusiasm for the Oracle database engine has been apparent from this chapter, and that it will help you to understand the background to a number of the Tales of the Oak Table that make up the rest of this book. Oracle's database engine is far from perfect but it is pretty good and it gets better with each release. We can get better at using it by understanding and allowing for Oracle's strengths and weaknesses as well as our own.

Dear Reader,

When I was asked to write the introduction to Mogens's chapter, I became worried. Having just been extensively late in delivering my own chapter for the book, my concern was that any worthwhile introduction to the World of Mogens could extend to many more pages than my entire contribution to the book so far. So I hope that you will forgive this somewhat condensed version of Mogens's metadata.

Mogens started as a DBA on Oracle version 5 for a Danish Bank in 1987. I don't know the name of the bank, but it was probably called Danish Bank, Royal Bank, or the Royal Bank of Denmark. You see, everything in Denmark follows this naming convention. When Mogens started Miracle in 2000, it was just typical of him to break the naming convention in this way.

After a few years as a real DBA, Mogens was tempted to the Dark Side, and joined Oracle Support in 1990, working on the RDBMS product on VMS. He then became head of RDBMS Support in Denmark, where he was working with many of the same guys he employs in Miracle today. After that, Mogens was manager of Premium Services in Denmark, where he was a noble piece of grit in the corporate oyster. So gritty, in fact, that he was fired in 1999, much to the disgust and surprise of nearly everybody in Oracle Denmark except the holder of the smoking gun. This was a big mistake; Mogens has so many friends, you see, that they were able to smother the Oracle management with thirty-five meeting requests and non-maskable interrupts over the next three days, resulting in a begrudging U-turn from the cowboy with the gun.

The condition of Mogens's rehire was that he should be sent to a psychiatrist for evaluation, presumably with the hope that he could be quickly dismissed once more on medical grounds. After a few sessions with the distinguished doctor, things started to backfire on the cowboy—not only was Mogens found to be completely and utterly sane, but of such mental strength and analytical ability that the psychiatrist offered Mogens employment himself ...

A year later in 2000, Mogens fired himself from Oracle, with no possibility of rehire this time, and founded Miracle with some old friends from Oracle and his old school friend Lasse. It was around this time that I quit from my employer and started Scale Abilities, and we finally met for the first time in a bar at Oracle World Berlin in 2001. Anjo Kolk made the introductions, possibly one of the first which ultimately resulted in the OakTable network.

Shortly after this time, Mogens introduced me into one of his large telecom clients for an extended period of work, much to my bank manager's relief. Mogens keeps telling me that it was because they needed my particular brand of expertise, but I only partially believe him—he was helping me out. This is a very typical attribute of Mogens's character, perhaps the most outgoing and friendly person I have ever met.

When I visited Mogens's house for the first time, it was part of a group of around forty-two people all staying on the floor of his house during one of the many Miracle Masterclasses that are run each year. During the day we studied Oracle internals and had offline discussions with others of similar mentality or lack thereof. By night we would write code, share hypotheses, and eat dinner from the temporarily closed laptops in front of us at Mogens's oak table. We may have also had one beer between us, and a drop of whiskey.

In Mogens's garden, he has some pets. Many pets, actually. What started out as a couple of small birds now comprises an average of eight chickens (depending on the level of success by the local fox), two goats, three box turtles, twelve small colorful birds, and an exponentially increasing number of rabbits. Somebody must explain to Mogens how this male/female rabbit thing happens one day.

Feeding all these animals would be expensive, if it were not for one of the many relationships Mogens keeps in the community. This particular one is with the local greengrocer, who sells Mogens enormous amounts of fruit and vegetables that have just rolled past their fitness for human consumption.

In addition, Mogens's neighbors include Naboo Peter, who was able to handle the shipping of a large NetApp filer for us one year, Kern the policeman, and Martin the carpenter and Torben the carpenter, who built Mogens's giant treehouse as a birthday present last year. You may be starting to detect Mogens's biggest strength— he is a natural networker, and expert builder of relationships for the benefit of all involved. It was this networking that was the genesis of the OakTable network.

In January 2002, while around Mogens's oak table, we put a name to the Oracle side of Mogens' networking—the OakTable network.

Since then, we jointly came up with the BAARF Party, as detailed in this book, and Mogens had had tremendous success with his "We Don't Use" website. Ranking in the top five of Danish websites, the "We Don't Use" (WDU) website started as a joke Mogens played on calling telesales people. If for example a stationery salesperson would call, Mogens would quite clearly explain that Miracle "Don't Use Stationery," being a fully electronic company. This was followed in other sales calls by "We Don't Use Detergents," "We Don't Use Training," and the ultimate "We Don't Use Computers." The concept has been so well received that salespeople actually start laughing even before they have finished their sales preamble.

As a motivator, Mogens is second to none. Throughout the many hundred ideas I have run past Mogens in the time I have known him, all have been encouraged as good ideas. From a pure Law of Averages perspective, this cannot possibly be true, and many have fallen by the wayside from natural causes. But sometimes ideas need encouraging in the early stages, before they can be seen in their full light; Mogens understands this better than most. Despite the fact that the correct pronunciation of his name (Moans), Mogens never Moans.

It is a privilege and an honour to introduce Mogens's chapter, and I hope that this short introduction to the man will give you some background into his officially sane Royal Danish mind. Enjoy!

—James Morle

CHAPTER 2

You Probably Don't Tune Right

... and perhaps you never will

By Mogens Nørgaard

To me, the Oracle performance optimization research carried out by the likes of Anjo Kolk, Cary Millsap, and several others, over the last 15–20 years can be summed up in two sentences:

- *If you don't know where the time is going on the session/job level, you cannot optimize.* You're reduced to guesswork. See Anjo Kolk's "YAPP-Method" paper (Anjo tells the story behind YAPP in Chapter 4 of this book) and Cary Millsap's "Oracle Operational Timing" paper, among others, for details. Also, of course, you should read Cary's chapter in this book and buy *Optimizing Oracle Performance* (O'Reilly & Associates, ISBN 059600527X).

- *Control your batch load, and realize that many online jobs/sessions behave (and should be treated) as batch jobs.* See Cary Millsap's "Batch Queue Management and the Magic of '2'" paper.

That was the executive summary. (I use Anjo's and Cary's names several times in this chapter, and from now on I've taken the liberty of using their first names.) Now for some details.

Correct Instrumentation Is Key

In the mid 1980s IBM realized that no matter how many counters and ratios they looked at, it was still pure guesswork (hence luck or lack thereof) whether a person managed to identify and remove the correct (in other words, the biggest) bottleneck of a given application or business unit.

So they instrumented the whole mainframe environment, including DB2, MVS (later OS/390, at present z/OS), and other components. The instrumentation aimed at providing time-based measurements on the session level, and proved so powerful that today, many years later, it's possible to predict within a very small margin what, say, a CPU-upgrade will mean in terms of response time for each application.

FUN FACT *The DB2 database code for AIX and Windows were written by different teams with little or no contact to the mainframe coders. Consequently, DB2 on AIX and Windows are not instrumented. Amazing, sad, and true.*

Around 1991 or 1992 Juan Loaiza and others from Oracle development were forced to instrument the Oracle kernel in the same way. Here's the story, as told to me by Juan (he's now vice president in Oracle kernel development). It is also my tribute to one of the truly great minds inside Oracle Development.

I think what you are referring to are the wait statistics that were implemented in 7.0. This stuff was developed because we were running a benchmark that we could not get to perform. We had spent several weeks trying to figure out what was happening with no success. The symptoms were clear—the system was mostly idle—we just couldn't figure out why.

We looked at the statistics and ratios and kept coming up with theories, the trouble was that none of them were right. So we wasted weeks tuning and fixing things that were not the problem. Finally we ran out of ideas and were forced to go back and instrument the code to figure out what the problem was.

Once the waits were instrumented the problem was diagnosed in minutes. We were having "free buffer" waits because the DBWR was not writing blocks fast enough. It's amazing how hard that was to figure out with statistics, and how easy it was to figure out once the waits were instrumented.

The "credit" for this should go to a number of people. I remember that Mark Porter was involved, and Keshevan Srinivasan did most of the actual instrumentation of the code. There were probably others involved but it has been so many years that I don't remember it clearly anymore.

Another time based measurement came about the same way. We had spent several weeks trying to figure out why a major customer's application performed so poorly. We had all sorts of theories and tried all sorts of things. Finally, after we had tried everything else we went back and wrote some tracing code for sql statements (sqltrace) and a little program to generate reports from it (tkprof). The problem was immediately tracked down to a SQL statement doing a full table scan and quickly solved by adding an index.

The common thread here is that generating the proper instrumentation was really the last thing we tried after trying everything else. If we had managed to figure out the problem using some other mechanism we would have just moved on. Fortunately (in retrospect) we were totally stuck and had to go back and do the right thing.

I guess the moral of the story is, when all else fails, do it right.

Of course right is a relative term. In retrospect I would have done this instrumentation somewhat differently. We are fixing some of this in 10g but I think there is still more work to do. I've always thought that diagnosing performance issues boils down to figuring out where the time is going in the system. If you can attribute the time correctly, then the source of the problem becomes obvious.

And yes, in retrospect a lot of the names could be greatly improved. The wait interface was added after the freeze date as a "stealth" project so it did not get as well thought through as it should have. Like I said, we were just trying to solve a problem in the course of a benchmark. The trouble is that so many people use this stuff now that if you change the names it will break all sorts of tuning tools, so we have to leave them alone.

It is worth noticing that if any of numerous suggestions from the "Guess & Grimacing" sessions held in Oracle Development had helped, the instrumentation of the kernel may never have taken place.

In the mid 1990s Anjo Kolk invented the YAPP method (as he describes in Chapter 4). In the process, he became the first human on Earth to take full advantage of the instrumentation.

Various folks in Oracle Development, Support, and Consulting might have heard about and fooled around with the various fixed views showing data from the Oracle Wait Interface, but since just viewing wait data is out of context (only the W in R = S + W), they never got the real picture.

NOTE *In the R = S + W equation, R is the response time, S is the service time, and W is the wait time. See Anjo's chapter for a full explanation.*

Anjo's idea of using Agnar Erlang's queueing theory, and the resulting YAPP paper written mostly by Shari Yamaguchi (Anjo was too lazy to write it himself, I'm sure) changed all that. Now it was possible to

- Use a method instead of a useless checklist. (Remember? "First, tune layer X, then tune layer Y ... ")

- Prioritize. Take the most time-consuming part and examine it first and consequently ignore the parts that are not contributing very much to the problem—in other words: conserve your energy by focusing only on changes that will make a difference.

- Quantify the possible performance gain (because it's time-based, and the information is available).

I was head of Oracle Denmark's Premium Services team back in 1997, when I first read Anjo Kolk's YAPP paper. It was as if everything fell into place (it didn't, but it felt like it). A groundbreaking paper, if there ever was one, in my Oracle World.

One of my very few claims to fame is that I insisted that the forty or so people in Oracle Denmark's Premium Services should stop using the layered performance tactics of the past, and instead focus solely on the YAPP method. Indeed, we were the first group within Oracle to do so. It was the right thing to do, except for one small detail: the typical engagement period for a performance problem at a customer site fell from days to hours, and that's certainly not good for a consulting practice. But it was good for the mind to do something that felt so instinctively right. The hardest part, as I always joke, was to force people in Premium Services to ignore the small contributors to the time spent, since they often knew how to fix those with, say, a parameter change. If, for example, the YAPP formula (R = S + W) indicated that 0.5% of the response time was due to latch problems in the log buffer, it could be tempting to fix this by setting a parameter controlling allocation of such latches.

It's All a Question of Focus

"Focus" and "it depends" are two key phrases for any consultant to help him get out of almost any tight situation or answer any difficult question from a client. I'll choose the first one for now ...

Focus on the most time-consuming part of the business function, the form, the report, the batch job. Reduce it as much as you can, or even better eliminate it. If your goal has been reached, stop. Otherwise, repeat. There is no other way.

Here's a wonderful story from Cary Millsap that I like to quote: imagine you have a teenage son with a driver's license, and you ask him to drive down to the nearby shop for a liter of milk. An hour later your son returns with a liter of milk. If you're a father with an IT background you will conclude one of the following:

- I need a faster car.

- I need two cars.

- Next time I'll only ask him to fetch half a liter.

- I'll try to convince the shop to only display one kind of milk.

- My driveway should probably be wider.

- My garage door should stay permanently open.

Cary's best guess (and mine) is that the young man has spent 58 minutes with his girlfriend, or on the highway, or both. However, if you don't *know* where the majority of the time was spent, you can't optimize. Profiling is everything.

So why the emphasis on job/session/thread/business function level? Because summaries hide details. Cary's famous question is this: if you see a pile of 1000 rocks, all of them gray except one, which is red, and you know the total weight is 1000 kilos—how much does the red rock weigh? The statistical answer is 1 kilo, of course. But if you have to carry it, you might be interested in the real answer.

My co-director (CEO) and long-term friend Lasse Christensen and I both studied Economics at the University of Copenhagen (Lasse finished his studies, which is only one of several differences between us). We do share, though, a certain wretched sense of humor, and if there's anything which is fun to watch, it's the annual release of the "Big National Summaries," in other words, the Gross National Product, the Gross Daily Product, the Money Supply One, and so on and on, from various Statistical Offices of the World. To put it into a mathematical context:

If N denotes number of economists, then N + 1 is the minimum number of interpretations of the same National Summary numbers.

If experts with approximately the same formal background and training come up with different conclusions based on the same numbers, then I would suggest they're not looking at the correct level of information. What good are inconclusive numbers and digits? What policy decisions exactly should governments make based on inconclusive national summaries?

Indeed, what optimizations strategies should you create based on summaries from your operating system, database, and so on? Here's something I often ask audiences of DBA's and system administrators: how come all system administrators have their own favorite tools and commands for these situations? Why haven't they been standardized a long time ago?

If the operating systems were correctly instrumented to find out where time is spent by what processes, would there not by now be one standard command or utility on, say, UNIX, to use when a system hits performance problems?

While we owe Anjo so incredibly much for the use of R = S + W in Oracle-based systems, we owe Cary big time for pointing out (indeed proving) that it needs to be used at the correct (not-too-summarized) level.

The Time Is Coming ...

To sum it up: counters don't count. Connor McDonald's wonderful utility which can give you any (higher) buffer cache hit ratio is one of the better ways of proving this (you can find it at http://www.oracledba.co.uk/tips/choose.htm). Cary even rewrote this utility in Perl in one of the appendices of his book.

Recall that time is money, and notice how we're able to focus correctly on so many other, non-IT related, things in life: it's not how many times Anjo's marvelous wife Astrid has gone shopping that worries Anjo. It's the amount of money spent in total, as he puts it.

It is also interesting to see that as the time-based measurements become available at more and more detailed levels of the Oracle code, the up-until-then use of summaries and averages prove to be flawed, and must be discarded, as the following examples illustrate.

Example 1: Don't Use the Counter Column

The counter and the time spent columns of v$session_event and v$system_event are never correlated. We have known that since around 1996, so we never use the counter. Yet if timed_statistics hasn't been set, we could be tempted to use the counter instead of the correct time column. Don't. There really is no correlation. I know, because I used it myself once. I ended up concluding that the customer needed to minimize number of IO's, when in fact they were spending most of their time waiting for latches because they had added more CPU's to the system (so, in fact, db_block_lru_latches needed to be increased).

Example 2: CPU Added to v$sql

When CPU was added as a column to the v$sql view in Oracle9i release 2, it immediately became clear that number of logical IO's (LIO's or buffer gets) and the CPU time didn't correlate at all. So whereas we had until then focused on finding the SQL statements with the highest number of buffer gets (LIO's) we were now forced to look at the statements that spent most time.

 NOTE *This means that, for example, the "Top 5" SQL statements in a STATSPACK report should be considered in terms of elapsed time and not any other category. It's somewhat ironic that they aren't listed in this way automatically.*

Workload reduction on a system is no longer a question of focusing on the statement doing most LIO/buffer gets, but on the statement spending most time.

It reminds me of Dave Ensor's "portable tuning kit" (here in pseudo code) that he showed at a conference in the UK in the fall of 2003:

```
select elapsed time, cpu time, statement id
from v$sql
order by elapsed time;
```

Anjo is currently working on, and looking at, the cost of LIO's, because an LIO is not just an LIO. There are many kinds of LIO's, and we'll need to look into that much more in the next couple of years or more.

Example 3: Timing in the Execution Plan

When timing for each step in the execution plan became available, it was obvious that number of rows processed (before 8.1.6.2) or rows returned (8.1.6.2 and later) did not correlate with the time spent in the step. So the method of focusing on steps where lots of rows were processed or returned in one step, only to be discarded or summed to much fewer rows in the following step (Martin Berg's Throw-Away Method, which he wrote, I'm proud to say, while working in my Premium Services outfit), also needs to be re-assessed.

Example 4: v$lock Is Instrumented

Until v$lock was finally instrumented in Oracle9i, all one could do was look at the number of times a lock had occurred (in the x$ksqst table), and from that deduce that the lock with the highest counter was indeed the biggest problem. As soon as the instrumentation was in place, it was obviously not true. Again, no correlation. In Oracle10g, by the way, each type of lock has its own wait event starting with Enq:, which is one reason why the number of wait events have gone up from 300+ in Oracle9i to 800+ in Oracle10g.

History Repeats Itself ...

To my knowledge, the IBM mainframe environment and the Oracle database are today the two "pieces" of code that are best instrumented.[1]

However, here is "My Big Observation #1":

> **INSIGHT** *Whenever a system or technology reaches a level of perfection (in other words, science is used as a rule), it will be replaced by something more chaotic that looks (and perhaps even is) cheaper.*

So the mainframe went out of fashion around the time it was correctly instrumented. A lot of know-how and experience disappeared with it. We know that now, but we didn't care then.

These days, I increasingly find myself talking to non-Oracle audiences about the need for time-based instrumentation at the correct level and the need to control batch. The audiences I'm talking to are setting up lots and lots of small Intel-based servers with SQL Server or MySQL, running Windows or Linux. None of these systems are correctly instrumented, none of them have the ability to control batch, and I find them inherently unstable and unpredictable.

What are they thinking? They're thinking that I'm an old fool, a dinosaur, a relic. Can't I see that these systems are so much cheaper, faster, and more fun, than all that big-iron, complicated stuff, complete with 100,000 pages of documentation? There's *no way* we will ever get a system up and running to solve our particular problem if we choose to use all those old-fashioned systems and tools, they think.

---

1. I'm probably wrong—there might very well be other folks out there who have done a better job. If so, then my apologies to the foremost instrumentors of the World, whoever you are.

Are they listening to what I say, you may ask? Only when I make fun of myself about how I missed the important messages from the mainframe guys when I started out in the late 1980s. So, no, I honestly don't think they care about my rantings!

Let me end this part of the chapter with my favorite quote from Karl Marx, to which the title of this section alludes:

History repeats itself. First as tragedy, second as farce.

Overhead

What about the overhead discussion? Imagine the following:

- IBM today announced that it was going to add 10% CPU-overhead to its mainframe environment because it wanted to instrument it correctly.

- Oracle announced an overhead of 10% for using timed_statistics. Or perhaps even a 20% overhead of using Active Session History in Oracle10g?

- UNIX vendors of the World announced today that they were going to instrument the UNIX kernel(s), and that it would cause an estimated 5% (or 10 or 20) in added CPU overhead.

- PeopleSoft instrumented their four tiers, but at a cost of an additional 15–20% CPU.

The truth is that, if these things were announced today, most customers would whine, yell, and scream, claiming a) that it isn't necessary, b) that the cost of the extra CPU should be covered by the company, and c) that it would cause a lot of applications to reach a threshold of unbearable slowness.

The point is that if a piece of software comes pre-bundled with instrumentation overhead, you don't argue or think twice before buying it. If it's added later it becomes a negative factor, and people are very hesitant to activate it permanently.

Recently someone asked me if I really was serious about having timed_statistics turned on permanently in an Oracle database. What about the overhead? Well, what about it? It might be 1%, it might be 5%, or even 20%, but the alternatives are much worse—Guess & Grimacing, trying this and that, buying too much hardware, buying too many consultants … but worst of all: Wasting a lot of time and energy.

Richard Foote, one of the technical reviewers of this book, puts it like this:

*At what point would the overheads be too much? 30, 50, 80%? My answer here would be that at the point when the instrumentation overhead is a significant contributor to any performance issues, then I would agree that perhaps the overheads would be worth consideration. However my final point would be that I have **never** come across an environment in Oracle (or IBM) where that has ever been the case. So if these instrumentations don't cause performance issues, but rather help to solve them, then any such argument is moot.*

Batch

We all know it. The three monumental, yellow tomes from Knuth told us that batch and online don't mix well. Batch jobs can eat all your CPU, and online jobs, such as forms, consequently become slow and unbearable to use.

We all know the signs: "Tuesday afternoons are horrible," "During month-end it's impossible to use the system for anything," and so on.

IBM decided a long time ago to separate batch from online. Their definition of batch was anything that used more than 8 CPU-seconds. With the ability to partition the CPU's on a mainframe, they could now run the batch jobs on certain dedicated CPU's while leaving the other CPU's to the online users.

The important point here is that a batch job doesn't have to run in a batch queue in order to behave like a batch job. Anything that runs for more than 8 CPU-seconds without any think time (human interaction, interruptions) is to be considered a batch job. Any report kicked off in the background by hitting F7, any long-running query that scans a large table, any file copy operation such as backup or restore—they're all to be considered batch jobs seen from the CPU's perspective.

As Cary has pointed out in his "Magic of '2'" paper, somewhere between 1 and 2 batch jobs (CPU-bound) will saturate any CPU. The more batch jobs that are being executed concurrently, the more CPU will be used. When the CPU's become saturated, you will have queuing delays on your system, similar to the situation where everybody wants to be in the fast lane on the highway. It slows down everyone, but it takes tough laws (Germany) or high moral standards (Denmark) to do the right thing in such a situation.

The operating systems themselves don't help much: with UNIX and Windows, the jobs will start when their time is up, regardless of the load on the system. VMS allows you to specify how many concurrently running jobs you want in a batch queue, which is much better, but still cannot take into account the actual load on the system.

Since Oracle8i it has also been possible to control batch via the Resource Manager facility. Although marred by several bugs, it has a very strong potential. The idea is that you can specify a number of "queues" and the number of concurrently running jobs per queue. Then you place users in groups with either a CPU-limit (Oracle8i) or an IO-limit (Oracle10g), and if a user/process exceeds the limit, it is suspended (thus the work done so far is not wasted), placed in a queue, and resumed when its time is up.

This, to me, looks so far as the best alternative to strictly managed systems (which are too costly for most to implement). I know that Microsoft wants to put this functionality into an upcoming release of SQL Server, and I strongly believe that it is a prerequisite in the future for serious players in the database field.

The dream of a predictable ad-hoc system lives on, though, but it is—and has always been—an oxymoron ☺.

The Wild West Systems: VMS, UNIX, Windows

I was never involved with mainframes myself. I was introduced to the world of VAX/VMS from Digital, and Oracle databases, in 1987, and it was a Wild West of systems, a time of true pioneer spirit. Guesswork and hearsay were used to a very large extent. Lack of skills and knowledge were evident everywhere. Kill It With Iron (KIWI) attitudes abounded (More CPU! More RAM! Bigger guns!). Nothing was impossible. We were invincible. And young.

Now and then I would talk to mainframe folks who would ask how we could control these systems. How could we optimize them? And how could we control batch? Since I didn't know what they were talking about, and didn't understand what they were saying, I just ignored them, while thinking they were rather strange.

Anyone could see that these new systems were much faster, cheaper, easier to change, and very much more fun. They also had *lots* of programming languages that were so much more fun, and solved certain categories of coding tasks much faster and easier than the traditional languages (Cobol, Fortran ...).

All this talk about minidisks, JCL, TSO, system programmers, COBOL, job scheduling ... it seemed so boring. They were just dinosaurs, them mainframe folks.

So we continued to build VMS-, UNIX-, and Windows-based systems. Bigger and bigger, busier and busier, more and more users. More and more unpredictable, too, since we didn't know about the need for proper instrumentation, nor the need to control batch.

Is There No Hope?

Not really. Chaos is increasing. More and more components enter your IT systems, and fewer and fewer of them are correctly instrumented.

Apart from the mainframe and Oracle, it seems that all other databases, disk sub-systems, application servers, operating systems, ERP/CRM systems, and so on, are at best incorrectly and/or incompletely instrumented, and at worst not instrumented at all.

Many of the folks working with mainframe development inside IBM are scientists. It shows in the ways you can make these systems incredibly scalable, stable, and predictable. It also shows in the way these systems are so very boring to work with. Working in IT Operations should indeed be incredibly boring. But in the VMS/UNIX/Windows world it isn't. Why? Because the systems are inherently unstable.

Any patch is a potential destabilizer, yet very few systems are capable of rolling back a patch or keeping track of interdependencies of patches and releases. Today, we've effectively given up, and just put on patches and patch sets and jumbo patches and one-off patches and releases like there's no tomorrow.

Yet, strangely enough, we never seem to reach that plateau of peace, insight, and sun that we yearn for. As Richard Foote explained it, in another of those "couldn't have said it better myself" moments:

> *In Oracle, there does appear to be a pattern. First release of a new version has more bugs than a honey jar in a South American jungle. Then the patches start flying in, some smaller (just the "right" significant numbers incrementing), some bigger ("left" significant numbers incrementing). Finally we have a version we're comfortable to implement in Prod, a few more patches and life starts to quiet down. Just as we get comfortable, Oracle releases a new version and the merry-go-round starts again ...*

The dream of the "technical fix" lives on. I don't think we can roll back the time, but we can at least try to understand the past and perhaps reuse some of the forgotten and ancient knowledge.

 NOTE *In the "good, old days" an engineer would receive a year's training inside IBM about these and many other things, before they were let loose on customer systems. Compare that to today.*

It is important to note that when I talk about mainframe environments, I'm talking about managed mainframe systems, with perhaps 12 people managing it. It is only fair to point out that I have also witnessed un-managed mainframe systems, in other words systems where the users could do anything they wanted, start any job they felt like, and so on—pretty much like the normal way a VMS/UNIX/Windows system is being managed ☺. Very powerful in some respects, but even on a mainframe this will create a situation where nothing can be predicted.

Add to the general lack of correct instrumentation what Cary kindly refers to as *Nørgaard's Law*: between one and two new components and/or tiers are added to any given system every year.

Furthermore, these new components and/or tiers are entering our systems faster than any instrumentation effort can keep up with. This leads to the conclusion that less and less of the work done in a database-centric system actually takes place inside the database, and to "My Big Observation #2":

INSIGHT *The value of the correct instrumentation of the Oracle database is ever diminishing because more and more work takes place outside the database in non-instrumented components.*

Therefore, in most situations, are you forced to use checklist tuning (a phrase invented, I think, by Cary Millsap), Guess & Grimacing, KIWI, and other inconclusive methods, then? Yes, you are.

In multi-layer, multi-component systems, where perhaps only the database is correctly instrumented, it's next to impossible to see exactly where the time is spent. When a system is slow, or a certain application is slow, the DBA's claim that the problem is not in the database (mostly rightly so), the developers point out that very little CPU is being consumed at the client end, and the network people *always* deny that the network is the problem! Keeping R = S + W in mind, and ruthlessly using that in your search for the missing time, can help, but sooner or later you will be forced to do the Guess & Grimacing exercise.

So if you know that your application's response time is 100 seconds, and the CPU spent is 42 seconds thereof, you still have to find the remaining 58. Maybe you can time your IO's, perhaps you can get the network to tell you how much time was spent there. But it will always be a puzzle, and the sums of IO time, network time, serialization time, and so on, might very well add up to more than 58, and that's when it truly looks hopeless.

Is there any hope at all? Not really. Systems today have more and more layers, tiers, components, and so desperately few of them are correctly instrumented.

The good news is that more and more people realize they have to instrument their code in order to be able to scale well (if you can't quickly tell where the bottleneck is, then you can't fix it and move on).

Also, the system management vendors (Veritas, Quest, CA, and so on) and the database and operating system vendors themselves (Oracle, Microsoft, IBM, HP ...) realize the need and the potential in these areas, so we should see a number of new products attempting to show the right information in the coming years.

But they are racing against the forces of change, and these forces always seem to succeed in increasing chaos (known as entropy to physicists).

As I write this (May 2004):

- **SQL Server** is partly instrumented (on the system level), and more work is under way (on the thread/session level). I have told various Microsoft people that they have a historical chance to instrument the whole environment, since they own so much of the stack. I hope they do it, but it is a huge task.

- The **MySQL** performance folks know they have to do it (but hesitate, because they're scared stiff of the overhead associated with any instrumentation—more on that topic later).

- At **PeopleSoft** they have done some serious work with respect to instrumentation of their four tiers, and not only to be able to troubleshoot internally, but to enable correct identification of bottlenecks. However, the task of time-based multi-tier instrumentation is awesome, and as I'm writing this they, too, have a long way to go.

- **Oracle** wants to do end-to-end performance monitoring and diagnostics, and might get very close to achieving it, as long as we're talking about a pure Oracle stack.

So I think we will see even more complex, multi-component systems in the future (I think it's what we in the OakTable network call a Cary Curve, in other words, an exponential function), which means more complexity, more problems, more chaos.

This is very good news for those who can keep up with the pace. Some old-timers with the right background to handle the whole stack will get tired, though, and find something else to do.

The younger generations will be full of energy and ideas, but don't care about the lower layers in the technology stack. When did you last hear a young man fresh out of school stating that he wanted to be the World's best system administrator or the World's best known DBA?

The fact is that the database is becoming a commodity. It would appear that the technology stack becomes commoditized from the bottom up: the disks were first. Nobody cares about them anymore, and they are mostly forgotten in incredibly complex SAN setups. The SAN itself will consist of eight or nine layers between the operating system and the disk platter, but no one knows about all of them.

Then came the commoditization of the operating systems. Most decision makers don't care anymore whether it's UNIX or Windows (or, increasingly, Linux). They just want the job done.

Now the time has come for databases to become commodities. I see IT system architects designing very complex systems, and then at the very end of the process ask the customer which database he or she would like to use. In the words of another OakTable member, Tom Kyte: the databases are being used as data dumps, not data bases.

Most graduates don't know much about databases when they get their first jobs, and most never will. They will use Java, .NET, and XML without really caring what goes on. Just as most programmers haven't cared much about the underlying operating system or disk layout in the last ten years.

The Instrumentation Panel

The correct instrumentation of components is critical to our ability to detect, diagnose, and repair (DDR) performance problems. It is also very useful in aiding us with general workload reduction on any system, thus potentially saving lots of money by delaying hardware and software upgrades.

With the correct information available in the correct format, it becomes possible to automate the task of optimizing. Witness the incredibly clever work that Graham Wood (the main architect of Oracle10g performance and availability features) and his team have put into ADDM (Automatic Database Diagnostic Monitor), ASH (Active Session History), and the AWR (Automatic Workload Repository) used to store data from both facilities. When the right information is put into a well-structured repository, you can then begin to automate.

Lots of work remains to be done by Graham and his team, but from now on it's "only" a matter of continuous improvement and refinement.

But apart from this splendid example, how many other splendid examples of this kind of instrumentation and performance-related thinking are there? Not many, I'm afraid. Not yet.

I have therefore decided (along with Anjo) that the World needs yet another group of people, this time dedicated to the instrumentation of components.

The working title of the group is The Instrumentation Panel. We will evaluate systems' instrumentation, and publish our findings. We will also work with anyone who would like to instrument code correctly. By the time this book is published in the summer of 2004, this initiative should be well under way.

State of the Nation

So, what of the future? Just because Oracle has (probably) the best, most highly instrumented database in the world, this unfortunately does not necessarily mean that it will prevail. We have all witnessed good products lose. DOS wasn't nearly as good as DR-DOS, CPM, or Mac in terms of user-friendliness, commands, and features. Windows certainly wasn't better than OS/2 in terms of multi-tasking capabilities, and so on. The SQL standard was the poorest possible implementation of a relational language (says Chris Date himself, one of the most important "fathers" of the RDBMS revolution, and author of several landmark books on the subject, not me). We still badly miss the ability to view code in WordPerfect. And so on.

After a while, the winners (mostly Microsoft products) reach a level of good enough, or even very good, functionality. The SQL standard today is quite sufficient, and almost elegant. But it's hard to say what could have been achieved if competition had lasted a while longer, or if the best product or idea had won.

A quote from an article in *Harvard Business Review* (April 2004):

> *Winners have a word for complaints about unfair practices and lost battles: They call it whining.*

In the tough world of business you either play hardball to win or softball to play. So there is not much use in complaining about the best marketing or sales strategies winning. Trust me when I say that without those ingredients Oracle wouldn't have gone far in its early days, for instance.

What about our database world? What will happen to the various databases and operating systems available today? These are my predictions, and I suspect most readers will disagree on one or more of them.

VMS Is Dying

It is one of the best operating systems ever, created by an impressive engineering effort, and further enhanced and developed with feedback from thousands of users. Perhaps the most stable OS ever, perhaps the most secure OS ever, and certainly the best clustered environment ever. Little did it help.

True, there are many, many VMS sites still out there, but new sales have all but stopped several years ago.

Proprietary UNIX Is also Dying

Observe how it's now possible to partition CPU's on the mature UNIX boxes, and how they're reaching levels of perfection and stability you never dreamed about (still lacking correct instrumentation, but so are all other operating systems). That's when they start to die.

The first UNIX flavors to die will be Solaris. Hugging Microsoft boss Steve Ballmer after secretly playing golf for a year with him is not going to save Sun, I think, but they might survive as a niche player.

Also Tru64 will die. It is a very good, very stable, and very cluster-savvy OS. But Digital was first bought by PC maker Compaq. That removed focus effectively from both VMS and Tru64, in the process killing DECUS, one of the most faithful and strong user groups ever. Then Compaq merged with another UNIX vendor, HP. HP says it will roll the cool features of Tru64 into HP/UX. No they won't, because they can't.

By pure coincidence these two UNIX variants (Solaris and Tru64) are the best UNIX variants currently available, but the rest will follow.

HP/UX is also excellent, and as Tru64 is removed, it's moving up to become the leading UNIX along with IBM's AIX. The battle between these two will be fierce. IBM might very well win, but has at the same time announced that all their operating systems will be Linux in the future.

Let's end this section with a database-related detour: in 1994 Oracle bought Digital's relational database, Rdb, along with a series of other products. In the beginning, the idea was to merge the Oracle Call Interface (OCI) layer and Rdb's equivalent, thus the two products becoming one. That approach turned out to be impossible, so instead Oracle opted to let the Rdb Development guys do what they were best at, namely developing new features for Rdb, while at the same time making sure that a certain level of interconnectivity was possible between the Oracle and Rdb databases. To this date, Rdb continues to be a very good and stable product, and I don't think Oracle lost one single Rdb customer in the process. Instead of taking over and killing the product (which is what IBM is going to do with the splendid Informix database product), they let the good product live, and kept supporting it. This, I think, is one of the best takeovers I have ever witnessed in the IT industry. Most Rdb customers have responded to this continued support by opting for Oracle as their long-term database strategy. Among them LEGO of Denmark.

Linux and Windows Are on the Rise

UNIX is being replaced by Linux and Windows, but the replacement period will be long. HP will keep HP/UX for as long as possible. IBM will be able to support AIX for an indefinite period. But those are exceptions. Besides, both IBM and HP are pushing Linux aggressively.

Since a vendor can now make as much money on a Redhat Advanced Server license as on an HP/UX license, there are fewer and fewer reasons for keeping up the R&D race for your own, proprietary UNIX. The biggest fight at the moment is between Dell and HP, and if HP wants to win that game they will have to focus strongly on Linux. IBM, meanwhile, looks on with semi-happy smiles on their faces.

VMS and UNIX will certainly not die overnight. They will die the same way Novell Netware is dying: slowly, over many years, with many believers sadly following the trend, but nobody thinking that it would one day suddenly revive.

What About Oracle?

Now, the Oracle database is by far the best database around, technically speaking. Most customers really only need Oracle version 7.3 with respect to features (although some larger users probably do need the partitioning option for manageability), and with Oracle10g they have all the features and instrumentation they could ever hope for. New features being introduced are either refinements on existing ones or features needed by the UPS's and eBay's of the World.

New sales at Oracle are slowing down dramatically. License renewals (buying the same software on a perpetual license again) provide a large part of the license revenue, and that is not the same as new license sales. The summary hides the details ...

So Oracle needs to reinvent itself, and fast, but that's a very hard thing to do when you're sitting on the top of the World with the best product around.

The fact is, though, that in a world where you currently don't get fired (sacked, as the English would say) for choosing Microsoft, it's also a real problem that Larry wants everybody else to fail, including third-party vendors with Oracle-based add-on products. These days (2004) the goal is to "Kill Weblogic" using license trade-ins and aggressive marketing. My personal view of the software world is this: 50% of it is Microsoft, and the rest of the software vendors are busy fighting each other while Microsoft is looking on with amusement. Take the Java versus .NET situation. Oracle is saying "J2EE is the way ahead," Weblogic is saying "J2EE is the only way forward," and IBM is saying "J2EE is the best choice," while Microsoft says ".NET is the future. Forget Java, although we will provide some basic interconnectivity things for it." Then Larry Ellison says that IBM is a hopeless company (why did he suddenly stop criticizing Microsoft and start hammering away at IBM? I never understood that), and that Weblogic should be killed. If you need to make a business decision based on "happenings" like that, you might very well decide that Microsoft and .NET looks like a safer bet.

Closing Thoughts

Oracle is technically the best database around. Apart from DB2 on the mainframe, Oracle is also the only database that allows you to correctly (repeatedly, scientifically) identify performance bottlenecks.

But Oracle needs to reinvent itself. No company can survive on a database-only revenue stream in the next 10 years. Unfortunately, Larry has made many enemies along the way (Microsoft, IBM, BEA, SAP to name a few) and will have a hard time breaking into new markets. Buying companies (that is, buying people and alternative products) seems the only way that Oracle can remain big enough to be a really important player in the market. Oracle still has the cash to buy other companies, but time is running out.

Oracle and DB2 are now legacy databases: very few truly new sales compared to license renewals and add-on sales to existing customers, very few young people coming out of schools wanting badly to learn about them. SQL Server is the safe choice that won't get you fired, and the open source databases such as MySQL will prevail when they can deliver the necessary (rather few, basic) functionalities that the developers of tomorrow will require (such as handling transactions correctly, have good backup methods, and so on).

MySQL founder David Axmark, in his own words, is "not in the invention business." They know what a database should be able to do, and they will get there by copying ideas from Oracle, DB2, and SQL Server.

Instrumenting code correctly is vital for any piece of software that needs to be able to scale well. Microsoft knows it, MySQL AB knows it, and most ERP vendors (PeopleSoft, SAP, and so on) know it.

But at the same time, more and more components are entering your systems, and this chaos is very hard to instrument in a complete and comprehensive way. The irony of it all is also that just when the Oracle database is near perfect in this respect, most of the real work taking place in a system is moved out of the database. I'm even beginning to see integrity constraints being enforced in the applications (sigh).

As long as you have the energy to stay on top of all the new developments in the IT world, *and* at the same time retain solid knowledge about the lower layers in the technology stack (disks, OS, database) there will be plenty of things to do in the future. Few of us, though, will be able to do that without strong personal networks, immense self-discipline, and perhaps the occasional beer.

Dear Reader,

Connor McDonald was born in Australia; lived for several years with his won-derful girlfriend, Gillian, in the UK; and then moved back to Perth, Australia, where his beautiful girlfriend, Gillian, quickly became his beautiful wife, Gillian.

Why on Earth a world-class programmer, writer, troubleshooter, optimizer, and humorist would want to live so close to Antarctica is beyond my comprehension.

It is not so much a question of WHETHER Connor can survive in Perth, since he shares the ability of the Australian Aboriginal to survive in the harshest conditions available on the Planet. He can find Oracle-related work and convince people to hire him into pure IBM mainframe environments devoid of any Unix, Windows, or Oracle software. No, the real problem is that we miss Connor terribly here in Europe. He used to do incredible presentations at various UKOUG UNIX SIG meetings and conferences, and now it is only once a year we get to see him, if that.

Apart from having the brightest smile of all Oakies, his wicked sense of humor has so far spawned at least two memorable achievements:

First, his PL/SQL script, which can give you any Buffer Cache Hit Ratio you want, is now a classic. By showing how to generate any BCHR, Connor probably put the final nail in the Hit Ratio coffin. It makes people laugh heartily at themselves and others, and ultimately that is much more efficient than writing long, scientific (or not so scientific) rants about the evils of the Ratios of the World.

Second, speaking about nails, it is worth mentioning Connor's famous presen-tation where he took a squirrel and filled it with nails (much drama on stage, much noise, very entertaining) to hammer (!) home his point about reorganizations. It must be the funniest presentation I have ever seen. It was voted best presentation at that year's UKOUG conference, and justly so. It contained many, many good tips and tricks, including a clear documentation of the fact that shutdown abort is the best way to bring down an Oracle database!

Oh, Connor has also written an excellent book, Mastering Oracle PL/SQL: Practical Solutions. *Of course, it was the first book in the OakTable Press series. Connor was always so young and fast compared to the rest of us.*

Here's to you, Connor, with the sincere hope that you will one day return to live with the rest of us in rainy and cold Europe instead of that boring place you call home. We miss you.

—Mogens Nørgaard

CHAPTER 3

Waste Not, Want Not

By Connor McDonald

Life is too short to waste.

—*Ralph Waldo Emerson (1803–1882)*

MOST EVENINGS WHEN I get home from work, I typically relax for a while, read the newspaper, and crack open a stubby (for those readers not familiar with Australian colloquialisms, this means that I have a bottle of beer). It is this activity that earns me a rap on the knuckles from my wife; firstly because she gets to observe first-hand my ever expanding waistline, and secondly, because I always forget to throw the newspaper and (now empty) beer bottle into the bin marked "Recycling." I am fully aware of the importance of recycling, but it is the easier (and lazier) option to just throw glass bottles and newspapers out with the normal trash.

Now before you start to panic, rest assured I am not going to go "environmental" on you and spend this chapter pontificating on global warming, greenhouse gases, and the like. However, what is true is that the same elements of human nature that often lead us to perform wasteful actions within our society, because they are easier, quicker, cheaper, or we are simply ignorant of their consequences, have a similar effect on the applications that we build with Oracle (or any other software infrastructure).

So what is waste in the context of Oracle? A quick lookup of *waste* in the dictionary reveals the following definitions:

- To use, consume, spend, or expend thoughtlessly or carelessly

- To fail to take advantage of

And these definitions are equally valid within the context of Oracle. Put simply, it is making the database do work that it did not need to do, or failing to take advantage of a feature that would avoid that excessive work in the first place. This can manifest itself within a system in many different ways. Most commonly, it is simply inefficient or poorly tuned code, but it can also be perfectly legitimate code being run at an inappropriate time or in an inappropriate way. Both of these problems are often relatively easy to resolve. However, more difficult scenarios also abound. Poor design sometimes mandates that the only means of satisfying a requirement is via a hideously wasteful solution. Chapters 10 and 11, by Jonathan Lewis and Tim Gorman respectively, highlight some classic examples of poor design in Oracle systems.

In a perfect world, waste within database systems would be avoided entirely. Every single task would consume no more than the minimum CPU, memory, and IO operations required to satisfy the successful completion of that task. By its very definition, there is no Oracle implementation on the planet that meets this rigorous ideal of "zero" waste, simply because the moment a row is deleted, or an index block splits, or myriad other such Oracle operations takes place, some wastage occurs. However, I have visited many a customer site where they claim that all possible wastage has been removed from the system, a claim to which I typically respond, "So why have you brought me in to take a look at it then?" Zero waste is an unattainable goal, and attempting to reach the impossible results in *Compulsive Tuning Disorder*, as vividly described by Gaja Vaidyanatha in Chapter 7. Our aim thus becomes to trim wastage to the point where its impact is negligible. We can relax this even further by aiming to reduce waste to the point at which its impact is *acceptable* as defined by the boundaries set by business requirements and/or users of the system.

Jonathan Lewis has commented in the past that any Oracle system that is performing at more than 50% of its optimal capacity is probably doing better than the vast majority of Oracle systems implemented.

This chapter is *not* about those systems that have a little waste here and there. Beyond a certain point, the benefits of attempting to eliminate waste do not justify the cost in time and money that it takes to get there—there is always a law of diminishing returns. This chapter is about some customers and applications I have encountered that were crippled by waste. However, I do stress in advance that this chapter is not intended to portray a "lynch mob" mentality, whereby I vent my spleen on all of the poor practices that have ever been used against an Oracle database. No application vendor *deliberately* sets out to build and sell a performance disaster, but often what the vendor views as "slight overhead" is a far cry from what happens when that system is switched on in your production environment. Usually this is due to ignorance of the features available, insufficient or inappropriate testing, or just plain bad luck. Hopefully, by reading this chapter, you will be able to avoid making those same mistakes on your systems.

With each tale of woe that follows, I have included the actions that were taken for each of the problems encountered. Sometimes a complete solution to the problem was achieved, but at other times just the worst symptoms were reduced by varying degrees (a headache does not always require brain surgery, sometimes just an aspirin pill will do). With infinite time and money the optimal solution can be found to virtually any problem, but in reality, the "best" solution is typically the one that strikes the right balance between achievable benefits and the cost of implementing them.

As a final note before we move on, you will notice that in this chapter the term *tuning* is rarely used. This is merely personal preference, to steer you away from the conventional opinions related to tuning—those opinions espoused by many an "expert" that wastage can be resolved simply by tweaking a database parameter here and there, or rebuilding a couple of indexes, and other such knee-jerk reactions. The focus on reducing waste starts on day one, the day you cracked open the seal on the Oracle software CD, to the day you go live with your application.

As Bad As It Gets

Let's commence with possibly the most extreme example I have ever found of waste within a component of an application. The issue for this particular client was obvious: CPU capacity. I was asked to investigate why the database server CPU for the application in question was continuously pegged at 100% throughout business hours. No dips, no troughs, just a neat flatline on the CPU graph at 100% (something that you could almost consider "impressive" on a largish Sun box with six top-of-the-range CPU's).

Perhaps the most common cause of excessive CPU on an Oracle database server is excessive logical IO. That is, retrieval of data that is already present within the buffer cache. If the problem was indeed caused by poor SQL, then with a CPU problem this extreme, it should be trivial to pick out the offending statements. With this in mind, we probed V$SQL to obtain possible candidates for excessive logical IO. And this is what was found:

```
SQL> select sql_text, buffer_gets, executions
  2  from v$sql
  3  where buffer_gets > 1000000
  4  order by 2
  5  /


SQL_TEXT                                        BUFFER_GETS  EXECUTIONS
----------------------------------------------- ------------ -----------
SELECT SUBSTR(:b1,:b2,1)    FROM DUAL            1612856838   322571313
SELECT INSTR(:b1,:b2)    FROM DUAL               1612856497   322571313
```

Ouch! Hundreds of millions of executions of queries to DUAL. Across the entire system, some 35% of all logical IO was being performed by these queries. Furthermore, it is immediately apparent from the preceding output that these calls were totally redundant! You never need to visit DUAL to calculate INSTR and SUBSTR values (except if by some bizarre circumstance the coding environment in question does not implement the functions at all).

In any event, a quick hunt through DBA_SOURCE revealed the source of this code to be a simple validation routine called STRING_CHECK. Take a look at the following typical usage scenario, and then I will drill deeper to reveal just how much pain a server can be caused by such a simple functional requirement.

```
SQL> variable x number
SQL> exec string_check('123',:x)

PL/SQL procedure successfully completed.

SQL> print x


        X
----------
        0


SQL> exec string_check ('12C3',:x)

PL/SQL procedure successfully completed.

SQL> print x


        X
----------
        1
```

And that is it! At first glance, it is relatively straightforward to glean what the STRING_CHECK PL/SQL procedure is doing. It is a simple data validation routine whereby if the string (p_text_in) that is passed in is numeric, then it returns 0, otherwise it returns 1. Surely a simple validation routine to see if a string is numeric could not be responsible for the CPU crisis? It was. Let's take a look at the underlying code for STRING_CHECK, to reveal the wastage.

```
procedure string_check (p_text_in varchar2,
                        p_ret out number) is
  char_list varchar2(255);
  v_single_char varchar2(1);
```

```
  v_in_string number;
  cursor c1(m number) is
    select substr(char_list,m,1) from dual;
  cursor c2(v varchar2) is
    select instr(p_text_in,v) from dual;
begin
  p_ret := 0;
  for i in 1 .. 45 loop
    char_list := char_list || chr(i);
  end loop;
  char_list := char_list || chr(47);
  for i in 58 .. 255 loop
   char_list := char_list || chr(i);
  end loop;
  for i in 1 .. length(char_list) loop
    open c1(i);
    fetch c1 into v_single_char;
    close c1;

    open c2(v_single_char);
    fetch c2 into v_in_string;
    close c2;
    if v_in_string > 0 then
      p_ret := 1;
    end if;
  end loop;
end;
```

Without delving too deeply into the specifics, the routine builds up, by concatenation, a string called CHAR_LIST. The CHAR_LIST variable is a string that contains all valid ASCII characters *except* those that may comprise a number, namely the characters 0 to 9 (ASCII characters 48 to 57) and a decimal point (ASCII character 46).

It is at this point that the work, and the waste, occurs. Each character from the CHAR_LIST variable is extracted, via cursor C1, by a query to DUAL using SUBSTR. That is 244 queries to DUAL. The retrieved single character is then checked for existence within the incoming candidate string using INSTR, via cursor C2. That is another 244 queries to DUAL. Thus, each time a string is checked for numeric validity, the database has to execute 488 queries to DUAL. This client was running version 8, so each access to DUAL requires five logical IOs, thus 488 queries equates to 2440 logical IOs. Had the database being running on version 9, this would have been "only" 1464 logical IOs, since queries to DUAL have been optimized down to three logical IOs per access. In either case, it must surely rate as the world's most expensive TO_NUMBER function.

A couple of thousand logical IOs in a database routine is not necessarily any cause for alarm. It is only when that routine is executed hundreds of thousands of times that it becomes a disaster. Further analysis of the application revealed that this routine was run for every piece of text that was presented to the system via one of the interfaces from an external system or via many of the screens that allowed for user entry of data. For virtually every column in every row of data that was fed into the system, STRING_CHECK was executed. Interestingly, one of the reasons that the vendor did not foresee a problem was that "the DUAL table was so small," and thus they surmised that querying it should not be a problem.

Resolutions

Savvy readers will be no doubt be already aware that the absence of nonnumeric characters does not necessarily indicate that a string is a valid number, and this flaw in the code actually caused problems when it came to devising an appropriate solution. If the procedure had been named, say, IS_STRING_A_VALID_NUMBER, then it could be safely assumed that numeric validation was its purpose, and it could have been trivially been converted to a simple procedure, as follows:

```
procedure is_string_a_valid_number(p_text_in varchar2, p_ret out number) is
  x number;
begin
  x := to_number(p_text_in);
  p_ret := 0;
exception
  when others then p_ret := 1;
end;
```

But given the vague name, STRING_CHECK, and the fact that strings with multiple decimal points would be treated as valid, there was some hesitation as to what would happen if the code was replaced with a more "correct" version. Hence initially, the code was replaced with a version in which the queries to obtain SUBSTR and INSTR from DUAL were replaced with their native equivalents, leading to the version shown here:

```
procedure string_check_v2 (p_text_in varchar2,
                           p_ret out number) is
  char_list varchar2(255);
begin
  p_ret := 0;
  for i in 1 .. 45 loop
```

```
      char_list := char_list || chr(i);
    end loop;
    char_list := char_list || chr(47);
    for i in 58 .. 255 loop
     char_list := char_list || chr(i);
    end loop;
    for i in 1 .. length(char_list) loop
      if instr(p_text_in, substr(char_list,i,1)) > 0 then
        p_ret := 1;
        return;
      end if;
    end loop;
end;
```

This yielded an immediate drop in CPU in the vicinity of 30%. After further consultations with the vendor, they confirmed that indeed the function was intended to be a numeric validation routine. And we were able to safely implement the optimal solution using Oracle's built-in TO_NUMBER function, and the CPU problems ceased. Tellingly, the reason that they had initially implemented their own "generic" version of TO_NUMBER was so that their code could easily be ported to another database platform that they supported. You might be thinking that a vendor that implements such a routine probably has countless other areas where excessive wastage is occurring—and you are correct; reducing the CPU for this client is very much a work-in-progress. Who knows, maybe one day you will read about them in *Oracle Insights—The Sequel*.

From a consultant's perspective, there is always much enjoyment to be had out of this type of problem. It was trivial to detect, trivial to fix, and the benefits for the client were enormous. Being able to reclaim a third of a server's CPU capacity with a few minutes' work does lend itself to those theories that consultants have some "magic tricks" up their sleeves when clients call them for help. While it is always sorely tempting not to dissuade clients from that belief, it was just a simple matter of seeking and eliminating waste. That was the true "magic" for the client.

Although excessive CPU consumption caused by excessive logical IO is perhaps the most common form of wastage in Oracle systems, it can also manifest itself in more peculiar ways, as we will explore now.

"Ultra" Read Consistency

Before going into the details of the next particular problem, let's take a look at a little background on read consistency and isolation levels, background that would have proved invaluable to the developers who built the application in question.

The ANSI/SQL standard provides for various levels of isolation that defines the data that is visible to the query when it commences. The levels are

- *Read uncommitted:* "Dirty" reads are allowed, that is, uncommitted data from transactions that you did not issue are visible to you. Oracle does not support this level.

- *Read committed:* Dirty reads are disallowed, but changes to data that has been modified (updated or erased) by committed transactions become visible if you reread the data. Thus a read of the same data may not be guaranteed to be repeatable over time. Oracle supports this level and uses it by default.

- *Repeatable read:* Dirty reads are disallowed and, as the name of the level suggests, a read can be repeated exclusive of modifications to the data. New data, that is, data that satisfies your query conditions and is created/committed by another transaction (known as *phantom data*), can be picked up by repeated reads. Oracle does not support this level.

- *Serializable:* Dirty reads are disallowed, repeatable read is supported, and phantom data will never be visible. Oracle supports this level and a read-only hybrid, which in effect is serializable and also prohibits the creation or modification of data.

A full discussion of isolation levels and Oracle's implementation can be found in Chapter 13 of the 10g Concepts Manual. Alternatively, information on how isolation levels pertain to other databases can be found throughout the Internet, for example:

- SQL Server at
  `http://www.winnetmag.com/SQLServer/Article/ArticleID/5336/5336.html`

- DB2 at `http://www.developer.ibm.com/tech/faq/individual?oid=2:18730`

By defining what data is visible within a transaction, the isolation levels determine the duration of read consistency available. In default operation, Oracle implements the Read Committed isolation level, which provides *statement-level read consistency*. All data returned and examined by a statement is guaranteed to be consistent with respect to a single point in time, that is, when the statement commenced. Thus the duration of read consistency is that of a single statement.

Rerunning the same statement may return different data (committed by other transactions occurring within the database). This is perhaps the most "natural" duration for read consistency in that it gives the perspective that the database is "frozen" at the point in time that the data was requested. In effect, it gives the closest impression achievable to the statement starting and finishing instantaneously (the laws of physics surrounding CPU, memory, and disk drives being the only mitigating factors). The serialization isolation level extends the duration of read consistency across multiple statements, thus allowing multiple statements to be conducted with the data fixed at a nominated point in time. Oracle implements this as *transaction-level read consistency*, where the nominated point in time is the start of a transaction. All subsequent requests for data will be consistent with respect to the start of the transaction—the duration of the consistency continues until the transaction is ended.

While some databases support the Read Uncommitted level, it is hard to see a use for it in practice, as data is not consistent with respect to *any* point in time. There is no read consistency or, more correctly, the read consistency has a duration of zero. All data as it currently exists (committed or uncommitted) at the moment the statement encounters that data during execution is considered. If you happened to be a database software vendor, the Read Uncommitted level is probably an easy mechanism to implement: you simply read data as you find it. Every other isolation level will require a mechanism to manage whether data will be exposed to the requesting environment.

Perhaps the easiest way to implement any required read consistency duration (statement, transaction, or otherwise) is to lock data as it is read. As long as the data is locked for the length of the desired read consistency duration, you can be assured the data will not be changed should you choose to reread it. Of course, the ease of this implementation comes at a cost—you lose concurrency. This is perhaps the reason why some database vendors allow the dubious Read Uncommitted level described previously. You avoid locking the data to keep the concurrency level high, at the cost of never really being sure about the consistency of your data.

There is another way, and indeed, one of the most attractive features of Oracle when compared to many other relational database products is you "can have your cake and eat it too." The act of reading data does not lock others from reading that data, while *still* providing the desired duration of read consistency. Even today, many an Oracle developer or administrator fails to realize that the UNDO segments in the database do more than just allow a transaction to abort its changes—those same UNDO segments hold the precious history that allows Oracle to provide read consistency without introducing additional locking.

Back to the Problem Application

Let's return to the problem application. In any day where business activity was high, response time complaints were jamming the help desk phone lines. The vendor insisted that it was not their application. (Have you ever known a vendor not to claim this?) The problem "must be" in the database server or the network. As is customary in the world of information technology, what followed were several senior management crisis meetings in which a number of resolutions, each having absolutely no basis in fact, were weighed up. Buy more CPU? More network bandwidth? Do we need more disk? Should we upgrade the database version? This list went on. The sole benefit of all these meetings was that while all the ranting and raving went on, it did allow time for some genuine analysis of the problem and its source. Using some judicious tracing, such as that described in Chapters 4 and 5 we were able to gather some concrete data on the nature of the problem. Typical user actions were traced as well as some of the batch programs that ran hourly on an application server. From tracing user activity, the key observations were

- Very little CPU was consumed on the database server.

- A great deal of time was lost on SQL*Net events (SQL*Net message to client, SQL*Net message from client, SQL*Net break/reset to client)

It is commonplace for tracing on user activity to see time lost on SQL*Net traffic. Often, this is simply idle time. Whenever the database is waiting upon a request for action from the client (that is, from somewhere across the network), the time is attributed to the "SQL*Net message from client" event. While our tracing team had endeavored to trace just "active" user time, the initiation and termination of tracing user sessions had been done over the phone, so it was concluded that some miscommunication had probably led to the capture of all that SQL*Net idle time (more on this later). Therefore, we put aside the user trace files and considered the batch program files. Since we had total control over their launch, we could accurately define the tracing time window to remove any spurious SQL*Net waits. The response time breakdown for the batch programs revealed some very interesting results:

- Very little CPU was consumed on the database server.

- A great deal of time was lost on SQL*Net events (SQL*Net message to client, SQL*Net message from client, SQL*Net break/reset to client).

A very similar profile to that obtained for user activity. But why would batch programs have idle time attributed to SQL*Net? Certainly, monitoring CPU on the application server did not indicate that the batch programs had any particular sleep time built into their infrastructure. Why were we losing all this time on network events? Did we indeed have a network problem? A search on Metalink revealed that large amounts of time lost on these SQL*Net events were caused by "an underlying network problem"(Note 160451.1). Perhaps the vendor was correct after all: time to dig a little deeper.

A *Closer Look at the Trace Files*

In the trace files for both the user activity and the batch programs, much of the work was accounted for by query and DML activities on tables named TMP_pp_qqqqqq_xxxx, where pp and qqqqqq were numeric ID's and xxxx was a piece of text that appeared to indicate what the table contained (for example, msum for data that seemed to be relevant to a monthly summary). It did not take too long to deduce that the two numeric ID's were simply the session identifiers, SID and SERIAL#, taken from V$SESSION.

Although the tables were tagged with the session ID and serial number, the tables were not transient; they simply remained on the database forever, or at least until a cleanup job was run. This cleanup job had never been scheduled, which turned out to be a blessing in disguise since it became possible to take a look at the tables' structure and the data that they typically contained. With some further analysis, their usage became apparent. Each time a user or batch program required a result set for a query from the database, this result set would be transferred to one of these TMP-prefixed tables. Typically the result sets were small but, for the batch programs, occasionally the tables would contain large sets of data. The duration of the data in the tables was not well defined. Examination of the trace files showed that sometimes the data would be regularly recycled with standard DELETE and INSERT DML throughout the session. Other times a table would be populated once and the data used for the duration of the session.

It was the mechanism via which these tables were created that finally revealed the explanation for our initial trace file diagnosis, that is, a "network problem." The application logic for using these temporary tables was as follows:

1. Wipe any existing data from the temporary table.

2. If an error is returned indicating that the table does not exist, then create the table.

3. If no error is returned, populate the table with the new data that has been requested.

4. The application can then query the temporary table to display results to the user.

Thus, each time one of these temporary tables was accessed for the "first" time, a parsing error would appear in the trace file, this error being the trigger for the application code to dynamically create the table and then populate it. Delving into the raw trace files to locate a typical occurrence of these parse errors revealed the following information:

```
PARSE ERROR #1: ... err=942
DELETE FROM TMP_12_34567_MSUM
WAIT #1: nam='SQL*Net break/reset to client' ela= 428 p1=1413697536 p2=1 p3=0
WAIT #1: nam='SQL*Net break/reset to client' ela= 189 p1=1413697536 p2=0 p3=0
WAIT #1: nam='SQL*Net message to client' ela= 4 p1=1413697536 p2=1 p3=0
WAIT #1: nam='SQL*Net message from client' ela= 26290 p1=1413697536 p2=1 p3=0
```

Notice that the statement failed to parse with an error code of 942. This is the "object does not exist" error. The DELETE statement was issued against the *nonexistent* table TMP_12_34567_MSUM.

 NOTE *The reason why the vendor used* DELETE *and not* TRUNCATE *will, I am afraid, remain forever shrouded in mystery.*

Each time a parsing error occurred on a statement issued from a client remote from the database server, whether this be a user or batch program, the database undertook some work to "resync" itself with the client program. There was not a network problem at all! The "network problems" were a manifestation of the continual parse errors the client programs invoked by attempting to query nonexistent tables (which they would then dynamically create on the fly, and populate).

Why would the vendor dynamically create a table and populate it with data from the database? They were not exactly forthcoming with explanations, but as conversations with the vendor support staff progressed, it became apparent that this approach was necessary because when their product had been implemented on other relational database platforms, ad hoc reads on large sections of the database (in particular by the batch programs) would cause locking and hence concurrency issues for the rest of the application (examples of which you can see in Chapter 10). By taking a copy of the data, the locks on the original data could be released and concurrency maintained. The vendor had, in effect, built their own custom (and very expensive) implementation of read consistency. In a typical user session, there would be perhaps 40 to 50 such tables created in quick succession, as a consequence of merely navigating through the common parts of the application.

Of course, as well as the overhead of creating the tables, there was the massive work of copying the data from the source table(s) to these temporary tables.

As discussed earlier with Oracle's implementation of the ANSI/SQL isolation levels, this work was not required. When work is being performed that is not needed, you have wastage. In this example, the application could have read the data with no fear of creating locking problems for the other users of the system, because these locks simply do not occur within Oracle. Whereas for some other databases, dynamically creating objects is commonplace, on Oracle, "on-the-fly" DDL is vastly more expensive than simple DML operations.

Resolutions

Having identified the source of the problem, where to from here? As is becoming more commonplace nowadays, this was a third-party application package. One cannot just rip open the source code and make the appropriate changes. In fact, we could not see the source code at all. Any database activity had to be deduced from what was exposed within the Oracle trace files. But let us briefly ponder what could have been done in a fantasy world, where we are sitting side by side with the application developers who are keen to make improvements to the implementation of their product within the Oracle infrastructure. (I did say it was a fantasy world ...)

Theoretical Solutions

Simply the act of opening a cursor on the desired result set would have satisfied the vast majority of requirements of this application. Regardless of how long you wait after you have opened the cursor, any rows that are fetched from it will be consistent with the point in time at which the cursor was opened. If coding was being performed at the OCI level (and the database was at version 9 or above), then it would be possible to repeatedly scroll back and forth through the result set in a consistent fashion.

Another alternative could be to explore the read-only isolation level that is provided by Oracle. Obviously, most users and batch programs would require the capacity to perform DML, but this could be performed autonomously, thus preserving the read-only isolation level and any desired duration for read consistency. Approaching from the opposite direction, all DML could be allowed as per normal, but read consistency for the queries could be explicitly enforced using the flashback features (if version 9 had been in use).

All of these operations have their own overheads that would need to be benchmarked and catered for. The longer the duration of read consistency, the greater the likelihood that more undo information must be retained in order to "roll back in time" the data for the result set. Reconstructing this data from the undo might in itself become an issue of wastage if the number of undo operations required to get consistent data becomes large. However, although this is not a solution that could be ever be benchmarked for this application (remember, we are in a fantasy world here), it is unlikely that the overheads of undo would be as drastic as those of repeated parse errors and constant DDL calls throughout the application.

Solutions in Practice

So, without access to the source code, what was done for this particular customer application? A partial resolution was quite simple to implement, although this was more down to good luck on our part than anything else.

Since no one had ever run the cleanup job to get rid of the tables for sessions that were no longer present, we could make a reasonable assessment of all of the different types of tables that were populated. There were only 70 or so different tables that were populated, each with a unique suffix (the tag MSUM, and so on, from before). Our aim was to use Oracle global temporary tables and "fool" the application into never having to issue a CREATE TABLE statement.

A global temporary table was created for each of the 70 or so possible different table structures that were being used within the application. The table was set to preserve rows on commit to mimic the behavior of the current tables to allow data to be retained for the duration of the session. Thus, if you consider the original example from the trace file where the table name was TMP_12_3456_MSUM, this would become a global temporary table called TMP_MSUM.

As each user connected to the database, a suite of synonyms was created at logon, one for each of the global temporary tables. The synonym names contained the session identification details that had been used for the original temporary tables (note that I say "temporary" because they held temporary data, but of course they were in fact permanent tables in the conventional sense). Following the preceding example, as the user connects, a synonym TMP_12_3456_MSUM is created for the global temporary table TMP_MSUM.

Naturally, this did have some impact on the logon process, and we were still breaking one of the cardinal rules about Oracle performance ("do not do DDL on the fly"), but the users typically logged on no more than a couple of times per day and, once they were logged on, performance for them during the day was significantly improved. We had certainly not eliminated the wasteful practice of copying data from the database repeatedly, but we had reduced wastage in many key areas.

There was a reduction in redo by using temporary tables instead of permanent tables, a reduction in parsing errors, a reduction in overall recursive SQL—simply a consequence of creating synonyms instead of creating tables, and, of course, a reduction in disk space usage because the cleanup of temporary data was automatic. As a user disconnected, their temporary data vanished automatically. A custom cleanup job was written to remove obsolete synonyms instead of dropping the original tables, and unlike the original cleanup job, we made sure it was scheduled on a regular basis!

Was it a complete solution? No. As time went on, scenarios were discovered in which the application attempted to drop the temporary tables and then re-create them on the fly. Needless to say, this caused some problems with our synonym/global temporary table approach. But the vendor has assured us that the "next release" of the product actually implements many of the customizations that we had ourselves implemented—hopefully this will provide a closer to optimal solution.

The Reference Code Dumping Ground

In the data warehousing world, careful distinction is made between dimensional data and fact data:

- *Dimensional data* are the elements that remain relatively static and typically are descriptive information that define the various categories of data that exist in the warehouse.

- *Fact data* is the raw detail within the warehouse along with the associated references back to the dimensional data.

Even in the non-warehousing environment, where the distinction is not as concrete, most database applications will contain some components of static or reference data: data that provides descriptive detail for surrogate key data stored within the database. For example, in the customer application I will be discussing in this section, a multitude of reference data domains were required for storing attributes about people. There were domains of reference data for

- Gender (male, female, and so on)

- Marital status (single, married, and son)

- Religion

- Primary language

and so forth. In total, there were some 700 domains of reference data. The vendor apparently did not want to create 700 individual tables, so a single table was created, the ubiquitous REFERENCE_CODE table.

```
SQL> desc REFERENCE_CODE
 Name                            Null?    Type
 ------------------------------- -------- -------------
 ID                              NOT NULL NUMBER(18)
 DESCRIPTION                     NOT NULL VARCHAR2(100)
 DOMAIN                          NOT NULL NUMBER(18)
 SORT_ORDER                               NUMBER(8)
```

There is nothing inherently flawed in this approach—but it is vital to remember that the rows in such a table *belong* to a domain. Further investigation revealed that over time thousands of rows had been added to the REFERENCE_CODE table, each with a domain of 0, signifying (ID, DESCRIPTION) pairs that apparently had "no domain." The table had become a dumping ground for any data in the application where a numeric ID needed to be associated with a textual description. Of course, no vendor ever admits to a table being called a "dumping ground"—an alternative term is typically used, such as "flexible" or "generic." In my view, generic is a proverbial "four-letter word." Relational databases are all about providing form and structure to data, whereas "generic" suggests the opposite. Whenever a table starts to contain miscellaneous data simply because the column data types seem to suit, the risk of wastage is high. So where did the vendor go wrong with their usage of the REFERENCE_CODE table? Two problems occurred with this particular application.

Problem 1: Lookup Function Pervasion

Many an application developer is taught that there are advantages to encapsulating SQL functionality within a suitable API, typically PL/SQL packages, and there are numerous components in the development of a large-scale application for which this is an intelligent strategy. However, does this automatically mean that, for the REFERENCE_CODE table, it makes sense to build an API to return the text description for a given ID within a domain? Where would such a function be useful? It is unlikely that a user would ever enter an ID—after all, it is just a meaningless number. The only time an ID would be known in advance would be if it has been retrieved from a table. For any column in a database table that references an ID from the reference table, a simple join to REFERENCE_CODE would suffice to retrieve the description. Unfortunately for this application, a PL/SQL lookup function had been created whereby an ID was passed in and the function returned the description. Notice that I have dropped the reference to domain—more on that shortly.

Recall from earlier in this chapter that massive numbers of executions of queries to DUAL were causing CPU problems. For this client, a similar scenario existed. Much of the server CPU came from a single SQL statement:

```
SQL_TEXT
---------------------------------------------
SELECT DESCRIPTION FROM REFERENCE_CODE WHERE ID = :b1
```

This SQL was contained in the REFERENCE_CODE lookup function, called GET_REF_DESC, which was a simple lookup routine.

```
function get_ref_desc(p_id number) return varchar2 is
  retval reference_code.description%type;
begin
  select description
  into retval
  from reference_code
  where id = p_id;
  return retval;
end;
```

A scan through the application source code revealed why this query was so prevalent. The vast majority of all queries to fact tables within the application were of the form

```
select
    <<columns>>
    get_ref_desc(gender_id) gender,
    get_ref_desc(eye_color_id) eye_color,
    get_ref_desc(occupation_id) job,
    ...
from PEOPLE
where <<conditions>>
```

Most readers will correctly identify the two main problems here.

- There is an inherent cost to calling PL/SQL from SQL, so calling GET_REF_DESC will incur a performance penalty.

- It is reinventing the wheel. The functionality being implemented is just a home-grown version of an outer join.

There is actually a third issue with the code and that is how Oracle exposes the execution plan for such statements. When you explain the preceding query, you see an execution plan looks similar to the following:

```
PLAN
------------------------------------------------------------------
SELECT STATEMENT
  TABLE ACCESS BY INDEX ROWID PEOPLE
    INDEX RANGE SCAN PEOPLE_IX
```

In this case the predicates allowed the use of an index on the PEOPLE table, but notice that there is no evidence that the REFERENCE_CODE table will be queried. In fact, it is queried several times per retrieved row. The plan is missing any clues as to how the access to the REFERENCE_CODE table will perform. Oracle does not expose plan information about recursive lookups (that is, those that result from PL/SQL calls within SQL). For the same reason, use of scalar subqueries, for example:

```
select
    <<columns>>
    ( select description from reference_code where id = p.gender_id) gender,
    ( select description from reference_code where id = p.eye_color_id) eye_color,
    ( select description from reference_code where id = p.occupation_id) job,
    ...
from PEOPLE p
where <<conditions>>
```

is probably not the best solution here. It is very hard to tune queries when you cannot get an accurate representation in the execution plan of what work is actually happening.

Problem 2: The Loss of Domain

Time to go back to the vendor. Armed with some benchmarking results, we were able to convince them that lookup functions were not appropriate in most of the SQL code. Let's take another look at the REFERENCE_CODE definition:

```
SQL> desc REFERENCE_CODE
 Name                          Null?    Type
 ----------------------------- -------- -------------
 ID                            NOT NULL NUMBER(18)
 DESCRIPTION                   NOT NULL VARCHAR2(100)
 DOMAIN                        NOT NULL NUMBER(18)
 SORT_ORDER                             NUMBER(8)
```

Each reference code text is assigned a unique numeric ID, populated by an Oracle sequence. Armed with this information, the example query to PEOPLE can be replaced by a series of joins to the REFERENCE_CODE table instead of calls to the GET_REF_DESC function. For mandatory ID columns in the PEOPLE table (for example, gender), an inner join is appropriate, and for optional columns (for example, job), an outer join is required. After a great deal of prompting, the vendor supplied a modification to the preceding SQL, with joins instead of calls to the lookup function, which referenced REFERENCE_CODE for each ID lookup:

```
select
   <<people columns>>
   gender.description,
   eye_color.description,
   job.description,
   ...
from PEOPLE,
  REFERENCE_CODE gender,
  REFERENCE_CODE eye_color,
  REFERENCE_CODE job
where <<conditions>>
and gender.ID = people.gender_id
and eye_color.ID = people.eye_color
and job.ID(+) = people.job_id
```

During testing, the revised approach from the vendor performed poorly. Certainly a strange result, given that the changes from lookup functions to outer joins should have yielded a considerable benefit. The probe to locate a reference code with a known ID should have been very efficient—after all, "it is a unique key lookup—nothing could be faster."

Notice the mention (or lack thereof) of domain in the preceding SQL statement. The problem lay with the fact that the query does not reflect what the REFERENCE_CODE table was modeled to do. For example, it was trivial to query the database to discover that any values for JOB in the PEOPLE table will always be one of only 60 reference code ID's that had a domain value of 577 (the designated domain for jobs). However, because the ID for every reference code was unique, the domain had become viewed as simply a categorizing convenience, and therefore deemed redundant to the query. After all, given the fact that the ID was unique, then a JOB value from the PEOPLE table could only ever map to a single row in REFERENCE_CODE. Why then bother with adding the appropriate predicate to indicate the job domain into queries?

The fact is, however, that whenever you hide information from the database, you are risking poor performance. The developer knows that someone's job will also map to one of the 60 ID's with domain 577, but if the query is joining on just ID and not domain, the database is not privy to that information. Even considering a simpler version of the query—probing for just one of the reference code lookups— revealed an interesting access path:

```
select
   <<people columns>>
   job.description,
   ...
from PEOPLE,
  REFERENCE_CODE job
where <<conditions>>
and job.ID(+) = people.job_id

PLAN
-----------------------------------------------------------------
SELECT STATEMENT
  HASH JOIN OUTER
    TABLE ACCESS BY INDEX ROWID PEOPLE
      INDEX RANGE SCAN PEOPLE_IX
    TABLE ACCESS FULL REFERENCE_CODE
```

A full scan on REFERENCE_CODE perhaps would not normally be a problem, but combined with the fact that the table has been used to dump some 20,000 entries, the full scan caused CPU problems even worse than the lookup function problems that we were trying to solve. The problems were exacerbated when (as was the case in the original PEOPLE query) multiple joins to REFERENCE_CODE were included with additional full scans.

The vendor very nearly reverted back to the lookup functions. But look at what happens when the *database* is given the information that we already knew—that is, we are only interested in the reference codes from the job domain.

```
select
    <<people columns>>
    job.description,
    ...
from PEOPLE,
  REFERENCE_CODE job
where <<conditions>>
and job.ID(+) = people.job_id
and job.DOMAIN(+) = 577
PLAN
-----------------------------------------------------------------
SELECT STATEMENT
  HASH JOIN OUTER
    TABLE ACCESS BY INDEX ROWID PEOPLE
      INDEX RANGE SCAN PEOPLE_IX
    TABLE ACCESS BY INDEX ROWID REFERENCE_CODE
      INDEX RANGE SCAN REF_DOM_ID_IX
```

Oracle chose a different access path and a more efficient entry into the REFERENCE_CODE table. In this case, the index REF_DOM_ID_IX, as the name suggests, was an index built on the DOMAIN and ID columns. Although you can never really tell just from the execution plan that this path is better than the full scan, benchmarking revealed significant benefits, and of course the key thing here is that Oracle has a far greater chance of choosing a smarter access path when it is given better information to work with. As a general guideline, you can never give the cost-based optimizer too much information, only too little.

Problem 2a: The Loss of Domain for Validation

Because the REFERENCE_CODE table had been given a primary key on the ID column, all referential integrity constraints on other tables within the application that referred back to REFERENCE_CODE could only refer to the ID. Thus the constraints only enforced that a valid ID was being used, not a valid ID *within the appropriate domain*. The application code was responsible for that additional validation. The consequences of this approach were as predictable as they were dire. A number of table columns contained ID values that referred back to *multiple* domains, and not only did we have performance issues but data integrity violations as well.

Resolution

There are still some 20,000 thousand entries in the REFERENCE_CODE table, many of which are still "domain-less." However, the preceding changes to remove the excessive calls to the lookup function and include the domain where appropriate have reduced CPU significantly in many parts of the application. A number of queries still do not include the domain due to the multidomain issue described, but our end goal is to get to the stage where perhaps one day the domain will be (correctly) placed as the leading column in the primary key for REFERENCE_CODE, something that will only occur when we have finally identified all queries that do not specify the domain and all of the data that maps to single domain.

Perhaps more importantly, both the vendor and local application developers are starting to embrace the important philosophies of using SQL, not PL/SQL, to solve problems where possible, and to give the Oracle optimizer as much information as possible to assist with its decision making.

Parsing Proliferation: From XML to Oracle

Every day, week, or month in the information technology workplace, a new piece of technology becomes the "next big thing." A few years back, Java was the latest and greatest thing since sliced bread. Today, anything that relates to XML seems to be all the rage. The capacity to provide a consistent mechanism to give a representation of any data and its attributes is a very powerful and compelling argument for using XML as the means for passing data between applications.

With any piece of technology, use it inappropriately and it will come back and bite you hard later, and XML is no exception. Being from a relational database background, for me perhaps the most important component of any application is the data model—the careful analysis that yields the entities and relationships between those entities. The data model drives the application that will encompass it. Data modeling is all about providing form and definition to your data. However, with XML it is easy to become lazy with the structure of your data. This is not a criticism of XML in itself, more the philosophy of believing that simply wrapping data within some XML tags somehow magically makes that data "well defined."

This clash between well-defined data within a relational database and arbitrary data represented within XML is the source of my next exploration of wastage.

Background

The application in question had a number of core tables (such as PEOPLE, PROPERTY, CARS, HOUSES) to store information about people, their property, the car that they drove, the house that they lived in, and so on. For each of these core tables, API's were provided via which data could be added to the system from external sources. Each API was implemented as a suite of calls within a PL/SQL package. For example, to maintain information about a person, the available package calls were along the lines of

- API_PERSON.ADD

- API_PERSON.MODIFY

- API_PERSON.REMOVE

Each API took a number of parameters representing the various attributes of each entity, and passed back a status code to the calling environment indicating whether the operation was successful. Thus, the specification for the API_PERSON package looked like this:

```
SQL> desc API_PERSON
PROCEDURE NEW
  Argument Name                   Type                     In/Out
  ----------------------------    ----------------------   ------
  SURNAME                         VARCHAR2                 IN
  FIRSTNAME                       VARCHAR2                 IN
  DATE_OF_BIRTH                   VARCHAR2                 IN
  JOB                             VARCHAR2                 IN
  GENDER                          VARCHAR2                 IN
  RELIGION                        VARCHAR2                 IN
  ...
  STATUS_CODE                     NUMBER(38)               OUT

PROCEDURE REMOVE
  Argument Name                   Type                     In/Out
  ----------------------------    ----------------------   ------
  SURNAME                         VARCHAR2                 IN
  FIRSTNAME                       VARCHAR2                 IN
  DATE_OF_BIRTH                   VARCHAR2                 IN
  STATUS_CODE                     NUMBER(38)               OUT
etc
```

Each API would return a STATUS_CODE parameter indicating the success or failure of the API call. A myriad of external systems, on a set of diverse architectures, were required to pass data to this application and thus use these provided API's. This data would be provided via XML, and thus the challenge became how to transform this XML into calls to the appropriate API's. To achieve this transformation, the development team took a shortcut to cut their coding time, a shortcut that was to come back and haunt them later.

The Problem

The structure of the XML that was presented from external systems would map to an API that would need to be called to pass that data to the application. Thus to add a new person to the system, the incoming XML data would look something like this:

```
<xml>
<person>
  <oper>ADD</oper>
  <surname>MCDONALD</surname>
  <firstname>CONNOR</surname>
  <dob>27011968</dob>
  <gender>MALE</gender>
</person>
```

And with this, a call to the API_PERSON.ADD procedure would then be made, passing the appropriate parameters. So an interface program to perform the task for the preceding example needs to perform the following work:

1. Extract the following data from the XML:

   - Surname

   - First name

   - Date of birth

   - Gender

2. Bind that data into appropriate variables.

3. Call the API_PERSON.NEW_PERSON, passing those variables as parameters.

4. Check the STATUS_CODE out-parameter to ensure that operation was successful.

A program (or subroutine within a program) would hence be required for each of the different API's that might need to be called. Diagrammatically, the program structure looks like the following:

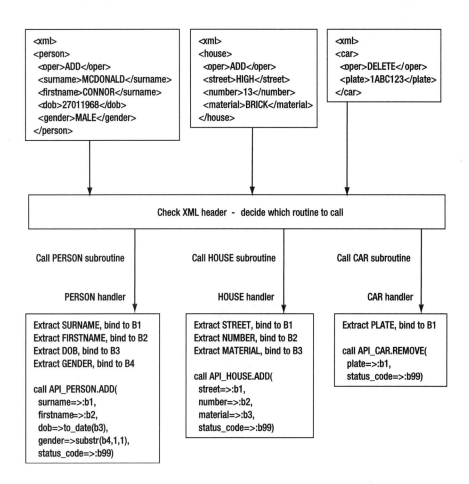

However, the developers realized that for each of these different entities (person, property, car, etc.) and the possible manipulations (ADD, MODIFY, REMOVE), the code for each subroutine was very similar—just a call to a different API, depending on the first fields within the XML, and so they took a shortcut. Rather than have an explicit routine for each of the possible API's, a single routine was built that would dynamically build a call to the API. Now the main problem with this approach is that each API may require a different number of values to be bound to the call, and the data types for each of those values may differ. "No problem!" thought the developers. The binding was skipped and all parameters would be passed as strings. In fact, this made the developers' job even easier. Now the incoming XML was a simple character string that needed to be transformed into an outgoing character string that represented a PL/SQL call. An XSL stylesheet is perfect for such a task. Thus the developers managed to a build a single program that would handle any incoming XML data and automatically convert it to a set of PL/SQL calls using the appropriate stylesheet. The program structure now looked as follows:

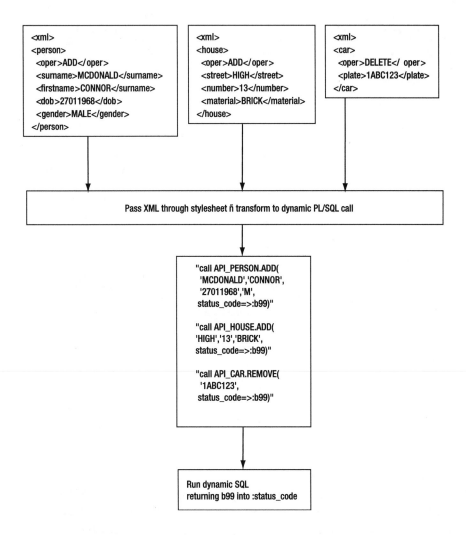

This saved the developers lots of time by having a single generic (there is that "four-letter word" again!) solution. Testing of the various data feeds with sample data did not reveal any problems, and thus the system went live with 40 concurrent data feeds on an environment with approximately 500 concurrent users on the system. The data feeds worked fine, but the server CPU went through the roof,

and online responsiveness for the system users slowed to a crawl. A quick examination of the system statistics showed a huge amount of CPU being consumed by
parsing and user sessions being significantly impacted by "latch free" waits.

What the developers did not know is that, just like standard SQL statements,
calls to PL/SQL also have to be parsed by Oracle. Even if the code *within* those
PL/SQL routines contains reusable SQL with efficient use of bind variables, failure
to *call* those PL/SQL routines in an appropriate manner will cause problems. This
can be demonstrated with the following simple example. Create a very simple procedure, P, which accepts a single numeric parameter:

```
SQL> create or replace
  2  procedure P(x number) is
  3    l number;
  4  begin
  5    l := x;
  6  end;
  7  /

Procedure created.
```

Then you can investigate the cost of calling this procedure, passing in parameter X as a literal string, in the same way as the XSL stylesheet mechanism was
doing. Measure the amount of CPU time spent on parsing the call by measuring
the "parse time cpu" session-level statistic before and after the test.

```
SQL> alter system flush shared_pool;

System altered.

SQL> col value new_value parse_cpu_before
SQL> select value
  2  from v$mystat
  3  where statistic# =
        ( select statistic# from v$statname where name = 'parse time cpu' ) ;

    VALUE
----------
    2306

SQL> set timing on
SQL> begin
```

```
 2  for i in 1 .. 1000 loop
 3    execute immediate 'call p('||i||')';
 4  end loop;
 5  end;
 6  /
```

PL/SQL procedure successfully completed.

```
Elapsed: 00:00:11.03
SQL> select value-&parse_cpu_before TOT_PARSE_CPU
  2  from v$mystat
  3  where statistic# =
         ( select statistic# from v$statname where name = 'parse time cpu' ) ;


TOT_PARSE_CPU
-------------
          903
```

Thus in 11 seconds of elapsed time, 9 seconds (903 centiseconds) was due to parsing the CALL statement. Compare this to what the developers could have achieved if they had remained with their approach to explicitly bind each parameter for the API calls.

```
SQL> alter system flush shared_pool;

System altered.

SQL> col value new_value parse_cpu_before
SQL> select value
  2  from v$mystat
  3  where statistic# =
         ( select statistic# from v$statname where name = 'parse time cpu' ) ;


     VALUE
----------
      3225

SQL> set timing on
SQL> begin
  2  for i in 1 .. 1000 loop
  3    execute immediate 'call p(:b1)' using i;
  4  end loop;
  5  end;
```

6 /

PL/SQL procedure successfully completed.

Elapsed: 00:00:00.06
```
SQL> select value-&parse_cpu_before TOT_PARSE_CPU
  2   from v$mystat
  3   where statistic# =
         ( select statistic# from v$statname where name = 'parse time cpu' ) ;


TOT_PARSE_CPU
-------------
           25
```

If only the developers had not taken the shortcut to reduce their development time, the payoff would have been tremendous.

Thus for this client, the wastage was excessive parsing. Although the SQL within the API's was coded well and used bind variables where appropriate, the act of *calling* the API's without appropriate regard to parsing was causing headaches. Parsing in particular is always a nasty issue to resolve, because although the problem is most often observed as a CPU issue, it cannot typically be resolved by increasing CPU capacity. Along with excess CPU consumption, parsing also induces contention issues, namely contention for the library and dictionary caches, or more precisely, contention for the latches (shared pool, library cache) that protect those structures. Adding CPU to such a system may have little benefit, and may even cause damage due to the increased contention. Similarly, the knee-jerk reaction of increasing the size of the shared pool—a common "technique" when the parsing hit ratio is low—merely defers the onset of the contention and typically makes it worse when it finally does occur.

Resolutions

My first proposal, namely to rewrite the data feed programs without the generic processing, was (understandably) met with some resistance, so the task then became how to minimize the damage with the least possible effort.

Option 1: Cursor Sharing

Since this particular client was running on version 8.1.7.4, cursor sharing was considered as an option. Since version 8.1.6, the cursor sharing facility has been available to assist with applications where parsing is having a significant impact. Full details of cursor sharing are covered in Chapter 7 of the Oracle 10g Performance Tuning Guide in the standard Oracle documentation, but in essence, the database attempts on-the-fly to replace occurrences of literal strings within a statement with bind variable equivalents. It is a quick-fix option to applications in which bind variables have not been considered during development. To demonstrate its function, I will repeat the preceding example with cursor sharing enabled:

```
SQL> alter system flush shared_pool;

System altered.

SQL> alter session set cursor_sharing = force;

System altered.

SQL> col value new_value parse_cpu_before
SQL> select value
  2  from v$mystat
  3  where statistic# =
       ( select statistic# from v$statname where name = 'parse time cpu' ) ;

    VALUE
----------
     8273

SQL> set timing on
SQL> begin
  2  for i in 1 .. 1000 loop
  3    execute immediate 'call p('||i||')';
  4  end loop;
  5  end;
  6  /

PL/SQL procedure successfully completed.
```

```
Elapsed: 00:00:00.14
SQL> select value-&parse_cpu_before TOT_PARSE_CPU
  2  from v$mystat
  3  where statistic# =
       ( select statistic# from v$statname where name = 'parse time cpu' ) ;


TOT_PARSE_CPU
-------------
          42
```

This looked extremely promising, so a trial was conducted with the true data feed programs. The results were disappointing; in fact, there was no benefit at all—no cursor sharing was taking place. Further investigation revealed that this was caused by the references to the STATUS_CODE parameter, which returned whether the API call was successful. Remember that although all inbound parameters to the API's were being translated to literal strings by the stylesheet, the STATUS_CODE parameter was still being bound—it had to since it was an outbound parameter. Thus whereas the preceding cursor sharing demo worked fine when a call looked like

```
call P(123)
```

cursor sharing does *not* take place when that call contains a bound variable, for example:

```
call P(123, :b1)
```

This makes sense—Oracle probably assumes that if developers can use bind variables in one of the parameters within the call, then they could just as equally use them for other parameters if they wanted to. Conversely, the assumption may be made that if a mixture of literals and bind variables are present, then the literals were deliberately used and hence they should not be replaced with bind variables.

Given that every API contained the outbound STATUS_CODE parameter, all calls to the API's were of the form

```
call API_NAME (<sequence of literal parameters>, :status_code)
```

no cursor sharing would ever take place.

It is probably a good thing that the STATUS_CODE parameter stopped us from implementing the cursor sharing option with the data feed. The system is currently in the process of being upgraded to version 9. Look what happens when a CALL statement is processed under CURSOR_SHARING = FORCE in version 9 (or version 10 for that matter):

```
SQL> alter session set cursor_sharing = force;

Session altered.

Elapsed: 00:00:00.00
SQL> begin
  2    execute immediate 'call p(1)';
  3  end;
  4  /
begin
*
ERROR at line 1:
ORA-01008: not all variables bound
ORA-06512: at line 2
```

Had cursor sharing worked for us in version 8, no upgrade to version 9 would have been possible until this bug had been resolved.

 NOTE *The preceding problem also occurs in 8.1.7.3 but not 8.1.7.4, so it would be reasonable to assume that at some stage there will be a fix for version 9 and 10 of the database.*

Option 2: "Manual" Cursor Sharing

If the cursor sharing facility provided by Oracle was not useful, could we build our own without having to entirely rearchitect the data feed programs? This was our next challenge. The approach being considered was to take the CALL string that was produced by the XSL stylesheet and pass that entire string to a PL/SQL routine, which would then examine the string and attempt to extract the individual parameters out of the string, and then call the desired API with the parameters once again appropriately bound. The data feed program would then only need a small modification, to allow it to call this "auto-binder" PL/SQL program and pass the entire CALL string as a parameter along with the status code. The auto-binder would then form a new CALL string to the API that included bind variables, and handle the actual binding of value to the appropriate parameters.

Since the number of parameters would not be known until run time, the PL/SQL routine would need to use type 4 dynamic SQL to process the incoming call string and bind the appropriate variables. Diagrammatically, the process is relatively simple.

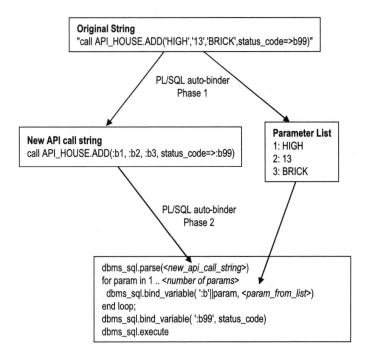

Most of the complexity in this solution was in the scrutiny of the incoming string. Initially the code started by simply looking for commas as separators between parameters, but as the code evolved, additional smarts to handle commas within parameters, nested quotes, nulls, and the like were all built in. This in itself adds up to a significant amount of processing time to parse (no pun intended) the string into its component parts.

Amazingly, even by adding this additional layer of processing, the implementation of the "auto-binding" PL/SQL routine yielded a 20–30% reduction in CPU consumption by the data feeds. But far more importantly, there was a direct benefit to the users of the system, not just in the CPU that had been reclaimed, but also with a vast improvement in the effectiveness of the reuse of their cursors (that is, those from the application). Parse times for user sessions dropped because their cursors were not being forced out of the library cache by a plethora of individual

CALL statements. This is an important issue. Eliminating wastage, in particular wastage due to contention, in one part of a system often leads to even more efficiencies in other parts of the application.

This solution is not particularly pretty or elegant, but it is getting the job done for now. Probably the most beneficial outcome of this exercise was a realization by all involved of the enormous cost that parsing can have on an Oracle system. Until the developers were shown some of the statistics that documented the massive cost their initial coding shortcut had on the system, most of them had been unaware that the concept of parsing even existed. Ironically, they have now been convinced of the pain of parsing to such an extent that some of my time is spent ensuring that some parts of the application code *retains* literals strings and does not excessively lean toward bind variables. As a performance consultant, that is a nice position to be in.

Hidden DUAL Access

One row ... one single row—how can that be a performance threat to your database? You have seen from the first example in this chapter that just because DUAL is small, it cannot be discounted as a performance threat. I like to think of access to the DUAL table as being akin to a snowflake. One snowflake that rolls down a mountainside is insignificant, almost undetectable. Put several billion snowflakes rolling down a mountainside, and your entire ski resort and its occupants are about to be wiped out.

Access to the DUAL table is no different, but one place where customers can be caught out by the DUAL table is that it may be accessed extensively even though an application makes *no explicit reference* to it. This is the topic of this next problem application.

Background

This was an Oracle Forms 6 application running on version 8.1.6, deployed throughout Europe and entirely generated from Oracle Designer. This was no mean feat in itself—for years I had read the marketing hype that entire enterprise applications could be produced with a "click of a button" using Oracle Designer, but to actually be at a site where both management and the development team had committed to producing a 100% generated application was very impressive. If a requirement could not be met within the constraints of Designer generation, the requirement was recast into something that was possible.

This discipline had actually produced a very successful system in terms of budget, schedule, and user satisfaction. However, there were problems with CPU load on the servers, although given that the client was running several hundred concurrent users on an original Sun Enterprise 450, this was perhaps not unexpected. If anything, the system was probably running much more efficiently than most I had seen. However, the client was seeking some solutions without having to drift away from the code generation model to which they had so rigorously been adhering, or to upgrade the hardware.

A quick look at high logical IO SQL statements, as per the first section in this chapter, revealed the following two statements:

```
SQL_TEXT
-------------------------------------------
SELECT USER FROM DUAL
SELECT SYSDATE FROM DUAL
```

When presented with this evidence, the development team immediately responded, "We don't query DUAL for the user or date," and they were right. Their code was not querying DUAL, but the database was doing it for them on their behalf. The problem lay not with their application coding, but with some of the internals of the Designer code generation. To allow a consistent means for auditing changes to tables (known as *journaling* within Designer), every table within the system had the journaling table API triggers built on them. With the version of Designer that was in use, even if journaling (in other words, auditing) was not going to be performed for a particular table, the triggers still existed to call to the journaling procedure, but Designer simply generated the procedure as a simple NULL statement. Hence every row that was ever created, removed, or updated within the system, regardless of whether that row would be audited or not, resulted in a call to the trigger code.

Fully delving into the contents of their table API triggers is outside the scope of this book, but every table API trigger commenced with the following two lines:

```
declare
  current_date date := sysdate;
  current_user varchar2(30) := user;
begin
  ...
  ...
```

Hence, in alignment with what the developers had said, there were no references to DUAL. However, when a trace was performed on the application, the following was observed within the trace file:

```
PARSING IN CURSOR #2 len=25 dep=1
SELECT user from sys.dual
END OF STMT
...
PARSING IN CURSOR #3 len=28 dep=1
SELECT sysdate from sys.dual
END OF STMT
```

Two recursive SQL statements to obtain the value for USER and SYSDATE would be run. Within PL/SQL (under 8.1.6), the USER and SYSDATE are not *directly* available, and thus SQL is run to retrieve their values via the SQL engine. Typically this is a problem that is trivial to solve: simply change the code to avoid or minimize the references and we were done. However, add in the requirement not to alter the generated code, and the exercise became a good deal more complicated.

Resolutions

As seen earlier in this chapter, under version 8, every access to DUAL yields five logical IOs. Since the references to DUAL could not be avoided, the challenge then became to minimize the cost of each access. A number of options were explored.

Option 1: DUAL As an IOT

Whereas a full scan through a heap DUAL table requires five logical IOs, if this table is converted to an IOT, then this can be reduced to a single logical IO. I will create an IOT mirror of DUAL to demonstrate:

```
SQL> create table IOT_DUAL ( dummy primary key)
  2  organization index
  3  as select * from dual;

Table created.

SQL> analyze table iot_dual compute statistics;

Table analyzed.
```

```
SQL> set autotrace on
SQL> select * from iot_dual;

D
-
X

Execution Plan
----------------------------------------------------------
   0      SELECT STATEMENT Optimizer=CHOOSE (Cost=1 Card=1 Bytes=1)
   1   0  INDEX (FULL SCAN) OF 'SYS_IOT_TOP_52448' (UNIQUE) (Cost=1 Card=1 Bytes=1)

Statistics
----------------------------------------------------------
        0  recursive calls
        0  db block gets
        1  consistent gets
        0  physical reads
        0  redo size
      375  bytes sent via SQL*Net to client
      499  bytes received via SQL*Net from client
        2  SQL*Net roundtrips to/from client
        0  sorts (memory)
        0  sorts (disk)
        1  rows processed
```

This all looks very impressive, but it masks one extremely important detail. Notice from the preceding execution plan displayed from the autotrace output that any use of an IOT immediately mandates the use of the Cost Based Optimizer (CBO). This would probably be fine in version 10, but in version 8, when the IOT DUAL option was tested, the application itself appeared to run fine, but a number of other components within the Oracle dictionary started to display some erratic performance behavior. Any query that references DUAL immediately falls under the CBO control. If other tables in that query do not have statistics (as is the case with any data dictionary tables), then good performance is more good luck than good management. For this reason, DUAL as an IOT was discounted.

Option 2: X$DUAL

Steve Adams, a renowned Oracle expert, had proposed the possibility of replacing the DUAL table with a view that accessed X$DUAL instead. X$DUAL is a fixed table that allows Oracle access to a "DUAL-like" table before the database is fully opened. Since X$DUAL is a fixed (or virtual) table, querying it requires no logical IO. Or more accurately, it requires none of the memory protection mechanisms that are associated with logical IO. To replace the DUAL table with X$DUAL required the following steps:

1. Create a view, QUICK_DUAL, as SELECT DUMMY FROM X$DUAL.

2. SELECT privileges on QUICK_DUAL are given to public.

3. The DUAL table is renamed to OLD_DUAL.

4. A public synonym DUAL points to SYS.QUICK_DUAL.

5. A private synonym SYS.DUAL is created for SYS.QUICK_DUAL.

Once this has been performed, the cost of querying DUAL becomes "zero" (in terms of logical IO):

```
SQL> set autotrace on statistics
SQL> select * from dual;

D
-
X


Statistics
----------------------------------------------------
          0  recursive calls
          0  db block gets
          0  consistent gets
          0  physical reads
          0  redo size
        375  bytes sent via SQL*Net to client
        499  bytes received via SQL*Net from client
          2  SQL*Net roundtrips to/from client
          0  sorts (memory)
          0  sorts (disk)
          1  rows processed
```

The real measure of success, of course, came with what CPU reductions were achieved by the customer application. Converting to use of X$DUAL resulted in approximately a 50% reduction in CPU time *for these two particular queries*. The net gain across the entire application was in the vicinity of 5–10%. This is a reasonable result but admittedly not as good as we initially hoped. However, given the constraints of not changing a line of code, this gain did allow the customer to defer the expense of a hardware upgrade, at least in the short term.

Option 3: X$DUAL with Additions

This is an option not explored with the customer, but some information I recently came across from an Oracle consultant, Tanel Poder. While use of the X$DUAL table did not cause any problems with the customer application above, Tanel has displayed some issues with X$DUAL that you may need to consider when queries to DUAL are included within queries that run under the cost-based optimizer.

Like any X$ fixed table, there are no optimizer statistics held for the X$DUAL table, and thus when querying X$DUAL under the CBO, the optimizer must make assumptions about the size of the table. Thus, if you activate Explain Plan and then run a simple query to the QUICK_DUAL view, you will see the following:

```
SQL> set autotrace traceonly explain
SQL> alter session set optimizer_goal = all_rows;

Session altered.

SQL> select * from quick_dual;

Execution Plan
----------------------------------------------------------
SELECT STATEMENT Optimizer=ALL_ROWS (Cost=11 Card=100 Bytes=3200)
  FIXED TABLE (FULL) OF 'X$DUAL' (Cost=11 Card=100 Bytes=3200)
```

While (for single instance Oracle) there will only be a single row in X$DUAL, the optimizer assumes 100 rows. This might have an adverse impact on any queries that reference your newly converted DUAL table in a CBO environment.

There are a couple of resolutions to this problem that you may wish to explore. The first one is to include WHERE ROWNUM = 1 within the view definition for QUICK_DUAL. Including ROWNUM ensures the view is always resolved before being applied to other parts of the query. As a result, the execution plan more accurately reflects the true cardinality.

```
SQL> create or replace
  2  view quick_dual as
  3  select dummy from x$dual
  4  where rownum = 1;

View created.

SQL> select * from quick_dual;

Execution Plan
----------------------------------------------------------
   0      SELECT STATEMENT Optimizer=ALL_ROWS (Cost=11 Card=1 Bytes=2)
   1    0   VIEW OF 'QUICK_DUAL' (Cost=11 Card=1 Bytes=2)
   2    1     COUNT (STOPKEY)
   3    2       FIXED TABLE (FULL) OF 'X$DUAL' (Cost=11 Card=100 Bytes=200)
```

Alternatively, for Oracle 9, the CARDINALITY hint can be used to explicitly nominate the number of rows, as the following example demonstrates:

```
SQL> create or replace
  2  view quick_dual as
  3  select /*+ CARDINALITY(x 1) */ dummy
  4  from x$dual x;

View created.

SQL> select * from quick_dual;

Execution Plan
----------------------------------------------------------
   0      SELECT STATEMENT Optimizer=ALL_ROWS (Cost=11 Card=1 Bytes=2)
   1    0   FIXED TABLE (FULL) OF 'X$DUAL' (Cost=11 Card=1 Bytes=2)
```

Things to Note

Whereas the customer application made no reference to DUAL, if you choose to re-create the DUAL table in a more efficient manner, you will find that great swathes of the delivered Oracle features do in fact use the DUAL table, and thus will all immediately be marked as INVALID and require recompilation. For this reason, plan on altering DUAL during a outage and recompile anything that becomes invalid.

Remember that DUAL is one of the most ubiquitous tables in almost any Oracle system. If you do intend performing any manipulation on it, then you need to take tremendous care and be extremely thorough in your regression testing. Playing with DUAL is nearly always treating the symptom not the problem. Such problems will be lessened in version 10, in which Oracle has introduced a new FAST DUAL optimization method whereby the retrieval of SYSDATE, USER, and other such pseudo-functions from DUAL are automatically optimized to avoid logical IO.

Conclusion

As I stated at the beginning of this chapter, cataloging a list of vendor disasters does tend to lead to the lynch mob mentality, but this is not the aim. Most problems with wastage are a direct reflection of how we conduct ourselves as developers, designers, and database administrators; namely, when faced with timing and budgetary pressures, we often take shortcuts when implementing Oracle systems—shortcuts that can turn into a performance nightmare when those systems change in size or scale, or if we have not tested them appropriately.

If there is a single thing I hope you can take away from this chapter, it is that *avoiding* a wastage problem is so much cheaper in terms of money, time, and your own peace of mind than running around like a headless chicken trying to fix it when the proverbial brown stuff hits the fan. It is not the technical aspects of the IT profession that are critical for successful applications. It is having a passion for understanding the Oracle infrastructure, sticking to your guns when someone wants to cut the testing cycle short, being honest with yourself and your colleagues when scrutinizing your proposed solutions, and sometimes having a little luck fall your way as well. Severe wastage always ends up as pain for you and your users. Avoidance or, at worst, early detection is the cure.

Dear Reader,

I don't know how to do Anjo justice. I really don't. He is exceedingly intelligent, innovative—and restless. He has a phenomenal memory, a huge network, a strange but wonderful mind for cross-references—and a tremendous sense of humor.

His all-round knowledge about the World and its going-ons is incredible, his ability to solve (all sorts of) problems un-matched, and it is almost impossible to persuade him to write anything, especially on time (I can vouch for that—Ed.). Guess who turned in his chapter for this book after everyone else did ...

Here is a brief biography: he was hired by Oracle right after his Dutch technical high school days, and very quickly found himself being part of the European development organization. His sheer grasp of code and database issues ensured him a place in Oracle development as one of its premier troubleshooters and fault analysts.

After having done work with Oracle Parallel Server (and written several notes about it that at least I still recall as being very helpful as an Oracle Support member back in those days), his Big Break came when working in Japan, where he was forced to invent the YAPP method. Note, though, that it was really the very bright lady Shari Yamaguchi (who is still in Oracle Development) who actually wrote most of the paper ☺.

The YAPP revolution has been a quiet revolution with an exponential development over the past few years, and Anjo was never the one to loudly go out and try to make a name for himself (which is why he is only rich, but not incredibly rich). Now, with Oracle10g, all the timing philosophy and the formal abandon of the silly buffer cache hit ratio (you can't see it in Enterprise Manager anymore!) is official. It is very good to see that Anjo is enjoying the respect he deserves for this, and that the number of people trying to steal the idea and take credit for it themselves is lower than usual.

His OraPerf.com web site is brilliant, and has hundreds of visitors every day, each of them uploading a bstat/estat or statspack report and getting in return some useful advise back. What is perhaps less known is that behind the web site is a database with a huge collection of statistics from all the uploads that Anjo uses to spot trends and further refine his advisory services. It has always been surprising to me that so little of all the information written to flat ASCII files by Oracle is used in this manner: parse the information into a repository, then generate the reports and the statistics that everybody can benefit from. To make OraPerf a public, free service is, I guess, just proof of the way Anjo is.

As a friend and business partner, Anjo is invaluable, and we in Miracle A/S sincerely hope that one day we will have enough money and exciting projects to be able to afford to hire him. Until then, he just keeps coming up with ideas. He suggested the OakTable network name, he suggested the Miracle Database Forum and the Miracle Master Class concepts, and he's currently occupied with the idea of OakTable events around the globe, especially in the Far East where he sees a huge market for that sort of activity (and probably rightly so).

He's also the owner of one of the most profound shopping genes we know of in the OakTable network. That's one bug. His second bug is his—err—ability to deliver written stuff on time. The third is about him getting up in the morning.

Apart from that I can't really find anything to criticize him for. A true friend if ever there was one. I count myself very lucky for that.

—Mogens Nørgaard

CHAPTER 4

Why I Invented YAPP

By Anjo Kolk

IN 1992 ORACLE **RDBMS** Development ("the kernel group") introduced a new feature in the Oracle7 database that wasn't really planned. It was kind of sneaked in at the last minute. This new feature was the Oracle Wait Interface. The reason for this "stealth project" was that an Oracle system had encountered a performance problem and it had been difficult to locate the cause. The system wasn't using any CPU, it seemed to be waiting on something but they couldn't work out what, and this is why Juan Loaiza decided to instrument the waits in the Oracle kernel (as described, in his own words, in Chapter 2). Maybe this is also why the waits got instrumented so well but the same level of detail for the CPU is missing.[1]

Discovering the Wait Interface

I had seen the interface and read some internal documents about it,[2] but, other than that, hadn't given it a lot of attention. At the time, I was responsible for porting Oracle to the NCR product line and most of my time was taken up running make,[3] changing the port-specific Oracle code, and finding C compiler problems.

At that time I was involved, together with Andrew Holdsworth (Oracle), in the largest benchmark on Oracle7 Parallel Server at that time; 2,500 users on a 3-node cluster running 7.0.12. That benchmark opened the door to Oracle Parallel Server and tuning large systems for me. This was the start of the famous Brushco project, as described in lurid detail by James Morle in Chapter 8. It was with this crazy Englishman that I took the night boat to France in the summer of 1993. It was a

---

1. Of course Oracle Corp. wants you to use more CPU (CPU licensing).
2. I worked for Oracle at that time so it was not illegal.
3. Unix utility

kind of a last minute decision and we had to do some speeding (120+ mph along the English highways).[4]

I spent the next couple of days at the Brushco site, watching these DBA guys (James and others) trying to keep a large production system up and running.

We used the wait interface a bit once in a while but without any real methodology (in fact, without much of a clue what we were looking at). It wasn't until a couple of years later when I met James again in Portland, while doing a benchmark for the same system (a couple of versions later), that we used a method (but I'm getting ahead of myself).

So, I started to get interested in the wait interface, even more so during my work for Oracle Japan in Tokyo, when I noticed that a lot more people were starting to use it.

It was around this time (1994), for example, that Kyle Hailey met Roger Sanders and was introduced to his m2 tool, which provided information on what sessions were currently waiting without the overhead of querying the v$session_wait (you can read all about this in Chapter 6). So, the interest was there, and work was being done, but public information and documentation were very scarce.

Documenting the Wait Events

Jeff Needham made the first brave attempt to document the different wait events in the Oracle version 7.2 Performance Tuning manual. But it was far from complete (if I remember correctly it was only 3–4 pages or so) and contained a couple of big mistakes. For example, it showed 4294967295 as the *actual* wait time on some of the events, when in fact this value represents -1 in decimal (in 32-bit systems), or 0XFFFF in hexadecimal, and the meaning of -1 is actually "waiting short amount of time."

 NOTE *I know Jeff Needham very well (I have worked with him for a couple of years) and he obviously didn't make this mistake on purpose. Documenting some of these events was just one of the things he had to do when he really didn't have any time.*

---

4. We had an interesting problem with the car: the fan of the motor would stop (blow a fuse) when you tried to use the left-/right-hand signal. This was discovered early in the trip and it was decided not to use any signals anymore. That didn't matter as we were going to France and, as would become obvious real soon, nobody uses signals there anyway.

In early 1995, my pregnant wife and I moved to Redwood Shores and I started working at Oracle Headquarters, in the Performance Group, for Juan Loiaza. Well that is what was agreed, but Juan moved on to another job and Jeff Needham, Doug Rady, and myself got a new manager. A few months after that, Graham Wood (future author of statspack) joined us.

At that time I found a paper by Greg Dogherty[5] that attempted to document all the different enqueue names that Oracle used. Greg wrote this internal paper to make sure that developers wouldn't be using the same names for locks that had different purposes.

So, I started to document the wait interface in more detail. Jeff was busy with TPC benchmarks and TPC council meetings, so I decided to start working on documenting the wait events alongside the enqueues that Greg had started doing. It became the never-finished "Oracle7 Wait Event and Enqueue" paper. It was written directly from the kernel code and, at that time, I didn't know what most of the events really meant. But documenting them felt important and it also gave me something to do (the birth of our first baby was drawing near, and I was getting more and more nervous the closer we got to the due date). One Sunday afternoon (May 7, 1995) I was actually working on the paper in my office at work when I got the phone call that labor had started. On Monday afternoon Michael Sebastiaan Kolk was born. Life has never been the same again after that.

Back to Oracle Parallel Server

I never got to finish the "Oracle7 Wait Events and Enqueues" paper. This was partly because of the baby but also because I shifted my focus to Oracle7 version 7.3 and back to my old friend, Oracle Parallel Server. And that wasn't a bad thing, because that opened the door to using the wait interface in new ways. Having documented most of the events, I felt that this was good enough for now, and it is kind of funny to still get requests for a later or updated version of this paper.

Mogens asked me why the enqueues were included. The reason for this was that, in Oracle7.3, Oracle Parallel Server was getting very popular (almost as popular as RAC today!), but many people didn't know how to set the different `init.ora` parameters related to Oracle Parallel Server. Another problem was that Distributed Lock Manager (DLM) needed to be configured just right. If this wasn't done right, you could run out of DLM locks and resources. At this point, when no more could be allocated, the database instance would crash.

So documenting the different locks (each lock is denoted in the database by a two-letter tag such as TX or ST) and their meaning was the start of finding out how

---

5. Greg Dogherty is one of those one of a kind guys that can move mountains. He was later instrumental in getting Partitioning and Object support into Oracle8.

many locks and resources were needed to run Oracle Parallel Server. The concept of locks and resources is used a lot in Oracle so an explanation of them here would probably be helpful.

Locks and Resources

A *resource* maps to an Oracle structure or some logical entity. Now any session that wants to use this resource has to have a lock on it.

For example, take the start of a transaction by a session. The session opens the transaction resource and then acquires a lock (TX lock) on that resource. So the start of the transaction means that there is one TX resource and one TX lock (on that resource). Another example is control file transactions. There is one resource for the control file (the CF resource), and if a session wants to do something with the control file, it will need to get a lock on the CF resource. In other words, in order to "own" the CF resource a user needs to acquire a lock (enqueue) in Shared or Exclusive mode.

Figure 4-1 shows different sessions trying to lock the same resource, in this case because different sessions want to update the same row.

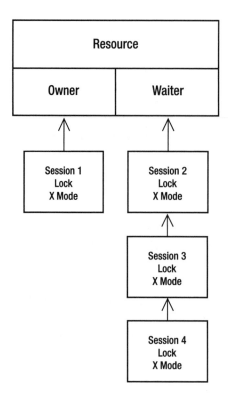

Figure 4-1. Four database sessions attempting to access the same resource

Session 1 has successfully acquired an eXclusive mode lock on the resource and thus the lock structure is placed on a linked list called owner. The lock structures for subsequent sessions (2, 3, and 4) are placed in a linked list called waiter where they'll remain until session 1 releases its lock. This diagram makes it obvious why we need more locks than resources.

In Oracle7 a lot of time was needed to figure out the right number of locks and resources because you needed to make these allocations statically at startup time. In later versions of Oracle this was all done more or less dynamically by the Oracle kernel. Oracle used to have a lot of parameters that dealt with setting resources and locks, now Oracle allocates them dynamically from the shared pool. This happens in RAC or Oracle Parallel Server mode or just plain single instance Oracle.

So that is pretty much why I set out to create a document about the need for calculating the number of resources and locks for Oracle Parallel Server.

OPS in Tokyo

My first year in the US was coming to an end and I decided to visit our family in the Netherlands over Christmas (1995) and show little Mikey the flat country.

During the first few of months of 1996, I became involved in a project for a large customer that was running Oracle Parallel Server, and it turned out to be very interesting. The problem was that they couldn't get the performance that they needed for their production system. So, together with a hardware manufacturer, I found myself on a plane to Tokyo to investigate this problem. That first fateful trip embroiled me in this project for the next three years: it took me a long time to convince the Japanese how to fix the problem! I had a gut feeling of what the problem was fairly early on, but I couldn't convince them with words. I had to prove it with numbers, and that took time.

On this project I worked with a lot of very talented people, such as Kuwahara-san, and Fujita-san (both from Oracle Japan) as well as Okawa-san from the hardware manufacturer. We spent a lot of hours working late in a very small room in an office in Tokyo. We had lots of fun, but there was also a lot of pressure to make it work. Giving your word in Japan has a completely different meaning than in the rest of the world. If you say, "Yes, I will make this work," you are basically committed for the rest of your life (if necessary!) to make it work.

So, as part of the task force assigned to improving the performance, I found myself sitting on the floor in a restaurant in Tokyo with a group of Japanese people. Everybody introduced themselves, and they were all experts in solving performance problems (OS, database, network, Tuxedo, and so on). I was very impressed by the company I was keeping. Listening to that group, it became clear that all the right people had been involved, so why hadn't they solved the problem? One thing that I realized at that moment was that solving performance problems is not all about technical know-how. This project had all the right people involved, but still no solutions. And this was not the only project that this was happening on.

So, when asked to say a couple of things to the group about myself, rather than proclaiming to be an expert in Oracle Parallel Server or in Oracle database performance, I simply said, "My name is Anjo Kolk, and I solve problems." I didn't want to "pigeonhole" myself, because then my focus would be purely on the Oracle database and not on the whole system.

Problems with Queues

The three-tier system in question consisted of COBOL programs submitting requests to a Tuxedo system that was connected to an Oracle database. Anybody who has waited at a checkout or bank teller window knows that queues can consume a lot of time. So seeing Tuxedo in this system already set alarm bells ringing in my head. Not that Tuxedo makes things slow, just that I knew from my experience that there can be wait time in the queues. So, one of my first questions was how many requests were there on the Tuxedo queues and what was the average time they spent on these queues? The answer that I got was that there was waiting time for the requests and that queues were actually filling up quickly.

Now, one of the tuning rules of Tuxedo says that if the queues are filling up or that the wait time of the requests starts to increase, then you need to add more server processes to the queue. They tried that and found actually that things didn't improve at all. In fact they got slower! How was that possible?

Figure 4-2 shows how this system was implemented.

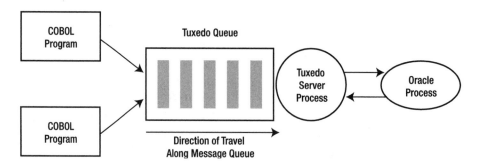

Figure 4-2. COBOL programs submit messages to the Tuxedo Server, which interacts with the Oracle database.

The amount of time that a request waits on the Tuxedo queue depends on

- The time it takes to process the request in the Tuxedo Server process

- The time it takes to process the request in the Oracle database

- The number of requests in the queue

Now, having just documented some of the Oracle events, I realized that some of this time would be wait time. After examining v$system_event and v$session_event it became obvious that most of the waiting time was on OPS-related wait events! By adding more Tuxedo Server processes to the queue, more Oracle processes could run in parallel (and did) and that only caused the waits for Oracle Parallel Server events to increase (the specific wait event was lock element cleanup).

So, my thinking was to *reduce* the number of Tuxedo processes: to actually run with fewer processes than they would have thought possible. But this was not the common way of thinking, and so they wouldn't believe me: "That can't be true, we need more, not less."

The Birth of Tuning by Response Time

I needed to convince the task force to try running with fewer processes. I was convinced that this would be the way to improve performance. I needed to prove to them that waiting time was the problem and not the CPU.

The R = S + W formula came to me because the system was using Tuxedo and Tuxedo is a queuing system. The formula can be applied very easily to a request in the queue. But first let us look at the meaning of the formula:

- R = response time

- S = service time

- W = wait time

So the service time is the time it takes the Tuxedo Server process to service the request and the wait time is the time that the request waited in the Tuxedo queue.

$$R_{Tuxedo} = S_{TuxedoServerProcess} + W_{Tuxedo}$$

The Tuxedo Server process is connected to Oracle, so the service time for this process also includes the service and wait time of the Oracle (shadow) process. If we break out the Tuxedo service time into its component parts, it looks like this:

$$R_{Tuxedo} = (S_{Tuxedo} + S_{Oracle} + W_{Oracle}) + W_{Tuxedo}$$

where

- S_{Tuxedo} is the service time of the actual Tuxedo Server process.

- S_{Oracle} is the service time of the Oracle (shadow) Server process.

- W_{Oracle} is the time spent waiting on Oracle resources.

This implied that the Tuxedo Server process wouldn't wait on anything other than Oracle, which was fine for me: I didn't have to be 100% correct.

So I had the formula. Now I needed to find the source of the service and wait times within Oracle and Tuxedo. We had some basic tools that allowed us to (manually) collect the response times for the different Tuxedo queues and server processes.

Having done that, we turned to Oracle. The Oracle waits were relatively easy to obtain; I could find them in v$session_event for the session, as follows:

```
select *
    from v$session_event
    where sid = <sid>;
```

However, there was one event that caused some trouble: SQL*Net message from client. If the Tuxedo Server process is working, Oracle is basically idle and is waiting on this event. So this means that we if include this event in the wait time and then add the service time for the Tuxedo Server process, we do some double counting. So that was when I decided that the SQL*Net message from client shouldn't be included. From this, the notion of an *idle event* was born. It turned out to be a bad name later on, but it was perfectly valid in this project.

I wanted to make sure we got a full picture of what was going on. What if there were no waits, or they were negligible? If that were the case, then chances were that we had a CPU problem, so I wanted to collect the CPU times for the Oracle and Tuxedo processes as well as the wait times.

Collecting the CPU times was easier. These processes existed prior to executing the benchmark and after the benchmark execution was complete. Therefore the CPU consumed in the interim (during the actual benchmark run) could be determined by using standard UNIX tools to examine the process statistics. So, we executed a `ps -ef` command just before and just after the benchmark.

It occurred to me that I could also obtain the CPU consumption by a particular session from v$sesstat view, as follows:

```
select value
   from v$sesstat
   where sid = <sid>
   and statistic# =
   (select statistic# from v$statname where name = 'CPU used by this session');
```

I could then compare it to the value obtained from the UNIX operating statistics. What I found was that the value obtained from v$sesstat was always lower. In fact, in this case, it was always likely to be lower since the value obtained from v$sesstat did not include the significant SQL*Net processing overhead that we were experiencing (and this was picked up using `ps -ef`).

However, while investigating further, I found out something else that was interesting. For every user call in Oracle, the CPU used by this session is calculated and the granularity of the timing is in centiseconds. So if a user call completes within a centisecond, Oracle thinks it takes 0 centiseconds. The opposite could also happen, when the user call starts at centisecond c1, and completes at c2, but the total time is 0.1 centisecond, Oracle still counts it as 1 centisecond. So there is a degree of over- and undercounting.

So, tuning by response time was born! We were able to drill down into the different wait events for the session and determine exactly why the session was waiting and, by collecting all the different response times, we were able to determine the exact impact of the waiting time on the total response time. We even did a 10046 level-12 trace (see Chapter 5 by Cary Millsap for more information about this) on some of the very slow running processes, but we found that the slowdown caused by the tracing had a negative impact on the total response time (writing the wait events to the process trace file is potentially a significant overhead, depending on the number of wait events). So we did this only a couple of times.

Our work included the CPU data alongside the wait time data, whereas other groups who had discovered the wait interface were focusing exclusively on that. In my opinion, this is the wrong thing to do. You need to collect and examine both sets of data at the same time, not one or the other.

Incidentally, the methods that were used on this project to collect the statistics and data from Tuxedo and Oracle were eventually integrated into a tool called AKTOOL.[6] It was developed in 1997 and is still in use at the time of writing.

---

6. Anjo Kolk TOOL

The Birth of YAPP Methodology

When I went back to HQ, I started to tell people in the Center Of Expertise and MPP support about this new method. Shari Yamaguchi worked in MPP (Massively Parallel Processors) Support at the time, and they were supporting all the Oracle Parallel Server customers. Shari also taught a five-day internals class that covered performance tuning and she asked me to explain this new response time method in that course. I started off with a two-to-three-hour presentation, but it attracted a lot of interest and the talk just kept expanding. The last time I gave it, it was for a one-and-half-day seminar.

Shari was taking notes during my presentations and was the person responsible for getting started with the YAPP white paper. Later on the Center Of Expertise got involved and decided to take ownership of it and they published the white paper. Shari also urged me to come up with a name for this method, and all I could think of was YAPP: *Yet Another Performance Profiling Methodology.*

Using YAPP Methodology

So the YAPP methodology is based on response time tuning. It was developed first on the session level, then on the SQL statement level, and then on the instance level. In 1998 I moved to back to the Netherlands to a little town in the forest area, with two churches and only around 1,800+ population. To my surprise, I discovered that they were going to offer high-speed Internet by December 1998. So I signed up and got a two-CPU Linux box, installed Apache, and my first web site (http://www.oraperf.com) was a fact.

Over Christmas 1998, around the time I decided to register OraPerf.com, I started thinking about something that I had thought about before: how to upload a file to a web site and how to process that file and return some HTML that could be displayed inside the client browser? After reading about it, it was time to actually do it. So I decided to write a bstat/estat parser that would accept uploaded bstat/estat files, break them out into their constituent statistics, and perform an analysis on them based upon YAPP. I knew that many people were using bstat/estat but didn't know how to make sense of it. By applying the YAPP method on the report.txt file (the result of running utlbstat and utlestat), people could make sense of the file for the first time ever.

In 1999, I started some email exchange with a guy called Mogens Nørgaard; he read the YAPP white paper and instructed all his people in Premium services in Denmark to follow the paper in solving performance problems. In the year 2000, we met for the first time[7] and I was invited to stay in his house, and that was the start of the interesting get-togethers that we have every so often. I think one of the more interesting things that we did was visit the Niels Bohr institute and look at handwritten letters between Niels and this other fellow called Einstein.

People like Mogens have made the wait interface popular. It wasn't me coming up with the response time tuning methodology. You need people to spread the word, and he definitely did that, and is actually still doing that.

The Wait Interface in the Mainstream

All this work on the wait interface started in 1992. I did the initial YAPP work in 1996/1997 and the YAPP white paper came out in 1998. It is only really now, however, that use of the wait interface is becoming truly widespread. You can't go to an Oracle conference these days without seeing quite a number of sessions on this topic.

While this is essentially a good thing, I believe that care is required. For a start, does the wait interface record all the information we need about waits in the Oracle database? What if a wait hasn't been instrumented? Oracle keeps on adding wait events (from around 100 in 7.0 to around 800+ in 10.1), so that means that a lot of things that weren't instrumented in Oracle7 are now, but still it isn't clear (we can't check) if everything has been instrumented. We have to trust Oracle (can we?). The wait interface is getting more important for Oracle due to Automatic Database Diagnostic Monitor (ADDM) and Active Session History (ASH), but there is always the question: does it show everything?

Another problem with the wait interface is that it only looks at database waits, not at waits caused by the OS due to, let's say, involuntary context switches, or waiting for memory to be paged in, or waiting for a CPU to become available. That level of instrumentation is missing.

More important than either of these, though, is the fact that the wait interface can only diagnose what is going on in the database. What if the problem is not in the database, where is the problem then? Sure, the wait interface can help you a bit by proving that the problem is *outside* the database, but it does not help you to determine in which tier/layer the problem really does reside. This becomes a bigger problem as systems become more and more complex, with more and more

---

7. I walked off the plane into the arrivals hall in Copenhagen airport and found a man standing there talking and walking around. It was Mogens on the phone. It has been proven by now: all Danes are born with a mobile phone attached to their right hand. This mobile extension to the arm can be replaced with a whisky or hotdog extension.

tiers, none of which are usually properly instrumented. So what good is a well-instrumented database going to be, if we don't have the same level of instrumentation in the other tiers?

 NOTE *Even when we can get statistics from other tiers, there are not that many tools that will actually correlate the statistics from the different tiers. Veritas i3TM is such a product,[8] but there are not that many.*

Just because you can prove that the problem is actually outside the database, this is only half the battle; all the other tiers must be instrumented in order to find the real root cause.

Looking Forward

So, ironically, just as the wait interface and response time tuning are getting more traction with DBA's, they are also in danger of becoming less useful, due to the increasing complexity of uninstrumented multi-tier systems.

How do we combat this? Firstly, look across the tiers and don't get stuck in the database, or any other single tier. This is exactly the problem in today's IT departments: there are plenty of experts on each tier, but they don't talk the same language. The network person talks in terms of the "number of network packages," the app server person talks about "number of requests serviced," and so on. More than once, I have heard about a task force that has all the brightest experts in it, but because they had no common language in which to communicate, they still resorted to trial-and-error techniques to solve performance problems. The word *try* plays an important role in that process. Let's *try* this or let's *try* that. We need a common language in which to discuss performance problems, and that common language is *response time*.

Secondly, we need full instrumentation across all the tiers. What we need is for every tier to show the response times, and for these to be correlated across all the different tiers (from the end user to the physical disk).

In this way, problems will have no place to hide in the application stack, and the common language (response time) should also help to remove some of the

---

8. I work for Veritas Software on the i3 products, just to let you know.

"walls" that exist between different IT teams, that make performance problems mostly political and cultural. This will improve productivity and efficiency of the IT department as a whole.

Summary

One of the good things of the wait interface is it can lead you to the symptoms of your performance problems, and that is basically a mechanical process. You can see the proof of that in Oracle10g; ADDM uses the wait interface to figure out what performance problems occurred and what was the impact of these problems on the total response time.

NOTE *For those who have not yet migrated to Oracle10g, OraPerf.com has been providing a similar service across different database versions since 1998.*

However, in order for the Oracle Wait Interface to remain successful, we need to remain focused on response times, and we need the same level of instrumentation across the other tiers. If we don't get this, the wait interface will lose some, if not all, of the potential that it has. The distinction between tuning the database and tuning the application, or tuning the network, may have some relevance within your IT department, but it has absolutely no relevance at all to the unhappy customer who has to wait ten minutes to order one of your products online.

Dear Reader,

Of all the heroes I get to meet in and around the OakTable network, Cary is the biggest. He is not "just" a friend of mine; he is a very dear friend of mine. To be in a position where I can introduce him, and his various claims to fame (he would never claim them himself), makes me feel incredibly privileged.

I first noticed his name on a number of (still legendary) papers that he wrote while working inside Oracle. His VLDB paper, his RAID paper (with the footnote about stripping), his Storage paper, and so on and on and on. All excellent papers, all well researched, all attempting to enforce good ideas and kill off bad ones. Oh, and not to be forgotten: the Optimal Flexible Architecture, which has become the standard for installing Oracle anywhere, first presented as a paper at IOUG in Miami in 1991. I was at the conference, but missed the paper. Few probably realized what this OFA idea would lead to.

The former Jonathan Lewis, a.k.a. Dave Ensor (who recently retired again), once remarked to me that "Cary is perhaps the best person Oracle ever had to disprove a theory."

The first time we met was at an EOUG conference in Vienna in 1996. He was in the presenters' lounge, and I went over and introduced myself. He glanced at me, shook my hand, and said some polite, American sounds, and then continued his work.

After perhaps 10 minutes he came over and said "Wait a minute—what did you say your name was?" So I repeated it, and then there was much joy and celebration over the next couple of days, because we had been communicating a lot across that intra-Oracle 2000-member mail list known as HELPKERN, and in the process generating some really interesting mail threads. Now, after several years of that, we met each other. (I also met his beautiful wife Mindy, and I felt envious of Cary for being younger, smarter, richer, more beautiful, and especially for having such a wonder of a wife—and that last part of my envy lasted right up until I met Anette. The rest of them are still with me.)

The next day we both had a seminar before the conference. Cary ran his VLDB seminar, and all of six people or so showed up for it. In the next room I was presenting some performance ragtag stuff or other for 30 or more attendees. Oh, and two of Cary's attendees left him around lunch to join my crowd. I don't think Cary has ever forgotten that experience, but in case he has, it felt good to share it with the rest of the Planet (Cary will usually talk about the Planet instead of the Earth—there's probably a scientific reason for it). Cary's obsession with math and laws of nature are evident in everything he does. In fact, OakTable members rarely talk about exponential curves—we call them Cary Curves. I think if it was legal he would speak in Perl, actually.

Some time later I attended a class of his (VLDB, I think) in Dallas in order to become a certified presenter of it in other parts of the world than Texas. By that time Cary had created the famous System Performance Group and he needed help in other parts of the World (sorry, Planet), because his team of 50–70 people could only just cover the need in the US region. So I volunteered my Premium Services outfit in the middle of one of Cary's sentences, he said yes, and thus we became the third SPG-associated group, along with the huge Mark Large in the UK and the other Mark in Australia. The contacts and knowledge we gained from that are still valuable to this date, and are the basis for several businesses around the World (Planet).

Then came the time when Cary (now a vice president) left Oracle to found Hotsos along with Jeff (also from SPG) and Gary Goodman (formerly of Oracle). One evening Jeff and Cary called me from a client site and needed to know about this strange tracing trick that could show you what the session was waiting for. It took a couple of hours before we got it to work over the phone, and the full credit for this should go to Miracle's own Johannes Djernæs, who finally got it to work for Jeff and Cary.

The rest is history. Many people knew about this way of tracing: Anjo had written the YAPP paper and put it to good use; I had, as usual, just talked for years about it; Kyle had actually used it; and so forth. But Cary? He couldn't just do like everyone else. Oh no. Cary had to create a method, a company, and a tool around it. His and Jeff's book is the only performance book I'll bring to the deserted island. There, in solitude and peace, I might finally find the time to understand that chapter about queuing theory that contains more Greek letters than the story of Odysseus.

Cary has a workshop the size of my garden (everything is big in Texas) where he builds beautiful things in wood (including an Oak Table, of course) and finds excuses for buying big machines that will take your arm off if you're not paying attention. He also used to train with the US Olympic team in Taekwondo, as a black belt. And as a boy he used to kill American box turtles (because they ate fish in the fish pond). The American box turtle is now an endangered species, and I'll leave it up to the reader to make the connection. By pure coincidence I'm currently the proud owner of three American box turtles, but I haven't dared tell Cary where I keep them yet.

Cary introduced me (during a seminar in Denmark many moons ago) to the notion of a mental break. It is not what you think. It is instead an interruption in a technical presentation of something completely unrelated (how insects die, or how Cary's table was constructed) to take your mind off the real topic in order to be able to absorb yet another 42 minutes of hard science. Ladies and gentlemen, dear readers—it is my great honor to present to you the one, the only, my dear friend, Cary.

—*Mogens Nørgaard*

CHAPTER 5

Extended SQL Trace Data

By Cary Millsap

WAY BACK IN 1992, Oracle introduced a new means of extracting detailed response time information from a database: the extended SQL trace mechanism. In 1995, I began to learn much more about this feature when my colleagues at Oracle Corporation used it to remove the guesswork from Oracle performance improvement projects. The magic of this new extended SQL trace feature was that it allowed analysts to predict the exact response time impact of a proposed system change. At the time, this predictive ability was revolutionary. Predictability and the resulting notion of "fully informed decision making" has been the foundation of my career ever since.

In 1999, I left Oracle Corporation to work full time creating a new performance improvement method that I hoped would far surpass the reliability and accuracy of traditional Oracle methods. In our book, *Optimizing Oracle Performance* (Millsap and Holt, O'Reilly & Associates, 2003), Jeff Holt and I have published the full technical details of our new method and the extended SQL trace tool itself. Here, I describe the story behind Oracle's extended SQL trace capability, its history, the people who helped develop it, and how and why you might consider using it.

Before the Microscope

In the days before the microscope, the fight against infectious diseases was brutally difficult. In the fourteenth century, for example, bubonic plague ravaged Europe and Asia. Between 1347 and 1352, the Black Death (as the disease came to be called) killed 25 million Europeans—one third of the region's total population.[1]

---

1. Source: http://www.byu.edu/ipt/projects/middleages/LifeTimes/Plague.html.

Medieval medicine provided no cure for the plague, but men and women of the time tried everything they could think of to combat the disease. The dominant response to plague symptoms was bloodletting practiced with extraordinary aggressiveness. When a patient lost consciousness from too much blood loss, the "caregiver" would revive the patient with cold water. When the patient reawakened, the bleeding would continue.

The list of responses to plague symptoms would sound like comedy if not for the magnitude of the suffering that motivated them. Wives nudged their husbands in their sleep, prompting a roll from one side of the body to the other to "prevent the liver from heating too much on one side." Scents were big. People would inhale virtually anything they could think of that might have a chance of "replacing" the plague-bearing air in their bodies with plague-free air, from aromatic spices to their own sewage pits. Neighbors exterminated cats and those cats' masters on the premise that perhaps it was witchcraft at the root of the epidemic. There wasn't much that a medieval neighbor wouldn't try, if he thought he could save himself or his family from the horrors he had seen befall other families.

Medieval medicine failed to stop the plague because medieval medicine failed to identify the plague's root cause. The root cause, we know today, was a bacterium called *Yersinia pestis*, which was transported and inoculated into humans with exceptional efficiency by fleas (... turns out that cat killing probably caused positive harm). Medieval "doctors" didn't know that *Y. pestis* existed. They didn't even know that bacteria existed—they couldn't *see* them. You can't see plague bacteria without a microscope, and the microscope wouldn't be invented until a Dutchman by the name of Anton van Leeuwenhoek did the job late in the seventeenth century.

The history of Oracle performance analysis looks a lot like the history of humanity's war on infectious disease. The nouns are different, but the story is familiar. Instead of people, it's Oracle systems that die before their time. Instead of leeches, cat killing, and vapor wafting, it's hit ratios, database rebuilds, and disk rebalancing. Instead of *Yersinia pestis*, it's `latch free`, `buffer busy waits`, `SQL*Net message from client`, and the hundreds of other code paths in which an Oracle system can consume response time. And instead of the microscope, it's *extended SQL trace data.*

Our story even has its own Dutch guy. We will get to that in a little bit.

The Dark Ages

In the days prior to Oracle version 7, Oracle professionals taught only one way to "tune Oracle." That way was to look at a variety of data sources, usually beginning with the output of a program pair called `bstat.sql` and `estat.sql`, and including anything else you could find, such as output from `sar`, `vmstat`, `glance`, `top`, and whatever other operating system tools you could get your hands on.

The game was to look at the output from all these sources and construct a theory that could explain the root cause of a given performance problem. You would address that root cause and then retry the slow program, in the hope that it would be sufficiently fast now that you could declare success, and move on to the next item of business. Often, however, you'd find that the thing you fixed had no bearing on the problem at hand, or worse, perhaps you'd find that your attempted repair had exacerbated the problem. If this happened, then you could do a good job only if you had kept good enough notes to allow you to undo your change, so your system would be at least no worse off for your efforts.

This was "tuning." It was a process akin to forensic pathology: like detectives who searched for blood droplets and clothing fibers, you'd search for numbers or combinations of numbers that looked unusual. The number that always looked unusual was the famous *database buffer cache hit ratio*. The database buffer cache hit ratio was a measure of what proportion of database buffer accesses could be serviced without the Oracle kernel having to issue an operating system read call. The formula with which people computed the cache hit ratio (chr) was

$$chr = \frac{requests - reads}{requests} = 1 - \frac{reads}{requests}$$

No matter what its value was, the number always looked suspicious. For example, a value of 0.1 would have been considered unconscionably low. Nobody wanted to think that 90% of the Oracle blocks used by his system involved the participation of the disk subsystem.[2] Of course, when your database buffer cache hit ratio is too low, the prescribed response was to increase the size of the database buffer cache, which in those days meant incrementing the value of the db_block_buffers Oracle instance parameter.

But low cache hit ratios weren't the only problem. Slow systems could have high cache hit ratios, too. Some people knew why, but most didn't seem to. Most people assumed that if a system had a high buffer cache hit ratio and the system was still slow, then the buffer cache hit ratio simply must not be high *enough*. So, even people with cache hit ratios in excess of 0.99 would presume that the way to remedy their problem was, of course, to increase the size of the database buffer cache.

---

2. Of course, this isn't exactly what a cache hit ratio meant, but it's what a lot of people were *taught* that it meant. The first important distinction between this statement and actual fact is that many systems have an OS buffer cache between the Oracle kernel and the disk subsystem, so many I/O calls that seem, from the Oracle kernel's perspective, to be "physical" are in fact serviced from memory.

The problem is that this technique often didn't work. Increasing the size of the database buffer cache made a system faster if its buffer cache was too small to begin with. But on many systems, increasing the size of the buffer cache didn't produce any improvement in end-user performance, even if it did happen to improve the database buffer cache hit ratio.

Some people knew better. In the early 1990s, two of my Oracle mentors, Willis Ranney and Dave Ensor, taught me that a really high database buffer cache hit ratio value—a value, say, in excess of 0.95—was usually an indication of a serious performance problem that demanded attention. The argument went like this . . .

Imagine that a given result set could be produced by any of three different methods: A, B, and C. These methods use different join orders and access methods, but they all return the same answer. Furthermore, imagine that use of these methods produced the operational statistics shown in Table 5-1. Which method presents the best way to produce the result set?

Table 5-1. Database Buffer Cache Hit Ratios for Various Numbers of Requests and Reads

Method	Database Buffer Cache Hit Ratio
A	0.7
B	0.998
C	0.99999

The naïve answer is that method C is the best, for the simple reason that it produces the largest buffer cache hit ratio of the three methods. But using only the information shown in Table 5-1, it is impossible to determine which method is the best. Table 5-2 shows why.

Table 5-2. Database Buffer Cache Hit Ratios for Various Numbers of Requests and Reads

Method	Requests	Reads	Database Buffer Cache Hit Ratio	Response Time (Seconds)
A	10	3	0.7	0.031
B	1,000	2	0.998	0.070
C	100,000	1	0.99999	5.010

The far superior answer is that method A is the best, for a couple of reasons. First, method A produces the best *response time*, which is a metric that is very well connected to a user's perception of how the system is performing. Second, method A does far less work than either of the other two methods. That "requests" count means something. Each time an Oracle kernel process requests the access of a block from the database buffer cache, the process executes potentially thousands of CPU instructions, many of which are serialized.

The argument continued that if a system showed a database buffer cache hit ratio value, say, in excess of 0.95, it was a pretty good indication that there were one or more SQL statements resembling method C that should be converted to method A. Doing this would have two effects: it would make the system perform better, and it would reduce the value of the buffer cache hit ratio.

This argument was, at the time, revolutionary, and history has borne out that the argument was entirely accurate.[3] The argument caused a horrible problem, though: The principal system metric that Oracle professionals used to measure the performance of an Oracle system didn't work. "Low" numbers were supposed to be bad, and "high" numbers were supposed to be good, but "low" numbers weren't always bad, and "high" numbers weren't always good. Worse yet, the values of "low" and "high" were completely subjective.

It was a mess. And the problem was even worse than I've let on. It wasn't just the database buffer cache hit ratio metric that was flawed; almost *every* system metric we had was flawed in a similar manner. Is a latch miss ratio of 95% a problem? It might be, but if a latch has been acquired only 20 times in the past two months, and the 19 misses have cost a grand total of 2.718 seconds of end-user response time over that period, then who cares? Is CPU utilization of 90% a problem? It might be, but if there's batch workload queued up for processing, and response time fluctuations aren't bothering the users, then letting a CPU sit idle would be a waste of good capacity. Similar problems existed for every single metric we looked at.

The only solution we had was to look at larger, more elaborate collections of statistics. Most of us tried to do our jobs by looking at dozens of pages, each containing hundreds of operational statistics. We'd try to single out our favorites. If one time we had made a system go faster by noticing too "high" a ratio of `table scan blocks gotten` to `logons cumulative`, we would check that ratio every time we analyzed a new system. If one time we had discovered that creating a certain index made things faster, we'd check for the presence of that index.

Basically, we would fix the things we knew how to fix, and then we'd pray that what we had done would somehow cause the things people were complaining about to run faster. It was akin to looking in the best-lit spot in the parking lot for the car keys you lost, regardless of where you dropped them. The "method" we were taught for "tuning" Oracle databases worked only when the problem was something that we knew in advance how to fix.

---

3. One of the reasons that the many people were slow to realize the truth of this argument on their own was the widespread and nearly debilitating myth that reading a block from the Oracle database buffer cache is "10,000 times faster" than reading a block from a disk. The correct factor is on the order of 10 or 100, not 10,000 (Millsap, "Why You Should Focus on LIOs Instead of PIOs," Hotsos, 2001).

The Enlightenment

The beginning of the enlightenment for me came when I was in charge of Oracle Corporation's System Performance Group in 1995. One of the more pleasant aspects of my work in those days, as it still is today, was keeping in contact with the leader of the Premium Support Services group of Oracle Denmark, one Mr. Mogens Nørgaard.[4] On one particular day, my dear friend[5] was telling me the news of a new thing in Oracle that people were calling the *wait interface*.[6]

Mogens explained to me on the telephone that this wait interface thing was a lot like watching someone buy groceries. Instead of guessing how long someone had spent in the store by investigating the contents of her shopping cart, the wait interface was like a timer that could tell you exactly how long the shopper had spent choosing potatoes, how long she had spent choosing orange juice, and so on. A mutual friend named Anjo Kolk, a Dutchman, also from Oracle Corporation, had written a very nice paper about it called "Description of Oracle7 wait events and enqueues." Mogens would of course send me a copy, and I of course would read it.

I was interested because my friend seemed to think it was important, but, frankly, I thought the news wasn't as interesting as Mogens seemed to think it was. I certainly wouldn't have guessed during that conversation that in the year 2000, I would give the next four years of my career over to the thing he was describing.

At about the same time, a young consultant in my group named Virag Saksena had begun sending client engagement reports that represented a *huge* advance in optimization effectiveness. Virag had always impressed me with his effectiveness as an Oracle optimizer. He had already established himself with me as one of the most efficient SQL query optimizers on the planet. But in 1995, Virag was doing work that took Oracle "tuning" to a completely different plane.

---

4. It looks like the name Mogens would be pronounced \mō´gəns\, but it's not. The Danes swallow their g's, so the name is pronounced \mōns\. That is, *Mogens* and *groans* rhyme perfectly.

5. Mogens is now not just my "dear friend," but my "award-winning dear friend" as well. Mogens has kidded me relentlessly about Americans' propensity to give so many awards to each other that everyone can advertise that they are "award-winning." Since *Oracle Magazine* named Mogens "2003 Oracle Educator of the Year" he doesn't kid me so much about it anymore.

6. Happily, as of version 10, Oracle Corporation no longer calls this feature the *wait interface*, but rather the *timed event* interface. This is a much more appropriate name for the feature. The word *wait* already has a specific technical definition in the field of queueing theory, and the "wait" statistics that the Oracle kernel produces are definitely not *waits* in the queueing theory sense (Millsap and Holt, *Optimizing Oracle Performance*, O'Reilly & Associates, 2003. pp. 239–242).

In the early 1990s, I fancied myself a decent Oracle "tuning expert." I did what most "tuning experts" in those days did. It's only slightly unfair to say that what we did was to follow these steps:

1. Listen politely as the client explained what the problem was. Take notes to prove that we're listening carefully.

2. Fix the ten or so problems that we knew how to fix.

3. Pray that the ten things we had "fixed" would provide some relief for the client's most important complaints.

4. Document the miracles we had performed, with *before* and *after* statistics, explain what changes we had made, and create a list of open issues that would have to be resolved later.

5. Send the invoice.

It usually took me three or four days to get through step 2, and then I would spend the remainder of the week praying and explaining. As I said, when I was doing this for a living, I had thought I was pretty good.

I wasn't.

What Virag was doing was *completely* different. He was listening politely, and then he was focusing his efforts on the client's most important complaints. He was making statements like this:

If you do x, *then you will reduce the response time of the thing you're complaining about by* y *seconds. Doing* x *will cost approximately* z.

This was completely revolutionary. He was providing exactly the information that a decision-maker would need to make a fully informed economic decision about whether to do x. Here was, for the first time in my career, a consultant who was informing his client about both the costs *and benefits* to be expected from an action. And he wasn't guessing. He was creating a spectacular track record of accurate predictions. When people did x, response times really did drop by y seconds, just like he'd said.

Before Virag, I had seen consultants specify only costs (which consultants are well-trained at estimating) and *guesses* about benefits:

Do x, *and we think it will help, but we can't really guarantee anything.*[7] *Doing* x *will cost approximately* z.

---

7. Of course, a consultant spends a lot of time figuring out ways to express such disappointments as this without sacrificing one's professional dignity.

To make Virag's predictions even more remarkable to me, he was making them on his *first day of a project*. Let me recap: I had thought I was pretty good, and I was often guessing even on Friday. Virag was making accurate and very detailed cost/benefit predictions about performance on Monday. I was blown away. I had seen the future.

Virag's extraordinary efficiency was an inspiration that would help drive my research into what I, and everyone else, might be able to extract from the Oracle extended SQL trace data that he was using.

The History of SQL Trace

Let me switch gears for a while and tell the story of Oracle's SQL trace feature, which would eventually become the *extended* SQL trace feature used today.

The Oracle extended SQL trace feature exists today because, fortunately, Oracle customers aren't the only ones who have to wrestle with Oracle application performance problems. The men and women who built the Oracle kernel fight the same problems too, both in customer situations and in competitive benchmarks. The following quote is from Juan Loaiza, an Oracle kernel architect, and at the time of this writing a vice president at Oracle Corporation (you can read the full story in Chapter 2, where Juan tells of the motives for inventing SQL trace and then extending it to the state in which we know it today):

> *I've always thought that diagnosing performance issues boils down to figuring out where the time is going in the system. If you can attribute the time correctly, then the source of the problem becomes obvious.*

Certainly our professional community is indebted to Juan Loaiza and his team for giving us the microscope to see how the Oracle kernel is spending *all* of our users' time.

Version 5

SQL trace is at least as old as Oracle version 5, which was released in 1986. The syntax to turn it on and off was simple:

```
select trace('sql',1) from dual
...
select trace('sql',0) from dual
```

Apparently, not too many people knew about SQL trace in Oracle version 5, and probably fewer than that actually used it. In an old Oracle internal document called "Optimizing," Oracle described the trace function as follows (quoted verbatim from the source):

> *The Kernel provides a trace function to provide information about internal operations.*
>
> *The trace function is essentially a debug aid for Oracle Software Development.*
>
> *—It is **not documented.***
>
> *—It is **not supported.***
>
> *—[It] will not be a function in ORACLE version 6.*

By today's standards, the version 5 SQL trace function didn't do a whole lot. All you could get from the 'sql' trace output was a stream of PARSING IN CURSOR sections that looked something like this:

```
=====================
PARSING IN CURSOR 3:
    "select tab$pid,tab$rba,tab$tbl,tab$type,tab$sowner,tab$sname"
    " from sys.tables where tab$owner=:1 and tab$name=:2"
=====================
PARSING IN CURSOR 4:
    "select idx$cky from indexes['1.f.1'] where idx$tbl=:1 and id"
    "x$cky is not null"
=====================
PARSING IN CURSOR 1:
    "select * from dept "
=====================
```

There were other trace functions besides 'sql'. With the trace function, an Oracle user could see information about access paths, sorting operations, and memory consumption.

Version 6

In Oracle version 6, SQL tracing became a core, documented feature for everyone to use. In version 6, Oracle introduced the syntax that also works in versions 7, 8, 9, and 10:

```
alter session set sql_trace=true
...
alter session set sql_trace=false
```

SQL trace was a significant step forward in power for the Oracle performance analyst. It allowed you to see the sequence of SQL statements that an application was executing, and it allowed you to see how much load each of these statements placed upon the database. Raw trace data was ugly, as you can see from Listing 5-1.

Listing 5-1. An Excerpt from Raw SQL Trace Data

```
=====================

PARSING IN CURSOR #1 len=103 dep=0 uid=5 oct=3 lid=5 tim=564568615 hv=3329006097 ad
='54a12578'
select count(*)
from (select n from dummy connect by n > prior n start with n=1)
where rownum < 100000
END OF STMT
PARSE #1:c=4,e=18,p=2,cr=34,cu=1,mis=1,r=0,dep=0,og=3,tim=564568615
EXEC #1:c=0,e=0,p=0,cr=0,cu=0,mis=0,r=0,dep=0,og=3,tim=564568615
FETCH #1:c=381,e=393,p=0,cr=100000,cu=0,mis=0,r=1,dep=0,og=3,tim=564569008
FETCH #1:c=0,e=0,p=0,cr=0,cu=0,mis=0,r=0,dep=0,og=0,tim=564569008
```

However, it didn't matter too much because Oracle Corporation provided a tool called tkprof that formatted raw trace data into a more convenient form for people to use (Listing 5-2[8]).

Listing 5-2. An Excerpt from tkprof *Output*

```
select count(*)
from (select n from dummy connect by n > prior n start with n=1)
where rownum < 100000
```

---

8. Listing 5-2 shows the form of modern tkprof output (the case shown here was generated using Oracle version 8.1.6.1.0). The format of tkprof output has changed a little bit since version 6, but the content remains materially the same as it was in the version 6 days.

call	count	cpu	elapsed	disk	query	current	rows
Parse	1	0.01	0.00	0	0	0	0
Execute	1	0.00	0.00	0	0	0	0
Fetch	2	3.81	3.93	0	100000	0	1
total	4	3.82	3.93	0	100000	0	1

```
Misses in library cache during parse: 1
Optimizer goal: RULE
Parsing user id: 5
```

In addition to the standard ratio-based stuff, the better Oracle "tuning" courses taught students how to interpret tkprof output. The rules for using tkprof output were pretty simple:

1. Reduce the numbers that appear in the count column. That is, eliminate all the database calls you could. The most powerful way to accomplish this was by manipulating whatever application code was making database calls with SQL.

2. Reduce the numbers that appear in the query and current columns (derived from the cr and cu fields in the raw trace data, respectively). That is, eliminate all the requests for blocks from the buffer cache that you could. Sometimes doing this was as simple as creating or dropping indexes. Sometimes you had to manipulate the text of the SQL itself to accomplish this.

3. If the query + current sum was at its bare minimum, and disk was nonzero, then consider using a bigger database buffer cache. That is, eliminate all the "physical" read requests that you could, but only after eliminating all of the memory accesses that you could.

Of course, these guidelines evolved over time as well. At the first Oracle "tuning" course I ever attended, our instructor taught that the way to tune SQL with tkprof is to do whatever it took to make the disk column's value be zero. We now know that the problem with this strategy is that it helps to promote a very serious type of performance problem: a SQL statement can work entirely within the confines of the database buffer cache and still be horrendously inefficient. Tables 6-1 and 6-2 show how. However, this advice was the "golden rule" of internal Oracle training courses at the time of Oracle version 6.

When bad SQL or bad schema design, missing indexes, too much parsing, or under-use of Oracle's set processing capabilities were the problem, SQL trace data was the microscope you needed to find the problem. But for some problems, SQL trace data wasn't enough. Standard SQL trace data is inadequate when the elapsed time of a SQL statement greatly exceeds the amount of CPU capacity the statement has consumed. For example, what do you do when you see this in your tkprof output?

call	count	cpu	elapsed	disk	query	current	rows
Parse	1	0.01	0.02	0	0	0	0
Execute	1	0.03	0.03	0	0	0	0
Fetch	20	0.13	22.95	11	39	0	20
total	22	0.17	23.00	11	39	0	20

This table says that the query consumed 23.00 seconds of response time, but it *explains* only 0.17 seconds of that time. What are you supposed to believe about the other 22.83 seconds? The answer, when you're using standard SQL trace, is that *you just don't know.*

Of course, not knowing doesn't keep people from guessing. The most popular guess was the usual suspect of all performance problems throughout the late twentieth century: disk I/O. This guess was certainly right some of the time, but it was wrong some of the time, too. The problem is that when your problem is *not* CPU consumption and it's *not* disk I/O, what then?

Listing 5-3 shows an example of the problem. In this example, the statement in question is a simple UPDATE statement that updates the value associated with a specified primary key value. The update manipulated only one row (r=1), yet the execution phase of the command consumed 10.56 seconds of elapsed time (e=1056). What took so long? It certainly wasn't CPU service, because the statement consumed only about 0.02 seconds of CPU time (c=2). The "it must be disk I/O" argument doesn't hold much weight in this case, because the raw trace data indicates that the kernel issued no OS read calls during the update (p=0). How can you find why this update consumed more than 10 seconds?

Listing 5-3. Raw Level-1 Trace Data Showing That Elapsed Time Greatly Exceeding the CPU Service Duration

```
=====================
PARSING IN CURSOR #1 len=31 dep=0 uid=73 oct=6 lid=73 tim=27139911 hv=1169598682 ad
='68f56dc8'
update c set v1='y' where key=1
END OF STMT
PARSE #1:c=0,e=902,p=0,cr=0,cu=0,mis=1,r=0,dep=0,og=4,tim=27139911
EXEC #1:c=2,e=1056,p=0,cr=3,cu=3,mis=0,r=1,dep=0,og=4,tim=27140969
```

Version 7

Oracle version 7 brought the solution to the problem of what to do when the value of e for a database call is much greater than the value of c. In version 7, Oracle introduced the feature that is the subject of this chapter: *extended* SQL trace. With extended SQL trace enabled, the Oracle kernel can tell you *everywhere* it spends your time. The prevailing hypothesis of the version 6 era would have been that the time was lost in disk I/O. However, Listing 5-4 shows exactly where that missing time from Listing 5-3 actually went: the Oracle kernel waited four times—for a grand total of approximately 10 seconds—on Oracle enqueue events. In other words, the update was blocked on the acquisition of a lock.

Listing 5-4. Raw Level-8 Trace Data Shows Where the Time Went

```
=====================
PARSING IN CURSOR #1 len=31 dep=0 uid=73 oct=6 lid=73 tim=27139911 hv=1169598682 ad
='68f56dc8'
update c set v1='y' where key=1
END OF STMT
PARSE #1:c=0,e=902,p=0,cr=0,cu=0,mis=1,r=0,dep=0,og=4,tim=27139911
WAIT #1: nam='enqueue' ela= 307 p1=1415053318 p2=393254 p3=35925
WAIT #1: nam='enqueue' ela= 307 p1=1415053318 p2=393254 p3=35925
WAIT #1: nam='enqueue' ela= 307 p1=1415053318 p2=393254 p3=35925
WAIT #1: nam='enqueue' ela= 132 p1=1415053318 p2=393254 p3=35925
EXEC #1:c=2,e=1056,p=0,cr=3,cu=3,mis=0,r=1,dep=0,og=4,tim=27140969
WAIT #1: nam='SQL*Net message to client' ela= 0 p1=1413697536 p2=1 p3=0
```

Do you think you would have guessed that? You might have. After all, this was an UPDATE statement, the kind of thing that might block on a lock. But it could very well have been something else. In Oracle version 7.3.4, it could have been any of 106 things, to be exact, because in version 7.3.4, Oracle had instrumented 106 distinct code paths in the Oracle kernel.

So, maybe you would have guessed that the dominant contributor of the update's response time was time spent blocked on a lock, but there would be about a 1% chance you'd have been right. But even if you had guessed that the problem was a lock, you couldn't have proven it. How much would you have been willing to wager? A few thousand dollars of your company's budget? Your career? And could you have guessed the lock type and lock mode? The trace data contains this information, too. It was an EXCLUSIVE mode TX lock, which you can determine by properly interpreting the value p1=1415053318, using Oracle Metalink documents such as 55541.999 and 62354.1 for guidance.

The Oracle version 7 syntax for activating extended SQL trace is, again, the `ALTER SESSION` statement:

```
alter session set events '10046 trace name context forever, level 12'
...
alter session set events '10046 trace name context off'
```

The level number for the extended SQL tracing event (event number 10046) is a binary encoding of three values, as shown in Table 5-3. You can combine the levels to combine effects, so using level 12 creates the effect of using both level 4 and level 8 at the same time. Curiously, manipulating the decimal 2-bit doesn't appear to have any effect.

Table 5-3. Extended SQL Tracing Levels

Binary Digit	Decimal Value	Description
0000	0	No tracing
0001	1	Standard SQL tracing
0100	4	Standard SQL tracing plus bind variable information
1000	8	Standard SQL tracing plus timed event information
1100	12	Standard SQL tracing plus bind variable and timed event information

Using an `ALTER SESSION` command is well and good if you have read and write access to the application code whose performance you're trying to diagnose. But what happens if you're trying to diagnose an application that you've purchased from a software vendor? If the application vendor wasn't thoughtful enough to give you the option to trace the application code (maybe a menu option), then what do you do?

One answer is to activate tracing with an `ALTER SYSTEM` command. However, this approach can cause more problems than it solves. Tracing a whole system can fill disks very rapidly, making it difficult to identify which trace data you want to study and which you want to discard.

A standard Oracle package, `DBMS_SYSTEM`, provides a much more elegant answer. The procedure `DBMS_SYSTEM.SET_EV` allows an Oracle session to activate extended SQL tracing in another Oracle session. The syntax is

```
dbms_system.set_ev(sid, serial, 10046, 12, ")
...
dbms_system.set_ev(sid, serial, 10046, 0, ")
```

With SET_EV, you could trace *any* Oracle session on your system. However, there was a drawback to using SET_EV: the procedure was (and still is) officially unsupported. This drawback was more of a political issue than a technical one. The justification for not supporting SET_EV was entirely rational. First, you probably don't want to grant the execute privilege on DBMS_SYSTEM to just anyone; there's stuff in there that you don't want most of your users being able to run. Second, misuse of SET_EV can cause serious harm to your system. For example, typing the event number 10004 by accident instead of 10046 could cause application of the Oracle kernel event that will simulate a control file crash . . . probably not what you wanted to do.

I'm not much of a rule breaker in real life, but the rule not to use SET_EV is, in my opinion, a rule truly worth breaking. For many, the feature is just too valuable not to use. There seem to be at least as many Oracle Metalink articles encouraging the use of extended SQL trace (see especially note 39817.1) as there are articles discouraging it. It appears that extended SQL trace is well supported, just not the means for turning it on.

Version 8

In Oracle version 8, Oracle Corporation supported the extended SQL trace slightly more, with the distribution of the /rdbms/admin/dbmssupp.sql script. This script creates the package called DBMS_SUPPORT, which insulates users from the dreaded effects of misusing SET_EV. The DBMS_SUPPORT package makes it very easy to activate extended SQL trace for a given session:

```
dbms_support.start_trace_in_session(sid, serial, true, true)
...
dbms_support.stop_trace_in_session(sid, serial)
```

An inconvenient aspect of DBMS_SUPPORT is the following note in the file dbmssupp.sql:

```
Rem    NOTES
Rem      This package should only be installed when requested by Oracle
Rem      Support. It is not documented in the server documentation.
Rem      It is to be used only as directed by Oracle Support.
```

Alas, still unsupported; however, Metalink note 62294.1 definitely provides encouragement to users of DBMS_SUPPORT.

Aside from the improved access mechanism, extended SQL trace data didn't change much in version 8. It really didn't need to, because it worked so well in version 7. The number of wait events did grow from 106 in Oracle version 7 to 215 in Oracle version 8.

A couple of Oracle bugs shook some people's confidence in SQL trace from time to time. Bug 1210242 affected cursor sharing when tracing was activated. Bug 2425312 caused the Oracle kernel to neglect to emit important information about remote procedure calls into the trace output. But with the appropriate patches installed, SQL trace in Oracle version 8 worked accurately and reliably.

Version 9

Oracle version 9 brought the first major changes to trace data that had occurred in a long time. Changes included the following:

- *Improvement of timing statistics resolution:* Oracle improved its output timer resolution from 1-centisecond (0.01-second) units to 1-microsecond (0.000001-second) units. With the finer resolution, we were able to learn even more about short-duration database calls and wait events.[9]

- *Option to include wait event information in the* tkprof *report:* Finally, tkprof began processing the extended SQL trace information. Not too bad for an officially unsupported feature.

- *Even more instrumented wait events:* The Oracle kernel developers instrumented many more code paths in the kernel, as the wait event count rose to 399 in version 9.2.0.4.

- *Inclusion of row-source workload and timing statistics:* This helped analysts determine how much time each row-source operation in a statement's execution plan was responsible for contributing to total response time for the statement.

---

9. It probably sped up the Oracle kernel a little bit, too. Most underlying operating systems had long since provided microsecond timing data to the Oracle kernel, but only in version 9 did the Oracle kernel cease integer-dividing the microsecond part of the OS timing statistics by 10,000 to convert the data from microseconds to centiseconds.

The inclusion of row-source statistics in version 9.2.0.2 created a bit of a brief plunge into darkness for SQL trace users. Since version 6, Oracle has emitted one or more lines beginning with the token STAT in the trace data when a cursor with an execution plan closes. You can easily assemble these lines into an execution plan, as shown in Listings 5-5 and 5-6.

Listing 5-5. STAT Lines Show Statistics About a Cursor's Row-Source Operations

```
STAT #3 id=1 cnt=0 pid=0 pos=0 obj=0 op='FILTER '
STAT #3 id=2 cnt=1068 pid=1 pos=1 obj=16351 op='TABLE ACCESS FULL ACCOUNT '
STAT #3 id=3 cnt=1067 pid=1 pos=2 obj=0 op='CONCATENATION '
STAT #3 id=4 cnt=1067 pid=3 pos=1 obj=19512 op='TABLE ACCESS BY INDEX ROWID
 CUSTHASPRODUCT '
STAT #3 id=5 cnt=213128430 pid=4 pos=1 obj=22903 op='INDEX RANGE SCAN '
STAT #3 id=6 cnt=1067 pid=3 pos=2 obj=19512 op='TABLE ACCESS BY INDEX ROWID
 CUSTHASPRODUCT '
STAT #3 id=7 cnt=1160025328 pid=6 pos=1 obj=22903 op='INDEX RANGE SCAN '
```

Listing 5-6. The Execution Plan Denoted by the STAT Lines in Listing 5-5

```
Rows returned  Row-source operation (object id)
-------------  -------------------------------------------------------
            0  FILTER
        1,068   TABLE ACCESS FULL ACCOUNT (16351)
        1,067   CONCATENATION
        1,067    TABLE ACCESS BY INDEX ROWID CUSTHASPRODUCT (19512)
  213,128,430     INDEX RANGE SCAN (22903)
        1,067    TABLE ACCESS BY INDEX ROWID CUSTHASPRODUCT (19512)
1,160,025,328     INDEX RANGE SCAN (22903)
```

These STAT lines are enormously helpful to you, the performance analyst, because they tell you (a) what steps the Oracle kernel has used to access your data and (b) how much work each step has done. However, the study of performance is the study of *time*, and you cannot determine how long something took by counting how many times it happened. While it is nice to see how much work is being done by each row-source operation, it would be nicer to see how much *time* each row-source operation consumed.

This is the new feature that Oracle introduced in version 9.2.0.2. A new STAT line looks like this:

```
STAT #1 id=5 cnt=23607 pid=4 pos=1 obj=0 op='NESTED LOOPS  (cr=1750 r=156 w=0 time=
1900310 us)'
```

Notice that the row-source operation name has been augmented with a parenthetical list of new statistics (compare this sample to the lines in Listing 5-5). The time=1900310 us field in this example tells you that this NESTED LOOPS row-source operation consumed 1.900310 seconds of wall time.

Time consumption by row-source operation is wonderful information to have. The problem was that the means by which the Oracle kernel obtained this information in the first release of the feature was so resource intensive that using SQL trace (either standard or extended) became unbearably expensive in many cases. Using SQL trace in Oracle versions 9.2.0.2 through 9.2.0.4 caused some SQL statements to consume five or more times the response time they would have consumed by using SQL trace in earlier versions of Oracle.

This is Oracle bug 3009359. Fortunately, Oracle Corporation responded rapidly to reports of this problem with a patch present in 9.2.0.5. The world of SQL trace was rocked only briefly before order was restored. With the patch, extended SQL trace continued to provide faithful and valuable service.

Version 10

There's a big functional problem with the whole version 6/7/8/9 tracing model. In the version 5 and 6 days, when the architects at Oracle designed the SQL tracing model, there was really only one kind of Oracle application: client-server. In the Oracle client-server model, an Oracle user application process connected to one and only Oracle server *session*, which was executed within one and only one Oracle server *process*, resulting in one and only one trace file. For this model, the design of SQL tracing made perfect sense. If you wanted to trace user Nancy's functional user action, you would activate tracing for the one and only one Oracle session to which Nancy's program connected. You would find the trace file and analyze it. The world was good.

However, the Oracle application architecture model has diverged significantly since the 1980s. Oracle's *Multi-Threaded Server* (MTS) feature[10] was one of the first complications to the tracing model, because this feature allowed a single user action to engage the services of potentially many Oracle server processes. With MTS, the trace of a single user action commonly results in the creation of two or more trace files whose contents have to be knitted together either by hand or with some kind of custom software tool. With MTS, SQL trace is still a perfectly usable feature; you just have to do a little more work to piece all the data together correctly.

Oracle's *parallel execution* (PX) features provide another complication because, again, a single user action will engage the services of several Oracle

---

10. Which, incidentally, has an odd name because it's not multithreaded, as Dave Ensor and James Morle explain in Chapters 1 and 8, respectively.

server processes. The trace of a parallel degree *n* user action will result in the creation of one trace file in the user dump destination directory, and up to 2*n* more trace files in the background dump destination directory. Again, SQL tracing (both standard and extended) still works great for PX operations, but it takes a good bit more work to piece everything together because the content of these files has to be knitted together by hand or with some kind of custom software tool.

The advent of multiplexing environments takes the problem to a whole new level. Multi-tier computing has evolved to accommodate the scalability requirements of today's online applications to which literally *millions* of users might connect. Today, it is possible for a single functional user action to speckle evidence of its database workload across dozens of trace files, distributed across dozens of computers. The biggest problem is that, because you can control tracing only at the Oracle *session*, when you try to trace Nancy's workload, you necessarily trace other users' workload as well—for all the users who are sharing Nancy's Oracle session (or perhaps even *sessions*, plural). How in the world are you going to trace a user action, then, without getting either a whole lot more trace data or a whole lot less than you really want?

The Oracle version 10[11] *end-to-end tracing* model promises to solve this difficult technical problem, and tracing's nagging political problem to boot. That's right, in version 10, the extended SQL trace function is fully documented and fully supported (and the event count is up to 808 in version 10.1.0.2.). Furthermore, in version 10, "is tracing" becomes an attribute of a specified *functional* unit of work. The package DBMS_MONITOR provides the syntax for activating and deactivating the trace:

```
dbms_monitor.serv_mod_act_trace_enable(service, module, action, true, true)
...
dbms_monitor.serv_mod_act_trace_disable(service, module, action)
```

With version 10, Oracle provides a new tool called trcsess, which does the work of knitting trace files together for you, so that you can see a linear sequential record of the work done by an individual user action.

Of course, it is the application's responsibility to identify its functional units of work in such a manner that DBMS_MONITOR can find them. In the old days, good application developers used the set methods in DBMS_APPLICATION_INFO to identify the diagnosable components of their applications. The problem with DBMS_APPLICATION_INFO is that, for example, setting an application's MODULE and ACTION attributes requires the execution of two stored procedure calls. Calling these procedures integrates extra database call overhead into the application.

---

11. Officially, Oracle version 10 is called *Oracle Database 10g*, but I'll refer to it as *version 10* in the same spirit in which I operate when I don't call Oracle version 6 *ORACLE V6*.

Oracle version 10 provides changes to the *Oracle Call Interface* (OCI) that allow an application developer to piggyback an application's identifying information onto database calls that the application already makes.[12]

If it all works correctly, the end-to-end tracing model of version 10 is exactly what we have been waiting for: the ability to answer Nancy's question, "What took so long?" for any application's functional unit of work running on a system of any arbitrary architectural complexity.[13]

The Revolution

The lineage of work beginning with Juan Loaiza and continuing through Anjo Kolk, Mogens Nørgaard, and Virag Saksena has had a profound influence upon my career and the careers of many others. In late 1999 when Gary Goodman and I founded this company called Hotsos that now feeds our families, we created a business that would set out to revolutionize the practice of Oracle performance problem diagnosis. The problem we saw was that the world's approach to Oracle performance optimization required a lot of experience, intuition, and luck to be successful. Of course, any process that requires experience to succeed is expensive, and any process that requires intuition and luck to succeed is impossible to reproduce and, of course, just as difficult to teach. We had seen hundreds of good people lead failed performance improvement projects in the 1990s.

What we sought was a performance optimization method for Oracle systems that produced economic value by being quicker, more reliable, and—perhaps most difficult of all—*teachable*. We found the most important attribute of such a method to be *determinism*. We wanted to create a method that began with the same step every time, and that progressed reliably using exactly the same decision-making criteria through every step, completely irrespective of the experience level or intuitive development of the practitioner. For a method to be a success, any two people from any two cultural backgrounds must be able to achieve the same desired end result with the properly executed method. Guesswork is out of bounds.

Jeff Holt and I worked full time on this assignment as a technical problem for more than a year. We spent an enormous amount of time pursuing the acquisition of performance diagnostic data from traditional sources inside the database, such as the V$SESSTAT and V$SESSION_WAIT fixed views. The problems with using data

---

12. See, for example, the descriptions of the attributes OCI_ATTR_MODULE, OCI_ATTR_CLIENT_INFO, and OCI_ATTR_ACTION in the "User Session Handle Attributes" section in Appendix A of the *Oracle Call Interface Programmer's Guide* for Oracle Database 10*g* Release 1.

13. At the time of this writing, the production version of Oracle Database 10*g* has just been released, so we're still trying to figure out exactly how it all works.

from these sources eventually overwhelmed us. I've described several of these problems in detail in my book (Millsap and Holt, *Optimizing Oracle Performance*, pp. 177–187). One dominant factor was simply the lack of drill-down capability: it is impossible to provide adequate detail-mining capability using V$ data without either forcing extra iterations of the data collection process or implementing an expensive-to-build and expensive-to-maintain SGA-attach mechanism. Having said that, if you know what you're doing and have the time to dedicate to it, an SGA-attach mechanism can provide very useful information. In fact, in the very next chapter, Kyle Hailey talks about his experiences in developing just such a mechanism.

This realization stopped the show for our pursuit of using the traditional V$ data sources. However, we learned very quickly that Oracle's extended SQL trace data suffered from no such restriction. Notably, in our research since 1999, we have learned to appreciate the following benefits of extended SQL trace data:

- *It's cheap:* The Oracle extended SQL trace feature is inexpensive both in terms of acquisition cost (it's part of the core Oracle database product) and operational cost (used properly, the feature is far less invasive than a data acquisition tool that samples your V$ data structures using SQL or attaches directly to an instance's SGA).

- *It's reliable:* Extended SQL trace bugs are extremely rare. On the rare occasion when we have encountered a bug in the interface, Oracle Corporation has been swift to provide a repair. Bug 3009359 is an excellent example.

- *It's complete:* There are several things you can learn from extended SQL trace data that are impossible to find in the V$ data sources, including the ability to view response time contribution by individual database calls (for example, parse, execute, fetch); the ability to determine recursive relationships among database calls; and the ability to derive the amount of response time consumed by process preemption. These days, the only operational timing data that my colleagues and I need in most performance improvement projects is extended SQL trace data.

Extended SQL trace simply works better at diagnosing performance problems than anything else we've seen. It is the critical link between the user's performance experience and the question that performance analysts have always needed to answer: "What *took* so long?" As simple as that question seems, the ability to answer it in Oracle is revolutionary.[14]

---

14. And still impossible to answer in other databases such as SQL Server.

Diagnosis Beyond the Database

Certainly not all Oracle system performance problems have their root causes within the Oracle database. Yet Oracle's extended SQL trace feature is very much a database-centric way to measure the response times. How much good does the feature do you when a performance problem has its root cause outside the Oracle kernel? A very curious benefit of Oracle's extended SQL trace data is its ability to inform you of actions that are going on *outside* of the database. It seems counter-intuitive that such problems could be fully diagnosable with only data collected from the Oracle database tier. But it works.

For example, application coding problems like the one shown in Listing 5-7 are trivial to find in extended SQL trace data. In this example, an application executes a parse call inside a loop.

Listing 5-7. Bad Application Code That Parses Too Much, and the Trace Stream That Results

```
/* BAD application code that parses too many times */
foreach value in (set_with_N_elements) {
    sql = concat('select ... where col=', quote(value));
    handle = parse(sql);
    execute(handle);
}


/* The extended SQL trace stream that results */
PARSE #1:...
WAIT #1: nam='SQL*Net message to client' ...
WAIT #1: nam='SQL*Net message from client' ...
EXEC #1:...
WAIT #1: nam='SQL*Net message to client' ...
WAIT #1: nam='SQL*Net message from client' ...
...
PARSE #1:...
WAIT #1: nam='SQL*Net message to client' ...
WAIT #1: nam='SQL*Net message from client' ...
EXEC #1:...
WAIT #1: nam='SQL*Net message to client' ...
WAIT #1: nam='SQL*Net message from client' ...
...
PARSE #1:...
WAIT #1: nam='SQL*Net message to client' ...
WAIT #1: nam='SQL*Net message from client' ...
EXEC #1:...
```

```
WAIT #1: nam='SQL*Net message to client' ...
WAIT #1: nam='SQL*Net message from client' ...
...
```

Applications that do this type of thing are slow, and they scale very poorly. With extended SQL trace data, it's easy to see why the code in Listing 5-8 is so much more efficient than the code in Listing 5-7. Not only does the good code save the database from the bother of having to process $N-1$ parse calls, the good code also saves the network from having to process $N-1$ network round-trips between the application client and the database server.

Of course, competent interpretation of standard SQL trace data would have revealed the possibility that excessive parsing might be causing a performance problem. However, standard SQL trace data cannot tell you *how much* of an impact fixing the problem might yield. The extraordinary value of the *extended* SQL trace stream is its *response time* data that allows you to determine exactly how much end-user response time you might save by fixing the problem.

This information is hugely important. Without it, you cannot evaluate the merit of a proposed repair without actually trying it first. Eliminating the trial and error is the magic that Virag Saksena brought to my group in 1995. Virag didn't just say that an activity like reducing the number of parse calls was a "good idea." With extended SQL trace data, he was able to tell us exactly *how* good an idea it was. In cases where he could see that a proposed repair would yield a poor return on investment, he would steer his clients clear of wasting their resources on it. In cases where a proposed repair would create extraordinary *positive* impact, he was more effective than most consultants at arguing his ideas into production, because he could demonstrate the merits of those ideas by using simple language that technicians and users alike could understand.

Listing 5-8. Good Application Code That Parses Once, and the Trace Data That Results

```
/* GOOD application code that parses once */
sql = 'select ... where col=:v';
handle = parse(sql);
foreach value in (set_with_N_elements) {
    execute(handle, value);
}


/* The extended SQL trace stream that results */
PARSE #1:...
WAIT #1: nam='SQL*Net message to client' ...
WAIT #1: nam='SQL*Net message from client' ...
```

```
EXEC #1:...
WAIT #1: nam='SQL*Net message to client' ...
WAIT #1: nam='SQL*Net message from client' ...
EXEC #1:...
WAIT #1: nam='SQL*Net message to client' ...
WAIT #1: nam='SQL*Net message from client' ...
EXEC #1:...
WAIT #1: nam='SQL*Net message to client' ...
WAIT #1: nam='SQL*Net message from client' ...
```

The New "Step One"

In the old days, step one of a performance improvement project was to guess which system metrics to collect (or perhaps it was to collect them all and then guess which ones to pay attention to). These days, an extended SQL trace of a business's most important functional action is the first diagnostic data collection I perform. The feature is so informative that usually it's the *only* runtime diagnostic data collection I perform. Perhaps contrary to many people's expectation, I do not even use other tools to identify which parts of the system to trace. Instead, I construct a list of user actions that the *customer* has identified as being unsatisfactorily slow and collect extended SQL trace data for those transactions. This top-down focus on *business* priority (instead of letting the system tell you what it thinks is wrong with itself) is the foundation of our new performance improvement method (Millsap and Holt, *Optimizing Oracle Performance*).

Using extended SQL as a primary diagnostic data source has worked phenomenally well in the field, even in circumstances where I would have thought, in 1995, that it couldn't work at all. Extended SQL trace is what my colleagues and I turn to, regardless of what expensive database monitoring software is on site when we land. With extended SQL trace, we're able to solve problems from a surprisingly broad domain of root causes, including the following:

- *Data design mistakes:* Lack of constraint declarations, poor entity relationship design

- *Application mistakes:* Excessive parsing, inadequate use of array processing, overuse of locks, unnecessary memory buffer access serialization

- *Query mistakes:* Poorly written SQL, faulty indexing strategies

- *Operational mistakes:* Poorly collected optimizer statistics, faulty purge processes, poorly sized caches, poor batch management strategies, data density issues

- *Capacity shortages:* Insufficient CPU, memory, disk, or network capacity for the required workload

- *Network configuration mistakes:* Poor protocol selection, faulty devices

- *Disk configuration mistakes:* Poorly distributed I/O patterns, faulty devices, poorly configured RAID architectures

The reason the feature works so well—and for so many different problem types—is simple:

1. A piece of workload has a performance problem if and only if its run time is excessive.

2. Proper use of Oracle's extended SQL trace feature shows you where a given piece of workload has spent *almost all* of its time.

3. Therefore, performance problems cannot hide from Oracle's extended SQL trace data.

The only gap in this logic is the *almost* in step 2. Extended SQL trace is not quite airtight. For example, even in version 10.1.0.2, there is no Oracle timed event that covers the total amount of time that an Oracle kernel process spends writing its trace data to the trace file (although I think this feature would be easy for Oracle to add).[15] But the evolution of the extended SQL trace feature has narrowed the gaps in Oracle timing data to a hair's breadth.

Extended SQL trace is, in my considered opinion, the most important performance diagnostic feature in any Oracle system. It is the microscope that has brought the management of Oracle system performance into the scientific age.

---

15. On first blush, the problem of instrumenting writes to the trace file seems like a recursive problem, but it's easy to avoid the recursion. If the Oracle kernel would store an aggregation of all the individual durations spent making write() calls to its trace file, it could merely print some kind of WAIT #0: nam='writing to trace'... event to the trace file upon the close() call for the trace file descriptor. Hotsos has actually implemented this solution as an add-on that doesn't require any modification to Oracle code.

References

Millsap, Cary. "Why you should focus on LIOs instead of PIOs" Hotsos (http://www.hotsos.com), 2001.

Millsap, Cary, and Jeff Holt. *Optimizing Oracle Performance*. Sebastopol, CA: O'Reilly & Associates, 2003.

Dear Reader,

Kyle is somewhat different from most of the other male OakTable members. For one thing, he actually seems to know how to dress. We also suspect that he has dozens of girls all over the World just waiting for him to stop by some day (but we've never been able to prove it).

Kyle used to work in Oracle Development before he moved to Paris, where he spent several years in Gold Support, along with a bunch of first class French supporters.

He was the first person to introduce me to the wait interface, having had it introduced to him by the legendary Roger Sanders, whilst on the Brushco project. Kyle always ruthlessly shares with others things that he learns about Oracle and IT in general, without ever hesitating.

Kyle worked for Quest for a while, then rejoined Oracle in an exciting project: the idea was to bring a dream team into Oracle Enterprise Manager (OEM) development. The four chosen ones were Gaja Vaidyanatha, James Morle, John Beresniewicz, and Kyle (all of them OakTable members), and they were to do exciting things with the product, its architecture, and much more. The thinking behind their work will show up in the coming years in the OEM family of products, I'm sure.

Meanwhile, as I'm writing these words, Kyle has disappeared. The editor can't find him, his Hotmail account is full and returns an error, and he's simply not available for comments, as they say. Rumors have it that he has gone surfing (again) in some exotic place, probably spending his spare time developing cool, visual applications for OEM. But we don't know for sure. One day he'll pop up again and pretend nothing has happened, and refuse to go into any details.

So there's Kyle for you: open, friendly, speaks French, incredibly intelligent and sharp, always polite, well dressed, cosmopolitan, sporty ... in other words, the typical OakTable member (just kidding!).

In this chapter Kyle gives you the background for the DMA (Direct Memory Access) work he's been doing besides his real work over the last couple of years. It's a very fascinating piece of work, and Kyle has achieved impressive results with it. As you may have guessed, Kyle has been eager to share his findings with the community, being the true scientist he is.

So if you ever get a chance to meet Kyle, take advantage of it before he moves on to the next beach!

—Mogens Nørgaard

CHAPTER 6

Direct Memory Access

By Kyle Hailey

IN THE EARLY 1990s there was no World Wide Web; in fact, many clients didn't even have email access, and Oracle patches were sent almost exclusively by postal mail. For those clients who did have email, binary attachments were not yet an option. Patches had to be compressed and uuencoded, and even this was pushing the technological envelope for most of the clients and support technicians.

This is just to put into perspective the work of an Oracle support technician by the name of Roger Sanders, who at around this time wrote a Direct Memory Access (DMA) program, called m2, to attach to the System Global Area (SGA) of an Oracle Database running on a UNIX platform. This allowed traversal of the SGA data structures at no cost to the Oracle kernel and retrieval of detailed wait time information, equivalent to that which can be obtained from v$session_wait.

This was considered an amazing feat over a decade ago, and in fact still is today, even with Google, binary editors, web pages by Steve Adams on Oracle internals, and so on. This chapter tells the story of how I first met Roger, became entangled in the world of DMA, and eventually succeeded in writing my own version of the program to support my Oracle performance optimization efforts.

On Site at Brushco

In mid-1994, while working as a support technician at the Oracle France office, I was asked to help out on a large development project for a customer called Brushco, a Europe-wide company that rented out toilet brushes.

 NOTE *Of course, they didn't really, nor was the company in question called Brushco. The names have been changed to protect the innocent and guilty alike.*

The Brushco project was on the bleeding edge, technologically speaking; they needed to support over 3,000 simultaneous users. This would have been impressive even for the IBM mainframes, but at this time, in the UNIX world, it was unheard of. The largest machines available at the time had 512MB of memory, less than many home PC's have today! The only way to harness enough computing power on a UNIX platform was to use Oracle Parallel Server, which could access memory and CPU on multiple machines for the same database.

So, we had a groundbreaking project whose ultimate success depended solely on two pieces of software, both of which were completely new: the Oracle 7 database and Oracle Parallel Server. The former had only just been released and was still rather "green" and the latter hadn't even cut its teeth in production databases on UNIX yet. On top of all this, the company that won the Brushco contract (TLA Systems) proposed that the whole online application be coded, using RAD technology, in just one year. Down the torpedoes, and throw caution to the wind!

Needless to say, the Bruschco project was plagued by bugs: lots and lots of bugs. In fact, my initial task on the project was to code a `makefile` to verify that any new patch that was to be installed didn't overwrite any of the object files from the other 150 or so patches that had already been applied!

I'm not going to give any further background about the Brushco project here, because the resulting Herculean struggle to get this application up and running is described in graphic detail by James Morle in Chapter 8. As James will tell you, Oracle, TLA Systems, and Brushco brought together a top-notch team of engineers and Database Administrators (DBA's) to overcome a huge potential for failure and make this application the success that it turned out to be. I give this brief summary, because this is where my story starts; it was on this project that I first met a man called Roger Sanders, at the time a Bruschco DBA. I remember showing up for the first time at the Brushco site early one morning excited, but having no real idea what to expect.

Meeting Roger Sanders

The first of the Brushco DBA's started showing up to work around 9:00 a.m. I sat at my desk drinking coffee and taking in as much as I could without getting in the way. The Brushco DBA's had made it clear that our presence was warranted, but that they were the ones in charge.

My first morning was an interesting one. All around me the Brushco DBA's began to tackle the first challenges of the day, and the atmosphere in the support center started to get a little more hectic. It was impossible not to be affected, even carried away, by their efforts to solve problem after problem that adversely affected the network response times of the largest brush rental conglomerate in Europe. The system slowed so badly at times that the rental offices were actually forced to revert to using pen and paper!

"The database will go down in five minutes," said someone sitting at a desk near mine to no one in particular. This person, I later found out, was one of the Oracle support technicians, Roger Sanders. I was surprised to see that no one else paid him any attention, and that he didn't seem to notice or care. I found out later that he'd been on site for a while before me; by now he'd grown accustomed to being ignored. I watched him intently. He sat calmly at his desk, completely unflustered and unhurried, in stark contrast to the DBA's who surrounded him. Curious, I walked over and stood behind him. He was so focused on his task that doubt he even realized I was there looking over his shoulder. I remember watching how he typed everything with two fingers on each hand and smiling at this. He never hurried, he was never flustered, and he worked nonstop. Aside from bathroom breaks and the occasional meal, he never stopped typing. Most people take a break every once in a while to stretch their legs or get some fresh air but not Roger; he just kept on typing with those first two fingers on each hand.

Because the Brushco project was so high profile, Oracle Corporation sent over three of their best and most esteemed kernel developers to help with the implementation. Juan Loaiza is famous as one of the main architects of the Oracle version 7 code. Jeff Needham and Doug Rady were the other two kernel developers Oracle sent. Doug Rady was quite a character in his own right; a brilliant kernel programmer with a very distinct look. The other French programmers used to call him "Jesus" because he always wore sandals and had a long, flowing beard. There we were in France, where image is very important and people often wore suits to the office, and in would walk Doug Rady looking like some hippy plucked fresh from the streets of Berkley. Only the Americans could get away with this—those crazy Americans.

It was remarkable to see the interactions between these kernel developers and Roger. I remember watching in disbelief as they would stop to ask Roger questions like, "What object module can I find this function in?" Roger was an Oracle support technician and shouldn't have known anything at all about the source code, but he had managed somehow to get access to it, and he knew it really well. These guys were the *elite* of Oracle's elite kernel developers and should have known the inner workings of the code better than anyone else on the planet, especially some lowly Oracle support technician. Still, here they were asking Roger questions about the code. And it was funny to watch Roger respond to their questions too. He'd just answer each question nonchalantly while continuing to work, never missing a beat. Most people were obsequious toward the kernel developers, but Roger was completely unfazed.

Roger and "m2"

June 15, 1994, it said on the top of an email that detailed Roger's current assignment. Oracle Forms was slow in starting up, and this affected every rental office across all of Europe. No one could find a way to pinpoint the problem. There only seemed to be two options, neither of which was acceptable. The first was putting the whole database into trace mode, which would have created thousands of trace files, swamping the disks and slowing the database to a crawl. The second option was to attempt to identify a Forms user as they were connecting and then trace their connection process, which was nearly impossible to do. When the problem found its way to Roger, he had an entirely different way of approaching it.

I watched as he copied the SQL*Forms binary onto his machine locally and opened it with a program I'd never seen before. I should point out that it was a big surprise to me that it was even possible to *open* such a binary. The fact that he happened to have a tool to do just that was still a distant second at this point. And neither of these would turn out to be the biggest surprise of the day.

To put this feat into perspective, at that time Oracle would not even allow its customers to edit the *textual* representation of a Form. A Form is a set of data entry pages based on tables and defined by a fairly simple-to-read text file—back then it was anyway—today it's binary. Since it was just a text file, customers would often go in and edit it by hand because it was quicker than using the interactive design tool. If Oracle Support found out that a customer had edited this file by hand, they would often refuse to help because there was a good chance that this hand edit may have broken something. And Roger wasn't editing this text file by hand, but rather the cryptic hexadecimal code of the binary that constituted the Oracle Forms executable! Merely opening such an executable with a text editor like vi could corrupt the output to the computer screen, as much of the binary data could be interpreted by the computer as commands to change the internal settings and cause the ASCII to turn into wingbats or worse. Also, if vi was used to open the executable and then save it, this simple act would corrupt the entire file, as vi didn't know how to handle such binary data. I was duly impressed and intensely curious.

"*What's that you're doing there?*" I asked.

"*I'm adjusting this binary so that I can get the trace running before the slow-down occurs. This should tell us where the problem lies,*" he answered without turning around.

I tried to act as if that made perfect sense, still wondering exactly how one made such an adjustment to a binary file. And what was that program he was using?

"*I haven't seen the program you're using before, what is it?*" I asked.

"*m2,*" he answered, pleasantly, without volunteering anything more.

I then watched him use this m2 program to access the Oracle Forms binary and locate a string for the startup SQL statement that set NLS parameters. He edited the statement, changing it to read `alter session set sql_trace=true` and then using this newly edited binary he tracked down the problem almost immediately and started typing up a response to the original email, detailing the problem and suggested fix. Roger had found, via the traces his new executable had created, that the data dictionary tables were missing an index needed for lookup. Given tens or hundreds of users this was hardly noticeable, but Brushco had created over 25,000 users, since every user had a dedicated account and users were never deleted!

m2, I thought to myself ... I definitely needed to familiarize myself with that program; it looked extremely useful. I left him to finish hunting and pecking his way through his email report and headed back to my desk. Halfway there chaos erupted all around me in the support center; the database had crashed. The only person who didn't seem surprised by this was Roger, who I noticed never even looked up from his screen. I still had no idea how he was able to predict that.

"That m2 program seems really useful," I said to Roger a little later in the day.

"Thanks," he replied. A pretty strange response.

"Where can I get a copy of that?" I asked.

"m2? Hmm ... No one's ever asked me that before."

"Well, where did you get it?" I asked.

"I wrote it," he answered matter-of-factly. Right there was the biggest surprise of the day. And that's the exact moment I realized the type of Oracle support technician that Roger was.

"Kyle Hailey," I said, offering my hand almost reverently.

"Roger Sanders," he said, *"Nice to meet you."*

I ended up spending a lot more time watching Roger work that day. At one point, I was amazed when I watched him attach his m2 program to the Oracle SGA and loop over all the users' information, showing the equivalent of `v$session_wait`. This system always seemed on the verge of getting severely bottlenecked, so almost any performance query caused significant slowdown, but with m2 that wasn't a concern. Also when the database did bottleneck such that queries would not respond, m2 would keep working just fine because it didn't depend on SQL to get the data. With this view, he could watch real time as waits began to stack up, enabling him to predict almost exactly when the site would be crippled several minutes before the other DBA's. This is how he'd predicted the earlier database standstill. The other DBA's had limited performance information since virtually any query on a `DBA_` view would make latch-free waits on the library cache latch go through the roof—there was only one library cache latch back then!

m2 and Direct Memory Access

m2 is an application based on *Direct Memory Access*. The access is direct in the sense that no system calls or other resource-expensive access methods are used to read the data. Oracle is built around the SGA, a shared memory area, which is used by all background and foreground processes to share resources. In particular, there is an area of the SGA called the fixed SGA that contains most of the latch structures, the database buffer headers, and state objects like the process state object array and the session state object array.

On UNIX, Oracle is a process-based architecture, where data is shared using UNIX System V Shared Memory. The memory is simply part of the address space of the Oracle processes.

 NOTE *My work focused on the UNIX platform. On the Windows platform, the implementation is different: the Oracle back and foreground processes are not "real" OS processes but Windows threads sharing one address space: the* oracle.exe *process space.*

The purpose of a DMA tool such as m2 is, as noted in the introduction, to allow traversal of these SGA data structures at no cost to the Oracle kernel (we'll see exactly how we do this later). From this you can obtain detailed wait time information, equivalent to that which can be obtained from v$session_wait (see Chapter 7 for details of this view).

Of course, the advantage of DMA over traditional v$ queries is that it's *fast*! If you realize what Oracle must do under the hood to parse and execute a query, the CPU usage, the building of library cache structures, acquiring and releasing latches, and so on, you may never consider a query again, if the alternative is a simple direct access instruction, which only takes a few CPU cycles. This is especially important when accessing (over)stressed, or even "hanging," Oracle instances or servers. In these cases, adding extra SQL influences the object of measurement in an unwanted manner.

Inevitably, every silver lining has its cloud. Much of the SGA data is very fluid; it changes a lot, and pointers are constantly changing, but that's all part of the fun! Oracle processes mostly acquire latches in order to make sure to have a consistent or atomic view of SGA structures, certainly when they need to be changed. By accessing the data directly without taking latches, you run into the risk of reading faulty data, invalid pointers, and so on. This can cause interesting problems, mostly weird output or a crash of your process. There are a few other things to watch out for as well, but we'll come back to that later.

Originally m2 just gathered information on session events/statistics and latches, which were the easiest to model. But once m2 retrieved the basic information, the door was open for investigating more esoteric and intriguing questions. An example of the esoteric, from the days of Brushco, was latch hold times. With microsecond clocks, it was possible to

a. Calibrate a sampling code path, and

b. Measure how long latches were held. This was done by statistical sampling—one second is an eternity at this level; here we're talking millisecond sample periods.

On a more practical level, m2 could be used to investigate wait dependency to derive a dependency tree (for example, a user is waiting for PMON, which in turn is waiting for DBWR, and so on). Today in 10g, all we have is a 10-row history buffer and no attempt at dependency analysis. Dependency analysis was added to m2 as a result of Roger's work at Brushco, and this is a good example of the benefits of direct access. Each event had a different cause, and many different data structures had to be traversed to build a wait tree. All this was only possible because everything was done unlatched.

The biggest drawback in implementing dependency trees was that the code needed to work with the specific kernel data structures, and so would have to be reviewed upon each major release. This led to Rogers's final project with m2: loadable SGA structure definitions.

You can think of the SGA as a large C structure or, at the next level down, as a collection of hundreds of structures, related together using direct pointers. So why not create a loadable file that describes all the structures in the SGA: struct names, field types (pointer, int, and so on), and offsets. A DMA program could just load this map file and traverse the structures without any hard-coded dependencies. This sort of map file is like an old-style Cobol cross-reference table. So Roger took the entire kernel source and preprocessed it, thereby building a complete structure map. This worked fine, but in reality the map file would have to be created at the time the kernel was built. Roger put this to Oracle Development at the time but it wasn't on their radar, which was understandable as it wasn't a priority for them.

 NOTE *Incidentally, this is why Roger eventually ceased work on m2; he didn't feel there was anywhere else he could go with it.*

---

m2 was useful in manifold ways, like a kind of Oracle Swiss Army knife; m2 was really was a whole Swiss Army knife for an Oracle hacker. It even had its own scripting language just like the UNIX shell. Roger had also programmed all the Oracle Call Interface (OCI) calls that were used in the C programs such that he could call them interactively in a script, i.e., there was no need to compile and he could interact with them at the command prompt instead of running them blindly in a program. He also had a binary editor in m2 and lots of other useful little functions like converting hexadecimal to decimal.

m2 in Action

By 1995 the Brushco site had started to stabilize and my involvement waned, but the contacts I made and the things I learned shaped my future involvement with Oracle and performance tuning.

Roger and I had become friends, and he agreed to let me use his m2 program so long as I didn't pass it around. It was fortunate for me, and for Oracle, that Roger agreed to let me use his m2 program. It would later provide me with a valuable advantage on future projects.

Benchmarks at Digital Europe

I first became involved in diagnosing some high-profile performance issues at Oracle sites through my connections with the consultants and DBA's at Brushco who knew my work and called me in personally to these other sites. Using m2 always gave me the upper hand in these situations. I was able to monitor statistics unnoticed and without using SQL on systems where the local DBA's were admonished for any performance statistics queries. On these bottlenecked systems even small perturbations would push them over the edge.

I used m2 most effectively in the mid to late 1990s for high-end benchmark testing, mainly at Digital Europe. I found myself going to Digital Europe about once a month for these high-end benchmark tests. I was pitching Digital machines against all the other vendors, and in these situations, whoever had the fastest machine won the contracts. During these tests, resources couldn't be wasted on querying v$ tables for performance data, but m2's SGA attach was so lightweight that it would go virtually unnoticed. It would be difficult to estimate the number of benchmark tests Oracle won and the amount of business that was, in turn, generated from these tests. All of this was thanks in no small part to Roger's m2 program.

Leaving Oracle

In 1999 I left Oracle and said goodbye to my access to m2. I went to work for an Internet startup company back in the United States in the midst of the dot-com boom. In what little spare time I had, I tinkered around a bit with writing a program that could attach to the Oracle SGA the way m2 did because it had proven so useful under so many different circumstances. It didn't take me long to write a program that could successfully attach to the SGA. I found the starting address of the SGA in UNIX memory using a file called SGADEF. At the time, this file contained information on the shared memory and semaphores. The file was binary, but Roger had showed me the structure and how to read it with a binary dump program such as od, which stands for "octal dump." The same information could also be found using UNIX commands like ipcs. I found that the view v$session_wait was actually a view on the fixed table x$ksusecst by running the query

```
SQL> select * from V$FIXED_VIEW_DEFINITION where view_name='V$SESSION_WAIT'
```

I then ran queries on the x$ksusecst table using SQL to get the memory addresses of the session waits. Then I dumped the memory at these locations from the SGA and attempted to match up the data in the dump with the information from the SQL query of v$session_wait.

I knew v$session_wait was getting its data from that memory location somehow, but I couldn't get the numbers to synch up. When I couldn't find the data I needed where I expected it to be, the only explanation I could come up with was that v$session_wait must contain pointers to other memory locations. I needed to know exactly how the memory was formatted; without that information the task would be impossible. Eventually I gave up on the project and started devoting what little spare time I had to more productive endeavors. After that I had an even greater respect for the work Roger had done in creating m2, if that was even possible. I was also glad that this was just a pet project, and not something I absolutely had to figure out how to do. The incredibly useful functions of m2 were not going to be duplicated by me; not yet anyway.

Moving to Quest Software

Eventually I found myself working at Quest Software, a company that made tools to help monitor Oracle databases. I needed something that I could use to identify the current waits on a system (together with their parameters) and my thoughts turned once again to m2. Fortunately, soon after starting work at Quest, I was sent to Oracle World where I ran into some of my old colleagues from Brushco. One of these colleagues was Anjo Kolk. When I saw him, I struck up a conversation about the SGA attach program I had given up on not so long ago.

"Hey Anjo," I said, *"I tried to rewrite Roger Sanders's program that attaches to the SGA and reads v$session_wait, but when I looked at the memory location for v$session_wait I couldn't correlate the data I saw in memory with the output from an SQL select query on the table. It must contain pointers to other locations in memory, but how can I decipher them?"*

"There aren't any pointers in the v$session_wait table to decipher," he answered.

"Are you sure?"

"Quite sure," he said, *"The v$session_wait is a fixed array of data. Actually, James has been working on a program to read the SGA directly via the view x$ksmmem, I remember discussing it with him."* x$ksmmem is a raw data dump of memory via the SQL interface. *"The v$session_wait table is definitely fixed."*

This didn't jibe with what I had seen, but Anjo seemed sure. If the v$session_wait table was indeed fixed, then the program shouldn't be as difficult to write as I had thought.

"Well, that's good to know," I said. *"I guess I'd better get in touch with James."*

"You know Mogens Nørgaard is putting together a convention in Denmark for some of the higher end Oracle tech folks; you should get yourself invited. He's getting together some of the best Oracle Performance experts in the world like Jonathan Lewis, Steve Adams, and James Morle. You could talk to James there."

I couldn't believe it. This convention sounded like a dream come true. What an amazing group of people. I'd met Steve, worked with James, and had recently gotten in contact with Jonathan, who had impressed me greatly with his recent book.

"That sounds like a plan," I said.

After this I had a whole new perspective on my SGA attach pet project. Just knowing for sure that the v$session_wait table was fixed gave me new hope for writing my own version of m2. Rewriting the program couldn't be that complicated if the table was fixed. I decided that when I got back from the convention I'd take up the project again.

Developing DMA in Anger

However, things were busy when I got back. I didn't have the time to start working on my own version of m2 straight away, and then was sidetracked for several months into investigation of a new program called the Oracle trace facility, which I was introduced to in Denmark, during Jonathan Lewis's Masters Class in February 2002. Although this facility has grown into an undeniably powerful tool, as comprehensively described by Cary Millsap in Chapter 5, at the time I found it to be little more than a very esoteric interface into Oracle statistics. It was clumsy and slow to put it kindly. Worst of all, it made the database crash every time I tried to use it.

I eventually gave up on the Oracle trace facility altogether and decided again to turn my efforts toward writing my own SGA attach program to get the job done properly. I was pretty sure I could write the program I needed in a day or two. It sounded simple enough in theory, but like they say, *"In theory there's no difference between theory and practice, but in practice there's a big difference."*

How DMA Works

Oracle's SGA is a dedicated chunk of memory shared by all Oracle sessions. Here this shared information is stored along with global information about how the database is performing, such as database-level and session-level performance statistics. For my DMA program to work

1. The program needed to attach to the SGA. On UNIX I needed the address and ID of the shared memory segment in order to attach to it (and I also needed permissions).

2. The program needed to know exactly where to get the information in the SGA.

I already knew how to access the SGA with the proper C code system calls; Roger had taught me that much while I was still at Oracle. Unfortunately, that was the easy part. Once attached, or "inside the castle," the real challenge was still locating the exact information I needed.

Finding the Data in the SGA

In order to access a shared memory, it needs to be added to the address space of the running program. On UNIX it is easy to write a C program that simply "adds" the shared memory segment to its address space, by calling shmat, which stands for *shared memory attach*. In order to do this, you need to provide a shmid, a *shared memory ID* and a *shared memory base address*, which defines the common starting point for all attached processes.

When the shmat succeeds, it's simply a matter of addressing the shared memory as you would any other object in local memory.

 CAUTION *Again, on Windows it's not that simple. In order to access the SGA in the* oracle.exe *process space, one needs to be part of that process: a thread. The SGA is not shared externally, so external access is not possible without using expensive (in terms of CPU and context switch overhead) Win32 system calls such as* ReadProcessesMemory().

Other than C, programming languages such as Java and Perl also provide shared memory access calls, which under the hood will do the same as shmat.

There are several ways of finding the shmid and the required base address. For example, you can use the UNIX command ipcs -m. Alternatively, an Oracle utility called Sysresv will show shmid(s) for the instance that's currently defined in your UNIX environment. It's available on most UNIX platforms (and on some platforms, such as on IA32 Linux, it even works as it's supposed to!). In any event, it's a far easier option than ipcs -m when you're running multiple instances on the same box because ipcs -m will show *all* shared memory segments of all running Oracle instances.

A good way to find the SGA base address is through the following query:

```
select addr from x$ksmmem where rownum <2
```

Another helpful utility is oradebug. When connected to SQL*PLUS, set your process to be the "active debug" process (oradebug setmypid) and do a oradebug ipc. This will dump shared memory information to the user dump destination, find the dump file, and pick up the shmid(s) and the base addresses. Depending on the maximum shared memory segment size defined on the UNIX level, Oracle can decide to use one or more shared memory segments.

Therefore, I knew where to go in memory to find what I wanted; I just had to figure out how to read it!

Reading the Data from the SGA

As discussed earlier, you can think of the SGA as a large C structure or, at the next level down, as a collection of hundreds of structures, related together using direct pointers. The first few megabytes of the SGA is called the *fixed SGA*. This is where you can find most of the latch structures located, the database buffer headers, and state objects such as the *process state* object array and the *session state* object array. The size of these arrays is determined by init.ora parameters such as processes and sessions. The oracle SID (Session ID) is an index into this array of state objects.

The process state object contains the following information:

- Which OS PID (process ID) is used for this Oracle process

- Which Oracle and OS user is using this process, and

- A linked list (a process can hold more than one session) to other state objects, such as sessions

A large part of the session state object is externalized through the x$ksuse view, on which the v$session view is based, and x$ksusecst, on which the v$session_wait is based. The first version m2 was a program that used access to this structure in order to get the session wait data: wait sequence number, wait event names, parameters, and times.

A lot of other x$ structures simply represent parts of this fixed SGA. However, there is a growing number of x$ views that only live for the duration of the SELECT query against that view: they are temporary tables based mostly on data in the variable part of the SGA, represented in heaps that are allocated and de-allocated constantly. Good examples of this are views on the library cache structures. It's normally quite easy to distinguish between the two: every x$ view starts with an ADDR column. If this column shows an address above the SGA base address, it's probably a real SGA usable address. If it's way below the SGA base address, it's most likely a PGA address in your process: a locally constructed view.

Fortunately the session structures are fixed and easy to locate. You can simply execute

```
select * from x$ksusecst
```

From this, you can see in the ADDR column, the absolute address of the session state object in memory. You can verify this if you execute

```
select ADDR from x$ksuse
```

It will show the exact same address. By subtracting the next address from the previous address, you get the size of a session state object.

So, finding the data in the x$ksusecst table is pretty easy. But this is where the fun starts. The x$ tables represent structures in the C code; they're just an externalization of the underlying C structure. The tricky part is that not all of the contents of the structure are externalized in the x$ table, so reading from the SGA it might be expected that field 1 would be followed directly by field 2 in memory, but that wouldn't necessarily be the case. Often in the C structure there are several other values between field 1 and field 2 that are not externalized into the x$ table, so instead of finding field 2, there could be some other value there that isn't recognized without having access to the code.

For example, say a given row was 400 bytes. Which bytes represented which fields in the table? And how many bytes comprised each field? Some flag fields might only be a couple of bits in a byte, while a character field might be many bytes wide. In memory it's all just one big soup of binary or hexadecimal. I decided to just poke around and match up what I saw using SQL and the values from the raw memory.

I managed to piece together parts of the v$session_wait view by dumping and using od (octal dump) to view relevant pieces of SGA memory and noting where the values found matched the values returned from an SQL query on v$session_wait.

Eventually, I arrived at a version of the program that would let me read the v$session_wait view directly from SGA memory, but I knew I had to find a way to make the program easier and more portable. At the moment, with hard-coded offsets, it wasn't at all portable and very Oracle version dependent. I had to find out how to determine the offsets of the statistical data in the session object. It was time to talk to James Morle.

The x$kqfco Goldmine

I sent the first draft of my program to James and showed him the C code of the program. He wrote back quickly, baffled as to why I would choose to hard code all the offsets that pinpointed the pertinent data inside a record field. James explained that all those offsets, which I found only by painstakingly comparing values I read out of memory to those I found using SQL, could be found in "some x$ table." Unfortunately, he couldn't remember the table's name. This rang a bell though, and I soon found an email from Jonathan Lewis where he named it. And there it was. This goldmine of information was a table called x$kqfco!

All the field offsets were there along with their respective sizes. With this information I could find the structure of any x$ table that represented a fixed array. I should add that Tom Kyte also chipped in, however unknowingly, because I used his SQL decimal to hexadecimal conversion function to help with the offset calculations.

```
SQL> select c.kqfconam field_name,
        c.kqfcooff offset,
        c.kqfcosiz sz
```

```
from
       x$kqfco c,  /* column  offsets and sizes */
       x$kqfta t    /* fixed table names */
where
       t.indx = c.kqfcotab and
       t.kqftanam='X$KSUSECST'
order by
       offset
;
```

FIELD_NAME	OFFSET	SZ
ADDR	0	4
INDX	0	4
KSUSEWTM	0	4
INST_ID	0	4
KSSPAFLG	1	1
KSUSSSEQ	1276	2
KSUSSOPC	1278	2
KSUSSP1	1280	4
KSUSSP1R	1280	4
KSUSSP2	1284	4
KSUSSP2R	1284	4
KSUSSP3	1288	4
KSUSSP3R	1288	4
KSUSSTIM	1292	4
KSUSENUM	1300	2
KSUSEFLG	1308	4

There are three interesting things in the preceding output:

1. What are all the fields at OFFSET 0? These are all calculated values and not stored explicitly in the SGA:

   ADDR is the memory ADDRS.

   INDX is the record number in the structure, like ROWNUM.

   KSUSEWTM is a calculated field.

   INST_ID is the database instance ID.

2. What happens between OFFSET 1 and 1276?

   Oracle doesn't always expose all the fields in the structure. Thus if there are gaps in the offsets that are bigger than the field sizes, there is other information in the underlying structure that isn't exposed in the x$ table. Coincidentally, in this case those addresses are exposed but in different views, such as v$session, the list of sessions, and v$sesstat, the session statistics.

3. Why do some fields start at the same address?

   KSUSSP1 and KSUSSP1R have the same address, i.e., V$SESSION_WAIT.P1 and V$SESSION_WAIT.P1RAW have the same address. This is because P1 is the decimal version of P1RAW, and the data actually comes from the same location. They are equivalent.

Putting the information from the mapping of v$session_wait fields to x$ksusecst fields and the field sizes and locations, the results are

Field Name	x$ Field Name	Offset	Size
SID	s.indx	calculated	4
SEQ#	s.ksussseq	1276	2
EVENT	s.ksussopc	1278	2
P1	s.ksussp1	1280	4
P2	s.ksussp2	1284	4
P3	s.ksussp3	1292	4

This table provides all the information needed to read v$session_wait or x$ksusecst from the SGA. Visually, we can describe it using the following series of diagrams.

In Figure 6-1, we see that the SGA represented as a chunk of machine memory, where 0x80000000 represents the SGA base address.

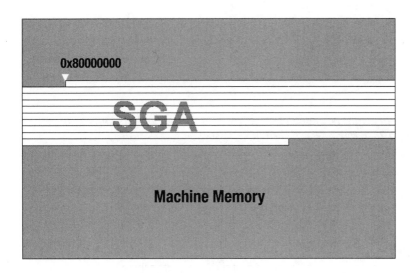

Figure 6-1. SGA is allocated as a chunk of machine memory.

In Figure 6-2, we see the location of x$ksusecst in the SGA, with 0x85251EF4 representing the start address of the first session object.

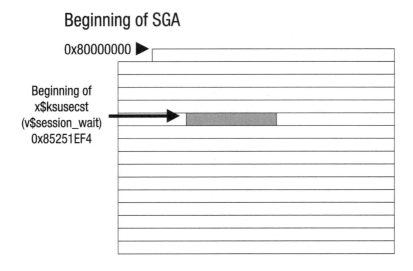

Figure 6-2. Location of v$session_wait, i.e., x$ksusecst in the SGA

In this example, as shown in Figure 6-3, each "row" is 2328 bytes in length; we can find where the next row starts by simply adding 2328 to the start address (0x85251EF4).

 NOTE *In actuality, these 2328 byte "rows" are session objects. Only a part of such a 2328 row is represented in* x$ksusecst.

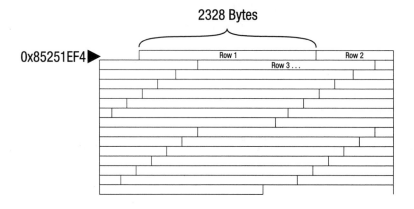

Figure 6-3. Rows in v$session_wait, *i.e.,* x$ksusecst

Within the "row" we found the column offsets using the x$kqfco table. In this example, the seq# column starts at byte 1276, as illustrated in Figure 6-4.

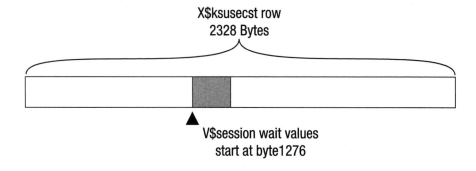

Figure 6-4. Location of the fields of interest in x$kusecst

By using the column offsets found in x$kqfco, it's now easy to see the column sizes, as shown in Figure 6-5.

1276	1278	1280		1284		1288	
Seq #	Event #	p1		p2		p3	

Figure 6-5. Field sizes in x$ksusecst

With this information it didn't take long to write an SQL script that generated the header files with offsets for a generic version of the C code.

Since event numbers and names change through Oracle release, I also used the following script to generate an event name table (events.h in the code) header file:

```
Spool events.hselect 'char event[][100]={' from dual;select '"'||name||'",' from
v$event_name;select ' "" };' from dual;spool off
```

Following is the simplified source code:

```
#include <stdio.h>
 #include <sys/ipc.h>
 #include <sys/shm.h>
 #include <errno.h>
 #include "event.h"


 #define SGA_BASE       0x80000000 /* SGA BASE ADDRESS */
/* as found in x$ksmmem or oradebug ipc  */
 #define KSUSECST_ADDR  0x85251EF4 /* START ADDR of KSUSECST */
/* the first ADDR in X$KSUSECST */
 #define SESSIONS        150       /* NUMBER of ROWS/RECORDS in */
/* init.ora parameter session.
   If not defined do a 'show parameter sessions' as sysdba */
 #define RECORD_SZ      2328       /* SIZE in BYTES of a ROW in */
/* subtract the second ADDR in X$KSUSECST from the first to get this number */


 #define KSUSSSEQ 1276     /* offset 1276  size 2 */
 #define KSUSSOPC 1278     /* offset 1276  size 2 */
 #define KSUSSP1R 1280     /* offset 1280  size 4 */
 #define KSUSSP2R 1284     /* offset 1284  size 4 */
```

```
#define KSUSSP3R 1288      /* offset 1288  size 4 */
/* the above can be found by querying the x$kqfco view */
/* start of the program */
main(argc, argv)
int argc;
char **argv;
{
 void  *addr;
 int    shmid;
 int    shmaddr;
 void  *current_addr;
 long  p1r, p2r, p3r, sqla;
 unsigned int   i, seq, tim, flg, evn;

   if (argc != 2) {
        fprintf(stderr, "Usage: %s shmid \n", *argv);
/* expecting SHMID as program argument */
        exit(1);
     }

  /* ATTACH TO SGA, using the shmid, sga base address, with read-only permission */
     shmid=atoi(argv[1]);
     shmaddr=SGA_BASE;
     if (  (void *)shmat(shmid,(void *)shmaddr,SHM_RDONLY) == (void *)-1 ) {
        printf("shmat: error attatching to SGA\n");
        exit();
     }
/* now we have access to the SGA, we can loop through the session structures: */

    /* LOOP OVER ALL SESSIONS until CANCEL */
    while (1) {
        current_addr=(void *)KSUSECST_ADDR; /* set the first session address */
        sleep(1);                          /* and sleep for a second */
        printf("^[[H ^[[J");               /* clear screen */
        printf("%4s %8s %-20.20s %10s %10s %10s \n",
            "sid", "seq", "wait","p1","p2","p3"); /* print the header to screen */
        for ( i=0; i < SESSIONS ; i++ ) {  /* start loop */
           seq=*(unsigned short *)((int)current_addr+KSUSSSEQ);
/* get all the offsets of the session wait information by adding the field offsets
   to the start off the current session object address */
            evn=*(short *)          ((int)current_addr+KSUSSOPC);
            p1r=*(long *)           ((int)current_addr+KSUSSP1R);
            p2r=*(long *)           ((int)current_addr+KSUSSP2R);
```

```
            p3r=*(long *)            ((int)current_addr+KSUSSP3R);
         if (  evn != 0 ) {
/* if event type does not equal 0, print the line for the current session wait.
   If evn is 0, the session might not be waiting */
              printf("%4d %8u %-20.20s %10X %10X %10X \n",
               i,
               seq,
               event[evn] ,
/* we use event type as an index into the eventname array defined in the
   header file: event.h */
               p1r,
               p2r,
               p3r
              );
         }
            current_addr=(void *)((int)current_addr+RECORD_SZ);
 /* bump up the address offset to point to the next session and continue loop */
       }
    }
  }
```

Running the program, with a `shmid` as the argument, we see

```
$ sga_read_session_wait 34401
sid     seq wait                       p1        p2        p3
  0   40582 pmon timer                 12C        0        0
  1   40452 rdbms ipc message          12C        0        0
  2   43248 rdbms ipc message          12C        0        0
  3   24706 rdbms ipc message          12C        0        0
  4     736 smon timer                 12C        0        0
  5      88 rdbms ipc message        2BF20        0        0
  8     177 SQL*Net message from   62657100        1        0
```

which shows the same output as would the following SQL query:

```
select sid,seq#,event,p1raw,p2raw,p2raw
```

DMA in Action: Reading Buffer Cache Handles

My first project with my finalized DMA program was reading v$session_waits, which allowed me to sample the user waits hundreds of times a second and get almost all the waits that the sessions were experiencing in the workloads I was testing and analyzing. This allowed me to study in depth the different bottlenecks. I soon expanded the program to read the session statistics, as well as the value of the SQL hash of the query the user was executing. These user statistics and SQL hash values were easy to get because they were also stored in the same structure, x$ksuse.

The next project I decided to take on was reading x$bh. The table x$bh is the list of buffer handles describing the datablocks in the Oracle buffer caches. Reading x$bh was loads of fun because with a small buffer cache of 50 blocks (this was in Oracle version 8) and a terminal display of 50 lines, I could see all the buffers in the cache and how they moved about. I could watch the midpoint insertion algorithm in action, and I found that full table scans only read into the very end of the LRU of buffers in the cache.

DMA Pros and Cons

I had pretty much achieved what I wanted to achieve. I had a working SGA attach mechanism that was portable and has proven itself in the field. It had numerous advantages over use of SQL and the x$ tables, especially when a system was under stress and the last thing it needed was additional workload due to investigating DBA's!

On the other hand, there were a few drawbacks too, the main one being that it's quite difficult to maintain. It's simply a lot of work to decipher different x$ views, and maintain it for different Oracle releases, or platforms (think of 32-bit and platform 64-bit differences for instance). Data locations can change from release-to-release, structure sizes can differ, or Oracle development can decide to change the complete implementation, which can cause your program to be worthless.

Another problem is that once you've found the base address or addresses, and the shared segment memory size is changed on the UNIX level, the number of shared segments used by Oracle can change (as explained earlier); in this case you need to go back to your DMA program and change it accordingly.

However, I still firmly believe that it's an immensely useful tool and encourage you to check it out for yourself. All the technical details regarding my Direct Memory Access program are currently available at http://oraperf.sourceforge.net.

Looking back at the roots of the current state of Direct Memory Access at Oracle, it's interesting to note how many members of the OakTable played a significant part in my efforts to write an SGA attach program similar to Roger's original m2 program. Without the help I received from Steve Adams, Anjo Kolk, James Morle, Jonathan Lewis, Tom Kyte, and Mogens Nørgaard, I may still have succeeded eventually, but it would certainly have taken a good bit longer.

Closing Thoughts

The future of direct memory attach is uncertain. In theory, the functionality should work on Oracle versions 7 through 10. Companies like Quest, Precise, and BMC already use DMA techniques for the data collection of certain Oracle statistics. Oracle Corporation has never supplied such functionality because it was felt that current methods of querying through SQL were sufficient. The one area where DMA is especially useful is in cases of a hung or slow database. Oracle is currently looking into the possibility of providing methods of reading data from the SGA in these cases. However, beyond Oracle version 10, it's always possible that Oracle Corp. will decide to obfuscate the structures and thereby prevent the method outlined here from working.

One thing you may be wondering, just before we close, is: Whatever happened to Roger Sanders? Among the world's Oracle tuning experts, one rarely hears of Roger, even though he came up with DMA over a decade ago. But far from being "put out to pasture," Roger's extensive kernel knowledge is currently being put to good use in the area of Oracle Applications. In the world of Oracle Applications, standard install databases are 70GB, which means it's impossible to support the sheer number of databases per person within the Applications group. Thus Roger wrote a utility called zipDB, which allows an Oracle database to run compressed. The dbf files are zipped up and use a set of replacement vectors to handle skg I/O (OS-dependent Oracle layer responsible for I/O). And it even works with RAC! For those who download it, you'll also find an old favorite: m2pxsql, which stands for *m2 privileged excluding SQL access* and is used to fix up the kernel symbol table. So m2 lives on!

Dear Reader,

Ah, yes, Gaja. There are several stand-up database comedians in the OakTable Network, but they all learned it from Gaja Vahatneyhatneyhatney. Whether it's inventing the term CTD (Compulsive Tuning Disorder) or making 500 people chant "Ratios are for losers!" Gaja is never afraid to seek new paths to other people's enlightenment.

He wasn't born Vahatneyhatneyhatney, by the way. I renamed him during a presentation at IOUG in 2001, and even Gaja realized the obvious benefits of this, and so has begun to call himself that at special occasions.

I met him first while he was an instructor in Oracle US Education, but soon he took off for higher and better things, becoming involved in curriculum development and product management. After several years at Oracle he left to join Quest, then joined Oracle Enterprise Manager Development, and later Veritas. Currently, he's doing independent work (which is what he always did, really).

But what Gaja really deserves credit for is this: at the Database Forum in 2003, James Morle and I had written "BAARF: The Musical." It starred Gaja as a confused young man (himself) who had been brought up to believe in the power of RAID-F systems, but was now having second thoughts.

The star role required a good deal of singing, and I happen to know that Cary Millsap told Gaja right before we started the show that he should give it all he had, even if he wasn't a world-class singer, or he would regret it for life.

That's exactly what Gaja did. He made the audience roll with laughter at his lines, but he also made them applaud wildly in admiration when he—loud and unclear—sang the various songs at the top of his lungs. Who else would have dared do that? He certainly deserved all the admiring girls that surrounded him after the show. Without him, the show would have been incredibly boring, I'm afraid.

If you think the following chapter by Gaja is fun to read, and has a fascinating rhythm to the text, just wait 'til you see this man live.

Gaja can also be serious, not least when his back is giving him problems. During the Tom Kyte master class in Copenhagen in 2004 it was killing him, so Anjo and Anette took him to an ex-wife of mine, who's a doctor that can do the acupuncture thing. I shall leave it to your imagination to figure out where exactly the needles were placed in Gaja, and what exactly the rest of us had to say about that later.

Gaja (with a couple of co-authors) wrote the Oracle Performance Tuning 101 book a couple of years ago, and it was the first good book on that topic. Of course, if you read Dave Ensor's (now somewhat dated) book on Oracle Design, or Jonathan's, or James', or Tom Kyte's, you will find most of the information you'll ever need in order to avoid performance problems altogether, but here was a book on perform-ance, and it was saying a lot of the correct things.

*Gaja has also written a number of very good papers and presentations, and is a sure hit at any conference, not least because of his insistence (and associated brav-ery) on telling the audience the **right** things, and debunking myths wherever he can.*

—Mogens Nørgaard

CHAPTER 7

Compulsive Tuning Disorder

By Gaja Krishna Vaidyanatha

AT THE RIPE AGE of 33, I had the pleasure of co-authoring my first book, *Oracle Performance Tuning 101*. It was published by Oracle Press in the wonderful month of June, during the year of the lord 2001. My first book was originally intended to be only 42 pages long, and that should have sufficed. After all, the answer to every question in the Universe is 42, so why couldn't the details about Oracle performance diagnostics be shared within 42 pages? For those of you who have absolutely no clue what I am talking about, I urge you to seek out sources of literary material other than your Oracle documentation. The essence of 42 can be retrieved from Douglas Adams's classic book, *The Ultimate Hitchhiker's Guide to the Galaxy*.

Under extreme pressure, duress, and coercion from the publisher, I along with my co-authors of my first book wrote 362 additional pages. The rationale the publisher gave to me was that a book with only 42 pages would not sell. Heck, according to some market research, it would not even be visible on the shelf of a large bookstore. Maybe that explains the vast number of doorstoppers that crowd and strain our bookshelves. This is true in general in the world of Oracle databases, and most particularly in the area of Oracle performance tuning and diagnostics. We are lead to believe that the more pages a book possesses, the better it is! Nonsense! The book you are holding in your hands (and which by the way should never leave your sight) does not have a single superfluous page. The content in every page has been carefully crafted, reviewed, and aged, like some classic single malts in our world. And that in my humble opinion is how books should be!

At any rate, in all of the 404 pages that we wrote, it took only three words—yes a measly three words—to get people to recognize the latent message of my first book. It makes me wonder why I gave up six months of my life, stuck in the dungeon of my home office, writing hundreds of pages on Oracle performance. I wasted approximately 180 days of my life on something that could have been done much faster, orders of magnitude faster! If only I had known, I would have completed my first literary conquest in 4.2 seconds flat. You can tell by now my favorite digits in the numeral system are 4 and 2. Mr. Adams has left an indelible mark on me.

The infamous three words revealed themselves to me one dark night in November of 2000. I was trying to come up with a creative phrase that would capture the reader's attention and yet send a strong message. The moment then arrived—it was a moment of absolute literary bliss. The phrase was short, but it said it all. It has subsequently been quoted many more times than I could have ever imagined during various Oracle performance optimization seminars (even by some of my esteemed co-authors on this book!). I thank everyone from the bottom of my heart for that!

These three words, *Compulsive Tuning Disorder*, have somehow struck a chord in the Oracle community and have become a humorous way to get the point across to a database administrator on what he or she should *not* do while engaging in an Oracle performance diagnostic effort. Given the words' unanticipated popularity, Tony Davis, our fearless editor (from Apress LP), made the executive decision during the planning stages of this book that I should write an entire chapter on those three magical words. So here it is: a thorough exploration of the condition now known as Compulsive Tuning Disorder, or CTD, as I affectionately call it.

Before we proceed any further, I need to make a couple of confessions. First of all, I am *not* an expert by any stretch of the imagination. I have been wrong many times before and will be wrong many times in the future. There is so much to learn, so many mistakes to make, and you can never know it all. But I know one thing for sure—CTD causes silent damage to your mental and physical health. Believe me, I speak from personal experience since I used to suffer from CTD. Now I am a reformed individual with renewed Oracle tuning problem solving skills. You've just got to trust me on this one!

Secondly, I am a simple engineer, *not* a scientist. Some of my co-authors are born database scientists. They spend their days (and nights) figuring it all out (the bits and bytes) and I salute them for that. My day job involves looking at the usability and the "real application" of a given feature within Oracle and the value that it will add to the user. Okay, confession time is over. I feel better already, lighter at heart. Time to move on!

What Is CTD?

CTD is an unofficial subcategory of a bigger mental ailment that many of us humans suffer. CTD is a branch of a common neurobiological disorder called Obsessive Compulsive Disorder (OCD) which consists of a set of obsessions and compulsions. This disorder can range from being mildly annoying to life crippling.

The definition of *obsession* (Zabenskie 2002) is a set of truly intrusive and fear or anxiety-producing reactions, images, impulses, or thoughts. Some common obsessions are fear of contamination, fear of blasphemy, fear of acting in a violent fashion, fear of unacceptable behavior, and of course the *fear of databases that require tuning*. Most obsessions are caused due to the "fear of the unknown." For many of us, we just cannot deal with unknowns. As a result, the need to know becomes a constant and never-ending exercise, so much so that one sacrifices sleep in exchange for being informed.

In contrast, a *compulsion* is an anxiety-reducing action in response to an obsession. Most compulsions are physical in nature, in the form of repeating an activity (or a set of activities) over and over again, especially in cases of individuals who have undergone trauma. Some examples are excessive washing of one's hands; excessive counting (just to double-check, triple-check, and so on); excessive checking of the status of household appliances, light switches, and locks; and of course *excessive checking of database cache-hit ratios*.

Yes, let there be no doubt that what I am referring to here is the trauma of the DBA faced with a "database that requires tuning" and armed only with the ability to check ratios. The other aspect of the trauma is that, even if the DBA used the Oracle Wait Interface, it still did not make him or her immune from this malady. This is because the obsession to eliminate every single wait in the database can result in the compulsion to resort to tuning activities that were really not required.

Theories proposed in the psychiatric scientific community (Kolk 1989) suggest that traumatic memories of traumatic events can persist as unassimilated fixed ideas, which then act as foci for the development of alternate states of consciousness, including dissociate phenomena, such as amnesia, and chronic states of helplessness and depression.

 NOTE *The individual with the surname Kolk referenced here should not be confused with my dear friend and co-author Anjo Kolk. Anjo is an Oracle database scientist, not a psychiatrist. Although I think he may be talented enough to be one!*

Kolk continues by stating that unbidden memories of the trauma may return as physical sensations, horrific images or nightmares, behavioral reenactments, or a combination of these. Traumatized individuals can become fixated on the trauma, and may experience difficulties in assimilating subsequent experiences as well. It is "as if their personality development has stopped at a certain point and cannot expand anymore …"

Our good old friend Sigmund Freud independently arrived at similar conclusions. He concluded that trauma permanently disturbed the capacity to deal with other challenges, and the victim who did not integrate the trauma was doomed to "repeat the repressed material as a contemporary experience instead of ... remembering it as something belonging to the past."

It is very evident from the various scientific sources in the world of psychiatry that compulsion arises due to fear and/or trauma. So if you are a database administrator who has been traumatized one or more times by the need to "tune a database" using the laundry list method of checking ratios, then this will be the defining and ultimate chapter for your therapeutic process.

Note, however, that CTD is not necessarily confined to those DBA's who check ratios. In essence, CTD can be defined as the mental and physical state of a DBA who tunes without any idea as to whether the benefit from such a tuning or optimization effort will outweigh the cost. One really needs to continually ask the question: what is the Return On Investment (ROI) of a tuning effort? If one cannot quantify it, one has no business engaging in it in the first place.

Why Do People Suffer from CTD?

From the dark ages (early 1980s), Oracle performance engagements have always been shrouded in mysticism and associated with black art (like witchcraft or voodoo) secretly practiced by an elite group of individuals. To compound and complicate this misperception, there are many thousands of pages of published material that propagate the idea of *tuning Oracle with cache-hit ratios and a laundry list of things to check.*

There are many references to how performance is "good" when the ratios are high, and to how ratios below a "desired level" are a great cause for concern. Historically, you have been required to check a laundry list of ratios (database buffer cache-hit ratio, library cache-hit ratio, dictionary cache-hit ratio, the miss-ratio for a latch, the get-ratio for a latch, to name a few). This was done repeatedly to ensure that the database was performing at optimum levels. All of this caused confusion, and very often got you no closer to understanding *the actual source of the bottlenecks* that are inflicting performance pain on the entire system.

Many such performance engagements wind up by randomly tweaking memory-related Oracle initialization parameters and/or by arbitrarily throwing more memory at Oracle, in an endless attempt to eliminate physical I/O; the vain hope being that any system performance problem will be magically cured when, by divine intervention, a parameter hits its preordained value or when enough memory is allocated to the SGA. The misguided reasoning behind the latter process goes something like this: the database buffer cache-hit ratio (BCHR) is below 90%, so we have excessive physical I/O. Reading from disk is "always bad for performance" and therefore we must allocate more memory to the database buffer cache in order to eliminate it.

 NOTE *This is not to say that all ratios are completely useless. If ever you are so inclined to check a ratio, it might be worth checking the number of executions a given SQL statement performed below its response time goal versus the number of executions it performed above its response time goal. Check out Jonathan Lewis' notes on the "Fan Hit Ratio" at* http://miracleas.dk/undskyld/fhr.pdf

---

This effort, when repeated enough times, results in inordinate amounts of memory being allocated to the Oracle SGA. "The more memory you allocate to Oracle, the better," right? This is a myth. A 95%+ BCHR is not necessarily an indicator of a performant system. In fact, it's often not an indicator of much at all. Allow me to refer you to Connor McDonald's buffer cache-hit ratio PL/SQL program, which you can find at http://www.oracledba.co.uk/tips/choose.htm. This program (I call it the database buffer cache-hit ratio genie) will provide you instant gratification by giving you the database buffer cache-hit ratio that you desire without tweaking a single parameter. Your desired ratio will be its command!

The point I am trying to make here is simple—tweaking memory-related parameters without understanding the true nature of a performance problem will set you on a journey to optimize Oracle that will never really end. If you have a background in programming, think of a program with a looping construct and no exit condition in sight. The individual who practices the cache-hit ratio and laundry list-based tuning method ends up entangled in the complex web of CTD, because he or she has no criteria or condition to cease such a tuning effort.

Oracle 10g Automatic SGA Tuning: An Oasis for a CTD Sufferer

All CTD sufferers should welcome the introduction of the *Automatic SGA Tuning* feature in Oracle 10g. With this new feature, you give Oracle (via an initialization parameter, SGA_TARGET) *x* GB of memory to be allocated to the various SGA components as needed.

In this setup, the database buffer cache acts as a memory broker and dishes out the required memory to each SGA component: Default Buffer Cache, Shared Pool, Large Pool, Java Pool, and may be even to your Swimming Pool. You may be interested in knowing that there is actually a *Streams Pool* in Oracle 10g. The

Swimming Pool I am told will appear as a new functionality in a future release. So if you compare Oracle 10g to a holiday resort, it has four exotic pools in it.

The Automatic SGA Tuning feature of Oracle 10g promises the benefit of reducing the number and frequency of tweaking instance-related memory parameters. This is especially true for those systems that require a larger than normal LARGE_POOL_SIZE during a batch window. What previously required a database and instance restart is now done automatically based on the demand for memory for the large pool. When the memory demand for the large pool decreases the excess memory is returned back to the database buffer cache. And as part of this setup, there is a built-in *Memory Advisor* in 10g that will inform you if you have over-allocated memory to various components of the SGA. More importantly, if you have over-allocated memory, the advisor will inform you the extent of such an over-allocation. Now there is a feature that warrants uncorking an aged bottle of Blackadder whisky!

So, Oracle 10g's Automatic SGA Tuning can alleviate some of the pain of a CTD sufferer by virtually eliminating the constant need to tweak initialization parameters. Having said that, it is important to understand that the only true cure for CTD is to leave cache-hit ratios behind, understand the ROI for any tuning effort, and adhere to a meaningful method that tackles Oracle performance problems.

 NOTE *At the time of writing of this chapter (May 2004), the true workings of this feature in "real-life" production environments were yet to be determined. The reader is advised to take all usual, normal, and customary precautions before deploying this (or any other new feature) in production environments. Also, it should be noted that in Oracle 10g Release 1, the redo log buffer, the* KEEP *and* RECYCLE *Pools, and any nondefault buffer caches (created post-database creation) are not automatically managed.*

Are You DBA Survivor Material?

During one of my long transatlantic flights many moons ago, whilst bored out of my mind, it occurred to me that is would be a great idea to produce a reality TV show that placed a bunch of Oracle DBA's on a tropical island—basically a *Survivor* show for the DBA. I'm not sure whether any network television company will welcome this proposal with open arms, but one never knows. Here is the underlying plot nevertheless:

1. Transport a bunch of DBA's to an exotic island in the South Pacific.

2. Remove all access to their GUI tools (hey, got to separate the true "men and women" from the boys and girls).

3. Ring their pagers, mobile phones, or PDA devices to inform them that there is a performance problem in one of their databases.

4. Provide them with nothing but an honest-to-goodness `telnet` session.

5. Given them the challenge to determine the source of the performance problem within three SQL statements.

How many DBA's will keep their jobs, and how many will be kicked off the island? If you suffer from CTD, I guarantee that you will lose your job on the island. At this point, I guess you're either intrigued by this statement or are starting to wonder whether I really need to "get a life." Believe me when I say that I am working on "getting a life" as I am writing this chapter!

The sole purpose of this chapter is to help you identify whether or not you suffer from CTD and, if so, to point you down the path towards recovery. But the first step towards any psychiatric recovery process is to get out of the denial phase. You have to first accept that you are suffering from CTD. Once you do that, I can show you the path to recovery, which by the way involves a behavioral change on your part. You need to alter old habits and start adhering to a new method, and this method uses the Oracle Wait Interface (OWI). Performance management is not about just allocating memory to the Oracle shared memory areas and eliminating physical I/O. It is all about identifying the root cause of an application-level response time issue. And that, ladies and gents, requires some *logical* thinking.

It Is Time to Get Logical ...

Okay, let's face it: the single-most significant factor in any Oracle database performance problem is SQL. I totally believe (and you may agree) that there are way too many people out there who should NOT be allowed to touch a keyboard but end up writing some *horrendous* SQL. Bad news comes in various forms, but at the end of the day a DBA needs to support the performance requirements of such applications. Don't get me wrong, this is not about bashing all the wonderful developers out there but about dealing with the reality of the situation. An Oracle wise man once said that the best performing Oracle database is one where there are no SQL statements being processed. I couldn't agree more!

From a performance optimization standpoint, there is no doubt that response time is the single most important indicator of a performance problem. Related to this is the reduction of logical I/O. Under normal circumstances, a query performing 1000 blocks of logical I/O (`db block gets + consistent gets`) is much better than a similar query (producing the same result set) performing 5000 blocks of logical I/O. This is because logical I/O in Oracle comes at a cost.

Cary Millsap (2001, 2003) eloquently describes the chronic problem of performing excessive logical I/O and its impact on system performance. He describes the pain that applications can inflict on the system in the form of contention for the `cache buffers lru chain` latch (this contention was eliminated by a significant change in the database buffer cache management algorithm in Oracle8i) and the `cache buffers chains` latch, when repeatedly performing large amounts of logical I/O across many user sessions. Cary also provides data that suggests that the performance difference between logical I/O and physical I/O (in the Oracle context) is *between 10 to 100 times faster than physical I/O, not 10,000 times faster* (which is the commonly accepted factor when comparing memory reads to disk reads). The salient point here is that performance problems cannot be solved just by eliminating physical I/O. Or to put it another way, an application that reads data only from memory may still possess performance impediments.

Logical Performance Optimization

Performance optimization is a systematic, deliberate, and managed effort to achieve a system response time goal by purposefully eliminating one or more bottlenecks with a well-defined ROI in mind. It is very obvious that accurate diagnosis of the bottlenecks in a performance optimization effort is a prerequisite: you must know that a certain bottleneck exists and then plan your course of action accordingly. You must not base your performance optimization efforts on opinion or on a "hunch." If you tuned based on "hunches," it will lead you back to CTD.

To attain any level of repeatable success in performance optimization, a reliable diagnostic method is required. So at this time, let us please spare ourselves the pain of using any so-called expert techniques. We have many world-renowned experts whose tuning methods lead us nowhere near the true problem. All they do is obscure the whole exercise beneath a layer of wizardry, thus making it impenetrable to the common DBA. Any advertisements for *Advanced Tuning, Turbo Tuning,* or *"Push Me for More Power" Tuning* are marketing gimmicks to sell consulting services. Plain and simple!

There is only one way to optimize Oracle performance and that is to determine the response time of a given application and break down the *service time* and *wait time* components. Although *service time* is usually determined by hardware specifications and common laws of physics, the *wait time* component has a varied set of sources. For example, I absolutely believe in the following—*you cannot control what people smoke before they code.*

As a result:

Wait Time = Fn (wasteful processing, resource contention, controlled substance smoked before application coding)

Now there is a mathematical formula to remember!

My dear friend and co-author Anjo Kolk, along with Shari Yamaguchi and Jim Viscusi, wrote about response-time-based optimization in great detail in their famous YAPP paper in 1996. Anjo explains the story behind it right here in this book (Chapter 4). The YAPP method is still very much relevant to the area of performance management. If we identify where the wait times occur for a given database component, we will be automatically led to the "bone of contention" and thus will reap significant and repeatable performance tuning benefits.

This is the basis of the methodology that can potentially cure CTD. We set well-defined and realistic performance targets and then we use the Oracle wait interface to determine exactly where the database is spending its time. No ratio checking, no endless parameter twiddling.

Bear in mind, though, that the point about having defined, realistic performance goals is central. Regardless of what bottlenecks are unearthed and what necessary changes are required, the following key fact still remains—CTD is a state where tuning efforts are attempted without heed to the associated cost of such an effort. The need to achieve the required response time goal is quintessential and all tuning efforts must cease when the *response time goal* is achieved. However, the cost and feasibility aspects have to be taken into consideration. Failure to recognize the cost aspect and cease performance efforts when response time goals are achieved is a classic sign of an individual suffering from CTD.

Don't kill yourself trying to eliminate all the waits in your Oracle database. It is a virtually impossible task. As long as the application is conforming to its response time goal, you should not bother with the waits. If the response time for a given SQL statement is not an issue, the corresponding waits should not be an issue either. Remember, you can and will suffer from CTD, if you attempt to (in vain) eliminate every single wait event in your database.

Okay, it is time to examine Oracle's wait interface in detail and find out what information it can offer us. We'll examine the interface itself along with the new diagnostic data sources and views that Oracle 10g has introduced in order to allow you to effectively gather and use the information that the wait interface has to offer. We'll then discuss how to use this information in a "2-pronged methodology" that will provide your once-and-for-all cure for CTD.

The Oracle Wait Interface

The symptoms of a bottleneck in an Oracle environment can be determined by looking at the *wait events* experienced by the database. A wait event, in its true sense, is Oracle kernel code instrumentation that facilitates the process of determining the root cause and location of bottlenecks inside Oracle. This code instrumentation began in version 7.0.12 of the Oracle database. There are approximately 215 events in Oracle8i (8.1.7.4), and this number has risen to about 399 in version 9i (9.2.0.4) and to approximately 806 wait events in version 10g (10.1.0.2). Cary Millsap's chapter, "Extended SQL Trace Data" (Chapter 5) provides the details on the history, the inventor, and other exciting snippets about wait events.

The Oracle Wait Interface is defined as the collection of information available in the V$SYSTEM_EVENT, V$SESSION_EVENT, V$SESSION_WAIT, and V$EVENT_NAME dynamic performance views and trace files generated by setting the 10046 session-level diagnostic event. The 10046 diagnostic event can be loosely defined as "SQL_TRACE on steroids." Basically when you enable SQL_TRACE at the session level you are enabling 10046 at level 1.

This 10046 diagnostic event is the one you will find yourself using most often in your logical performance analysis. It has many levels of tracing, which are covered in detail later in this chapter. However, before we move on, here are some additional diagnostic events that are useful to have in your diagnostic arsenal. These diagnostic events can be set exactly in the same fashion as 10046, using the DBMS_SYSTEM.SET_EV() procedure.

- 10032, 10033: Sort Tracing

- 10053: Optimizer Tracing

- 10060: Query Transformations Tracing (Query Un-nesting/View Merging)

- 10128: Database Partition Tracing

- 10391: Parallel Query Tracing

- 10730: SQL Statement Tracing with Row-Level Security

Types of Wait Events

Not all wait events are cause for concern. There are certain wait events that are more important than others. If you are familiar with the serenity prayer, you are already aware of the fact that you need to accept certain things in life and move on. Well, there are such wait events in the Oracle database: just accept them as part of life and move on.

The wait events in an Oracle database have been historically classified into two types, *idle* and *non-idle*.

Idle events are normally generated by background processes, although there are some idle events that are generated by foreground processes too. When generated by foreground processes (server processes), wait events usually indicate that the database is "waiting for some work." Idle events are not normally an indication of any database performance problem, although there have been exceptions to this rule in prior versions of the Oracle database. Some common idle events are pipe get, rdbms ipc message, smon timer, and pmon timer.

So, let's put this in perspective. Unless you plan on rewriting the code for PMON's timer (which by the way is illegal if you aren't employed in Oracle Corporation's development organization), just accept the fact that waits for PMON's timer are "part and parcel" of a functioning Oracle database, and move on.

Non-idle wait events are caused by inefficient SQL or inefficiencies in some subsystem in the configuration, and these are the waits that generally are a cause for concern. Some common non-idle wait events are free buffer waits, buffer busy waits, latch free, db file scattered read, enqueue, db file sequential read, and SQL*Net more data to client.

NOTE *A comprehensive list of the wait events and their description can be found in Appendix A of the* Oracle Reference Manual *for pre-10g releases. In Oracle 10g, the wait events are described in Appendix C along with a description of the various types of enqueues in Appendix D. Also, regardless of whether an event is idle or non-idle, if it is contributing to a significant portion of the wait time of a SQL statement, it requires attention.*

V$SESSION_WAIT: The Goldmine of Symptoms

The waits for the currently active sessions can be obtained from V$SESSION_WAIT. This view provides *the details* behind the event: in other words, the location of the wait event.

The V$SESSION_WAIT view is quite possibly the most complex dynamic performance view within Oracle. It provides low-level drill down information, at the session level, for a given event. Unlike some of the other views, which display totals, this view displays "real-time" session-level wait information. This is the real stuff, as it unfolds.

CAUTION *It is important to note that iterative querying of this view may show different results. This is attributed to the activity that is happening on the database.*

For example, if a session is waiting on a multi-block read event (db file scattered read), the file number, the data block number, and the number of blocks in the read system call issued by Oracle are provided in the three parameters, P[1-3].

The relevant columns in the V$SESSION_WAIT dynamic performance view are as follows:

Column	Description
Sid	The session identifier.
Seq#	An internal sequence number for the wait event related to this session. This column can be utilized to determine the number of waits for a given event that a session has experienced. If you need to determine the top session that is *suffering the largest number of waits*, look for the sessions with the largest Seq# value.
Event	The name of the event such latch free *or* db file sequential read.
P[1-3]	The goldmine of symptom indicators. P1..P3 provide more details about the specific wait.
State	The state of given session, which takes one of the four following possible states: Waited Short Time: The wait duration for the session was less than 1 centisecond. Waited Known Time: The wait duration for the session exceeded 1 centisecond. Waiting: Session currently is in the process of waiting for the event. Waited Unknown Time: The Oracle initialization parameter TIMED_STATISTICS is set to FALSE.

Wait_time	This column is only relevant for wait events that have completed waiting, thus when the value of State is Waited Known Time.
	If State = (Waited Known Time) then
	  Wait_Time = Actual wait time, in seconds;
	End If;

Seconds_in_wait	This column is only relevant for wait events that are currently in progress, thus when the value of State is Waiting.
	If State = (Waiting) then
	  Seconds_In_Wait = Actual Wait Time in Seconds;
	End If;

The OWI in Oracle 10g

As discussed earlier, the extent of kernel instrumentation for the waits has been significantly increasing with successive version releases, and Oracle 10g is no exception. Among other reasons, the significant increase in the number of wait events in 10g can be attributed to breaking down of the various types of latch free and enqueue events into their own individual events.

One benefit from the aforementioned "breakdown" is this: prior to 10g, a two-step process was required to determine which latch or enqueue was causing the performance problem. This is because the details for the wait event did not explicitly specify the latch or enqueue that was waited upon. In Oracle 10g, this has now been transformed into a single-step process in 10g. Read on for more details.

The Concept of a Wait Class

Oracle 10g has introduced the concept of a *wait class*. Wait classes are categories or buckets into which individual waits are classified. This effort was primarily undertaken to facilitate the use of a rule tree with meaningful branches for the Automatic Database Diagnostic Monitor (ADDM). Wait classes help to identify which "class of waits" contributes the most pain in the database. Thus the concept of logically storing wait events in a wait class was born.

There are 12 different wait classes in version 10gR1 (10.1.0.2.0), namely Administrative, Application, Cluster, Commit, Concurrency, Configuration, Idle, Network, Other, Scheduler, System I/O, and User I/O.

The Administrative class contains wait events that are related to normal functions in the database such as backups, buffer pool resizing operations, database writer operations, rollback segment/undo segment operations, controlfile operations, log switches, index rebuilds, and processes involving Oracle's Automatic Storage Manager (ASM). Examples are Backup: sbtread, buffer pool resize, switch logfile command, enq: TW - contention, and index (re)build online start.

The Application class consists of waits that are application-focused. A good number of enqueue waits are in this class. Examples of waits in this class are enq: TM - contention, enq: TX - row lock contention, SQL*Net break/reset to client, SQL*Net break/reset to dblink and waits related to the new Oracle-provided log-based replication functionality—*Streams.*

The Cluster class contains wait events associated with Oracle RAC related to the various global cache events, such as gc current request, gc cr request, gc cr multi block request, and so on. In an Oracle RAC configuration, the cluster-centric waits of RAC will be classified under the Cluster class.

The Commit class consists of a single wait event—log file sync. This wait event is associated with the rate of commit by the application. It may be useful to clarify here that your system may experience waits for log file sync if the I/O subsystem on which the redo log files are configured has underlying performance issues.

The wait class Concurrency consists of waits associated with multiple server processes attempting to contend for the same resource. This class stores all waits that require "serialization" in the database, i.e., only one process can execute that piece of Oracle kernel code. All relevant SQL-related latch waits show up in this class. Examples of wait events in this class are latch: cache buffers chains, latch: library cache, enq: TX - index contention, and buffer busy waits.

The Configuration wait class provides information on any configuration-related waits in the database. These waits are normally caused by improper configuration of a given component in the database. For example, if the redo log buffer is improperly sized, Oracle indicates this by surfacing the log buffer space wait event. Similar sizing and configuration-related issues are flagged as wait events, and these are bucketed in this class. Examples of other waits in this class are free buffer waits (indicates lack of enough buffers in the database buffer cache if write complete waits are not present), write complete waits (DBWR is experiencing difficulty writing dirty blocks to disk), and enq: ST - contention (indicates waits for the space management transaction enqueue due to the presence of dictionary-managed tablespaces).

The Idle wait class consists of wait events that usually don't require a great deal of attention. Of course there are exceptions to this, but normally these are waits that should not cause any performance bother. Examples of wait events in this class are PX Deq: Parse Reply, PX Deque wait, SQL*Net message from client, SQL*Net message from dblink, PL/SQL lock timer, pmon timer, and rdbms ipc message.

The Network wait class comprises of all those waits that indicate a network-related performance problem. There are some new wait events that related to ARCH and LGWR that are classified in this class. Some wait event inhabitants of this class are ARCH wait for netserver start, LGWR wait on ATTACH, SQL*Net message to client, SQL*Net more data to client, and SQL*Net more data from dblink.

The wait class Other consists of 554 events. According to inventors, the wait events in this class should normally never occur. Any "significant" occurrence of a wait event from this class that contributes to a response time problem should be considered as a code anomaly and reported as a bug. Examples are enq: JS - contention, MMON slave messages, and DLM recovery lock convert.

The Scheduler wait class consists of wait events that relate to the built-in Scheduler in the database. This class consists of two wait events and they are resmgr: cpu quantum and resmgr: become active.

The wait class System I/O comprises I/O-related waits generated by background processes (DBWR, LGWR, ARCH, CKPT). Some wait event examples in this class are ARCH wait for pending I/Os, LGWR sequential i/o, i/o done, db file parallel write, and kfk: async disk IO.

The User I/O wait class consists of I/O-related waits generated by foreground processes (server processes). The usual suspects (wait events) from this class are db file sequential read, db file scattered read, direct path write, and read by other session. Notable here is the new wait event in 10g—read by other session. This wait event illustrates one or more sessions waiting for another session to complete the physical I/O of a block from disk. Prior to 10g, this wait was obfuscated by a buffer busy waits wait event, which now lives in the Concurrency wait class in its own right.

The following listing provides some details on the various wait classes in 10g:

```
SQL> select * from v_$version;

BANNER
----------------------------------------------------------------
Oracle Database 10g Enterprise Edition Release 10.1.0.2.0 - Prod
PL/SQL Release 10.1.0.2.0 - Production
CORE    10.1.0.2.0      Production
TNS for 32-bit Windows: Version 10.1.0.2.0 - Production
NLSRTL Version 10.1.0.2.0 - Production

SQL> describe v_$event_name
 Name                                     Null?    Type
 ---------------------------------------- -------- -----------
 EVENT#                                            NUMBER
 EVENT_ID                                          NUMBER
 NAME                                              VARCHAR2(64)
 PARAMETER1                                        VARCHAR2(64)
 PARAMETER2                                        VARCHAR2(64)
 PARAMETER3                                        VARCHAR2(64)
 WAIT_CLASS_ID                                     NUMBER
 WAIT_CLASS#                                       NUMBER
 WAIT_CLASS                                        VARCHAR2(64)

/* Query displaying the number of wait events in this release */
SQL> select count(*) from v_$event_name;
  COUNT(*)

----------
      806
```

```
/* Query the various wait classes and the number of wait events in each class */
SQL> select wait_class, count(*)
  2    from v_$event_name
  3  group by wait_class;
WAIT_CLASS                                                         COUNT(*)
---------------------------------------------------------------- ----------
Administrative                                                          42
Application                                                            10
Cluster                                                                45
Commit                                                                  1
Concurrency                                                            17
Configuration                                                          21
Idle                                                                   58
Network                                                                25
Other                                                                554
Scheduler                                                               2
System I/O                                                             19
User I/O                                                               12

12 rows selected.
```

V$ACTIVE_SESSION_HISTORY: The New Diagnostic Data Source

Oracle 10g introduces a brand new performance diagnostic data source—Active Session History (ASH). This data source is exposed to us via V$ACTIVE_SESSION_HISTORY. This V$ view is based on two X$ tables—X$KEWASH and X$ASH.

X$KEWASH contains the metadata for ASH samples, and X$ASH contains the data currently in the circular buffer in memory. The following code listing is a formatted view definition of V$ACTIVE_SESSION_HISTORY in Oracle 10g Release 1 (10.1.0.2.0):

```
SQL> select view_definition from v_$fixed_view_definition
  2    where view_name = 'GV$ACTIVE_SESSION_HISTORY';

  VIEW_DEFINITION
  -------------------------------------------------------------------
  SELECT  /*+ no_merge ordered use_nl(s,a) */
    a.inst_id,
    s.sample_id,
    s.sample_time,
    a.session_id,
```

```
       a.session_serial#,
       a.user_id,
       a.sql_id,
       a.sql_child_number,
       a.sql_plan_hash_value,
       a.sql_opcode,
       a.service_hash,
       decode(a.session_type, 1,'FOREGROUND', 2,'BACKGROUND','UNKNOWN'),
         decode(a.wait_time, 0, 'WAITING', 'ON CPU'),
         a.qc_session_id,
         a.qc_instance_id,
         a.event,
         a.event_id,
         a.event#,
         a.seq#,
       a.p1,
       a.p2,
       a.p3,
       a.wait_time,
       a.time_waited,
       a.current_file#,
       a.current_block#,
       a.program,
       a.module,
       a.action,
       a.client_id
FROM  x$kewash s, x$ash a
     WHERE s.sample_addr = a.sample_addr
     and s.sample_id    = a.sample_id
     and s.sample_time = a.sample_time
```

So what makes a session active? An active session is a session that is in one of the following states:

- Parse

- Execute

- Fetch

- On the CPU—a server process is currently consuming a CPU resource

So for all practical purposes, ASH provides recent (short-term) historical wait information about sessions that have been "active." So, again, basically it is V$SESSION_WAIT plus history. The intended duration for this short-term history stored in the memory buffers is 30 minutes. The changing system load, amount of change, and the number of active sessions will have an impact on the actual duration on a given Oracle 10g database.

ASH also provides the capability to perform spot analysis on both foreground (server processes) and background processes (DBWR, LGWR, and so on). ASH logs session waits, along with SQL details and session statistics, in a circular buffer, using a dynamically adjusting sampling algorithm. This sampling algorithm samples the session state object structures in the SGA and writes the data in the circular buffer. The data is written to the circular buffer by a new background process called MMNL, which stands for "MMON Lite." Every 30 minutes, or when the circular buffer becomes full, the contents of the circular buffer are persisted to disk. The location of the persistence is WRH$_ACTIVE_SESSION_HISTORY, in the Automatic Workload Repository (AWR). Furthermore, the history of the recent in-memory system activity available in ASH is maintained on a snapshot-by-snapshot basis in DBA_HIST_ACTIVE_SESS_HISTORY. The following diagram, Figure 7-1, gives a high-level overview of the workings of ASH.

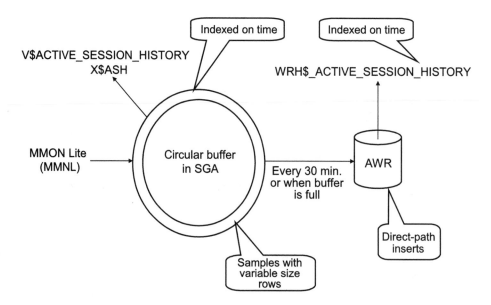

Figure 7-1. Overview of ASH

ASH does not require any setup or installation. It is installed and configured as part of the database creation. So if your database version is 10g or above, V$ACTIVE_SESSION_HISTORY should be a preferred dynamic performance view.

Following is a sample query that provides wait details and SQL details from ASH for a foreground user, DEMO_USER, in the previous 3 3/4 minutes:

```
SQL> select ash.user_id "USER",
        e.name "EVNAME",
        e.wait_class "EVCLASS",
        ash.twait_msecs"TWAIT_MSECS",
        ash.obj# "OBJ#",
        ash.file# "FILE#",
        s.sql_text "SQL"
from v_$sql s,
     v_$event_name e,
        (   select user_id,
            sql_id "SQL_ID",
            sql_plan_hash_value,
            sql_opcode,
            seq#,
            event#,
            p1,
            p2,
            p3,
            time_waited/1000 "TWAIT_MSECS",
            current_obj# "OBJ#",
            current_file# "FILE#",
            current_block# "BLOCK#"
        from v_$active_session_history
     where session_type <> 'BACKGROUND'
            and (session_id,session_serial#) in
     (
        select sid,serial#
            from v_$session
            where username = (upper('&&oracle_user_name')
        )
   )
     and wait_time = 0
     and event# <> 0
     and sample_time between sysdate-(0.125/24) and sysdate
    ) ash
where s.sql_id = ash.sql_id
  and e.event# = ash.event#;
```

USER	EVNAME	EVCLASS	TWAIT_MSECS	OBJ#	FILE#	SQL
67	db file scattered read	User I/O	8	48868	4	SELECT COUNT(*) FROM WAIT_OBJECTS_BIG WHERE OWNER = 'DEMO_USER'
67	db file scattered read	User I/O	7	48868	4	SELECT COUNT(*) FROM WAIT_OBJECTS_BIG WHERE OWNER = 'DEMO_USER'
67	db file scattered read	User I/O	8	48868	4	SELECT COUNT(*) FROM WAIT_OBJECTS_BIG WHERE OWNER = 'DEMO_USER'

The formatted output from the preceding code listing displays wait and SQL information for the Oracle user, DEMO_USER. It shows the user number, the event name, the wait event class, the amount of time spent waiting for the wait event (in milliseconds), the object number on which the wait occurred, the file number in which the object's wait was experienced, and the SQL statement that is causing the wait.

V$EVENT_HISTOGRAM: Wait Event Data Distribution

This brand new dynamic performance view stores very useful data distribution information about the various wait events including the total wait time and maximum wait. The histogram buckets are defined in milliseconds, and in the range of between 1 and 2^{22}, based on the actual wait times experienced for a given wait event. The following code listing and output sheds some light on this new and interesting V$ view.

```
SQL> desc v$event_histogram
```

Name	Null?	Type
EVENT#		NUMBER
EVENT		VARCHAR2(64)
WAIT_TIME_MILLI		NUMBER
WAIT_COUNT		NUMBER

The following query displays the breakdown of wait time in milliseconds for all events beginning with the string db file and having a occurrence frequency of 100 times or higher.

```
SQL> select event, wait_count, wait_time_milli
  2  from v$event_histogram
  3  where event like 'db file%'
  4     and wait_count > 100
  5  order by event, wait_time_milli, wait_count
  6  /
```

EVENT	WAIT_COUNT	WAIT_TIME_MILLI
db file parallel write	1655	1
db file parallel write	179	2
db file scattered read	801	1
db file scattered read	12041	2
db file scattered read	25420	4
db file scattered read	177160	8
db file scattered read	4502	16
db file scattered read	6104	32
db file scattered read	3598	64
db file scattered read	981	128
db file sequential read	3668	1

EVENT	WAIT_COUNT	WAIT_TIME_MILLI
db file sequential read	193	2
db file sequential read	228	4
db file sequential read	670	8
db file sequential read	1666	16
db file sequential read	1655	32
db file sequential read	996	64
db file sequential read	322	128

18 rows selected.

In the preceding query output, it is very evident that most of the multi-block read requests (DB FILE SCATTERED READ) in this database have a service time that ranges between 4 and 7 milliseconds. In this case 177160 (76.82%) multi-block requests out of the total of 230607 were serviced within 4–7 milliseconds. Also, note that there are a good number of multi-block I/O calls that exceed the normal I/O time of 20ms. Here we have 6104 calls in the 32ms bucket, 3598 in the 64ms bucket and 981 calls in the 128ms bucket. We clearly have I/O bottlenecks here.

Oracle 10g DBMS_MONITOR: The New Frontier in Session Tracing

In Oracle 10g, a new package, DBMS_MONITOR, can be used to perform session tracing. Oracle Corporation recommends that you use that package going forward instead of DBMS_SYSTEM.SET_EV. Here is the stub output from DBMS_MONITOR:

```
SQL> desc dbms_monitor

PROCEDURE CLIENT_ID_STAT_DISABLE
 Argument Name                   Type                    In/Out Default?
 ------------------------------ ----------------------- ------ --------
 CLIENT_ID                       VARCHAR2                IN


PROCEDURE CLIENT_ID_STAT_ENABLE
 Argument Name                   Type                    In/Out Default?
 ------------------------------ ----------------------- ------ --------
 CLIENT_ID                       VARCHAR2                IN


PROCEDURE CLIENT_ID_TRACE_DISABLE
 Argument Name                   Type                    In/Out Default?
 ------------------------------ ----------------------- ------ --------
 CLIENT_ID                       VARCHAR2                IN


PROCEDURE CLIENT_ID_TRACE_ENABLE
 Argument Name                   Type                    In/Out Default?
 ------------------------------ ----------------------- ------ --------
 CLIENT_ID                       VARCHAR2                IN
 WAITS                           BOOLEAN                 IN     DEFAULT
 BINDS                           BOOLEAN                 IN     DEFAULT


PROCEDURE SERV_MOD_ACT_STAT_DISABLE
 Argument Name                   Type                    In/Out Default?
 ------------------------------ ----------------------- ------ --------
 SERVICE_NAME                    VARCHAR2                IN
 MODULE_NAME                     VARCHAR2                IN
 ACTION_NAME                     VARCHAR2                IN     DEFAULT
```

```
PROCEDURE SERV_MOD_ACT_STAT_ENABLE
Argument Name                        Type                    In/Out Default?
------------------------------       ----------------------  ------ --------
 SERVICE_NAME                        VARCHAR2                 IN
 MODULE_NAME                         VARCHAR2                 IN
 ACTION_NAME                         VARCHAR2                 IN     DEFAULT


PROCEDURE SERV_MOD_ACT_TRACE_DISABLE
Argument Name                        Type                    In/Out Default?

------------------------------       ----------------------  ------ --------
 SERVICE_NAME                        VARCHAR2                 IN
 MODULE_NAME                         VARCHAR2                 IN     DEFAULT
 ACTION_NAME                         VARCHAR2                 IN     DEFAULT
 INSTANCE_NAME                       VARCHAR2                 IN     DEFAULT


PROCEDURE SERV_MOD_ACT_TRACE_ENABLE
Argument Name                        Type                    In/Out Default?

------------------------------       ----------------------  ------ --------
 SERVICE_NAME                        VARCHAR2                 IN
 MODULE_NAME                         VARCHAR2                 IN     DEFAULT
 ACTION_NAME                         VARCHAR2                 IN     DEFAULT
 WAITS                               BOOLEAN                  IN     DEFAULT
 BINDS                               BOOLEAN                  IN     DEFAULT
 INSTANCE_NAME                       VARCHAR2                 IN     DEFAULT


PROCEDURE SESSION_TRACE_DISABLE
Argument Name                        Type                    In/Out Default?
------------------------------       ----------------------  ------ --------
 SESSION_ID                          BINARY_INTEGER          IN     DEFAULT
 SERIAL_NUM                          BINARY_INTEGER          IN     DEFAULT


PROCEDURE SESSION_TRACE_ENABLE
Argument Name                        Type                    In/Out Default?
------------------------------       ----------------------  ------ --------
 SESSION_ID                          BINARY_INTEGER          IN     DEFAULT
 SERIAL_NUM                          BINARY_INTEGER          IN     DEFAULT
 WAITS                               BOOLEAN                  IN     DEFAULT
 BINDS                               BOOLEAN                  IN     DEFAULT
```

We will focus on the last two procedures, namely SESSION_TRACE_DISABLE and SESSION_TRACE_ENABLE. The PL/SQL procedure calls for SESSION_TRACE_DISABLE and SESSION_TRACE_ENABLE are very straightforward. The ENABLE procedure takes the session ID (SID), serial number (SERIAL_NUM), and Boolean values for whether wait data and bind variable data needs to be logged in the trace file. The session-level diagnostic event 10046 at level 8 is achieved using the following syntax:

```
exec dbms_monitor.session_trace_enable(sid, seriall#, TRUE,FALSE);
```

If bind variable values are required, the last argument in the procedure call will also be set to TRUE. One of the great features of DBMS_MONITOR is its ability to set 10046 at level 8 for your current session without taking any arguments. It is achieved by the following syntax:

```
exec dbms_monitor.session_trace_enable;
```

It's now time to see how we use all of this precious wait information as part of a new and effective 2-pronged performance optimization methodology

The 2-pronged Methodology: The Cure for CTD

The lack of a meaningful performance methodology can result in unnecessary time and effort spent on tuning the system without significant and/or measurable gains. Haphazard attempts to alter Oracle initialization parameters in an endless effort to allocate more than the required memory to the Oracle SGA is not only counter-productive, but can (in some cases) cause worse performance.

Furthermore, as we have already discussed, too many performance tuning engagements fall prey to the habit of configuring significant amounts of memory for the database buffer cache in an effort to attain high cache-hit ratios (upper 90s), only for the DBA to discover that performance has not improved one bit after such an exercise has been completed. In some extreme cases, such efforts resulted in significant levels of operating system paging, due to memory over-allocation and memory starvation on the said systems.

First, allow me to take you down your memory lanes. Do you recall your physics classes from your high school days? You probably did one or more experiments related on "sound" using the *tuning fork*. If you recall, the tuning fork in your laboratory had (still has) two prongs. Well, guess what, the tuning fork for your Oracle database performance optimization effort also has *two prongs*.

This *two-pronged* approach focuses on both the OWI on one side and the operating system (OS) on the other. When the information derived from each is "merged" and correlated, you have defined the complete performance problem. This two-pronged performance tuning methodology (Vaidyanatha 2000, 2001) and the positive results that come out of it are repeatable and predictable. One of the key strengths of this methodology is its consistency in getting you to the root cause of your performance problem.

The two-pronged methodology requires you to

1. Set reasonable performance goals.

   a. Not only is there a requirement to set reasonable performance goals, but also there is a need to prioritize the application(s) that requires tuning. This is relevant if there are multiple applications accessing one or more databases on the same host.

2. Measure and document current performance.

3. Identify the current Oracle performance bottlenecks using the OWI. Use the 10046 diagnostic event to trace the session—*Prong I*.

4. Identify the OS bottlenecks (CPU or memory)—*Prong II*. This prong is required as the OWI does not have the required data to surface CPU or memory issues within a system.

5. Correlate data collected in both prongs to define the *complete performance problem*.

6. Identify the SQL that is experiencing the bottleneck(s) using the wait data in step 3. This is done by running tkprof on the trace file.

7. Determine the root cause for the problem—too many full table scans, index overuse, contention for certain buffers, lack of enough DBWR processes, inadequate number of freelists or freelist groups, and so on.

8. Implement one change at a time purely based on the data collected. If you don't have the data to justify a change, don't pursue it.

9. Track and exercise change-control procedures.

10. Measure and document current performance.

11. Rinse and repeat steps 2 through 10 until the tuning goal is met.

In the coming sections, we will focus on steps 1–4, which are driving factors in your CTD rehabilitation program. Steps 5–11 have been outlined for completeness.

CAUTION *Do not change any component if it is not the source of your system-wide bottleneck. Doing so can result in unpredictable and potentially undesirable effects. For example, if the current system performance problem is I/O, do not upgrade the CPU's on the system, assuming that it can only get better. You may be in for a surprise. It is as important to cease all tuning efforts when the set tuning goals are attained as it is to begin a tuning engagement. Otherwise, we have a clear case of someone suffering from CTD.*

Set Reasonable Performance Goals

This is the first step in the rehabilitation program for those who suffer from CTD. It is not enough to say that things need to get faster. That statement is too subjective. One has to be very specific and objective about the goals one sets in any performance optimization engagement. As part of setting the performance goals for a given effort, it is very essential to set priorities as to which applications or application component has the highest priority in the larger scheme of things. For example:

Application X's SQL statement, Y, currently has an elapsed time of 465 minutes, and there are driving business needs that require it to run in 42 minutes.

Once you have a goal in mind, you need implement only the minimum number of changes that will allow you to meet the required performance goal (in other words, the required response time goal). As soon as you achieve your goal (in this case to get the SQL statement to run within 42 minutes), start practicing tuning abstinence! If you don't, then there is no hope that you will escape the vicious cycle of CTD. Imagine experiencing the movie *Ground Hog Day*. Imagine a state-of-the-art PL/SQL loop without any exit condition in sight! I think you get my point!

Measure and Document Current Performance

The second step in the method is to determine how "bad" the performance really is. This is accomplished by benchmarking the offending SQL statements in the offending session(s). There is an urgent need to use common sense here. If a given SQL statement takes 16 hours to complete, you don't have to benchmark it for 16 hours. A reasonable benchmark interval of 15 or 30 minutes (when the real problem is experienced) is adequate. Many a time, the luxury of benchmarking does not exist, as real-time performance problems require a performance practitioner to take immediate action. In scenarios such as these, the question of benchmarking does not even arise. The core idea of benchmarking is to identify resource hogs and take us to the next step of "revealing bottlenecks."

Identifying the Bottlenecks within Oracle: Prong I

Here is the roadmap for identifying the symptoms and performance bottlenecks within the Oracle database. It outlines the steps required to identify and trace performance problems as they happen:

Step 1: Identify the Sessions Experiencing Excessive Waits

Identify the session(s) that are experiencing excessive response times due to waits. You can do this by repeatedly executing the following query (Query #1) on V$SESSION_WAIT:

```
SQL> select event, seq#, sid, p1, p2, p3, wait_time    /* Query #1 */
from v_$session_wait
where state = 'WAITED KNOWN TIME';
```

If the waits on the system are predominantly less than 1 centisecond (1/100th of a second), then Query #1 may not return any rows. In such cases, the WHERE clause for this query should be modified as follows:

```
SQL> select event, seq#, sid, p1, p2, p3, wait_time    /* Query #2 */
from v_$session_wait
where state = 'WAITED SHORT TIME';
```

In Oracle 10g, V$SESSION_WAIT_HISTORY stores the last 10 wait events for every active session. This view is defined as follows:

```
SQL> desc v_$session_wait_history
```

Name	Null?	Type
SID		NUMBER
SEQ#		NUMBER
EVENT#		NUMBER
EVENT		VARCHAR2(64)
P1TEXT		VARCHAR2(64)
P1		NUMBER
P2TEXT		VARCHAR2(64)
P2		NUMBER
P3TEXT		VARCHAR2(64)
P3		NUMBER
WAIT_TIME		NUMBER
WAIT_COUNT		NUMBER

A very useful column of data, WAIT_COUNT, is available with this view. The following query displays session and wait information using V$SESSION_WAIT_HISTORY for all wait classes other than *Idle* and *Other*.

```
SQL> select sid, event, wait_count, wait_time
  2     from v_$session_wait_history
  3   where event# not in (select event#
  4                          from v$event_name
  5                         where wait_class in ('Idle','Other'));
```

Step 2: Consider Logical I/O

If you are running an application where every user logs in as the same Oracle user, it is much more difficult to pinpoint the actual resource hog session in the database. For that purpose, it is very meaningful to look at resource consumption from a logical I/O perspective. Given that logical I/O is where most of a foreground process's (server process) CPU time is clocked, it only makes sense to view the top CPU consumer(s) on your system. Of course, the number of waits for a given session can be repeatedly retrieved by querying V$SESSION_WAIT. Here are some additional steps that are required:

a. Run top or an equivalent command to determine the PID of the Oracle server process that is consuming the most CPU resources. The value of the session's process ID (SPID) from the query that you will see in step 3 will be the same as the value of PID in top. On Windows, the information provided by top is available in the Performance Monitor.

NOTE *Step 2(a) does not assume that the CPU is the bottlenecking component on the system.*

b. If one PID is hogging the CPU (again from a logical I/O consumption perspective), then you have the job bagged as you have identified the process consuming the most logical I/O.

c. If many PID's are equally hogging the CPU's, then pick one of those PID's as a candidate PID. In this case, they are all equally inflicting the same amount of pain.

d. If many PID's are consuming the CPU resources, but none of them are really hogging the CPU's, and no matter how much load you put on the system the CPU consumption does not increase, pick one of those PID's as a candidate PID. In this case, it is more than likely that your application is experiencing a system-wide I/O problem caused by some I/O subsystem configuration issue.

Step 3: Find the SPID for Offending Session

Using the SID value(s) obtained from step 1, identify the session's process ID (SPID) that is experiencing the most waits and that is therefore a trace candidate. Item 2(a) is for those environments where each Oracle user has an independent Oracle username. This is done to help you identify the trace file from USER_DUMP_DEST.

```
select s.username, p.spid, s.sid, s.serial#
from v_$session s, v_$process p
where s.paddr = p.addr and p.spid =<PID>;
```

Step 4: Obtain Session History

Once you have identified a given session or a set of sessions from the preceding query to be waiting more than others, it is very useful (although not compulsory) to get a historical perspective for that session from the time it logged into the database. Even for systems that use connection pooling and persistent database sessions, this query can provide a historical perspective of what sessions are waiting for.

```
SQL> set linesize 132
SQL> col event format a40
SQL> col avg_wait_secs format 99.9999
SQL> col wait_secs format 9999.9999
SQL> col connection_time format 9999.9999
SQL> undef oracle_sid_number
SQL>
SQL> select se.event, (se.average_wait/100) AVG_WAIT_SECS,
  2  sum(se.total_waits) TOTAL_WAITS,
  3  sum(se.time_waited/100) WAIT_SECS,
  4  st.connection_time_secs CONNECTION_TIME,
  5  (sum(se.time_waited/100)/st.connection_time_secs * 100) PERCENT_OF_CONNECTION
_TIME
```

```
 6   from v_$session_event se,
 7   (select ((sysdate-logon_time)*24*60*60) CONNECTION_TIME_SECS
 8      from v_$session
 9    where sid = &&oracle_sid_number ) st /* -1 needs to be added if relevant */
10   where se.sid = &&oracle_sid_number /*  -1 needs to be added if relevant */
11   group by se.event, se.average_wait/100, st.connection_time_secs
12   order by 4 desc;
```

If the preceding query does not return any rows while there are active sessions in your database, you probably are running into a bug whereby the SID value in V$SESSION_EVENT is "one less" than the input value of ORACLE_SID. If that is the case, please modify the aforementioned query by adding a "-1" on line 9.

NOTE *In an effort to put as little pain on your system as possible, the afore-mentioned queries and others used in this chapter are written directly on the view, rather than on the synonym. For example, I use* V_$SESSION *rather than* V$SESSION. *This obviates the need to resolve the synonym* V$SESSION *which in actuality points to the view* V_$SESSION. *Also, if the application environment utilizes connection pooling, multiple snapshots is required to determine the true nature of the current problem. This is because the data in* V$SESSION_EVENT *is cumulative since the start of the session.*

Step 5: Trace the Offending Session

In order to do this, carry out the following steps:

a. Set TIMED_STATISTICS to true (if not already set) for the session in question.

```
exec dbms_system.set_bool_param_in_session(sid, serial#, 'TIMED
_STATISTICS', TRUE);
```

b. Limit the amount of trace generated by modifying the default setting of MAX_DUMP_FILE_SIZE.

NOTE *You really don't want to get famous for the wrong reasons. Please ensure that there is at least 2GB of free space on the filesystem that supports* USER_DUMP_DEST.

```
exec dbms_system.set_int_param_in_session(sid, serial#, 'MAX_DUMP_FILE
_SIZE', 2147483647);
```

c. Turn on 10046 for the session in question at level 8. Crank it up to level 12 if you need bind variable values to be traced.

```
exec dbms_system.set_ev(sid, serial#, 10046, 8, '')
```

d. Run the application (relevant only if a given SQL statement is known to be problematic and has already been identified).

e. Turn off 10046 for the session in question.

```
exec dbms_system.set_ev(sid, serial#, 10046, 0, '')
```

f. Locate trace file in USER_DUMP_DEST using the SPID from step 3.

g. Run tkprof on trace file.

Using Prong I: A Simple Yet Powerful Example

Suppose that an application performance problem has been detected on an Oracle 10g database, and the root cause of it had to be determined. We'll work through an example, using the steps outlined in the previous section, to illustrate the power of using the Oracle Wait Interface.

Identifying the Bottlenecks

The following query on V$SESSION_WAIT_HISTORY ignores any waits in the Idle and Other class for the sake of simplicity.

```
SQL> select sid, event, wait_count, wait_time
  2    from v_$session_wait_history
  3  where event# not in (select event# from v$event_name where wait_class in
('Idle','Other'));
```

SID	EVENT	WAIT_COUNT	WAIT_TIME
144	db file sequential read	1	1
144	db file sequential read	1	0
144	db file sequential read	1	2
144	db file sequential read	1	1
144	db file sequential read	1	1
144	log file sync	1	0

```
        144 db file sequential read                           1          2
        144 db file sequential read                           1          1
        144 db file sequential read                           1          1
        144 db file sequential read                           1          2
        146 log file sync                                     1          6

        SID EVENT                                     WAIT_COUNT  WAIT_TIME
        ---------- --------------------------------- ---------- ----------
        146 log file sync                                     1          0
        147 db file scattered read                            1          0
        147 db file scattered read                            1          1
        147 db file scattered read                            1          0
        147 db file scattered read                            1          1
        147 db file scattered read                            1          0
        147 db file scattered read                            1          1
        147 db file scattered read                            1         11
        147 db file scattered read                            1          1
        147 db file scattered read                            1          0
        147 db file scattered read                            1          1

        SID EVENT                                     WAIT_COUNT  WAIT_TIME
        ---------- --------------------------------- ---------- ----------
        148 SQL*Net message to client                         1          0
        148 SQL*Net message to client                         1          0
        148 SQL*Net message to client                         1          0
        148 SQL*Net message to client                         1          0
        148 SQL*Net message to client                         1          0
...more rows of data

60 rows selected.
```

From the preceding query it is ascertained that session 147 is experiencing some serious I/O bottlenecks. It has a few *1 centisecond wait times* and one *11 centisecond wait times* for multi-block read requests. The normal wait times for I/O should be less than 20 milliseconds. Needless to say, we have I/O-related bottlenecks here.

Finding the SPID for Session 147

Next order of business is to determine the details for this session.

```
SQL> select S.Username, P.Spid, S.Sid, S.Serial#
  2     from V_$SESSION S, V_$PROCESS P
```

```
  3    where S.PADDR = P.ADDR
  4      and S.Sid = &&oracle_sid_value;
old   4:     and S.Sid = &&oracle_sid_value
new   4:     and S.Sid = 147
```

```
USERNAME                              SPID              SID      SERIAL#
----------------------------  ------------  ----------  ----------
DEMO_USER                             2360              147         60
```

Obtaining History for Session 147

The wait events for session 147 is retrieved to provide a historical perspective of what the session waited for and whether the waits that we have unearthed is a spike or is really a problem.

This query has been provided for completeness and is not be required in real life, once the decision to trace session 147 is made. The trace data and the generated tkprof output will allow the user to arrive at the same conclusion as this query.

```
SQL> select se.event, (se.average_wait/100) AVG_WAIT_SECS,
  2    sum(se.total_waits) TOTAL_WAITS,
  3    sum(se.time_waited/100) WAIT_SECS,
  4    st.connection_time_secs CONNECTION_TIME,
  5    (sum(se.time_waited/100)/st.connection_time_secs * 100) PERCENT_OF_CONNECTION
_TIME
  6    from v_$session_event se,
  7    (select ((sysdate-logon_time)*24*60*60) CONNECTION_TIME_SECS
  8       from v_$session
  9     where sid = &&oracle_sid_number ) st
 10    where se.sid = &&oracle_sid_number
 11    -- In the above, oracle_sid_number -1 many be needed on some releases of 9i to
deal
 12    -- with a bug in version 9i
 13    group by se.event, se.average_wait/100, st.connection_time_secs
 14    order by 4 desc;
old   9:   where sid = &&oracle_sid_number ) st
new   9:   where sid = 147 ) st
old  10: where se.sid = &&oracle_sid_number
new  10: where se.sid = 147
```

EVENT	AVG_WAIT_SECS	TOTAL_WAITS	WAIT_SECS	CONNECTION_TIME	PERCENT_OF_CONNECTION_TIME
db file scattered read	.0100	332456	2039.4700	2381.0000	85.6560269
db file sequential read	.0100	483	4.5800	2381.0000	.192356153
log file switch completion	.1400	25	3.5400	2381.0000	.148677026
log buffer space	.0000	59	.2600	2381.0000	.010919782
log file sync	.0000	56	.1000	2381.0000	.004199916
SQL*Net message from client	.0000	15	.0100	2381.0000	.000419992
undo segment extension	.0000	1	.0000	2381.0000	0
SQL*Net break/reset to client	.0000	2	.0000	2381.0000	0
SQL*Net message to client	.0000	15	.0000	2381.0000	0

From the preceding output, it is clear that more than 85% of the time spent by this session is in multi-block I/O requests.

Tracing Session 147

Time to turn on trace and get to the bottom of this. Oracle 10g provides the ability to turn on trace using the SESSION_TRACE_ENABLE procedure within the DBMS_MONITOR package. Let's make good use of it!

```
SQL> exec dbms_monitor.session_trace_enable(147,60,TRUE,FALSE); -- 10046 at level 8

PL/SQL procedure successfully completed.

SQL> -- Collect trace data for some time --
SQL> exec dbms_monitor.session_trace_disable(147,60);

PL/SQL procedure successfully completed.
```

The next order of business is to run tkprof on the trace file. The trace file has the SPID embedded in it, so we look for the trace file with the SPID value of 2360. The following is the tkprof output, which was sorted by Fetched Elapsed (FCHELA).

```
SELECT COUNT(*)
  FROM WAIT_OBJECTS_BIG
WHERE OBJECT_NAME LIKE 'T%'
```

call	count	cpu	elapsed	disk	query	current	rows
Parse	1	0.01	0.00	0	0	0	0
Execute	44	0.00	0.00	0	0	0	0
Fetch	44	65.49	491.46	936594	938476	0	44
total	89	65.50	491.47	936594	938476	0	44

```
Misses in library cache during parse: 1
Optimizer mode: ALL_ROWS
Parsing user id: 64  (DEMO_USER)   (recursive depth: 1)
```

```
Rows     Execution Plan
-------  --------------------------------------------------
      0  SELECT STATEMENT    MODE: ALL_ROWS
      0   SORT (AGGREGATE)
      0    TABLE ACCESS   MODE: ANALYZED (FULL) OF 'WAIT_OBJECTS_BIG'
              (TABLE)
```

```
Elapsed times include waiting on following events:
   Event waited on                           Times   Max. Wait  Total Waited
   ---------------------------------------   Waited  ---------- ------------
   db file sequential read                      43      0.09          0.94
   db file scattered read                    58183      0.20        429.29
***************************************************************************
```

The most offending query was identified and it was determined that the multi-block I/O waits were caused by the full-table scan on the WAIT_OBJECTS_BIG table. The execution plan for the SQL statement confirms that. The trace data categorically shows that out of the 491.47 seconds of elapsed time, 429.29 seconds were spent waiting for the multi-block I/O to be completed.

Resolution

Assume that there are valid business reasons for this query to have a response-time goal of 2 seconds or less. Given the available trace data, it is determined than

an index on the OBJECT_NAME column can provide the required response time. The
index is created and the query is traced again to verify whether the existence of the
index has helped us achieve our response time goal—2 seconds. The following is
the tkprof output for the same query after the index was created.

```
SELECT COUNT(*)
  FROM WAIT_OBJECTS_BIG
WHERE OBJECT_NAME LIKE 'T%'
```

call	count	cpu	elapsed	disk	query	current	rows
Parse	1	0.01	0.00	0	0	0	0
Execute	200	0.02	0.03	0	0	0	0
Fetch	200	0.77	1.45	171	4800	0	200
total	401	0.80	1.49	171	4800	0	200

```
Misses in library cache during parse: 1
Optimizer mode: ALL_ROWS
Parsing user id: 64  (DEMO_USER)   (recursive depth: 1)

Rows     Row Source Operation
-------  ---------------------------------------------------
    200  SORT AGGREGATE (cr=4800 pr=171 pw=0 time=1474140 us)
 687609   INDEX RANGE SCAN WAIT_OBJECTS_I_OBJECT_NAME (cr=4800 pr=171 pw=0
time=2733336 us)(object id 50414)


Rows     Execution Plan
-------  ---------------------------------------------------
      0  SELECT STATEMENT   MODE: ALL_ROWS
    200   SORT (AGGREGATE)
 687609    INDEX   MODE: ANALYZED (RANGE SCAN) OF
               'WAIT_OBJECTS_I_OBJECT_NAME' (INDEX)


Elapsed times include waiting on following events:
  Event waited on                             Times   Max. Wait  Total Waited
  ----------------------------------------    Waited  ---------- ------------
    db file sequential read                     171      0.08          0.57
********************************************************************************
```

It is very apparent here that the index solved the performance problem in the preceding scenario and facilitated us to achieve our response time goal. The elapsed time went down dramatically for the query in question and because the execution plan changed (it now uses an index), the waits for the SQL statement also changed from multi-block I/O to single-block I/O (db file sequential read).

Mission accomplished!

Identifying the OS Bottlenecks: Prong II

The OS prong of the 2-prong methodology is required for two primary reasons. First and foremost, CPU and memory bottlenecks at the operating system level cannot be diagnosed within the Oracle Wait Interface. This is because the OWI does not show any wait events that reveal a memory-related or a CPU-related wait. Secondly, any resource consumption and contention that is generated outside the realm of an Oracle database cannot be revealed by the OWI.

The Key Metrics: CPU Run Queue and Memory Scan Rate

The key OS metrics that are of significance and interest to us are the *run queue* for the CPU and the *scan rate* for memory pages. The run queue portrays the number of processes out there waiting in queue for the CPU service. Run queues increase as the demand for CPU resources increase, thus indicating "wait for the CPU resource." Scan rate indicates the number of pages the paging daemon has to scan before it can successfully service a given memory request. This is a very important metric to track as it indicates in an indirect fashion "waits while finding free memory pages" to service memory requests.

CPU Utilization: A Different Perspective

In this section, we'll consider two OS utilities for investigating CPU utilization: vmstat and sar -u.

 NOTE *Although there are specific references to UNIX commands in the following sections, the concept is very much relevant for Windows systems too. On Windows, the Performance Monitor provides the same information as* vmstat *and* sar *under the Processor and Paging sections.*

The vmstat Command

This is quite possibly the most important OS utility that a DBA needs. Consider the following command:

```
vmstat 5 10
```

This command provides virtual memory statistics and CPU bottleneck metrics every 5 seconds for 10 times and provides useful information such as rate of run queue for the CPU, paging rate, and the scan rate of the paging daemon.

When the first column of output, – r, (runnable queue of the CPU) portrays a value that is consistently and continuously greater than 2 times the number of CPU's, one can conclude with reasonable confidence that the CPU resource on that system is becoming a bottleneck.

As discussed previously, Oracle clocks most of its CPU consumption while performing logical I/O. Thus any effort to reduce and/or eliminate logical I/O on a system will go a long way in delaying the onset of a true CPU bottleneck. Other sources of CPU consumption within Oracle are parsing and SMON (pre-Oracle 10g). In Oracle 10g, background processes such as MMON, MMNL, and MMAN can consume a significant amount of CPU resources dependent on the number of sessions and the amount of activity in the database. The effect of these on production environments is yet to be determined.

Systems in today's day and age should be rarely paging, let alone swapping. Any indication of swapping or paging, and the apparent scarcity for memory that is created, is revealed by the sr(scan rate) column of the output. This scan rate should be zero (or as close to zero as possible), as this indicates that the paging daemon has not had the need to scan too many pages in the paging table, before serving up the requested memory.

Excessive paging on machines that host Oracle systems is caused by over-allocation of memory to the various Oracle memory structures, usually in a vain attempt to attain a high cache-hit ratio.

The following is a sample vmstat output.

```
$ vmstat 5 10
procs      memory            page            disk          faults         cpu
 r  b w   swap     free   re   mf   pi  po  fr de sr s1 s1 s1 sd   in    sy    cs us sy id
31  6 0 4542592 1747840 378 3631   94  262 245 0  0  0 25 25  0  2365 17793 4086 62 18 20
52  2 0 4446880 1556736 325 2474   35  300 294 0  0  0  0  0  0  1681 22277 2279 83 11  6
70  1 0 4451632 1557256 567 5702   35  404 390 0  0  0  2  2  0  1879 24490 2432 79 17  4
56  2 0 4461664 1562864 553 6001   60  289 265 0  0  0  1  1  0  1611 16779 2288 69 17 14
58  2 0 4454664 1562192 450 3765  179  374 356 0  0  0  0  0  0  1848 20948 2345 84 14  2
62  2 0 4457192 1561640 360 3179    9  504 491 0  0  0  0  0  0  1789 22680 2201 83 13  5
12  2 0 4448856 1553080 305 2701   22  216 208 0  0  0  1  2  0  1499 12331 1934 84 10  7
97  2 0 4448936 1556288 615 5030   43  582 571 0  0  0  1  1  0  2128 29096 2560 84 16  0
54  1 0 4453744 1559144 770 8629    3  286 272 0  0  0  0  0  0  1988 20503 2553 78 21  1
 6  2 0 4459680 1561424 272 2773   27  280 265 0  0  0  1  1  0  1373 10061 2027 63  9 28
```

The above vmstat output from a 4-CPU Sun Solaris machine indicates significant CPU bottlenecks during the sampling period. This is ascertained from the first column of output "r", which is the runnable queue for the CPU. It has risen as high as 97, implying that at one point there were 97 processes waiting for the CPU resource. This number is greater than 28 times the number of CPUs. The normal reasonable value for the run queue is less than or equal to twice the number of CPUs.

It should also be noted here that the "sr" column or "Scan Rate" is 0, indicating that there are no memory-related bottlenecks on this system. It is corroborated by the fact that there is not much paging activity on this system (indicated by the pi and po columns).

The sar –u Command

Although the vmstat command provides both the CPU Run Queue and the Scan Rate metrics for free memory pages, the sar -u command is still a very important utility with which to get familiar, as it provides performance practitioners with the ability to avoid being blindsided by certain system conditions. For example, it is common for an I/O bottleneck to be incorrectly diagnosed as a system-wide CPU bottleneck. This is because historically system administrators have always been taught to "have an eye" on the "% idle capacity" on a system. If %idle decreases and tends to zero, then every alarm, bell, and whistle is triggered. This again stems from the faulty thought process, i.e., 0% idle implies CPU bottleneck. Nothing could be farther from the truth. The sar -u command helps us clarify such anomalies, as it helps us identify the true nature of "idle CPU capacity." Let's take a look in more detail at this command.

Consider the following sar -u command:

```
sar -u 5 5
```

This command measures CPU utilization every 5 seconds, repeating it 5 times and categorizes the utilization of CPU into four buckets—%usr, %sys, %wio, and %idle:

- The %usr bucket is the proportion of CPU usage consumed by the users of the machine. From the OS'es perspective, Oracle is a user. Thus the CPU time spent by all Oracle processes will be accounted for under %usr.

- The %sys is the overhead of the OS on the system to perform the functions that one expects from an operating system. Functions such as interrupts, paging, and context switches are all accounted for in this bucket.

- The %wio bucket is the proportion of CPU resources that is potentially available on the system, but is not being utilized due to processes "waiting for I/O." %wio is idle capacity, just viewed in a different way.

- The %idle bucket represents the proportion of system CPU that is completely idle (and not waiting on I/O).

Operating system purists will convincingly argue for separating %wio and %idle, as in their minds %wio is not true %idle. From a theoretical standpoint that may be true, but from a practical perspective, it makes perfect sense to combine %wio and %idle on real production systems, as follows:

```
True Idle Capacity = %wio + %idle.
```

The following is a sample sar -u output.

```
#sar -u 5 5
#
SunOS europa 5.8 Generic sun4u    06/09/04

11:42:37    %usr    %sys    %wio    %idle
11:42:42      9       1      44      46
11:42:47      9       2      49      41
11:42:53      9       1      48      42
11:42:58      8       1      41      50
11:43:03      9       1      36      54

Average       9       1      44      47
#
```

The above sar -u output from another Sun Solaris machine (not the same machine from where the vmstat output above was obtained) indicates that there is not much CPU spent in %usr mode. This is understandable as most of the time is spent either in %wio or %idle. The amount of CPU spent in %sys mode is very low and that is a good thing, as OS functions are not contributing to significant levels of overhead on the system. This output clearly shows that there are significant I/O bottlenecks on the system, as literally 40% or more of system CPU resources are not utilized (waiting for I/O).

Upgrading the CPUs on this system has questionable value (if any). In fact, it may have a very detrimental effect to upgrade this system with faster CPUs, as the I/O problem will be much worse with faster CPUs. This is because a faster CPU will process instructions faster, and thus the application will get the "I/O system call" faster than before.

In this case, the relevant I/O bottlenecks need to be resolved. So to clarify my earlier point on "True Idle Capacity", that number is in excess of 80% on this system. Even if the %idle number falls, if the %wio number remains a significant number, the system should not be deemed as bottlenecking on the CPU. The bottlenecking component is I/O *not* CPU.

For example, if the aforementioned sar -u output revealed numbers such that %sys = 25 and %wio = 40, there would be every reason for concern and the true cause for such numbers should be determined. Relative high percentages of %sys indicate consumption of CPU cycles due to excessive context switches or a CPU time-slice setting in the OS Kernal that is not optimal to the workload that is supported on the system.

The point is plain and simple: if the CPU %idle capacity is 0 and there are significant numbers in %sys and %wio, then the root cause of that should be determined before any attempt to add more CPU capacity is made. If %wio is 40% and %idle is 0%, then there is no question that the system has an I/O problem, not a CPU bottleneck.

Alternatively, if the %usr bucket shows a very high number, knowing that Oracle clocks most of its CPU time on logical I/O, any reduction in logical I/O will automatically translate into a reduction in CPU consumption. Reducing resource consumption and avoiding wastage are essential elements of any proactive performance management strategy.

In the end, if all relevant SQL statements have already been optimized and there is very little %idle capacity, and nobody is complaining of performance problems, we really need to step back and ask ourselves the question—why do we care? Bottom line—if there is no response time issue, why tune anything?

CTD Case Notes

In my life as a consultant, I have had the privilege of witnessing some of the wackiest performance problems. I want to say that most of these problems were self-inflicted and were caused by people suffering from CTD. I could feel their souls crying out for help.

CTD Sufferer #1

If my Oracle instance attains a 99%+ library cache-hit ratio, any SQL-related performance problems will vanish.

My consulting services were summoned to fix a performance problem at a telecommunication services corporation. Minutes after entering the building, I was looking for "the signs." I discovered that the Oracle initialization file (initSID.ora) is 8 pages long. Right there I knew CTD was in the air ducts at this site.

The memory-related parameters of the database had been tuned to the extent the Oracle instance had turned blue and purple. And oh, by the way, the change history describing who changed a given parameter's value from value X to value Y on a certain date was maintained with utmost accuracy. The change history and the 8-page init.ora file resounded to me without any doubt that these folks had been suffering from CTD for over five years.

Before Image

The initSID.ora file has been tuned out of this planet. Memory has been systematically and periodically added to the SHARED_POOL_SIZE parameter in the vain hope that at some point magic and divine intervention will occur. SHARED_POOL_SIZE was 4.5GB when I walked in. The application was suffering from severe response time issues. I am not kidding when I tell you that select sysdate from dual; was taking 15 minutes to return a date value. And there was talk about the system potentially experiencing I/O bottlenecks! To get around the problem, the DBA had set up a cron job to flush the shared pool every 30 minutes. I was desperately seeking to meet another human being to ask them to *"Just shoot me ..."* and put me out of this pain.

Diagnosis

The Oracle instance was suffering from a serious parsing bottleneck. The response time issues were all stemming from parsing hiccups. The shared pool and library cache latches were the primary source of the waits. This was determined by tracing a set of sessions and analyzing the wait events in the trace file. The application had no trace of any bind variable usage. Literally, thousands of identical SQL statements were present in the shared pool. Setting the Oracle initialization parameter CURSOR_SHARING=FORCE was not an option on that version (8.0.5.X).

After Image

We entered the Dilbert School of Hard Knocks—*Stick to the Basics*. The application was rewritten using bind variables. Yes, in this case, the application code was not buried at depths that made scuba diving illegal. We could actually change the code and observe its immediate impact on the system. Response time issues had all but vanished. Eventually SHARED_POOL_SIZE was shrunk to 256MB. Did I mention that SORT_AREA_SIZE on this Oracle instance was not explicitly set, thus defaulted to a whopping 64KB? This was a classic case of feeding Peter to death, starving Paul, and wondering what ever happened to Mary! Get it?!

CTD Sufferer #2

As soon as my Oracle instance attains a 90%+ database buffer cache-hit ratio, all performance problems will be automatically solved.

Have you ever read the *Dilbert* cartoon where the employee is pointing out exactly the source of a problem, but the manager insists on hiring a consultant? Well, I had the pleasure of experiencing that cartoon in real life first hand. Here is how the story goes. The junior DBA at this large corporation had already identified the source of a performance problem. But the senior DBA was a CTD sufferer and thus everything came to a grinding halt with him. Management was obviously facing the pressure of bad application performance and was leaning on the senior DBA's recommendation for next steps. The senior DBA was overruling and ignoring the junior DBA's diagnosis. Management decided to hire a consultant to figure out what was wrong. In walked the consultant—yours truly. What I found was pretty much in line with what the junior DBA had found. I just gave him enough ammunition to tell everyone "*I told you so.*"

Before Image

The database buffer cache was 9GB, and signs of multiple iterations of editing the database buffer cache parameter were very evident from the Oracle initialization file. These folks were suffering from some faulty thought processes. Here were some:

- *Faulty thought process #1:* The more memory you allocate to Oracle, the better it will perform.

- *Faulty thought process #2:* If you eliminate physical I/O, your system will perform like greased lightning.

- *Faulty thought process #3:* Avoiding full-table scans is quintessential to significant performance gains.

Again, these faulty thought processes and the misplaced hope that was derived from them left the team, their database, and application performance in a quandary. Needless to say, application response time was terrible (way above the required response time goal), yet CPU consumption on the box was very high.

Diagnosis

Severe contention for database buffer latches (cache buffers chains latch). Moderate contention for single block I/O (db file sequential read) and buffers (buffer busy waits). The cause for severe latch contention stemmed from the fact that almost every SQL statement had a /*+ RULE */ hint. The general thinking went along the lines that every SQL statement will perform at its best if and only if it used an index.

The /*+ RULE */ hint provided an easy way to implement that thought process, as long as at least one underlying index was created on the table. So, with multiple sessions reading and rereading the same index blocks, cache buffers chains latch contention and CPU consumption skyrocketed. The buffer busy waits problem was caused by lack of freelists for one specific transactional table, into which many concurrent inserts were performed.

 NOTE *The definition of severe and moderate has been deliberately omitted as there are no magical numbers for these. In the preceding case, commonsense percentages (50% or more for severe and 15% for moderate) were used.*

After Image

The fix-it process was a bit painful, as every SQL statement had to be edited to remove the /*+ RULE */ hint. The transactional table identified previously was rebuilt with multiple freelists. All pretuning symptoms that were observed were now significantly lower. Lastly, the relevant OPTIMIZER parameters like OPTIMIZER_INDEX_CACHING and OPTIMIZER_MAX_PERMUTATIONS were modified to provide the optimizer some reasonable value (other than the defaults that it came with). This was done to provide some reasonable guidance for the optimizer, to use the index when appropriate, to opt for a full-table scan when appropriate, and to derive reasonable execution plans based on the most effective driving table in the FROM clause. The tuning or optimization effort ended when the application began responding within the prescribed response time goals.

Conclusion

After 48 pages of literary therapy, I hope I have impressed upon you why the Oracle Wait Interface is the single source of diagnostic information to solve Oracle performance problems. It is the key to curing CTD. I hope you are at the good state where you will no longer bet your life on the information provided by database cache-hit ratios. They are more often than not pretty meaningless numbers. The two-pronged performance tuning effort is repeatable and is far more consistent than any cache hit ratio in your database. It is your route out of CTD. Even though performance management is a continuous and iterative process, you don't want to find yourself in an infinite loop.

The effective management of Oracle database performance requires adherence to a systematic methodology—one that ensures that all the core components of a system are addressed in a systematic fashion. With the two-pronged performance management approach, you will experience repeated success in your performance tuning efforts and may even have time to spend with your family and loved ones. Discipline needs to be exercised in setting reasonable tuning goals and ceasing all efforts when the tuning goals are achieved. *When you achieve your tuning goals, cease all efforts to further tune any component. That is the only way you will be able to get out of the vicious cycle of CTD. Good luck and may the force be with you ...*

References

1. Holt, Jeff, and Cary Millsap. "Oracle System Performance Analysis Using Oracle Event 10046." Hotsos (http://www.hotsos.com), 2002.

2. Van der Kolk, Bessel A. "The Compulsion to Repeat the Trauma." *Psychiatric Clinics of North America* 12, no. 2 (1989): 389–411.

3. Millsap, Cary. "Why a 99%+ Cache-hit Ratio is NOT Ok?" Proceedings of the International Oracle Users Group—Americas, 2001.

4. Millsap, Cary, and Jeff Holt. *Optimizing Oracle Performance*. Sebastopol, CA: O'Reilly & Associates, 2003.

5. Shallahamer, Craig. "Direct Contention Identification Using Oracle's Session Wait Virtual Tables." OraPub white paper, 2001.

6. Vaidyanatha, Gaja Krishna, Kirtikumar Deshpande, and John A. Kostelac. *Oracle Performance Tuning 101*. Emeryville, CA: Osborne McGraw-Hill, 2001.

7. Vaidyanatha, Gaja Krishna. "Oracle Performance Management." Proceedings of Oracle OpenWorld 2000.

8. Zabenskie, Audrey. *Life Behind Bars: Living with Obsessive Compulsive Disorder*. Winnipeg: 2002.

Dear Reader,

*I met James at the Oracle World conference in Berlin in 2001, where Anjo grabbed me and said "Hey, you **have** to meet James! He's written a very good book, and he's very smart ..." And then I met this young man (well, young compared to the rest of us), who turned out to be a) rather pleasant and b) rather smart.*

Since then it's been uphill. We have hired him in to work at a few Danish customer sites, and it's always a big success. His presentations (Sane SAN, Unbreakable, etc.) are always hits, and his troubleshooting abilities are simply fantastic.

With James, it's either computers or music. He started coding when he was 10 and sold a program (Lawn Mower Man?) when he was 13. Meanwhile, he learned to play, had a band (a tape with James singing exists somewhere, his brilliant wife Elaine claims), and probably did a million other things.

His book—Scaling Oracle8i—is among the five Oracle-related books you should bring to the deserted island if you're ever so lucky as to end up there for a while, and I think it was published when he was only 30. It took him two years to write it simply because he did real research for it, and it shows.

I think he's 34 as this book is published, and by sheer coincidence I'm sitting in his house in Cirencester in England while writing this (June 2004). Guess what? His garage space is taken up by 1) a huge rack with his 4–5 node RAC cluster and an EMC SAN and 2) several HUGE loudspeakers that he bought a couple of days ago.

The loudspeakers are marked Turbosound and each of them is the size of Miracle's headquarters. They require about 5,000 watts of output from the amplifiers. James's idea is to have a respectable PA sound system that he can rent out for concerts and other events. After that I think it will be a small step for him to start playing in a band again (to the utter horror of his teenage daughter Becky, whose nightmare vision is her father playing for her teenage friends at a school gig).

Meanwhile, in his parallel IT universe, James has just prototyped a program that might very well become an instant bestseller in the Java/database world.

His baptism of fire was the Brushco experience that he so vividly describes in this chapter, and it made him even stronger. In the insane multi-multi-component and -tiers environments of today, he's one of the few who can keep up with all of it, and that includes the physical properties of network cables and the latest version of Suse Linux.

Remember the Matrix movies? When the heroes needed an escape they called the operator named Tank and said "Tank—I need an exit." I call James with that phrase whenever I have a problem I don't know what to do about. He's either solved them, or led me down the correct path, in every case so far.

As you can perhaps deduct from the BAARF appendix and other remarks in this book, James is also a lot of fun to be around. He can't stop inventing, be it the BAARF acronym, the OakTable Press label, or a software program.

I think we have many beers and associated ideas ahead of us, mate.

—Mogens Nørgaard

CHAPTER 8

New Releases and Big Projects

By James Morle

RARELY DO SINGLE PROJECTS provide such opportunity for learning. "Insight through pain," one of the proposed titles for this book, seems to encapsulate perfectly the impact of this project on my life. Like a parasite, the insights from this project have been a permanent part of my life ever since, involved in every technical instinct and decision made.

To protect the innocent and the guilty alike, the description of this project has been heavily fictionalized. None of the names, places, or industries have been allowed through unmodified, though all of the technical details are verbatim. This project is described throughout this chapter, but it's worth a fast, broad-brush introduction at this stage.

During this project, I was working as a DBA for a relatively small systems integrator who was in turn contracted to provide all IT services to their customer. The deal was heavily front-loaded with a large development project, and this development followed the usual phased release process of developing code in functional blocks and releasing it into production. This meant that the rollout of the users onto the new system could also be staged accordingly, thus reducing the risk compared to taking the alternative "big bang" approach. Despite this approach, and despite having many very smart people working long weeks, the project encountered many serious difficulties, some of which will be highlighted here. The intent is twofold:

- To emphasize approaches and attitudes to new software

- To explain specific lessons learned in technical terms

The Arrival

In the summer of 1993, I got married to my wonderful wife, Elaine. To this day, however, we have been denied the traditional form of honeymoon. By traditional, I mean one where we can relax and reflect upon our new joint existence. Instead, I was informed by my new employer that it was impossible for them to wait another week for me to start my duties, and that my first day with them should be almost immediately after my wedding day. After an impromptu few days in Cornwall, in a tent, it was time to find out what it was that couldn't wait.

Upon arrival at the offices, near a major UK airport, it became apparent that my immediate manager, Mark, was not in the office. Well, not in this office at least. He was in our data center office, near a major French airport. He also did not know of my employment because nobody had informed him. A strange sensation was building inside me, one which had actually started during my interview. The sensation was one of a company on fire. Not completely on fire, but the trouser legs were certainly burning. You see, I had actually attended the interview for a position as a UNIX systems administrator, but had spent the whole interview answering Oracle-related questions. It turns out that the DBA team had "got to me first" in the office reception, and thus shaped the rest of my career so far.

As it turned out, the first week was relatively sedate. The UK office was occupied by developers and development DBA's, not to mention the usual plethora of overhead. For them, life was comparatively good, having recently released the first delivery of code into production (a *code drop*). Telephone calls with Mark were a little different, to say the least. The very first batch of users was live in production, and things weren't exactly going to plan, to put it mildly. In fact, this was the IT equivalent of the Apollo 13 moon mission.

This is as good a time as any to describe a little of the detail behind this project, and why it was such a big deal at the time. It will also give us our first two *Insights* of this chapter.

The Project

The project had a codename, as all projects do. For the purposes of this book, and the fact that it was carried out near two major airports, we will call it *Project Runway*. We'll call the systems integration company for which I worked *TLA*, because most modern SI companies appear to have three letters. TLA had a multi-year deal with the end customer, which was in the business of renting out toilet brushes. Of course they weren't really, but remember this is fictionalized. We will call the end customer *Brushco*.

Before describing the attributes of Project Runway, it's worth revisiting 1993 and setting the scene. You see, that year marked the end of Oracle version 6, and the beginning of Oracle7. This is a significant point, because prior to Oracle7, the Oracle RDBMS was really best suited to what we would now classify as a workgroup solution. With notable exceptions that were a few times larger, Oracle version 6 installations typically served 30–50 concurrent users. As with all major Oracle releases, Oracle7 was full of amazing innovations that allowed it to scale to never before seen heights. As with all major Oracle releases, you aren't actually meant to believe it until you have tried it. This is nearly an *Insight*, but a few more elaborations and a different intervening *Insight* are needed first.

The Runway team really did believe in the potential of Oracle7. Yes sir, they believed it: they had to, it was the underpinnings of the whole project, and this project needed to support 3,000 concurrent users!

> **INSIGHT 1:** *Scalability should never be taken for granted. It should also not be the sole responsibility of the RDBMS software—it is an architectural problem, not the domain of any single component. Whenever sizing numbers grow by a number of multiples, and particularly when they grow by orders of magnitude, ring the fire bell. If you don't, nobody else will: lives depend on it.*

Project Runway was designed to unite a fragmented IT solution that was fundamental to the success of a company borne of acquisition. Eighteen totally different and incompatible applications spread over nine countries, hosted on various mainframe architectures, meant that Brushco did not have any central view of the operation of their business. Worse than that, if a customer rented a toilet brush in Italy and returned it in Germany, the systems could not handle that situation at all. This resulted in a relatively high level of toilet brush theft.

So, Brushco went to market to find a systems integrator to help them unite these systems, and to do so with a new application that would give them such corporate power that they could crush their competition. The end goal was a single, centralized system that could support 3,000 users distributed across 450 different sites all over Europe.

In order to win this business my company, TLA, needed to come up with something radical. It needed a solution that could be delivered cheaper, faster, and with more functionality than the other contenders. TLA looked to the current favorite in the IT business—Rapid Application Development (RAD) and Client/ Server technology. Oracle had a really good story in this area (see Dave Ensor's Chapter 1), having practically invented it, and so were selected as the technology provider.

Rapid Application Development

Rapid Application Development is the Nirvana of software development. Ever since the birth of software, scientists have been trying to find simpler and faster ways to produce it. By and large they have succeeded, though each success so far has carried with it a degree of baggage. The underlying principle is very simple: make the computer do as much of the actual programming work as possible, leaving the developer to just define the required solution.

To understand this a little better, consider that all computers execute binary instructions. This is true whether the computer is a server running Oracle or SQL Server, or a Nintendo Gamecube running the latest cute game. To develop such complex software from scratch as binary code would be incredibly time consuming, so much so that software is no longer ever created this way. The lowest level of software development is now *assembly language*, which is a mnemonic representation of the actual instructions that the CPU executes. Even so, assembly language quickly becomes unwieldy for all but the smallest of low-level tasks; much of the development is concerned with moving data between registers and memory, and other such administrative functions associated with the execution of the actual task.

The lowest level mainstream development language used today is C. This is the language that was used to develop the Oracle RDBMS and, with modern compiler technologies, is nearly always as fast as or faster than the best efforts of assembly programmers. However, it is still very close to being a native machine language, and so developers still have the burden of carefully navigating the finer points (such as memory allocation and de-allocation) rather than applying their minds to the actual solution required.

The logical next step was Fourth Generation Language (4GL) technology, the spirit of which most database development environments adhere to. A 4GL is designed to allow the programmer to concentrate on implementing the actual required logic, rather than be concerned with much of the underlying detail. Often, a 4GL is geared towards a specific goal, such as database-centric programming. SQL*Forms is one of these, as is PowerBuilder and Delphi. For a more modern example, Java is a 4GL too, once the many frameworks and development environments are applied.

RAD is the next level of abstraction above 4GL. RAD endorses an approach where solutions are described in relatively abstract terms, and code is generated for the 4GL below. CASE*Designer/Generator fits into this mold, and was the mainstay of Oracle's RAD solution. Though the terminology is no longer used, RAD still exists today in the form of such things as J2EE "frameworks," 3D game "engines," and many ERP systems' pseudo-code. And now back to the project, where the use of RAD was both a triumph and disaster concurrently!

RAD-ical Runway

The central idea behind Project Runway went something like this: define the business problem and requirements adequately in CASE*Designer, press the "Go" button on CASE*Generator, and out comes a complete application. The scalability would all be provided by the new features of the Oracle RDBMS.

It is worth mentioning at this point that two very fine and distinguished fellows, Dave Ensor and Graham Wood, had already spent some time with TLA explaining that this was madness. Not that they didn't believe in RAD and client/server—they were Oracle employees after all. They merely pointed out that, of the numerous areas of concern in this plan, the use of client/server and RAD would mean that the database would need to perform more work than it would if a three-tier solution were developed. TLA decided that a three-tier model would prevent them from delivering the project within the time and budget constraints, and so all eyes were on the new Oracle7 product.

Of the many new features of the new Oracle7 product, which ones would TLA need to adopt to make this work?

The first big adoption was *Multi-Threaded Server* (MTS). For the benefit of those not familiar with this technology, I will explain the principles shortly, but for now just work on the basis of it providing a way to share database connections.

Fair enough, the idea of sharing connections to the database made it sound more than a little TP-monitor-like. Surely this would at least save on one of the very scarcest resources in system like this in 1993, namely memory. We'll get back to that one shortly.

The next big area of concern was processor capacity—even some terribly optimistic initial testing had shown that the largest machine available at the time (an eight processor i486 machine) was only able to provide half the required capacity. Ah, that's where the wonders of *Oracle Parallel Server* (OPS) were to save the day. When the largest machine is not large enough, OPS is your friend. The same is still true today with RAC, where it makes very good sense when the largest single server available to you will not provide sufficient processor capacity.

You don't need a crystal ball to guess that there were problems with this approach. Even taken individually, MTS and OPS are more extensive features than any others built into the product in recent years. Combining the use of these two new features with yet another very complex change to the product, the new *SQL cache*, was perhaps not the wisest move for a new project. That brings us at last to the next *Insight*.

> **INSIGHT 2:** *Using new functionality before you have comprehensively tested it is almost always a path to failure. Worse still is relying upon such technologies for the success of the project. Databases are software, and as such subject to bugs. The larger the feature (in terms of engineering), the more potential there is for bugs.*
>
> *It's worth pointing out that the people making these decisions were not stupid people in any way. In fact, they are some of the smartest people I have had the pleasure of working with, and they taught me an enormous amount about the data center business. However, when projects get large enough, decision processes become affected by many influences, including some that should not have any bearing at all. Financial, political, and technical issues all get thrown into the mix. That's all the more reason to stand firm behind risk adverse principles of systems engineering.*

Perhaps one of the reasons this didn't occur was some kind of implicit trust in the software vendor, in this case Oracle. My esteemed colleagues had come from the mainframe old-school, where stability and testing are given a higher priority. In fact, they are given such a high priority that this frequently results in restricted flexibility and a lower number of features in order to maintain stability. The worlds of open systems, Oracle, and even of closed operating systems such as Windows do not operate this way—for good and bad reasons. It's important to reap the benefits of this flexibility while maintaining prudence of judgment in terms of stability.

Multi-Threaded Server[1]

Much of the time at this point of the rollout was spent investigating the strange side effects of running MTS. Let's take a quick look at the MTS architecture before proceeding. In the standard "dedicated server" mode of operation that most are familiar with, Oracle creates a private connect process (or thread on the Windows platform) on the database server for each connection to the database, one which is used exclusively for the requests from the session that created it. That is, if there are 50 database connections, there will be 50 processes on the database server to handle those requests. In MTS, there are fewer processes than there are connections to the database, and a new set of processes to handle incoming requests and marshal the work to one of the *shared servers*. Figure 8-1 will help to clarify this concept.

---

1. Renamed to Shared Server in release 9.0.1 and later

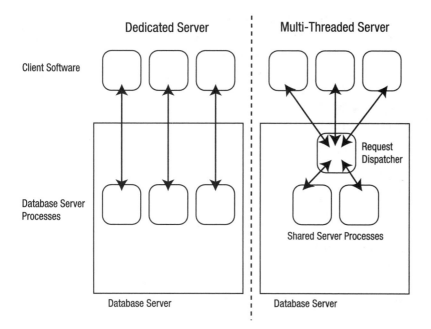

Figure 8-1. *Dedicated Server vs. Multi-Threaded Server*

In Figure 8-1, it can be seen that, in the Dedicated Server model, there is a 1:1 ratio between client programs and database connection processes. In the case of the Multi-Threaded Server, the client programs are only directly associated with a new process called a *dispatcher*. It is the role of the dispatcher to receive incoming requests and to pass them on to the next available database server process. The idea of this architecture is that, if users only have relatively short transactions, a fewer number of server processes can service the entire workload.

During the implementation of Runway, it quickly became apparent that these so-called multithreaded servers were not in fact multithreaded, but rather serially reusable. In other words, the server processes were not capable of executing different requests concurrently, but rather could only service one at a time.

One significant side effect of this was that the Oracle locking model dramatically restricted the servers' ability to service the needs of other users. For example, if User1 performs an update on a row (thus taking out a TX lock on that row), the shared server used would be held in context by that user session (what is now named a WAIT(ENQ) state), and thereby be unusable for other sessions. This meant that, for this very OLTP workload, shared servers were very often held for longer than desirable periods, simply because of lock duration rather than the actual time spent executing real work. This implied that more shared servers were needed than had been estimated, thus increasing the memory footprint on the database server.

It should be noted that the entire previous paragraph was written without mention of bugs. That does not mean there were no bugs. In fact, there were many, many bugs associated with this first release of MTS, nearly all of which were related to its dependence upon the shared pool for the allocation of session memory. Between MTS and non-shared SQL, I experienced my first introduction to the dreaded ORA-04031 error, one which I am still seeing today!

For those not accustomed to the ORA-04031 error, the error text is as follows:

```
04031, 00000, "unable to allocate %s bytes of shared memory (\"%s\",\"%s\",\"%s\"
,\"%s\")"
// *Cause:  More shared memory is needed than was allocated in the shared
//          pool.
// *Action: If the shared pool is out of memory, either use the
//          dbms_shared_pool package to pin large packages,
//          reduce your use of shared memory, or increase the amount of
//          available shared memory by increasing the value of the
//          INIT.ORA parameters "shared_pool_reserved_size" and
//          "shared_pool_size".
//          If the large pool is out of memory, increase the INIT.ORA
//          parameter "large_pool_size".
```

This is the new version of the message, and presents very much more help than the "increase the size of your shared pool" message from prior releases. What it still fails to explain is the actual cause of the error. This error is triggered when

1. A request is made for space in shared pool, perhaps for the purpose of parsing a new cursor

2. No space is available in the shared pool

3. After flushing every object in the pool that is eligible to be flushed, there is still insufficient space

By implication, this error means bad things to all users of the database, because it is highly likely that this request has resulted in the flushing of a significant quantity of potentially reusable cache in the pool. Frequently this error is actually pointing to a seriously fragmented shared pool, which leaves Oracle with difficulties in finding usable space.

System Sizing

So now my second week started. Perhaps unsurprisingly, it started in the data center office in France, as would become the trend for the next two years. If you own a stout pair of ear defenders, please feel free to ask my then-new bride about this commuting-to-France experience.

The first 300 of the 3,000 users were happily using the system. These users all worked in call centers, taking reservations for toilet brush rentals. They were using Forms v3, connected using MTS to an Oracle7 v7.0.13 database running on an 8-way NCR 3600 server. This server was connected to two other 3600s in a cluster, but no users were running on the other nodes. Each 3600 had eight 50 MHz (yes, fifty) Intel 80486 CPU's. The significance of the 7.0.13 version of the database is that it was the very first release of Oracle7. Version 7.0.12 was a "Developers Release," and almost to the day of the release of 7.0.13, Brushco went live in production.

In addition to the dysfunctional nature of MTS, upon which the success of Project Runway depended, something else was clearly wrong. The NCR 3600 had 512MB of memory, which was quite a lot in those days (if you had 4MB of memory in your PC, you were doing well). The trouble was that only about 50MB of memory was actually free once the SGA, Distributed Lock Manager (DLM), and process memory were taken into account—the server was more or less fully utilized. You might be wondering why we were running a DLM at this point—the answer is simple: we were planning ahead for OPS, and didn't want to require a systems outage to bring up the database in multi-instance mode. This overhead was extremely significant in terms of system memory, as memory was needed in both the DLM and the SGA to maintain lock state, thus leaving very little memory on the server once all the allocations were made.

So, let's do some elementary arithmetic on the data points we have. Three hundred users were more-or-less consuming a whole node in terms of memory (and CPU, for that matter), and we needed to support three thousand users. Doesn't that mean we would need ten nodes, not three? I seem to recall asking the same question myself. So what was going wrong?

The answer is that nothing was going wrong at all. The wrongness had all happened many months ago during a proof of concept that was fundamentally flawed. Giving credit where it is due, at least there was a proof of concept, and the intentions were good. The problem was that it was performed using a simplistic simulation of the application, written before the application was even designed. This simulation was written in Pro*C, whereas the real application was written in Forms, and its definition of a transaction was impressively simplistic. It was like the difference between a naval destroyer and a movie-set model: apart from looking quite similar, the model bears no relation at all to the real thing.

The net result of this was that the system was dramatically undersized, which brings us to our next insight:

> **INSIGHT 3:** *Do the necessary preparation for your system sizing—generate representative tests in order to produce meaningful baseline data. Check it. Double check it, Triple check it. Test it. Check the tests. Repeat the tests. It's this sizing stage where the budgets are set, and mistakes made here can be very difficult and expensive to rectify.*

We Need Bigger Guns ...

In the case of TLA, action had to be taken and fast. NCR were the first to jump in with their kernel engineers and their best technicians. They brought their latest hardware in their luggage (seriously) from the States, but they were unable to provide a system powerful enough to complete the user rollout. Oracle sent in their most senior NCR porting engineer from Blackrock in Ireland, which was the first time I met with Anjo Kolk. In between discovering plenty of bugs in the software, Anjo introduced me to this useful new view called v$session_wait, which proved to be a turning point in the way I approached Oracle performance and diagnostics. Anjo was a great evangelist of time-based tuning even then, something which would eventually be called the YAPP-Method (see Chapter 4 for Anjo's description of how the YAPP-Method came into being).

It was time to talk to other hardware vendors. The only two that were even remotely capable of delivering on the newly calculated hardware requirements were Sequent and Pyramid. I mourn the loss of both of these companies most profoundly, by the way. Between them they shaped the high-end UNIX server market as we know it today. Sun, HP, and IBM were floundering way behind these guys at this point.

The first replacement platform candidate to land in France was a *Pyramid Nile* series. Several very large servers sat shrouded in bubble-wrap inside the raised floor area for approximately one week, until it was determined that a fundamental restriction in the operating system would physically prevent the connection of more than one thousand users! I'm not sure where that information came from, but around the same time Sequent appeared with a good story, great attitude, and some of the best software technicians I have worked with from a hardware company. They were proposing a two-node cluster of 16-way SE60 servers, boasting mind-numbingly fast Pentium processors running at 60 MHz.

More importantly, the machines would support 1.5GB of memory each, and had a highly effective and configurable virtual memory system which could milk the maximum from the available memory.

They also proposed an upgrade of Oracle to the significantly more stable 7.0.15 release, and also to ditch MTS in favor of a dedicated server solution. The logic behind this was simple; we would benefit from losing the MTS functionality and memory management bugs and, by moving the session memory back out to the operating system, adopt a rational virtual memory management strategy.

Sequent stood behind their pitch, and partnered with TLA to produce a realistic benchmark, using the proposed hardware and software, on site in the French data center. The project was highly successful, and Sequent secured the business with TLA.

Migrating to Sequent

It was time to migrate the database servers from NCR to Sequent. Once the hardware was installed and configured (and Sequent also had some of the best hardware engineers I have worked with), we were ready to start the migration. This was a real/proper/hardcore 24×7 system, where toilet brushes could be rented at any time of the day or night, and so downtime had to be kept down to the strictest minimum. Luckily, one of the smart things TLA had worked on with Brushco from the early days was the development of strong manual front office procedures:

> **INSIGHT 4:** *Manual procedures are not always possible. However, the vast majority of business can exist for short periods with some well-thought-out procedures. Trading applications and automated systems such as ATM and web applications are impossible to define manual procedures for, of course, because there is no human interaction. For counter-based systems, however, the pen can be mightier than the sword when there needs to be a system outage!*

Changing Character Sets

During all the shenanigans of testing new platforms and running the first batch of users in production, another problem had come to light. This was a pan-European application, and thus required all 8-bits of the ASCII character set in order to handle accented characters such as ü, ñ, and ø. Unfortunately, however, the database had been erroneously created in US7ASCII mode, and so this presented something of a challenge. The challenge was not, as you may think, storing and retrieving the required 8-bit characters. In fact, that was working perfectly because of a little-known optimization of Oracle's NLS facility, which means that if the database *and* the client both have identical NLS environment variables set, *no* conversion takes place upon the transfer between the two. Therefore, if the Forms application was running with a US7ASCII character set, everything worked perfectly.

The bad part of this is that we were migrating from one port of Oracle (NCR 3600) to another (Sequent DYNIX/ptx), and so the only way to do this was via export and import. If we exported the production database using the required 8-bit WE8ISO8859P1 character set, the export facility would kindly intervene and strip all the accented characters because it was coming from a 7-bit datasource. If we exported using a 7-bit US7ASCII character set, everything was fine until we came to import it into our target WE8ISO8859P1 database! When combined with a limited time window, and a large (for the time) 100GB database, we needed some nonstandard solutions. The answer was to use a combination of techniques.

We could not wait for exports to finish before importing, because the allowable downtime was too short (seven hours), so it was clear that we had to use some kind of streaming mechanism. The conventional-path export was too slow on its own to march through the entire database, so we also had to have multiple exports running concurrently. It turns out that the optimal number for our 10MB Ethernet networks was seven, which we ascertained during a dry run the weekend before. So now, with a little plumbing expertise, we could run seven export jobs into named pipes, which were read by gzip executed from the remote node by a remote shell, which fed into another named pipe on the target end, which was read by imp using the indexes=n setting. Phew. That didn't solve the character set conversion, though, so we developed a new piece of plumbing (in the form of a very simple C program) which listened for the appropriate byte (by offset and value) in the export header and "nobbled" it on the way through. This allowed us to export the 8-bit characters by using a US7ASCII character set, but fool the receiving database into thinking the export had been done with WE8ISO8859P1.

The data migration phase of the platform changeover took three hours, and the multiple streams of serial index creation took a further three hours. We had achieved a platform migration within our allowable time window.

Problems with RAID

Further changes took place upon the migration to the Sequent platform. I did not mention this previously, probably because I was just too embarrassed, but the disk subsystem on the NCR was the dreaded RAID-5. In actuality, the problems of the system hadn't yet got to the point where the disk system was the main bottleneck, but nevertheless it was time to do things right. Or, at least, almost right …

The disk configuration proposed by Sequent was RAID 0+1, providing quite a performance boost compared to the old RAID-5 system. However, there was still one subtle flaw in this configuration, one which would cause untold operational problems in the future. The RAID levels were backwards!

To elaborate this statement, it would be useful to refer to Figure 8-2.

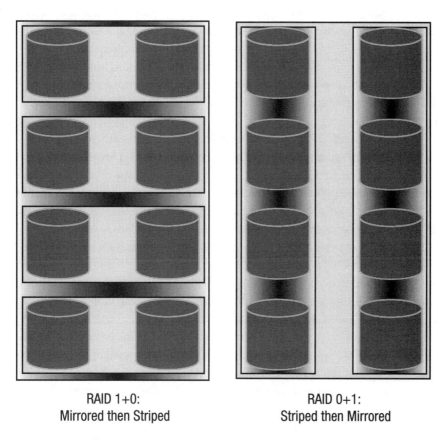

RAID 1+0:
Mirrored then Striped

RAID 0+1:
Striped then Mirrored

Figure 8-2. Differences of RAID 1+0 and RAID 0+1

In the case of RAID 0+1, each individual disk is first striped with its fellow members, and this whole stripe is then mirrored to an identical stripe. Conversely, RAID 1+0 starts by mirroring each individual disk, and then builds a stripe on top of those protected disks. Theoretically, both configurations should provide identical performance, given the same number and configuration of disks and controllers. Any write will result in a write to at least two disks, and any read can occur from either of two disks. Large sequential reads and writes can effectively maximize the performance of all disks in the stripe, all at once. However, there is an important difference in reliability ...

Consider the failure scenario where one disk fails in the array. In the case of 0+1, the failure of a single disk renders *the whole stripe* offline. In addition to effectively halving the read capability of the array, if one of the members of the surviving stripe were now to fail, complete data loss of that array would be experienced.

Now consider the case of 1+0, where one disk has failed. In this case, all other disks will remain operational, both protecting the data and providing full I/O capability less just one disk. If a further disk were to fail before the first disk was replaced, the impact would now depend upon which disk failed: if the second failure was the mirror-pair of the first disk, complete data loss would occur, as in the 0+1 case. However, if *any other* disk failed, the data would remain intact. In the case of Figure 8-2, it is theoretically possible to lose four active disks before any data loss is felt. It's extremely unlikely you would be that lucky, but theoretically possible nonetheless!

So, the RAID level was backwards. In addition, this was an early implementation of a logical volume manager, one without the concept of a Dirty Region Log (DRL). A DRL is used in modern software mirroring implementations to keep track of areas of disk that have potentially been written to. This is the first operation that occurs when issuing a write, and is a kind of safety net for use in failure situations. The particular failure situation in question is where multiple writes must be performed to satisfy a single logical write by the operating system such as, notably, to a mirrored disk.

When the operating system issues the physical write I/O's for a single logical write, these must be issued as two individual writes—there is no concept of an atomic (unbreakable) multiple I/O operation. This means that, should the operating system crash, there is no way to determine whether both the writes associated with a single logical write were successfully initiated and acknowledged before the operating system had the rug pulled from under it. Therefore, it is highly possible that some of the writes were only made to one side of the mirror, making the mirror inconsistent.

There are two simple ways to remedy this problem. The first remedy only applies when some kind of journaling technology is employed, either by a filesystem or by a database. In a journaled filesystem or a database, the journal (or redo log, in the case of Oracle) is written to before the actual data is written out. Using a journal, the mirroring software could hand off the responsibility of making sure both sides of the mirror are consistent to the filesystem or database, forcing a replay of the writes that occurred just before the mirror became inconsistent. Therefore, both sides of the mirror are now consistent. However, this method never really took off, and has largely disappeared.

Instead of replaying logs or journals, the most common method of making the mirror consistent is by copying the contents of one side of the mirror to the other. In fact, this was the only method available at that time anyway, and the concept of a Dirty Region Log was not yet born. Therefore, whenever there was a system crash, there was a high chance that the whole database would have to be copied from one side of the mirror to the other, because all the mirror sets had been marked inconsistent! Though this was an online operation (the database could be started and users working while it took place), it was also a highly CPU- and I/O-intensive operation. The implication of this was that the mirror refresh (known as resilvering) often had to be throttled back to run very slowly, thus leaving the disk subsystem open to secondary errors (and thus data loss, because the RAID levels were backwards) for entire business days at a time. If this had happened very rarely, it might not have been too terrible, but as we get onto the Parallel Server implementation it will become clear that this was not the case.

Bugs

Another of the changes when switching platform to Sequent was the upgrade of the Oracle software to release 7.0.15, away from the 7.0.13 version we had been running on the NCR platform. As 7.0.13 was the initial release of the product, this made good sense; an attempt to improve the stability of the product in our operation.

While we are on the subject of version numbers, it makes sense to explain how hard we were to eventually be hit by bugs on this project. The move to the 7.0.15 release was certainly a step in the right direction, but it was still far from bug-free. Some of these bugs will be covered in more detail later, and some were more architectural in nature than just code defects, but for now we can just focus on the statistics.

This project suffered from many bugs. Many, many, many bugs. So many bugs, in fact, that we had to resort to some rather strange practices on occasion, just to manage the bugs. We had so many bugs that Oracle could not keep up with merging the fixes into the main trunk of their source control system. This resulted in the creation of a special version of the source tree, which was labeled 7.0.15.TLA and resided on the workstation in the office of a member of the Oracle kernel group. At one stage we had around 50 open P1 bugs with Oracle, and Oracle development had to become directly engaged in the project, as we shall see in a little while.

The problem with bugs is that the fixing of them requires change. It is not too surprising, then, that sometimes the change itself can cause new problems. In those days, all patching was done by replacing object files in the Oracle libraries and relinking the product using the makefile in $ORACLE_HOME/rdbms/lib. As the number of patches increased, one of the strange development subprojects was started to deal with the complexity. Kyle Hailey was tasked with the project of making a version-controlled make system, one where a makefile could be produced for a specified set of patches. By checking out the correct version of makefile, different patches could be quickly applied or backed out, and binaries rebuilt. This was a capability that was required on numerous occasions.

In addition to Kyle's `makefile` project, we had to take special measures to deal with core dumps. A side effect of some of the bugs was that the user's server process would dump a core file. There was no concept of partial core dumps at that time, and so each one would contain the entire addressable space of the process, including the SGA. It wasn't unusual for hundreds of processes to core dump simultaneously, which meant that the system would become completely swamped in I/O requests to dump huge pieces of useless memory to the filesystem. Not only that, but each of these dumps were going to the very same file location named "core," so they were overwriting each other. The real icing on the cake was that these processes would often start dumping while they were holding a latch, thus effectively freezing the database until they were finished with the core dump and `pmon` could clean up their latch structure. So, this was a self-compounding problem that would cause huge outages during the production day, outages which were frequently overlapped in time!

The solution to this problem was simple. Oracle had more than enough diagnostic information for diagnostic purposes, so we didn't actually need any of these files. Therefore a simple but effective solution was to create a file named `core`, with permissions that would forbid Oracle processes from writing to them. Whenever an Oracle process went to dump `core`, whether holding a latch or not, it would immediately fail without more than a few cycles of CPU, or holding latches for long periods of time.

To cut a very long story short, the 7.0.15.TLA release lived until the release of Oracle 7.3, when the last of the bug fixes were finally incorporated into a production release.

No More MTS

Sequent convinced us of one other important thing: remove MTS from the equation. The memory management of the Shared Pool was extremely poor in the 7.0 release, and the heavy reliance of MTS upon this for session memory produced many of the dreaded ORA-04031 errors. The combination of the locking model side effect and the impact of this memory management problem meant that MTS was not serving us at all well. The main selling point of Sequent was that their Virtual Memory system was very mature and flexible, allowing us to squeeze the very most out of their maximum memory configuration of 1.5GB. The limit was this low because of the 32-bit address limitation of the IA32 architecture on the Pentium processor (Pentium v1, this is), combined with the allocation of the top 500MB of addressable space to kernel memory. The limit still exists today on IA32 architectures, where operating systems such as Linux have to employ the services of a kswapd daemon to bring high memory back into the addressable range on demand.

Memory was the big resource problem back then, both from a cost and a system limit perspective. It turns out that escaping from MTS at this early stage saved us from a really nasty unforeseen problem which we later discovered in subsequent benchmark testing of MTS. That problem was one of Page Table Entries (PTEs).

When a UNIX process is created, one PTE is created for each page of physical memory that the process has mapped. In the case of MTS, each process actually mapped all the session memory for all the processes in the system, by virtue of it being located in the SGA. This meant that a huge number of PTEs was being maintained for every process, all of which are allocated from the paltry 500MB of kernel memory. As the number of processes increased, kernel memory would become depleted! This meant that the system would crash, of course, and heralded Sequent's introduction of shared PTEs for shared memory—all processes would refer to a single set of PTEs that mapped the SGA shared memory.

Two Nodes: Using OPS in Anger

So that was week two. Not really, more like week 12 or 42 or something that I can't remember any more. At least we were now running on a system that was not ludicrously undersized for the requirement!

The user rollout was going very well. All the back office functionality had been rolled out to all the regional headquarters. The front office rental outlets across Europe now needed to start using the new system so that the bidirectional bridges between the multitudes of legacy mainframes and Runway could be closed, and the expensive maintenance contracts and people costs cut. In terms of user count, though, this was the vast majority, by a factor of two. Two thousand concurrent users from all over Europe now need to be added to the already-live thousand, and for the first time, Parallel Server was to be used in anger. The addition of these users was to be carried out on a country-by-country basis. The largest countries by a significant margin were France and Germany.

At this stage, we were relatively confident that we had done everything "by the book," and felt the system should deliver at least a close approximation of our expectations. Part of the Sequent proposal had even included a benchmark "proof of concept," and so we had seen our actual production system supporting the desired user load. The reason that we had scaled well over both nodes was because the application had been partitioned by design.

It makes sense at this stage to look at the application design for data separation that was employed, as all these principles are equally valid with RAC as they were with OPS.

Functional Partitioning

The heading of this section is carefully worded so as not to mislead. In those OPS days, pre-Oracle8, it was referred to as data partitioning, but that terminology is now adopted by the Partitioning Option, which is not directly related to this topic. Functional partitioning is the act of logically grouping the data access of particular application functions together so that they don't frequently share volatile areas of the database. The whole secret of getting good scalability on OPS (and for RAC, incidentally) is to minimize the concurrent read/write access to the same areas of data. The nice thing about using Oracle and OPS/RAC is that full separation of data access is not required, unlike a shared-nothing database such as MS SQL Server. However, the closer each instance gets to operating on its own islands of data, the better the system will scale.

> **INSIGHT 5:** *Scalability of OPS/RAC is maximized by reducing the frequency at which the instances must coordinate read/write access to common areas of the database.*

In the case of the Runway application, a good example of functional partitioning is the reservation function and the rental function. For the most part, these can be modeled as completely separate applications: the reservation function needs to access some of the same data as the rental function, but the volatile portions of this data are mostly written to by only one of these application functions. For example, during the reservation phase the details of the reservation are written to the database. This reservation is read at the time of checkout, but the chances are that this is some time after the actual reservation was written. The impact of this is one of the lesser known "get out of jail free" cards of OPS, RAC, and synchronization in general—*temporal locality of reference.*

> **INSIGHT 6:** *Temporal locality of reference is where shared access to a piece of data is separated by a significant length of time. The definition of "significant" varies dependent upon exactly what is being synchronized, but in the case of application data it is typically a few hours. The implication in the case of OPS and RAC is that the read/write accesses from two different application areas do not compete with each other because they access different data regions at any one time. This in turn reduces the synchronization required to keep the cached data coherent.*

The underlying reason for the temporal locality (or *lack thereof*, to be precise) helping to keep accesses separate is that there is an implicit lack of *spatial locality of reference* occurring as a result. Both spatial and temporal localities of reference are highly desirable when single caches are employed, or when the access is all read-only. In the event of read/write access by multiple caches, we actually want to keep *any* locality of reference to a minimum: by doing so, the impact of synchronizing the caches is kept to a minimum.

If we use the reservations functionality as an example, consider the following fictional operational profile (using smaller numbers for clarity):

- There are 5,000 new reservations per day.

- Reservations are made for an average of three days in the future.

- One reservation equates to one new row in the reservations table.

Figure 8-3 shows the operational profile of the actual table in this case.

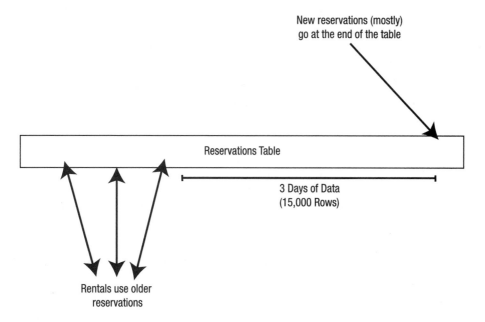

Figure 8-3. Operational profile of the reservation table

It can be clearly seen that the accesses to the reservation table by the two application areas are to different physical areas of the table. If we now assume that each of the application functions is performed on a different instance of an OPS or

RAC database, the ranges accessed by each instance are also separate. Therefore, the checkout operations from the "checkout instance" can read and write to the relatively older reservations without the need for much cache synchronization with the "reservations instance."

So that's the "get out of jail free" aspect of functional partitioning. In addition, of course, there are many techniques that can be employed to keep read/write access physically separate between the instances. Some of these are database implementation techniques, such as

- Partitioning

- Freelist groups or Automatic Segment Space Management (ASSM)

- Reverse key indexes

Of these database techniques, only freelist groups and reverse key indexes were available in the Oracle7 product (and even reverse key indexes did not come along until much later).

Some of the partitioning techniques are in the middle tier, such as Data Dependent Routing (DDR) in Tuxedo. The best place to plan for functional partitioning, however, is *in the application*. For example, if there is a table that many functional areas of the application write to, but *data is never shared between functions*, then make a table for each functional area and eliminate any coherency overhead implied by many instances accessing the same table!

Germany!

Most of the production users were now live, with the very notable exception of the German rental outlets. This represented a large proportion of the rental users, around 800 of the 2,000 rental operation users, and so there was still quite a big push needed to get the whole system live. We wanted to make sure that this final stage of the troubled rollout went as smoothly as possible, and so we deployed key TLA management to the larger German stations to intercept problems. One of these people was my manager's manager, Jerry, who accepted the ultimate suicide mission—to sit on site at the Frankfurt rental station, the largest and busiest in the country.

Jerry was the perfect person for this mission. One of a number of American citizens deployed into the management team from TLA's headquarters, Jerry was also implicated in the original platform selection. Karma does exist after all.

The German users were highly efficient, and had been extremely well trained—one of the big successes of the project had been the "train the trainer" training program. They were also not going to suffer fools gladly, and if they were impeded in any way whatsoever in their renting of toilet brushes, there was going to be hell to pay. So, Jerry was sitting in a room full of high explosives, hoping nobody would light a match. Bad luck!

As the number of German users increased, the number of problems increased. Most notable of these were problems in the shared pool, and problems with OPS. In fact, it was during this period that it really hit the fan, and the infamous 50 concurrent P1 bugs were open with Oracle. The system was spending more time down than it was up, and when it was up there was terrible response time.

We were also running out of CPU on the servers, which exposed us to a new phenomenon called *cluster shootdown*. When a node in the cluster determines that its peer is not responding to heartbeats, it assumes it must be down/crashed/failed. Therefore, it shoots the other node out of the cluster, and "fences" its access to the shared disk array. This fencing prevents the other node from performing any I/O, and also signals the operating system to "panic," the system call to immediately crash, and fall over in a heap. This crashing in turn requires a full resilver of all the mirrored disks that had outstanding writes (most of them), which put more pressure on the CPU for the rest of the day.

This was a system that never made it out of the inferno—we were constantly in battle. On top of all this, we had hardly started the German rollout, and Jerry was in danger of being murdered by hordes of angry frauleins. At this point the German rollout was halted, and the project put onto an immediate Defcon 1.

For historical interest, I will list some of the problems we encountered. Notably, one of them is still relevant today. The problems we had were mostly divided into two broad categories: OPS and the shared pool. It's hard to say which of these was the most impacting, but the OPS problems were certainly the most difficult to rectify.

Shared Pool Problems

The shared pool problems were largely caused by dynamic SQL. Yes, there were also many, many Oracle bugs—this was pretty much the first production release of the product that featured a SQL cache. But, the bulk of the pressure on the shared pool was caused by the fact that virtually none of our SQL was sharable. There was a reason for this, however.

As you may remember, the Brushco application had been completely generated from CASE*Designer. Not only that, but most of the development had taken place against Oracle version 6 databases, as Oracle7 was not yet available. In version 6, bind variables were not a concern, because there was no concept of a shared SQL cache. Likewise, most SQL*Forms version 3 SQL that was generated by default from base table queries did not use bind variables either. This resulted in a great deal of SQL that used literals instead of bind variables. In addition, Forms had a nasty habit it retained from Oracle v6 where it would close cursors very aggressively, causing more parsing on the server when they were reopened shortly after.

The result of this was that the shared pool was like a war zone. Not only were we not getting any benefit from the ability to reduce hard parsing through the reuse of shared SQL, but we were imposing the full penalty of at least making the attempt to do so. This penalty is extremely high—not only must the statement be parsed to generate the execution plan, but it must have hash values generated, and pass through several serialization points (latches) in order be stored for subsequent reuse. The net result of this was extremely significant contention for the library cache latch. Oh, yes, there was only one library cache latch at this point of history, and so it proved to be the ultimate serialization point.

The combination of a single library cache latch and massive fragmentation in the shared pool, because of both dynamic SQL and a number of management bugs and immaturity problems, led to enormous amounts of time being spent waiting on the library cache latch. By the time ORA-04031 errors were evident, the performance problems had already gone beyond the point of being funny.

> **INSIGHT 7:** *Please, please, please make sure that all your SQL is sharable. Although we currently live in a world of multiple library cache latches (first implemented in release 7.2, if memory serves correctly), we also live in a world of much higher workloads. It is also true that a cache that rarely achieves hits is just an overhead. This seems particularly true in the case of the library cache, where a small number of dynamically generated SQL statements can easily topple the most powerful machine.*

OPS Problems

The other big problem was that OPS was not working. Period. There was something fundamentally wrong with it, beyond the huge array of ORA-00600 errors. It was just not scaling at all, despite our valiant attempts to construct the application properly. Huge waits were evident in the database for "DFS lock" conversion, the main global cache synchronization method. Combined with the huge quantity of P1 bugs and the library cache problems, it was time to get some more of Oracle's attention.

The Juan and Andy Show

TLA had some good allies in the right places. The UK support organization, headed by Bob Dunsby, was representing TLA in the right way within Oracle. Bob had already deployed Roger Sanders as an on-site resource, which was a tremendous help in terms of helping us to understand the internal workings of Oracle and prioritization of problems. Roger was, and is, an incredibly understated fellow, with an amazing grasp of the Oracle internals.

NOTE *Much of Roger's work was carried out using his SGA attach tool (m2), as described by Kyle Hailey in Chapter 6.*

With his help, many problems were quickly resolved, or at least understood. In the same way, Bob had escalated the severity of our troubles within Oracle, to the point of waking senior development leaders in the middle of the night. Once TLA's senior executives contacted their old colleague Ray Lane, Oracle was well aware of the issues at hand.

As it happened, around this time, Juan Loaiza and Andrew Holdsworth were traveling to Europe to visit an Oracle expo. Juan is one of the relatively small number of people in Oracle Development that have a true grip on the whole product. He is also responsible for many of the finer features in the product, and is good to enjoy a margarita with. Andrew is currently the Director of Real World Performance, and has written the foreword to this book, but even back then was heavily involved in fixing many high-end performance problems and benchmarks. How fortunate, then, that these two chaps just happened to be on the right continent?

It turns out that Juan and Andy had already received a warning shot about this system when they were trying to rent a toilet brush at their initial destination in Europe. They had coincidentally elected to use the services of Brushco for this rental, and received an interesting reception from the rental clerk upon presentation of the corporate credit card.

Oh, you work for Oracle? Oracle is sh*t.

In those days, the login screen for SQL*Forms contained all the copyright notices for Oracle ...

Juan and Andy duly obliged the request of their management to stop by our development office in Heathrow to take a look at the problems we were experiencing. It would be fair to say that what they found was quite enlightening to them. One immediate realization dawned upon Juan, for example, when he was trying to join v$sessstat to v$session. The queries would take unacceptable amounts of time, because the joins of the underlying x$ tables became seriously problematic when large numbers of sessions were connected to the database. Whereas joining a hundred or so sessions to a couple of hundred session statistics was no problem, joining over a thousand sessions (per instance) to the same couple of hundred resulted in higher CPU, disk sorts, and longer elapsed time. Until this point, all access to x$ virtual tables was the equivalent of a full table scan. In our case, this was a really big deal, and not primarily because of the CPU requirement; the disk sorting area was a much bigger concern. I will try to explain.

Before the advent of sort segments, which are predominantly latch controlled once they are fully operational, the creation or cleanup of a temporary segment required the use of the ST (Space Transaction) enqueue, just like any other space allocation in the database. When this fact is combined with that of having a relatively small (64KB) sort area, which was entirely appropriate for our OLTP system with memory constraints, it means that even modest sorts require the allocation of the ST enqueue to create a disk-based sort area. The ST enqueue is, of course, a single lock that is shared across all instances of the database. This means that if we wanted to query some session waits or statistics, with a few hundred sessions connected to the instance, we would need to allocate the singleton ST lock from the database. This would probably not be a problem if the ST enqueue were only needed for x$ related sorts, or if the access to the ST were a First In, First Out (FIFO) queue ...

Access to the ST enqueue is not FIFO. It is, in fact, LIFO—Last In, First Out. This has some performance-theory-related grounding, but caused more harm than good in our case. The compounding problem in all this was SMON, the background process, which was alive and well on ALL instances, allocating the ST lock very frequently to perform free space coalescing and temporary space cleanup. All the SMON processes were effectively competing to perform this housekeeping work, and so the ST enqueue was being bounced all over the OPS instances. The impact of this, of course, was that there were times where it was nigh on impossible to run a query that required an on-disk sort area! For example, if a large batch job, or even a modest "online batch" (oxymoron) job had created a series of disk sort segments, and SMON was busy cleaning up, the DBA's would be totally unable to run any diagnostic queries as to the performance of the system ...

One of the fixes for this problem was implemented by an event that disabled SMON from performing certain cleanup activities. This event was set on all but one instance in the cluster, which certainly cut down on the contention for ST, but caused other problems when the instance that did not have this event set was not running: no cleanup was performed at all. In those cases, we had to manually re-enable the cleanup by turning off the event on one of the surviving nodes. The other significant fix took until version 7.3, which was the implementation of sort segments, which allow an instance to allocate a pool of temporary segments using the ST enqueue, and then manage them locally using latches.

Juan's take on the x$ problem was slightly different: We needed indexes on the x$ tables. When Juan got back to the office, he started work on a type of virtual index to manage access to the x$ tables. These indexes are, like the x$ tables themselves, not real indexes, and sometimes need special care in their use. However, their existence removed the need for large SORT MERGE joins when joining just a few rows from large x$ tables such as v$session and v$sesstat.

> **INSIGHT 8:** *When constructing queries against* x$ *tables, always try to use the virtual indexes for optimal performance. On very large systems, the* x$ *tables can become extremely large, and using the virtual indexes gives the optimizer the best chance to produce an efficient plan. The composition of the indexes can be viewed using the* v$indexed_fixed_column *view, which is very useful as the index definitions can and do change between releases.*

The other significant implication of Juan and Andy's visit was that Oracle development had firsthand experience of the problems at TLA.

Oracle Escalation

At last, we had the full attention of Oracle. Oracle France installed Kyle Hailey on site with Roger Sanders (Oracle UK), where they worked on various diagnostic procedures. Oracle Development responded by sending Jeff Needham, a member of Oracle Development, to the UK and France for a number of weeks. Jeff, now an OakTable member, was tasked with the triage duties for Oracle Development, defusing an incredibly volatile situation and organizing almost nightly conference calls with the correct development leads in California.

This kind of accelerated path to the right people was exactly what the project needed, and also allowed Oracle Development a closer look at the scalability problems we were experiencing with OPS. One of these became referred to as the *Buffer Fairness* issue, and was one example of a number of naiveties in the implementation of the OPS code.

Buffer Fairness

Imagine a situation where more than one instance of an OPS database wants to write to the same block of the database. Or rather, because OPS at the time was exclusively based upon hashed lock elements, imagine more than one instance wants to write to a relatively large set of blocks covered by one PCM lock. This is, of course, a pretty common occurrence: updating an index leaf block, inserting into the end of a table, and so forth. The way OPS (and RAC) manage the consistency of the cached representations of these blocks is through the use of escalated lock levels on the PCM (or Global Cache) lock elements. If an instance wants to write to a buffered version of a block, it must first of all escalate the mode of its global cache lock to become eXclusive. If another instance already has this buffer in eXclusive mode, it must downgrade it to Null mode before the lock can be upgraded on the other side.

Once the downgrade is completed by the former holder of the eXclusive mode, the upgrade to eXclusive mode on the other side can take place. Only at this time can the current holder of the eXclusive lock initiate a read of the current data. In OPS this implied a write to disk by the previous holder, followed by a read from disk by the new holder. In RAC, this is improved by the cache fusion process, where the current buffer is shipped directly between the instances.

The point of all that was to explain that, in OPS and even in RAC, the process of granting more than one instance write access to a block is quite an intensive process, one of significant serialized duration. This is particularly true in OPS, of course, because of the physical I/O which had to take place. The problem with the Buffer Fairness issue was that, for each and every write to the block, the writing instance would upgrade the lock mode, do the write, and then check whether other instances had requested a downgrade for its own update needs. This meant that, on a busy OPS cluster, each instance performed exactly one modification to the block before the lock was downgraded and the other instance allowed to perform its update. Let's now look at *Little's Law* (*The Practical Performance Analyst*, Neil J Gunther. Pub: iUniverse.com, ISBN 0-595-12674-X), which shows the relationship of queues to service times and response times:

$$Q = \lambda R$$

In English, this means that the queue length (Q) is equal to the arrival rate (λ) multiplied by response time (R). The queue in question is the queue for the global cache lock that covers the buffer we need to write to. So, in order to keep the queue as small as possible, the response time for the operation should be less than or equal to the arrival rate. The problem in this case was that every request for an eXclusive lock on a busy global cache lock was paying the full price of a cross-instance ping. This made the value for (R) artificially high, and thus the queue would increase. In fact, we would frequently see so many hundreds of users waiting in line for a single lock element. We then need to apply the other half of the simplistic queuing model to this:

$$R = S + W$$

Once again, in English: (R)esponse Time is equal to (S)ervice Time plus (W)ait Time. The service time remains constant as the time taken for a ping. The wait time, however, is defined as the service time for all other requests ahead of you in the queue, multiplied by their service time. So, if we had 500 requests ahead of us in the queue, and a service time of 300ms, this yields a response time as follows:

$$R = 300 + (500*300)$$
$$R = 150300ms$$
$$R \approx 150s$$

A response time of 150s, or 2.5 minutes, for just one part of a user's request, was clearly not acceptable: something had to change.

The response from Oracle was simple. The cost of a ping could not be readily changed, because all those steps were fundamental to the architecture of OPS at that time. The only thing that could be changed was how often it occurred (_). Oracle introduced a Buffer Fairness algorithm, which looked a little bit like this:

- Instance A upgrades a global cache lock to eXclusive, and takes a note of the timestamp (ts).

- Instance A starts processing all requests that are waiting for that lock element in exclusive mode.

- Instance B requests eXclusive mode lock on the same lock element.

- Instance A ignores instance B's request until it has processed all local requests received prior to (ts), then downgrades the lock element and grants instance B's request.

The impact of this is to break the aggregate coherency service time into two components: a local component and a remote component. The local component is relatively fast, and so can keep up with a high arrival rate, whereas the remote component is slow, and so is performed less often. This batching of remote coherency operations vastly improved the performance of Brushco's application.

When Jeff finally returned to the US, another member of Jeff's team, Doug Rady, joined us in France for many weeks of madness. A significant part of this was the implementation of yet another platform (nicknamed Bigfoot), which will be discussed soon. But for a minute let's step out of the frontline trenches, in the battle to get OPS up and running, and take a look at a skirmish that had been occurring nearby.

More Trouble at the WANch

While all these server-related fun and games were occurring, another issue was haunting the project: the network. The project had required a relatively large and complex Wide-Area Network (WAN) to support the hundreds of sites that needed access to the application. These sites were spread across the whole of continental Europe, using the only available technology at the time: X25.

Very early on in the project, the intent had been to run the Forms logic on local PC's, and to use SQL*Net over the WAN to the database server. This idea was abandoned very quickly (actually prior to any substantial hardware rollout), as SQL*Net was remarkably "chatty" at that time, requiring perhaps several hundred round-trips between the user's PC and the database server for each transaction, which brings us quite neatly onto the subject of *latency*.

Latency

Latency is the measure of time between two points. In the case of networks, latency is the time taken for a unit of data to travel from source to destination. In the case of rotational latency in a hard drive, it is the measure of time between a disk head being ready to read, and the disk platter rotating the required data portion under the head. Understanding the effects of latency is crucial in understanding response times.

The trick with latency is to always look for multipliers:

> **INSIGHT 9:** *A seemingly low latency can soon become excessive when multiple iterations of the latency must be made. For example, if a write to the redo log disk takes only 2ms, but you are committing for every row of a 1,000,000 row insert, you will be spending 2,000 seconds purely on the latency of 1,000,000 synchronous writes to disk.*

In the case of our network latency using SQL*Net, it can be clearly seen that this is a classic "multiplier" problem. The latency of the network was not awful, but the number of round-trips that SQL*Net required at that time multiplied this latency many times over for each transaction, thus yielding a high response time when viewed from the user perspective.

SQL*Net has been dramatically improved in later releases to significantly cut down on the number of round-trips required. This is achieved by delaying many of the required API calls from being sent to the server until they cannot be delayed any longer. At this point, all the API calls would be bundled into a single network packet, thus reducing the number of round-trips. Specifically, Oracle now bundles parse, bind, execute, and fetch calls into one request, if possible. In a statement with many bind variables, this could result in an enormous reduction in round-trips.

Centralized Client/Server

In the absence of bundled API calls, the solution to this problem was to host all the Forms processing on relatively large UNIX servers in the same data center as the database servers. In this way, all the client/server traffic would travel over extremely low latency Ethernet links. The WAN was then reserved for the shipping of character mode data to user's terminals, and the transmission of keystrokes.

This solution seemed to produce reasonable response times for the users, and everyone was happy. Everyone except the bean counters, that is, because a new problem had come to light: *cost*.

The invoices from our network provider were getting excessive. As in many near-monopoly situations, our provider was charging premium rates for the use of their WAN, and Brushco were not at all happy about this large footprint on their IT budget. The service provider were charging for used bandwidth, and doing so at exorbitant rates. It was time for action, and new lessons to learn.

Satellite Networks

TLA's response to the monopolistic tendency of the network provider was to find a way around the monopoly, thus disarming the opponent. In order to do this, TLA spent time investigating geostationary satellite technology. This seems like a good time to bring up the immutable laws of physics.

> **INSIGHT 10:** *Light speed is a significant one of these laws of physics that cannot be broken, and is particularly applicable to networking. When using satellite technology, the transmission and receipt of data is all subject to latency; that of sending the data up to the satellite and back down to earth at the target location. Geostationary satellites orbit approximately 35,000 kilometers, and the electromagnetic radio waves used in satellite communications travels at the speed of light, 300,000 kmps. This yields a latency of just over 110ms for each hop, and two hops are required for each send or receive. Therefore, satellite networks have a latency of around 220ms for each packet.*

Once this fact is combined with the fact that Forms applications rely upon host echoing of characters over telnet (as opposed to local echo), we have a there-and-back time of almost half a second between a user pressing a key and the character appearing on the screen. This effectively prevented satellite from being a potential alternative to the existing WAN, *except* through the use of some ingenious software. The software in question was called *EcoPad*, and it provided local echo functionality for certain Forms fields, and the ability to cache screen rendering information locally on the client side of the WAN. Not only did this hide much of the character echo latency from the end user, but also drastically reduced the bandwidth required.

The combination of these two attributes made the satellite option extremely viable, which in turn smashed the monopoly to pieces. Of course, the effect of this was that the network provider drastically lowered their prices, and the satellite technology was never implemented! This was also a special case where satellite technology could be made to work with a latency-sensitive application: the latency of satellite networking remains, and needs to be carefully assessed when making networking decisions. Light speed remains a constant ...

After that deviation into the world of networking, it's back to the arduous task of scaling the application on the database server.

A Multi-Prong Attack on OPS

Time to rejoin the OPS battle. When we left it, most of European sites were running with almost reasonable levels of performance and stability, but the rollout of the application to Germany had been stalled by the OPS problems. A multi-prong attack was initiated in order to reach a resolution.

We already had significant attention from Oracle on the issue of bugs in the software and architectural problems with OPS. Internally, we were attacking the issue of shared SQL (a crucial element in stabilizing the system) through the use of simple queries which I am still using variants of to this day. More on this in a moment. In addition, we had initiated a large benchmark at Sequent's head-quarters in Beaverton, Oregon, to test their latest and greatest platform which would allow us to have *four* active nodes in the cluster. The test system was nick-named Bigfoot.[2]

Shared SQL

I'm not going to dwell on the issue of shared SQL too much, but I am going to mention it one more time. I only mention it at all because I am still coming across problems that are caused by unshared SQL!

In the case of the Runway project, fixing the unshared SQL was one of the essential steps in getting the system stable, and so we produced weekly reports from the production shared pool, showing statements that were mostly similar but still unshared. These reports were run the day after the weekly migration of code into production, and showed the current big offenders. Affectionately known as the Top 50 list, the developers would pick up this report each week and thrash through the statements, in order of memory footprint in the shared pool, to fix the guilty statements. Many of these were a side effect of using base table queries in SQL*Forms v3, where it produced unsharable dynamic SQL. Others were just bugs in the Runway code. Whatever the source of the problem, they all had to be fixed.

The query we used looked something like this:

```
SELECT      substr(sql_text,1,40) text,
            count(*) cnt,
            sum(sharable_mem) mem
FROM        v$sql
HAVING      executions<1000
GROUP BY    substr(sql_text,1,40), executions
ORDER BY    sum(sharable_mem) desc
```

Of course, we did not have v$sql in those days, only the aggregated v$sqlarea. It's almost always more appropriate to use v$sql if possible, as it avoids an extra step of redundant aggregation.

Using these reports, we were able to find and fix all the offenders in the shared pool as a side task to the large effort required in testing and implementing the new Bigfoot servers.

---

2. This was the real name of the system. It also had an enormous basketball player's boot on top of it, just to make it clear.

Bigfoot: Splitting the Rental Users

One of the reasons that we took on the expense of running long benchmark tests at Sequent's headquarters was the fact that nearly all of the components of the new system were completely new. A new server architecture, support for greater than two nodes in a cluster, and a new operating system were all significant risks to a production implementation. However, there was an implication of going to more than two nodes that kept us awake at night. The application had been well designed to provide good data separation between the functional areas, as all OPS-destined applications should have been, but now we faced an implementation where we must split the rental users equally across two instances of OPS. Whereas we had previously hosted reservations and all other back-office users on one node, and all rental users on another node, we now had our first experience of running a completely unpartitioned workload across two nodes.

Though many, if not all, available application design techniques were used to scale the application on OPS, this only catered for running different application functions on different nodes. It categorically did not cater for hosting the rental users on greater than one node concurrently. This required a combination of techniques to be deployed, both operational and database-centric, in order to tip the balance in our favor.

The system was implemented after a number of weeks of on-site configuration and intensive performance and integration testing. We spent many weeks in France, seeing our usual quota of tourist attractions and beautiful countryside (zero—the hotel and the office were separated by an industrial estate). Doug Rady was with us from Oracle Development, maintaining the communication channel back to development. The last few weeks upped the ante to the point where we had an 8 on/8 off shift pattern in order to get all the tasks done, such as finalizing the system benchmarking, stabilizing the cluster, and preparing and executing the cutover.

The cutover was effected by means of a *rollforward* of a hot backup, starting two weeks prior to the go-live. I clearly remember a slow-motion moment as one of the operations staff at the data center insisted on grappling with the X-terminal we were using as the master console for the rollforward. This all happened less than seven hours before the final switchover, and was something to do with asset tags. Needless to say, this chap was lucky to escape with his life, never mind the asset tag number!

Tuning the Operations

In parallel to tuning the physical nature of the database to mitigate the increased coherency overhead of hosting two nodes of rental users, we also spent some time tuning the system operationally. We tried many things, but the most successful all came down to the placement of workload on specific instances to reduce the need for coherency operations.

The first thing we did was to connect users to a specific database instance based upon their geographical location. We wanted to make sure that users in a given rental location, for example, would be connected to the same database instance. This was an incredibly successful change, one that dramatically reduced cross-instance activity simply by minimizing it from a logical higher level. This is a technique that is still completely valid in RAC systems, just because it is so logical—doing less of something (coherency operations in this case) will always be faster than doing more of it.

> **INSIGHT 11:** *Locating logical pools of users on common instances of an OPS or RAC database will make your database run more efficiently. Despite Oracle's official party line with RAC that it doesn't matter, they have dramatically improved the service-based connection and statistics capabilities of the product in 10g. This facility is designed to make your life easier when doing exactly what they say is unnecessary—placing users of certain types on specific instances.*

In addition to the surgical placement of users, we made a decision that may seem counterintuitive at first. Every evening, before the start of the batch window, we would migrate all of the users to one node. There were fewer users at that time of the day, so one node could easily support the required load. That's not the counterintuitive part, though; this is: we then ran all batch processes on that instance also.

This may seem odd at first, because this server was made extremely busy by hosting nearly everything[3] on it. The reality, though, was that the large table scans inherent to batch processing resulted in significant cross-instance activity. This in turn resulted in response time problems for the user and throughput reductions for the batch jobs themselves, making both activities *slower* than on a CPU-constrained single node!

---

3. The backup process was always run on one of the other nodes in the cluster. This procedure had no bearing on the cache coherency of Oracle (though it did impact the shared I/O system) and so could happily consume all the CPU of one of the idle cluster nodes.

Tuning the Database

With two instances hosting the rental side of the application, there were now areas of significant overlap of the data needed by each of the nodes supporting these instances. Although this had been minimized through the operational procedures previously discussed, there were certain things that could not be separated without intervention at the database level. There is not sufficient space or scope in this book to go into the detail of all the techniques used, so I will simply outline the most important ones we used.

Large Sequence Caches

In an application that uses artificial keys, as was Runway, the use of sequence generators with large cache sizes is one of the most important changes to be made to minimize coherency requirements. The reasons for this are twofold. First, and most simplistically, the large cache means that the instance can pull numbers from local memory without going to disk and updating the underlying SEQ$ table (with its own resulting cross-instance activity). The second (and most important) reason is that it creates large areas of numeric separation between the key values used by each instance.

For example, if instance A allocates a cache of 5,000 numbers for a sequence used to generate primary keys, then instance B allocates its own cache, the numbers in instance B's cache will be 5,000 greater than those of instance A. As the index leaf block fills, it will split into two through a standard index growth patterns—one for each of the instances' ranges. This yields a very good chance that the instances will need to update *different index leaf blocks* for inserts. Different leaf blocks means that the instances do not need to spend a lot of time pinging current versions of blocks between instances.

Alternative methods of index leaf block separation also exist, notably reverse-key indexes and "instance prefixing." These are mostly unusable facilities, though, because they limit the subsequent access to the data! In the case of reverse key indexes, the digits in the key are reversed before the insert or later access. This means that an index range scan is no longer possible without, at best, a full index scan. In the case of instance prefixing, the instance number of the inserting index is prefixed to the index key, thus making inserts to the index effectively local to the inserting instance. However, fetching the data is then dependent upon knowledge of which instance inserted the data in the first place.

The beauty of the large sequence cache solution is that it yields almost all the advantages of these two methods, but with none of the drawbacks[4], and *no application changes.*

Multiple Freelist Groups and Preallocated Extents

The other component of the INSERT operation is that of the row allocation in the data segment, as opposed to the index segment: upon insert, Oracle must find space for the new row in the segment. Of course, this is also necessary with the index segment, but it generally happens much less often than with the data segment due to the row size compared to the key size, and also because an index has a much more distributed nature for inserts, especially when large sequence caches are used.

To find this new space, Oracle will use the standard mechanism of checking the freelists, and if necessary bumping up the high watermark of the most recent extent and allocating within that space. If multiple instances are allowed to use this standard mechanism, contention is observed for a) the segment header (which contains the freelist) and b) the "hot end" of the table, where there is space for inserts.

The solution is to use two mechanisms—multiple freelist groups and preallocated extents. Creating an object with multiple freelist groups creates an extended segment header with one additional block for each freelist group defined. These freelist groups are assigned to instances on startup, thus giving each instance a different freelist block to work on, and giving a good chance that the blocks listed within the freelist will not be contended for by the other instances.

By preallocating extents, Oracle allows the DBA to explicitly allocate extents to specific instances. These extents can be in totally different files, thus eliminating insert contention for PCM locks. However, this adds another dimension to the art of space management in the database, where space must be monitored across multiple extents for each object that is prone to heavy insert. If an extent for a particular instance was depleted, Oracle would automatically allocate an extent that was not assigned to any particular instance, thus creating contention when another instance spilled over into this extent!

---

4. The largest single problem with this technique is a nontechnical one. Large sequence caches (or any size sequence cache) can lead to gaps in the numbers actually allocated. Auditors can be very displeased about missing invoice numbers, for example. This "number loss" is especially true in OPS and RAC, but can also occur in single instances if they have a very volatile shared pool or if the instance crashes.

Automatic Segment Space Management[5] holds much promise in this area, though there are still some secondary issues with it. However, the design goals of ASSM mean that instances gain the advantages of multiple freelist groups and reallocated extents without any intervention from the DBA, saving significant amounts of administration.

GC_FILES_TO_LOCKS

The famous OPS parameter, gc_files_to_locks, was the nerve center for controlling the phenomenon known as *false pings*. A false ping is where a global cache synchronization occurs where it is not necessary because of an access to a block that is coincidentally protected by the same global cache lock. In pre-7.3 Oracle7, all global cache coordination was carried out in block ranges based upon the hash value of the block. This was to reduce the number of permanently allocated memory structures for managing these "lock elements," but resulted in a number of data blocks being covered by the same lock element. If any block covered by the lock required a lock escalation, and another block covered by the lock element has been written to on another instance, all dirty blocks covered by the lock element must be written to disk before the lock can be escalated on the current instance. This phenomenon is a false ping.

The gc_files_to_locks parameter assigned a number of locks to a specified file in the form <filenumber>=<lock count>. File number ranges could be specified, but in a moderately large database this parameter would quickly become very complex. In fact, we discovered the file size limits of an init.ora file because of this parameter.

With a combination of scientific methods, luck, and a large piece of time, we eventually produced a lock allocation scheme that kept false pings to the minimum.

Modern Day

Regardless of the marketing message for RAC, much of the tradition OPS techniques still apply to RAC. It is still a multi-instance cache coherency exercise, and so anything that can be done to minimize the required synchronization will make a RAC system run more efficiency. This includes the now-taboo topic[6] of application/functional partitioning and large sequence caches. It also includes many of the new features to make life easier, such as ASSM, and the new infrastructure (in 10g) to connect and monitor users by workload.

---

5. Available in release 9i and upward

6. The official message from Oracle is that modifications to application design are unnecessary for RAC.

Putting the Project to Bed

In 1997, the Runway project was finally migrated onto a new platform, the last migration in our charge. Despite the tremendous amount of effort expended, and the great successes in making Oracle7 and OPS work optimally, we felt that the exposure to failure implied by running with OPS was still far higher than running on a single instance with a cluster node in standby in case of failure. The failover time would still be superior to OPS, in fact, and the complexity and management overhead of the system would be tremendously reduced.

After a long period of system testing, Runway was migrated to a Sequent NUMA-Q server, running a single instance of Oracle7. Time and technology had progressed, and the highly tuned application could now be hosted by a database running on a relatively modest 12 Pentium Pro processors at 180 MHz. In fact, the database server had significant amounts of idle CPU, did not have the 1.5GB memory limitations we had been dealing with, and was considerably more stable than any prior production system that Runway had been hosted upon.

So, was all that time and effort wasted because of this? Absolutely not. The lessons learned by this project will stay with me forever, and have given me an entirely healthy skepticism of new features in a production context. In addition, I would not have had such a feast of knowledge presented to me if this had been yet another small project. And I would not have met the many great people that I am delighted to still call friends.

Dear Reader,

Having served in the Danish Army (these days that's pretty much an oxymoron) during the Cold War, it's really hard for me to introduce someone from DDR.

But David is not really from East Germany—he just looks like he is. He is in fact from the rather elite Diagnostic and Defect Resolution group, which resides in the exciting space between Support and Development, and helps decide what bugs to fix in what order, etc.

David has been around in Oracle Support for decades. One of his claims to fame is the creation of the precursor to the WebIV tool called TechRep, which everybody who ever worked in Oracle Support (and beyond) has the utmost respect for. It indexed all bug texts, bulletins and notes, initially using SQL*Textretrieval, allowing us to search for matching cases. It's hard to describe how useful it was, unless you can imagine a world where MetalInk (sic.) doesn't have any search facility at all, except for the fixed fields.

I started in Oracle Support in 1990, and once a month the Dutch Support chief, Andre Bakker, would ship a tape with the bug database to us. That was our support system, period. The technical bulletins were not available to us, since they belonged to US Support, and we belonged to the (also US-based) International Support. I'm not kidding.

A Danish legend—Martin Jensen—once went to visit his friends in the US Development organization in the late 1980s and came home with a complete collection of the bulletins, which the Danish Oracle User Group (OUGDK) then copied and handed out to our members—AND to the Support chief in Oracle Denmark, Jannik Ohl. Because Jannik hadn't been able to get access to those bulletins! That meant, for instance, that the RPT/RPF messages were not—I repeat NOT—available to international customers.

TechRep and the subsequent WebIV tool, developed by Richard Powell, was pure magic to us. Our productivity and learning curves rose faster than Oracle's stock price in 1999. For that, we all owe David (and the other crazy geniuses in Oracle UK Support) a great deal.

As head of DDR in the UK, David is a trough of knowledge, tricks, and workarounds. If it wasn't for his Scottish accent, we could all learn so much from him ☺. Seriously, though, David is always good to consult on technical matters when you're stuck. Always another thing to try, always another trick to pull, always another person to ask. Giving up is not an option, of course.

He's also a very structured person, but we—The Oakies—like him anyway. If you can use the rather American term "soft spoken" of a person from Scotland, here he is. Enjoy his thoughts and insights in this chapter.

—Mogens Nørgaard

CHAPTER 9

Testing and Risk Management

By David Ruthven

MANY THINGS HAVE CHANGED and improved over the last twenty years in software engineering. However, the following stand out with remarkable consistency:

1. Poor engineering practices remain the root cause of application failures and,

2. There is usually very little in the way of contingency planning to avoid and minimize the impact of such failures.

In spite of improved development tools and mature software components, there is no escaping the need to develop systems that avoid predictable risk by using tight engineering practices. A colleague of mine once observed that some software development practices are more akin to "basket weaving" than any recognizable flavor of engineering. Modern development tools and languages decouple the developer from the fundamental underlying concepts. Like giving a calculator to someone who cannot add up, the results you get may be unreliable.

I have worked in many development environments ranging from completely ad-hoc to red-tape-gone-mad. At one end of the scale you have a maverick environment where one or two gifted programmers produce a raw stream of source code with nothing else: no coding standards, no testing, no documentation, and, for the project at least, no tomorrow (no personal hygiene or social skills is a stereotypical view and is no guarantee of the presence of a maverick). At the red-tape-gone-mad end of the scale, such as I encountered when developing a secure suite of applications for central government on an infinite (time and materials) budget, you have templates and standards for literally everything. You can have rooms full of filing cabinets, filled with functional, design, hardware, and interface specifications. You have templates and standards for coding, for testing for revisions to specifications, for revisions to revisions of specifications, and on and on.

If you had to choose a life-support system built using one or other of these development environments, it would be a tough choice. With the former, your initial pleasant surprise at early completion would give way to a mild panic, leading to a tightening in the chest, as you realize you are entering the initial (and in your case final) test phase. With the latter, you would die waiting. Long live the project manager.

How often do you hear of software projects where the costs overrun and the application falls short? Almost all of us have either worked on, or know of, software projects that have either completely failed or have only managed to deliver limited benefit. Even many of the projects that appear to be effective are often delivered after disproportionate investment and overinflated deployment and administration costs. One of the primary reasons to build an application in-house is to tailor it to the needs of the business. However, in too many cases the resulting application is far from what the users require or expected. Too frequently the project release cycles extend beyond changes in business requirements.

Any software project that is worth undertaking will be vulnerable to risk. Since greater risks bring greater rewards, a company that completely avoids application development risks will face the business risk of lagging behind its competition.

This chapter pulls together some of the testing and risk management strategies that I have used over the years to develop successful applications. Somewhere we have to strike a balance between over- and under-engineering and to recognize budgetary and time constraints. We want to adopt software engineering and project management practices that will yield the best results without sinking the initiative with expensive and joyless procedures.

The areas that we will look at are

- The principles underpinning an effective development environment

- Design practices that navigate the project around familiar stumbling blocks

- Staying focused on business benefits

- Effective testing to aid short release cycles

- Code instrumentation for accountability and shorter fix cycles

While the topics covered here are broadly applicable to all software development environments, I will be focusing particularly on getting the most out of those based on the Oracle database.

A Little Background Muse

Edsger Dijkstra told us the truism that "software never fails"; I would add "the only problem is we don't know when it is working." When software is compiled and linked into a program it will execute with brutal pedantry. This is both its blessing and its curse: software never fails, so when the code is correct it never fails to succeed, and when it is incorrect it never fails to fail. It has an attractive predictability.

In common with all products of engineering, software is designed to work in a certain way, and all designs and implementations have their own compromises and limitations. Components used in electrical and mechanical engineering have published tolerances and operating requirements. These boundaries are more difficult to define and describe in the less tangible world of software engineering. Partly, this is due to the direct influence of the performance of the hardware and because resources used by software, CPU, memory, I/O, and network bandwidth are shared resources used by each process for varying periods of time. Database systems and application servers also manage their own sets of shared resources, and judicious use of these more granular resources is also important.

Algorithms typically define software performance tolerances. Such tolerances are usually quite wide in the sense that the algorithm will not necessarily fail, it will just become suboptimal when handling conditions outside of its "comfort zone." For example, a linear scan may be adequate for searching an in-memory data structure, but if the data set to be scanned is too large to fit in the allotted memory then the performance of the algorithm may be compromised by the need to read from persistent memory. If the algorithm allocates more memory, then the tail off in performance may be reduced at the expense of increased resource usage.

Over time we have moved up the programming food chain from assembler, through batch and online compilers, and on to interpreted 4GL scripting languages. This coupled with Moore's Law, stating that computing power doubles every eighteen months, has led to a decoupling of the programming process from an apparent need to understand what happens under the hood. Even so, strict software engineering practices are still essential to any company developing software products for a living, or to anyone involved in systems programming environments (developing, for example, operating systems, databases, and compilers). In-house development environments for non-IT companies are often more lax.

The driving force behind advancements in programming languages, development environments, and tools, including databases, is to allow customers to write less code to implement their business rules and workflow with more accuracy, reliability, and scalability. This does not obviate the need to understand precisely how these tools deliver their promise. You may not need to know the bits and bytes, but you still need to learn how to build applications through appropriate use of the tools on which they depend.

The importance and complexity of production business applications has led to a requirement for even more programming than before. Applications need to be secure, resilient, accountable, and scalable, and they often need to interface to multiple systems and integrate multiple technologies. As such, the development process has to encompass prototypes, evaluations, benchmarks, scale tests, and regression tests, whilst the code itself needs to be instrumented and maintainable. Advances in programming tools and environments are needed to absorb the increased volume of programming necessary to produce a production system rather than shorten the cycle to produce a bloated low-quality solution.

A database system allows you to build scalable, concurrent, and resilient applications. It also reduces the amount of code you have to design and write if you invest time studying its features and capabilities. However, databases like other tools can be used in many unpredictable and not always appropriate ways. A database application is an extension of the database itself. To get the best out of a database system requires that you understand how it operates and that you build applications that are in tune with its design principles.

Avoiding the Avoidable

Building a software business application is an engineering process. So why is it that many applications too often hit predictable and avoidable problems?

Strategic Problems

At the strategic level, the problems start with the management and culture within the organization. Often the root cause of a problem that is afflicting an application can be traced back to poor management decisions. Many of the deciding factors in the success or failure of a project are directly controlled and influenced by management (for example, personnel, skills and training, budget and budget constraints, timeframes and deadlines). Many projects suffer badly at the hands of unrealistic time constraints, insufficient resources, insufficient resources of the right type, poor project management, and so on.

Of key importance is the relationship between the IT department and its hosting organization and the influence that the IT director has at senior management level. Unfortunately, the IT department is often seen as subservient to the rest of organization and consequently does not always have the influence to demand the resource investment required for a project to succeed. (How often do you have to walk *upstairs* to visit the IT department?)

The attitude of an organization becomes very visible when handling escalated problems with third parties. I recall, several years ago, a customer whose method of escalation was to invite his account manager and myself out to dinner. We talked about all sort of things, but the escalated problem itself was never mentioned. After that I felt obliged to get the issue resolved as quickly as possible. This remains my favorite escalation method.

Operational Problems

Meanwhile, back at the coalface, we can categorize four types of software problem:

1. Incomplete—some more code needs to be written

2. Inappropriate—some different code needs to be written

3. Incorrect—an untested set of preconditions have manifest a flaw in the logic or implementation

4. Poor performance—burning too many resources

Whilst all software is prone to these problems, many projects increase their exposure to these risks through

- Inadequate use of features (reinventing the wheel)

- Overly complex solutions (too many wheels)

- Inappropriate use of features (wrong-sized wheels)

- Cumbersome manual testing (need some wheels?)

- Very large releases (maybe it will float?)

We all know that problems detected early cost less to correct because earlier on in the project they cause less disruption, as there are more alternative solutions and more remaining phases in which to correct problems (it's much easier to add in that vital "third bedroom" during the drawing of the plans rather than after the brickwork has been completed). Unfortunately, the last two items in the previous list tend to delay detection of problems arising from the first three items.

In the extreme case, where an application or some of its features are inappropriate, the costs are the highest. In my experience this does not happen often but is generally caused by lack of user involvement and by very long release cycles (see Figure 9-1).

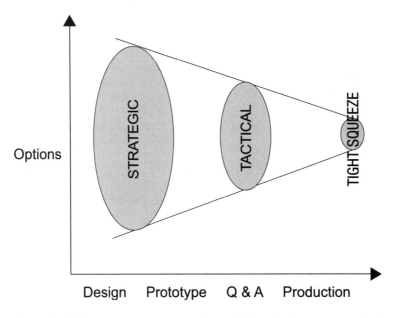

Figure 9-1. The narrowing tunnel of available solutions, as a project progresses toward production

Handling Change

Applications are generally not resilient to change or unexpected circumstances. Any change to an application or its environment can have undesirable side effects, and yet applications run in environments highly prone to change and are permanently exposed to the most unpredictable component of all, users. Non-legacy applications need to be continually changed to add functionality and correct faults in the application itself, and to upgrade the software and hardware components on which it depends.

It is perhaps not surprising, therefore, that the majority of problems occur after some change to the application, its environment, or usage patterns, or when some unanticipated circumstances arise: in other words, after either an explicit or implicit change. Some people, however, still seem surprised when problems occur after a change is introduced to a production system without being tested at all!

The only explanation is either that the implications of the change were not considered, the change could not be tested, or the costs of testing were too high (higher than the costs and risks of failure).

In short, software applications are exposed to a lot of risk, both during their initial development and when they are changed. Since we cannot prove that software works under all circumstances (at least not cost effectively), and since we can only perform a finite set of tests, the best we can do is to reduce its probability of failure. In order to do this, we have to

1. Detect problems at the earliest stage, during design, development, and production.

2. Identify, test, and code all plausible scenarios.

3. Ensure that changes to the application have no unwanted side effects.

4. Understand resource usage and pressure points which may impact scalability.

5. Be prepared to handle failure conditions.

6. Perform all the preceding steps without infinite resources, budgets, and timescales.

By taking this approach at least you will have an identifiable set of risks and a few constraints. So how do you build a high-quality application on which you have to rely but can never trust—carefully is the short answer. The next sections explain some methods to implement these steps.

Rules of Engagement

Before we get into the details of the development process we need to grasp a few thorns that wound the flesh of an otherwise potentially healthy application.

For most organizations there are only two valid reasons to build a software application, either to save money or to make money. It is therefore essential to minimize the costs incurred when building the application and to maximize the value of all the deliverables. The ability to maximize Return On Investment (ROI) is based on the ability to ensure that the development, maintenance, and deployment costs do not swamp the value returned by the application.

An effective development environment needs to

- *Stay focused:* Focus on delivering only the top components that deliver the key functionality that provides the maximum ROI for the business.

- *Implement short release cycles:* Avoid long release cycles that will increase project risk through

  - Delaying delivery of business benefit

  - Increased likelihood of deviating from intended requirements—user feedback will be on hold until the software is released

  - Being less able to respond to changing requirements—the longer the cycle, the greater the exposure

  - Spiraling costs and likely delays due to "biting off more than you can chew"

- *Build automated tests:* Develop automated tests in parallel with code development. The return on this investment cannot be overemphasized. Automated tests underpin the short release cycle, which is crucial to develop high-quality applications within budget and with reduced risk.

- *Instrument for visibility:* It is essential to instrument code for both performance and accountability. Building in instrumentation as part of the coding standards will reduce the time to debug application bugs and performance problems.

- *Avoid reinventing the wheel:* Many customers believe they are more in control if they implement functionality themselves. This may be true in some circumstances, but the costs and risks of implementing production quality scalable functionality should not be underestimated. Time not spent reinventing the wheel is time that can be spent making sure that your application will scale and implement your business rules accurately.

- *Use the wheel correctly:* Reduce risk by ensuring that your application is tightly coupled with the database architecture and design philosophy. In particular, for any feature or facility that you intend to use, ensure that your team fully understand

  - The design philosophy

  - How the feature is implemented

  - How the feature is intended to be used

  - Potential limitations and operating boundaries

  - How it is instrumented

- *Leave margins for error:* There will always be a need to revise an implementation sometimes at a late stage. This may be because of a change in requirements, an inability to scale, or a need to implement a workaround or an alternative code path to avoid a problem, which cannot be corrected in the required timescales.

- *Avoid unnecessary costs:* Avoid increasing any costs significantly without giving a real business benefit. For example, if you hit scalability problems with your own implementation of a feature, it may appear cheaper to throw hardware at the problem. Getting the most scalability out of Oracle is just a matter of correct usage. The database will cost you the same whether you avoid using its features or not.

Cycle Faster

Few successful mature applications would have been granted approval or budget clearance had the evolved functional specification been presented as the initial set of requirements. Software development is an iterative process involving successive development cycles, each culminating in a new version or release. So it is always surprising to learn from customers that their tests will take weeks or even months of effort. Test cycles of such duration are clearly delaying the success of their applications and increasing the costs of each release. A knock-on effect of these long cycles is that each release will contain much more functionality than perhaps originally intended, thus exposing the application to increased risk when initially used in production. Of course, there are also no business benefits accessible until the application is released.

I believe that a cornerstone for improved success developing business applications is to implement a relatively short release cycle. Releasing early and frequently will

- Yield a fast return on investment.

- Ensure the application stays on track with user requirements and business benefits.

- Ensure detection and correction of more problems early.

The main reason why this approach is not more widely employed is due to the lack of *integrated* testing during development and the absence of *automated regression tests*. Integrated testing requires that tests are built and used right from the start of the project, sometimes even being built before writing each piece of code. Automated regression tests are tests that can be run as batch scripts to ensure that no unwanted side effects are introduced to the project as code is added or changed. Automated regression tests are difficult to build but enable each step of the project to be fully tested as soon as it is coded. These key elements fundamentally change the development process, making it viable to shorten the release cycle and build higher quality releases with less risk.

Design Principles

The design stage of a project has a greater influence on the success, performance, and scalability of an application than the implementation phase or even the choice of components used to build the application. The following sections highlight some solid design practices that will help ensure the success of your application.

Design Accurately

The longest journey may start with a single small step, but if that step is in the wrong direction the destination may remain elusive.

Design a solution that benefits the business and meets the objectives of the business, rather than a solution that benefits the IT division, or the IT developers or the DBA's. The potential differences between these can be worlds apart with what IT thinks the business needs and what is actually required.

NOTE *A classic (if rather extreme) case of what can happen when there is a vast gulf between what customers need and what the IT developers want to produce is described in Chapter 11.*

The design of the application must match the fundamental requirements of the business, which in turn must match and deliver on the user expectations. If both the business requirements and the user expectations are not appropriately designed, then the project is doomed.

Whilst short release cycles can help ameliorate divergence from business objectives and user expectations, they cannot stop the project from heading off in the wrong direction from the outset.

Keep It Simple

Aim for a simple design and avoid complexity as much as possible. Simple designs are easier to explain, easier to implement accurately, easier to extend, and reduce application and system maintenance. However, every silver lining has a cloud: "simple" is not the same as "quick." It takes time and effort to ensure that you arrive at the simplest effective design for the given requirements.

Avoid Cumbersome Approaches

When you have a choice, try to minimize the number of components and interfaces used in your solution. The more components and interfaces, the more difficult the system is to construct, debug, and administer, and the more expensive it is to replicate for failover and volume testing.

I have encountered highly complex designs for delivery of even the simplest requirements (for example, a booking application of labyrinthine complexity which could have been implemented with a couple of forms). Sometimes it's just plain poor design. Occasionally the designer appears to be fashion conscious and is keen to use new technologies regardless of how appropriate they are. At others, it seems to be almost a point of pride with the designer that the design be so elaborate that only a handful of people in the company can understand it. The net result is always the same: an application that is unlikely to succeed or last, or at the very least will cost much more than necessary.

Other examples of poor design that I've encountered include

1. Building a web page like a jigsaw with each piece requiring a separate connect, query, and disconnect.

   We could reduce the load by adding connection pooling; however, this would be symptom fixing and adding unnecessary complexity. It would be far better to build each page using a single connect, query, and disconnect "transaction."

2. Implementing an OLTP system that requires data from one or more remote databases for some of the most frequently executed transactions.

   In most cases, rather than constantly querying the remote data, which is subject to variable performance from the network and the workload of the source database, it is better to co-locate the data or adopt a suitable replication method.

3. Writing programs to load data because the data has to be manipulated before going into the database.

   Isn't data manipulation what databases are designed for? It is almost always better to load data into some staging tables using SQL*Loader and then manipulate the data using SQL or PL/SQL. You will have less code to write and maintain, and tuning the SQL will be easier than recoding your application.

4. Running a standby against a database whilst it is being seeded with terabytes of data that is being pulled from other sources, using database links. If you are seeding a database, then this is presumably a repeatable and resumable batch operation, so there is no need to have an up-to-the-minute failover.

   Sometimes using an administrative procedure, in this case exporting, shipping, and importing transportable tablespaces, is better than absorbing a process within the application itself.

Some complexities are sometimes forced on an application because of the need to integrate with existing systems. Inheriting such a scenario is acceptable, but to engineer one will increase risk for no good reason.

Reward Code Clarity

Various published reports tell us programmers spend between 20% and 30% of their time writing code. The remaining portion of a programmer's time is spent reading, reviewing, and "reverse engineering" program code regardless of who was the original author. In general, code written by others, and older code, is more difficult to follow. Whilst the source code may implement the intended functionality, it only represents a fraction of the logic and thought processes required to design and build the software system, and documentation almost always gets out of step. This is a key reason why design and code clarity is of utmost importance to the overall costs of developing and maintaining an application.

It is a myth that complex applications require "clever" programming and that the inevitable price to pay for this is poorly documented, highly obfuscated code, understood only by a handful of programmers with nerdish skills. Investing in or accepting such a stereotype is too risky for production software.

In my opinion, complex code is difficult to maintain and, if understood only by a few people, expensive to maintain. At some point you will need to replace it with something more manageable and this will probably require major rewrites. My advice is to invest in simple, clear code that will avoid risks and reduce costs for the life of your application.

Code clarity is often compromised by

- *Small development audience:* Small teams often produce code not intended for publication to a larger audience and hence there is no perceived need to make it clear outside of the small community who read and the even smaller community who write or modify the code.

- *Narrow focus:* The development community is broken down into small teams with narrow focus. Being intimately involved with a small portion of code further reduces the perceived need for published clarity.

- *Protection:* Knowledge is power and cryptic coding is inherently seen as job security.

- *Skills:* Programmers who are unfamiliar with a language will tend to write code in a style more reminiscent of the language they are most familiar with. This also applies to their choice of algorithms and implementation methods.

- *Maintenance:* Code logic implemented in later versions may be compromised as the result of logic design from older versions hacked to work around previous issues and add support for new features. This results in the structural decay of the code logic, making it very difficult to predict how the code will behave in all situations.

- *Timescales:* There is always pressure to release code within certain timescales. Inevitably this leads to the dropping off of any activity seen as nonessential. Writing code takes time; writing clear code takes even longer. Rewriting code, which is often necessary for future clarity and scalability, may not always appear affordable at the time—when it makes most sense.

Ideally you want to avoid writing complex code in the first place because you will waste time having to simplify and rewrite it. Also bear in mind that the code will likely need to be amended and possibly debugged at some time in the future, and we all know what it is like trying to understand code, even code written by ourselves, long after it was originally written. A key development process priority should be to reward clarity. Have developers present their design and implementation with the audience tasked to offer advice on how to simplify it. Peer recognition is a great motivation for programmers.

It can be done. One of the public lessons from the open source community is that programmers can write clear code and even document it (note this does not apply to all open source developments) without being forced. It is all a matter of incentive. Open source programmers are measured not just by the quality of their application but also how easy it is for a third party to extend, port, or correct. This is a true measure of code clarity. Adoption of this philosophy within your development team should help lead to high clarity.

Identify Bottlenecks

It is imperative that you identify the main transactions that the application will support *before* you design the database schema necessary to support those transactions. You should assess each component from the perspective of

- *Frequency of execution:* Even an efficient query can become a bottleneck if run thousands of times per second. If the results of such queries are almost always the same, then refreshing a stored result or using a materialized view would be a better approach.

- *Resource usage:* High resource usage is a bottleneck to scalability. Tuning is not solely a retrospective activity. Use statspack to monitor resource usage as you implement the application. As a side benefit, efficient applications typically run into fewer application faults and product defects.

- *Likely concurrency:* Allied to resource usage, concurrent transactions may compete for resources and delay each other. Identify which transactions will execute concurrently and spend effort ensuring they hold onto mutually exclusive resources for the minimal time possible.

You'll need to invest the most effort on the most commonly executed transactions, as they will likely have the most influence on the schema design and the biggest impact on performance and scalability. These transactions should be the first to be prototyped.

Generalize

Have you seen what you can do with LEGO these days? You can now build much more realistic and aesthetically pleasing models, but the new bricks are more complex and less flexible and you need more of them to build a range of models. I buy my kids the traditional LEGO bricks because they are simpler to use and you can build a greater range of models by reusing the same bricks. If I write simple, reliable code "bricks" that are easy to understand and reuse, I can build a wide range of sophisticated, reliable applications. In this manner I also reduce the overall cost to build. All analogies break down, and this is no exception. For LEGO it may be important for the models to look realistic, but software is built for function not form.

You can identify opportunities to reuse code by isolating generic components from scenario-specific clients. A shared procedure reduces coding and maintenance and is implicitly better tested because several code paths will execute it during testing. For a generic, shared procedure the code path executed should be much the same for every caller.

For example, if you have more than one query differing only in the SELECT lists, it is often beneficial to have a single SELECT statement that supports all of these client queries. This approach guarantees that there is only one source of the SELECT statement and that the SQL areas in the SGA can be shared. The overhead of selecting more columns than is strictly necessary is usually negligible, and aside from reducing the overall number of distinct SQL statements, it makes application maintenance easier since you have fewer SQL statements to modify should the underlying schema change or if the SQL requires tuning.

Like all other code, generic procedures should be compact and simple. If you find yourself extending a generic procedure to handle more specific cases, for example, adding more parameters that are only used by a few callers, then it would be better to implement a separate procedure for those specific cases.

Design for the Rule Rather Than the Exception

Those of you who have used block mode terminals will remember that they are very fast for data entry, specifically because the user is only talking to the terminal and not interrupting the server until a block of data requires validation and execution. This approach works on the premise that regular users rarely make data entry mistakes and therefore can avoid field-level validation that slows up data entry and interrupts the server too frequently. The validation is performed at block level, which is a minor inconvenience since the likelihood of failed validation is very low.

Parameterize

Make your applications as flexible as possible by ensuring that almost nothing is hard coded. Everything that can be, should be table- or parameter-driven. Parameters allow you to control your applications at run time. You can enable and disable functionality, reschedule activities, or change quotas.

If you have a choice between putting a parameter in the process environment or in a parameter table, then use the table. It is easier to control and audit table-driven parameters since these are recorded in the database. Example uses of parameters would include

- Setting application workflow and environment choices such as banners, reminders, default printer, and so on, which are user specific or which the user can override (known as user-level parameters).

- Setting default application workflow choices (application-level parameters).

- Setting performance thresholds. For a given transaction or stored procedure you can record an acceptable execution time. The procedure can check this threshold and raise a warning. Such checking might itself be enabled and disabled by an application or user-level parameter.

- Setting which reports or batch processes are run at which dates/times.

- Setting debugging and tracing levels.

Work with the Product, Not Against It

A deep understanding of the key concepts underpinning Oracle will provide a foundation for using the database successfully and avoiding painful lessons. An advantage of a feature-rich product like the Oracle database is that there are often many ways to achieve the same result. However, the reason why there are so many options is because each has its own benefits and limitations. The downside, then, is it is sometimes too easy to make the wrong choice.

The first thing that you need to do is to gain an understanding of what the feature does conceptually and how it is implemented. This process also helps you confirm the feasibility of your requirements specification. Next, ensure that the feature is compatible with any dependent components, especially third-party components.

Study the documentation, even if you think you understand how to use a feature. Do not ignore any documented limitations. If the documentation seems incomplete, unclear, or ambiguous, then perform some specific tests. The correct choice becomes most critical when scaling the application, which is why I recommend some *prototyping* during the design stage (see the section "Prototyping" later in this chapter).

It is essential not to work against the product. For example, the database assumes that the vast majority of transactions will commit. If your application relies heavily on rollback, then it is working against the product by performing a lot of unnecessary work, which is thrown away, and this will result in poor performance, lack of scalability, and even failure, in pathological cases.

The most common example of working against the Oracle database is the use of literal SQL. Oracle7 implemented shared SQL to avoid the overhead of hard parsing, which is an expensive operation. Wherever possible, SQL needs to be written using bind variables. The cursors for all SQL statements are stored in the shared pool, so if the parser recognizes that two SQL statements are the same—or essentially the same, differing only in their bind values—the cursor can then be shared. Applications require to parse and bind once followed by an assignment of bind values and call to execute for each subsequent invocation of the same SQL statement.

Other key features of Oracle that must be worked with rather than against include Oracle's handling of locking, read consistency, undo, and redo (as discussed in Chapter 10, by Jonathan Lewis).

Instrument Your Code

It strikes me as odd that a major component of business applications is to provide visibility of key business processes, and yet the applications that provide this insight are often unaccountable themselves. If users are the first to know about poor performance, then it means that your instrumentation or production application monitoring are not up to scratch. The latter of these is the easier to correct. A key design goal is to ensure that you will be able to see what is going on when your applications are running live. See the "Instrumentation" section later in the chapter.

Less Is More

The less code you have to design, write, test, execute, and maintain, the better. It may sounds obvious, reading this here, but the only thing obvious to me about this rule is that it is too easily and too often forgotten, so here are a few reminders.

Prune Early (for Healthy, Vigorous Applications)

Prioritize your application's functionality by business benefit and choose that which can be implemented as a cohesive initial release. The 80-20 rule kicks in here: the majority of the business gain is usually provided by a fraction of the requirements specification (although admittedly usually the bigger elements). For the initial release, discard anything that adds little business value. Be more brutal on what to discard if its inclusion would compromise the project deadline or the quality of the initial release.

Defer any functionality that is valid but is not required in the initial or current release. Deferral of functionality can only be achieved if you have an effective release process.

User Tuning

Ensure that what gets delivered meets user expectations. The success of an application is met not only by technical criteria (i.e., "it works") but also in ensuring that what the user expects gets delivered. Tuning user expectations is the most important part of the tuning process. If users expect and accept a one-minute response, and your code already achieves that, then you're well on the way to delivering the requirements.

Use It or Lose It

Do not implement your own version of an available database feature, if that feature could potentially meet your requirements. It's amazing how many customers do not know about, let alone use, core database features that could reduce development time and take care of a lot of application logic. The most common examples are integrity enforcement, security, and stored procedures. If a feature does not work as you had anticipated, then the trade-off might be to adjust your dependency and ensure you fit within the operating boundaries of the supplied feature. If this is not an option then you may have to evaluate alternative third-party products. Only as a last resort should you build the feature yourself. Note that if a feature is available in the database, then implementing your own version of this feature is not going to be a business differentiator for you since it is also available to your competitors.

In some instances customers avoid using functionality that is not present in alternate databases in the belief that this will make their application database independent (there are some classic examples of this, and the resulting carnage, in Chapter 3, by Connor McDonald, as well as in Chapter 10, by Jonathan Lewis). If your application is database independent, the chances are it will not work well with any database. Ironically you end up with an application that is portable but not worth porting. Building database-independent applications is only tenable for ISV's who deploy and sell their applications with alternate database back ends and who only get a fraction of the benefits available from the databases used. Some ISV's build to the lowest common denominator, i.e., the functionality that all their intended target databases support with minimal interface differences. Their customers almost always pay for this in the long run (again see Chapters 3 and 10, which have some great examples of this and the subsequent difficulties involved in trying to tune without the application source).

Core Competency

Design and implement code that only your organization can write, namely the code to implement your business rules. It has become accepted practice not to write operating systems, databases, compilers, and debuggers, so extend this philosophy and avoid writing other major components and tools like source code control systems, bug applications, or automated testing tools. Implementing these will dilute your resources. Focus on your core competency, where your code can add the most value.

Stay on Course

Keeping the code uncluttered is a continuous process. The three main reasons why extra code can start creeping into the implementation are as follows:

1. *Deviation:* Programmers can rarely resist deviating from the requirement. It is always tempting to improve the application by adding neat ideas and functionality particularly when it appears easy to implement at the time of inception. Only 10% of that extra stuff will ever get used, so you are wasting 90% of that time.

2. *Duplication:* Avoid writing duplicate functions. This is made easier if each function is documented and that documentation is easy to search. If your development environment lacks documentation tools then, on Unix systems, writing manual pages is quick and effective. If you want full text retrieval capabilities, then you can store your function descriptions in the database and use Oracle Text to perform indexing and retrieval.

3. *Dabbling:* Care should be taken not to undertake any performance tweaking enhancements before some real-world performance and resource usage tests have been run. Attempts to enhance performance at the coding stage often leads to writing extra code to implement more sophisticated algorithms and extra code to maintain complex in-memory data structures. A slight improvement in performance is not usually worth a decrease in code maintainability and readability.

It may seem brutal, but a combination of enforcing test coverage for all code paths and pruning clutter (unused code) during code review should help. Only implement what is essential, with no bells and whistles.

Instrumentation

In the medical profession it is said that "symptoms are the last sign of disease." I think this applies to software systems where many problems are noticed until too late. In general the later a problem is identified, the fewer options there are for damage limitation and correction. When a serious problem is first encountered in a production environment, there is increased urgency to find a solution, whilst the "meter is running" on the financial impact to the business.

We already know that software is sensitive to change and does not always do what was intended or hoped for when presented with unanticipated conditions. We need to expect the unexpected. We need to instrument applications with sufficient information so that we can detect potential problems early and isolate the circumstances that will lead to failure.

One instance where instrumentation is sometimes used is where a response time limit is set. Here the programmer anticipates a potential problem and does not trust that the operation will necessarily complete as expected. This philosophy needs to be applied throughout the application but unfortunately it usually isn't. In fact, although code instrumentation is one of the most important components of a production application, it is also quite rare. I suspect that many application developers underestimate the value of instrumentation and view it as additional work. Often developers say that adding instrumentation will get in the way of developing the application, perhaps even delaying its release, and will anyway incur performance overhead at run time. As far as I'm concerned, even if it does add a little CPU overhead, the benefits far outweigh the costs (which should simply be factored into your testing).

In fact, basic instrumentation is relatively east to implement. It often involves simply printing or dumping additional information about progress and the results of certain phases of execution.

NOTE *As always, Tom Kyte provides excellent examples in his books,* Expert One-on-One Oracle *(Apress, ISBN 1590592433) and* Effective Oracle by Design *(McGraw-Hill Osborne Media, ISBN 0072230657).*

One of the best places to retain and analyze the information gathered by instrumentation is clearly in the database itself. Let's take a look at an example. The following database table will store details such as user, application name, transaction name, and record type, e.g. (ERROR, TIME).

```
create table metrix_tab (
        m_usr   varchar2(48)
,       m_sid   number
,       m_app   varchar2(32)
,       m_txn   varchar2(32)
,       m_typ   varchar2(32)
,       m_date  date
,       m_txt   varchar2(128)
);
```

We create a package of PL/SQL routines that allow an application to record start and end times, or errors (note it is often useful to gather errors reported to users centrally to identify problems with or using the application). Clearly additional routines could be added for other record types.

To try and make the instrumentation less intrusive on performance, the records are stored in a PL/SQL table and flushed to a database table when the PL/SQL table exceeds a certain row count threshold. Note we use an autonomous transaction to ensure that the commit in the flush does not interfere with an application transaction.

```
create or replace package metrix_pkg
as
  procedure mtx_reg(i_user IN varchar2, i_appln IN varchar2);
  procedure mtx_txn(i_txn IN varchar2);
  procedure mtx_err(i_err IN varchar2);
  procedure mtx_rec(s_time IN number, e_time number);
  procedure mtx_sav;
end;
/


create or replace package body metrix_pkg
as
  type metrix_typ is table of metrix_tab%ROWTYPE index by binary_integer;
  audit_tab      metrix_typ;
  user_txt       varchar2(48) := NULL;
  appln_txt      varchar2(32) := NULL;
  txn_txt        varchar2(32) := NULL;
  FlushCount     number := 200;
  mysid          integer;

  -- record user and application name in package variables
  procedure mtx_reg(i_user IN varchar2, i_appln IN varchar2)
  ...

  -- record the transaction name in package variable
  procedure mtx_txn(i_txn IN varchar2)
  ...

  -- record start and end time for a timed transaction
  procedure mtx_rec(s_time IN number, e_time number)
  is
    i binary_integer := 0;
  begin
    i := audit_tab.count + 1;

    audit_tab(i).m_usr := user_txt;
    audit_tab(i).m_sid := mysid;
```

```
  audit_tab(i).m_app := appln_txt;
  audit_tab(i).m_txn := txn_txt;
  audit_tab(i).m_date := sysdate;
  audit_tab(i).m_typ := 'TIME';
  audit_tab(i).m_txt := 's='||s_time||' e='||e_time;

  -- flush audit table?
  if audit_tab.count >= FlushCount then
    metrix_pkg.mtx_sav;
  end if;
end;

-- record error details
procedure mtx_err(i_err IN varchar2)
is
  i binary_integer := 0;
begin
  i := audit_tab.count + 1;

  audit_tab(i).m_usr := user_txt;
  audit_tab(i).m_sid := mysid;
  audit_tab(i).m_app := appln_txt;
  audit_tab(i).m_txn := txn_txt;
  audit_tab(i).m_date := sysdate;
  audit_tab(i).m_typ := 'ERROR';
  audit_tab(i).m_txt := i_err;

  -- flush audit table?
  if audit_tab.count >= FlushCount then
    metrix_pkg.mtx_sav;
  end if;
end;

-- Flush plsql audit table to database table
procedure mtx_sav
is
  pragma AUTONOMOUS_TRANSACTION;
  i binary_integer := 0;
begin
  -- ignore if no rows
  if audit_tab.count != 0 then
    -- copy contents using direct path insert
    forall i in audit_tab.first .. audit_tab.last
```

```
          insert /* +append */ into metrix_tab values audit_tab(i);
        audit_tab.delete;
     end if;
     commit;  -- commits only the work in this procedure
   end;
end;
/
```

Following is a demo client for our simple instrumentation package:

```
declare
  s_time  number;
  e_time  number;
  rc      number := 0;
begin

  -- register user and application name
  metrix.mtx_reg('scott', 'example');

  begin

    ------------------------------------------------
    -- Example 1: timing

    -- record txn name
    metrix.mtx_txn('txn-1');

    -- record start time
    s_time := dbms_utility.get_time;

    select count(*) into rc from scott.emp;

    -- record end time
    e_time := dbms_utility.get_time;

    -- record start and end time in plsql table
    metrix.mtx_rec(s_time, e_time);

    ------------------------------------------------
    -- Example 2: error recording

    -- record txn name
    metrix.mtx_txn('txn-2');
```

```
  -- force ORA-01476 error
  rc := 20 / 0;

exception when others then
  metrix.mtx_err(sqlerrm);
end;

  -- flush metrics to database table
  metrix.mtx_sav;
end;
/
```

After running the preceding code the database metrics table shows

STAMP	M_SID	M_APP	M_TXN	M_TYP	M_TXT
040518031526	7	example	txn-1	TIME	s=25319601 e=25319601
040518031526	7	example	txn-2	ERROR	ORA-01476: divisor is equal to zero

To get a complete view of activity you may want to pull information from alert logs and from various O/S reports such as vmstat, netstat, and so on. Data from these sources can be loaded into the audit table using SQL*Loader or referenced as EXTERNAL tables and queried chronologically based on their timestamps.

For database applications, transactions are a good unit of work to bracket with instrumentation, but we should also bracket other program segments that may be prone to variation including user responses and any long-running activity not included in a transaction.

If you let the database perform most of the work and use stored procedures to implement as much application logic as possible, then the bracketing becomes straightforward. It is likely that the 80-20 rule applies again here, meaning that 80% of your application run time and resource usage is incurred by only 20% of the code. This makes it less of an overhead to locate the program segments that should be instrumented. These program segments are also the ones that you will likely have to tune, but wait for the performance test results before unnecessary tweaking.

Although there are many passive "polling" methods for monitoring database usage, there is no substitute for application instrumentation. Application instrumentation can be used to

- *Detect changes in performance:* Record transaction name and response time for later trend analysis.

- *Detect increases in resource usage:* For similar reasons to performance auditing.

- *Audit activity:* For usage trends and event sequences.

- *Provide tracing on failure:* Aids debugging.

- *Provide initial sizing:* Resource usage and activity rates will help assess system sizing.

These forms of instrumentation are discussed more in the following sections.

Changes in Performance and Resource Usage

The only sensible place to capture the user's response time experience is to monitor response times within the application. An increase in resource usage does not necessarily mean poorer performance, but it may indicate that the transaction has become less scalable. If a warning is to be raised by the application itself, then the application needs to have access to benchmark data and a threshold value to trigger the warning. The alternative is to passively record the metrics, perhaps using some threshold to reduce the volume of recorded data, and use a separate report to perform trend analysis. This second option is simpler, can be integrated with information captured from other monitoring utilities, and also supports auditing.

If the application is doing a lot of resource-hungry work outside of the database, then it may need to provide methods to query those resource usage levels. The database manages all of its own resources, and the majority of important database and server-side O/S resource metrics can be queried via V$SESSTAT. This is another good reason to put as much of your application logic in the database as possible because it is already instrumented.

Clearly not all changes are directly implemented by the application, and many of these changes are recorded elsewhere. For example, a given transaction run twice, in quick succession, may take longer for the first run. It could be that the second run benefited from caching performed as a side effect of the first one, or maybe there was a redo log switch and the log archiver delayed the switch. In multi-user scenarios the possibilities are endless. For a complete view of the system you need to integrate information reported in several places.

Auditing

Recording and labeling some instrumented activity in an audit trail provides a history to be used for performing trend analysis. Your application may already need to record usage levels, particularly if it supports highly variable user activity. If you have a customer sales portal then, aside from recording the sales transaction, you ought to also record the performance of each component of the sale transaction.

An audit trail can also be used to help with debugging functionality problems. When a failure occurs, one of the most important but elusive pieces of information that you need to pin down is which activities were running immediately prior to and during the time of failure. An audit trail of user, process, and transaction/activity start and end times will show what was running at any point in time.

Ideally each significant code segment or transaction should have a unique label. A user or application parameter can be used to enable/disable recording of these high-level steps completed by a given process. This information can be expensive to capture and accumulate quickly so some levels with different degrees of detail may be warranted. Such an audit trail is best stored in the database using PL/SQL procedures such as those described previously.

Tracing on Failure

Providing trace information on failure is an essential debugging tool. Ensure that your application

1. Reports the full error stack, not just the top error

2. Has the ability to switch on database and other third-party tracing

3. Can provide a code path trace

Your coding standards should define how errors are handled once detected and how they percolate up to the routine that reports the error. Make sure that you have a method for recording and reporting all the errors raised in the stack, in particular the first one that is often the most important. If the first error was reported by a third-party component, make sure to grab and report all the information that component has about the failure.

It is often more important to know what sequence of events a process executed prior to failure than the actual state of the process at the time of failure. For more granular information than may be provided in the audit, you can record, in a buffer, important details such as "touch points" throughout the code, which would help debug a failure by highlighting the code path executed. This buffer would be flushed to the trace file on failure or cleared at some success point, say after a successful commit.

Sizing

Initial performance and resource usage metrics will help identify the necessary hardware sizing requirements and any particularly slow or resource-hungry areas of code that will need to be implemented differently. These can be gathered during prototyping when using realistic data (or as close as can be manufactured).

Some might say that the Oracle database provides too much instrumented data, requiring expertise to interpret all of the statistics and ratios. However, in the absence of instrumentation and tracing you are effectively flying blind. If you implement instrumentation first, you can use it as a permanent part of your application from prototyping onwards.

Testing

We have all heard that "genius is 1% inspiration and 99% perspiration." The same applies, to a degree, to the development of production software systems. As the importance of the application to the business increases, the stakes clearly get higher. You will have to contend with more users or customers and reduced scheduled downtime.

Unfortunately writing tests (perspiration) is not deemed to be as constructive as writing code (inspiration) and is generally viewed as less glamorous. Sometimes, it is even perceived as getting in the way of producing the application. However, since we cannot prove that software works under all conditions, the best that can be done is to perform a variety of tests that exercise the design and implementation and pushes its boundaries. We want to confirm that the software works, performs, and scales as intended and handles boundary conditions gracefully. The need to ensure the correct balance of inspiration to perspiration during development becomes key.

Ironically, properly written tests are likely to last longer than the application they are designed to test. An application will be modified extensively over time but the tests tend to be retained and extended. Hence the investment in developing tests persists for a longer period than most revisions of the application components.

Functionality Tests

Functionality tests are tests used to check that the code performs its intended purpose. There is no way of knowing if the code works without some form of functionality tests.

The usual way to confirm whether a test has passed or failed is to compare the results with some generated output. The required output, known as the reference output, is created and stored in an O/S file, database table, or sometimes within the test script itself. The output generated by running a test is then compared with the appropriate reference output, and any differences result in a test failure being reported.

For functionality that does not generate output, the tests may require the code to be instrumented with diagnostic output for comparison purposes.

A common dilemma is how to generate reference output. You can either

1. Generate output from an initial test run.

2. Handcraft the expected results.

Generating reference output by running the code is okay for detecting changes in output after modifications to the application code but is no guarantee that the code worked correctly in the first place.

It is much better to handcraft the input data and results. This approach makes the programmer or tester think more about the application and often reveals the need for additional tests. Generating reference output in this way may appear expensive, but it only has to be done once for each test.

White Box Tests

White box tests aim to exercise all the code paths and are sometimes known as *code coverage* tests. White box tests can only be written by someone who understands the implementation at the code level and are hence typically written by the programmers themselves. The "Extreme Programming" methodology suggests that programmers work in pairs where one writes the tests as the other writes the code, sometimes swapping roles.

White box tests pull at the seams and joins of the coded implementation. For example, an array may be sized adequately to handle 99% of all cases, however for the remaining 1% the code may have to extend the array. It may be quite difficult to set up the preconditions necessary to force execution of this exception code and so the programmer may add some event or parameter triggered code to artificially force the logic to execute this code path, making the test easier to achieve. This is another benefit of testing whilst coding; sometimes the code may need to be changed or extended to make the tests easier to perform.

All programmers perform some sort of functionality tests on their code and often these tests are thrown away, like removing debugging statements once you have fixed a bug.

Black Box Tests

Black box tests are functionality tests based solely on the application documentation. These tests are built by independent testers who assume no understanding of how the application is implemented, hence the name black box tests.

Programmers are the best people to write white box tests, but third parties are much better at writing black box tests. Since programmers understand how the functionality is implemented, they tend to write tests that are implicitly more likely to succeed. They use the application as *they* intended. A third party has no such baggage and will test an application from a user's perspective. The independence of testers is a valuable asset and they should not be distracted from pedantically testing the functionality as documented.

Test Suites

Test suites are collections of functionality tests, which together test a particular aspect of the application. Large projects will likely have many separate test suites.

For any code change it is useful to know which tests execute code paths that depend on the code you have changed. By generating code coverage maps, using for example, tcov on Solaris, you can build a mapping of which test suites execute which code paths. This mapping can be used to identify the minimal set of test suites to be run after any code change. Code coverage analysis is also used to ensure that all code paths are tested by one or more tests.

Regression Tests

Black and white box tests are both essentially functionality tests used to test the correct operation of the application. Functionality tests are called *regression* tests, when they are used to detect side effects of changes made to the application code or its environment.

Regression tests are not used for scalability or benchmark testing, they are used solely for testing application functionality. Regression tests should be autonomous, meaning they can run on any machine having the same processor and O/S. They can be run on machines with different performance characteristics and are not dependent on complex coordination with other tests. To ensure that test results are deterministic, even when run on different machines, the regression tests must check the environment and versions of components on which they depend.

For small projects it may be possible to run the entire set of regression tests for every code change, depending on the resources and execution time required. For large projects, the full set of regression tests should be run after each build of the release, daily is good!

Automated Testing

Any form of testing is expensive and, when performed manually, definitely falls into the perspiration category. Manual testing is a boring, repetitive, and time-consuming task requiring precision execution: all in all, an ideal candidate for automation. Many customers test their applications using manually keyed test scenarios and do not have automated testing tools or regression test suites. With manual testing the costs of reexecuting tests are high, more so if the development team are involved in performing those tests. If the cost of testing outweighs the benefits of correcting problems, then the cost of testing has to be reduced and not by performing it less frequently.

Investing in automated tests may increase the costs of developing the tests, but the test execution costs drop dramatically. Being able to execute tests without incurring substantial incremental costs means you can test more comprehensively and more frequently and shorten the development cycle. A small change in an application, particularly in a generic procedure, may have side effects elsewhere. The ability to run regression tests quickly and easily increases your chance of detecting these problems early. From an operational point of view automated tests make it easier to accommodate patches and upgrades to any part of the application environment.

Automated tests provide the foundations for a stable and frequent release environment.

Scalability Testing

Scalability is defined as how well a solution to some problem will work when the size of the problem increases. In application terms the size of the problem is directly related to the number of concurrent users, processes, and data volumes.

Application scalability needs to be built in at the design stage. Designing with performance in mind will avoid a lot of time trying to retrieve performance from an implementation wrestling with poor data schemas and algorithms. It is essential to identify which transactions will be executed the most frequently and which will be the most prone to execute concurrently. If a given transaction will run in "splendid isolation" at all times, then it can happily use as much resource as it likes; the resource/throughput trade-off does not then exist. In the majority case, transactions will need to share resources amicably. Use your application-level instrumentation to keep tabs on resource usage right from the outset.

Thankfully the Oracle database can take care of a lot of concurrency and scaling complexity, but the database client processes need to use it efficiently. It is easy to design and implement a process or transaction that runs adequately on a dedicated single user system. The challenge is always in identifying how concurrent processes will interact and to avoid coding anti-social (resource hogging) application processes.

Ensuring scalability is generally achieved by reducing resource usage, namely CPU, memory, and disk or network I/O and by holding onto mutually exclusive resources for the smallest possible duration. It is also essential that resource usage will grow, at most, in proportion to workload. Most algorithms have an operating zone in which resource usage scales in proportion to workload; however, all algorithms degenerate at some point when presented with excess workload and this manifests itself as excessive resource usage or contention.

The more work you can let the database perform, the better; this reduces the amount of code you have to write and maintain. Using database features will also avoid the need to implement the generally more complex algorithms necessary to reduce resource consumption whilst improving throughput. However, in spite of careful design and implementation, the only way to reduce risk is to perform scalability or volume testing.

Scalability testing (a.k.a. volume testing) is intended to simulate planned workloads by extrapolating results from a sample workload and dataset. It is a difficult and traditionally expensive process and can only sensibly be performed when the application has reached a degree of maturity. Since volume testing magnifies the resource profile of the application, small changes in the application or transaction sequencing can make a big difference in resource pressure points. It is easy to get lulled into a false sense of security having done volume testing only to discover that the tested application scales but the slightly modified production application yields different results.

Volume testing uses random time intervals generated on-the-fly to simulate realistic interactions, and this means that each volume test run is not identical. Whilst volume testing does not explicitly test functionality, if a failure does occur it will make identifying a reproducible test case a realistic challenge! This in itself can be a good opportunity to test if your instrumentation is sufficient to effectively assist in debugging.

Due to the costs it is quite rare for a simulation workload to be built and more common to have real end users either enter scripted instructions or play with the application while a few experts monitor the behavior of the system to capture the consumption of resources. For an application intended to support 200–300 concurrent users it is viable to have a representative sample of users perform concurrent testing in this way and then extrapolate the results to assess the impact of increased volume. The resulting risks can be addressed by an additional hardware capacity margin, plus some tuning expertise during the first few days of production when the application goes live.

The problem with this approach is that it does not scale and is also not easily repeatable from a logistical or cost perspective. To achieve this you need to deploy automated volume tests. Preparing automated volume tests is a difficult process; you require

- Realistic transactions

- Realistic data

- Realistic timing profiles between interactions and processes

- Data generation capabilities

- Hardware matching the target system, including a matching network topology

- Hardware to drive the tests

In general we are not interested in the scalability of a PC client since if we assume a single user per PC, there is no shareable resource to compromise scale.

Whatever tool you use to perform volume testing, the calls made by that tool to the application server or database need to be identical to those made by the real client application. HTTP clients are straightforward to simulate as are published interfaces such as OCI, ODBC, or JDBC, but many of the older Oracle client tools including earlier versions of the precompilers use the unpublished UPI interface. If most of your OCI or precompiler programs run as batch, then they can be used directly in the simulation.

Even armed with process and client capture capabilities, it is still difficult to construct a realistic environment. Like all testing the best we can do is attempt to predict and simulate as realistic a workload as possible. There is no harm pushing the application a little harder than it will be exposed to in reality, as long as you do not invest a lot of effort tweaking anything unless you know that the scenario is not artificial.

In spite of the need to simulate a mature version of an application, some volume testing should be performed during prototyping to get some ballpark figures. It is also a good opportunity to get familiar with the stress testing tools during that stage, assuming you have not decided to build your own (see the previous "Core Competency" section).

Keep It Real

All forms of testing need to remain as realistic as possible. You can get carried away and test increasing unlikely scenarios. We only want to test probable event sequences and usage levels and avoid artificial tests that inflate costs and add no value.

A dangerous side effect of (invalid) testing is that it can lull you into a false sense of security. This can happen particularly when performing unrealistic volume tests. Complacency sets in, more load is introduced onto the production environment in the "fool" knowledge that the application can handle the workload and the system has been sized correctly. You should only add extra workload progressively and constantly monitor the impact regardless of how much preproduction testing has been undertaken, or at what expense.

For manual testing, end users provide the most realistic feedback. Not being so close to the application, they have a broader view on what can/cannot be done and come up with interesting and surprising results. Providing access to the project at prototype and beta stages and through short release cycles increases the opportunities for end users to get their hands dirty and feel involved.

Testing Culture

Years ago I was a developer for a text retrieval product that was sold via partners. One of those partners was really keen to help us test our product, so they sent someone out to work with us. He was only with us for two or three weeks (it seemed longer at the time), but his tenacious testing improved the product quality immensely and made us much more confident in it. Well, we were confident before, but now we had some evidence!

The important project management mindset is to treat any investment in testing as an investment in the building itself, not in the "scaffolding." Continuing the building analogy, we already have some of the foundations for developing test suites, namely tests written alongside the code by programmers. We need to retain those tests and implement them so they can be run in batch mode and provide reference results that can be checked by an automated test harness.

Building and maintaining tests is essentially another programming task. Rather than use ad-hoc methods for writing disposable tests, you should use testing tools for writing persistent tests. Proper testing tools will simplify the process of developing, executing, and maintaining tests.

Test suites should be part of the project deliverables. They are equally important to the projects as application source code and should be managed using similar procedures including source code and version control. Do not attempt to implement what you cannot test.

Prepare to Fail

The nirvana for problem solving is to be able to fix on first failure. That means capturing all relevant information at the time of failure to be able to investigate and fix offline without the need to expose production systems or users to the problem again after we put more diagnostic "torches" in place. Unfortunately most diagnostics are reactive and triggered by a failure condition. Very often it is the steps prior to the failure that are necessary to understand the cause of the problem.

In high-throughput software systems it is difficult to implement the level of auditing required without being too intrusive to the overall performance. The volume of data generated may also be prohibitive. Circular buffers provide a good compromise since they only involve memory writes and limit the volume of recorded audit. If a failure is detected, the circular buffer can be dumped to trace. The limitation is the variable period of time that the buffer can support, which is obviously shortest when the process is busy.

Problem solving is easy if you have all the facts. In software terms the facts are best encapsulated in a test case. To paraphrase witnesses sworn in during all those TV courtroom dramas, what you require are "the preconditions, the whole (set of) preconditions, and nothing but the preconditions." We need to instrument our code with witnesses. We can then piece together the relevant witness statements, determine what really happened, reenact the crime, and, since this is only software, build a "repeat offender," namely a portable and minimal reproducible test case.

The most difficult problems to get a handle on are those that manifest intermittently, usually misquoted as an intermittent problem that is not possible in a software system. Recalling our first principles, software works exactly the same way everytime; the result can only differ with different inputs. Even the hardware supporting the software is an input, which is typically consistent except in the event of a hardware failure. The exact set of preconditions necessary to manifest a problem may appear random, rare, and elusive, but given that set of circumstances the problem will reproduce at will.

I estimate that for long running problems around 80–90% of the time is spent isolating a test case. It is rare to find escalated issues where a test case exists. Whilst problem solving may be relatively straightforward given a test case, problem isolation is where most of the time and effort are consumed. The process of identifying and separating the failure inducing circumstances from the irrelevant ones is also constructive to identifying the cause. In fact, given a reproducible test case the problem solving can become a systematic process of comparing the failing case with a working case, generated by a minimal change to the failing case.

We need to identify all the inputs to the problem, including user actions, user and program input data, attributes, configuration parameters, environment, and relevant concurrent activity. It is sometimes very beneficial to physically sit next to a user who might be experiencing a problem or to simply determine exactly the actions and operations they physically perform. Examples of users who complain of bad performance but end up searching for unrealistic volumes of data or use the application in an unexpected way are all too common.

Once we have ascertained there is a genuine problem and the problem reproduces at will, the task is to reduce the test case down to the minimal set of preconditions. If the problem occurs intermittently, the focus is on identifying the contributory factors for the problem to manifest. It is also useful to know if the failing activity has ever worked or continues to work sometimes.

Our instrumentation can be used to determine which activities were running immediately prior to and during the time of failure. If the same failure happened several times, then a pattern may emerge from an audit report. Either way we should start to model the conditions on a test environment using our closest matching unit test to build the framework for a test case to reproduce the problem at will.

Once the cause of the problem has been identified and corrected, our test case can be added to our automated test suite to ensure that the problem will be avoided in future releases of our application.

Prototyping

There is no accurate way of calculating the resource requirements needed to support a bespoke application: there are simply too many parameters. The only effective method is to prototype major components with realistic data and transaction types. Data captured from prototyping together with estimates of transaction concurrency can then be used as a basis for calculating the likely machine sizing. However, even those numbers will need to be verified with accurate volume testing.

The SQL language and database development tools make prototyping database transactions relatively straightforward. However, essential to realistic prototyping is to use real-world data, ideally in the expected volumes. This will ensure that the data schema supports the anticipated transactions, data loading, archiving, and replication requirements.

Prototyping also helps us quench our thirst for hands-on activity and more importantly can help answer the following:

- Which features are sufficient and appropriate, what are the implications of using them, and do we understand them?

- Does our instrumentation help us solve and detect problems?

- What are the pressure points that might prevent scaling?

- Does our development environment work?

- Does our test harness fulfill our testing requirements?

- Will it suit the users, assuming we give them access to prototypes?

- What are the minimal system sizing requirements?

- What evidence is there that the project is feasible?

Software and tests developed during prototyping are not wasted. Infrastructure code such as the instrumentation code and reports will be used in the final application, as will some of the tests. If any aspects of the development or test environments are new or untried, then using them during prototyping has the additional benefit of gaining expertise in their use.

Conclusion

Few of the techniques discussed in this chapter will be unfamiliar to software engineers and architects. The aim of this chapter has been to remind us that some software engineering techniques that are too often treated as overheads ought to be treated as investments. Software engineering is the application of scientific techniques to the design and construction of applications used by many.

Design and implementation simplicity makes applications more reliable, scalable, and easier to understand, correct, and maintain.

Instrumenting code makes visible what is happening in a live system, helps us size the hardware and isolate performance bottlenecks, lets us detect when something has changed and when something might go wrong, and tells us as much as possible about the circumstances surrounding a failure or deviation from the norm.

Prototyping provides the earliest opportunity to prove the concept and design, gain understanding of implementation options, ensure instrumentation works, highlight scalability bottlenecks, and get a handle on sizing.

Functionality testing identifies potential gaps between design and implementation and ensures the application is reliable. Volume testing ensures the application is scalable and resilient. Regression tests ensure that changes to the source code do not introduce unwanted side effects.

Automated testing makes it possible to publish high-quality releases quickly, getting an early return on investment, and makes it safer to extend and improve our applications and apply upgrades to supporting components.

Dear Reader,

The first time I heard about Jonathan was in a short email from Cary Millsap (after he left Oracle and formed Hotsos) with a pointer to Jonathan's sexy and easy-to-remember web address http://www.jlcomp.demon.co.uk/ *and a short question: "Ever heard about this guy? Seems pretty smart."*

Pretty smart, indeed. I have called Jonathan "the future Dave Ensor," but even that is not doing him full justice. He writes incredibly well. He even has the guts to tell an audience of more than 500 people that he considers his book the second-best on the market, with Tom Kyte's first book being, well, the first. That might be so, but reading his book is still pure pleasure to me, and it would still be one of the three Oracle-related books I would bring to the famous desert island.

He forces the rest of us to ever higher standards when it comes to testing, testing, and testing (to destruction) before we write or claim anything. And he constantly reminds us that this or that experiment or observation is only true for this or that version of Oracle under this and that condition.

He shares any insight he gains with the World, and is in that and other respects the scientist we all want to become one day. He somehow also finds time to answer more questions on comp.server.databases.oracle *and the Oracle-L list than most. He teaches as if he used to be a teacher (a teacher, that is, who cared about his job). Which he was, by the way. His presentations are always well prepared, well timed, and well worth your time.*

He has, of course, a brilliant sense of humor. In fact, I think it is a requirement if you want to stay on top of the various Oracle features and variations across releases and patch levels. He has, for instance, on several occasions brought fun and entertainment to the Database Forums and Master Classes in Denmark in the form of his trombone (he plays rather well), the adoption of Haiku verses to the Oracle World, and as the perfect game-show host.

With what little time is left (must be less than 42 minutes per day) Jonathan somehow manages to turn in a full working day as a consultant, while also having time for his wonderful wife and fantastic family. Somehow Jonathan must have invented the 48-hour day, without ever looking tired or irritated.

It is imperative that I mention Jonathan's daughter Anna, who is still very young, yet is capable of apologizing profoundly for several minutes about any topic you throw at her. She is brilliant, she reminds me of Harry Potter, and I would have expected no less from a daughter of the Mighty Jonathan.

Don't be fooled by his friendly looks and ways, by the way. Jonathan knows his soldiering, and will fight if it's his last option, or if an experiment proves it's the right thing to do under the circumstances.

—Mogens Nørgaard

CHAPTER 10

Design Disasters

By Jonathan Lewis

I OFTEN GIVE presentations at meetings of Oracle User Groups around the world, and one of the most frequent requests on the feedback forms for these meetings is for more war stories, or real end-user experiences, or examples of real problems and solutions. You won't be surprised to hear, though, that very few real end users stand up to describe how they did everything wrong, had a complete disaster with a system, or spent a fortune fixing mistakes that shouldn't have happened.

If you feel you've been deprived too long of the comfort that other people have also had to put up with all the problems you must face, this is the chapter for you—you may have seen "The World's Worst Car Chases" before, but now prepare yourself to read all about "The World's Worst Oracle Project."

The Environment

Everyone makes a few mistakes with Oracle. It's not really surprising as there is so much to learn and (inevitably) so little time to learn it. There are plenty of wonderful features, but never enough time to work out which features are most appropriate for what you want to achieve. And there's never any time for testing your ideas properly. So if you've got a choice of strategies, you have to take the one that seems to allow for the quickest, easiest development.

So errors do happen, and you can usually survive a couple of suboptimal design decisions. But if you want to maximize your opportunities for getting it wrong, you need to raise the stakes and broaden your horizons. Don't just go for Oracle—bring in a third-party application, customize it heavily, integrate it with an existing data warehouse, but not until you've hired a team of consultants and a team from the application supplier to sit alongside the in-house developers. The greater the diversity in the project components, the more chance there is for unsuitable practices to be introduced.

Summary of Errors

It is usually impossible to put a finger on a single design defect and say, *"This is the show-stopper, this should never have been done."* Every error that appears in this chapter is one that I have seen at several sites, but my response at one site might have been something like *"You shouldn't have done this, but it's not worth worrying about at present,"* whereas my response to exactly the same error at another site might have been more like *"If you don't fix this, there is no point in going on."* All projects are different, with different critical requirements, so something that is bad in theory isn't necessarily the big issue in practice. For example, this chapter describes the issue of home-grown sequences—they're always bad practice, but if you only request a few thousand sequence numbers per day, you may not notice a problem; if you try to request 10,000,000 sequence numbers per day, that's a very different matter.

An Oracle project is a bit like a duck faced with a 12-bore shotgun. One unlucky pellet (from the duck's viewpoint) might be all it takes to bring it down, but it may survive being clipped by a couple of pellets. Against a full load, however, it doesn't stand a chance. This chapter is about the project that took every pellet.

As you read the following headline description of the project, take a moment to predict where, and why, there are going to be problems:

- The third-party application was "database independent."

- The database was used as a bit bucket; validation, constraints, and consistency were handled only in the front-end code.

- All keys were surrogate keys (generated as meaningless sequence numbers) to "protect" the code from changes in the real key and make it "more flexible."

- The third-party application needed heavy customization.

- The existing data had to be migrated into the third-party application.

- Custom data feeds had to be reengineered for the third-party application.

- The third-party application wasn't designed with any change tracking features.

- The third-party application had to feed changes to an existing data warehouse.

Given the frequency with which the expression "third-party application" appears, you may think that I tend to assume that all third-party applications are automatically bad. It is true, of course, that if a project does not have control of the database design and supporting code it is much harder to change things in a timely fashion, and a lot of effort can be wasted working around issues that could, in an ideal world, be removed. But in this case, my constant repetition of the phrase is just a way to avoid naming any one product—which hereinafter I shall simply refer to as the application.

Database Independence

An application that is database independent is automatically an application that will perform badly at high levels of concurrency or large data volumes. It may do the job adequately, but you may spend all your time and money struggling to push the software into meeting Service Level Agreements (SLAs) and the users' expectations.

Of course, some software is only independent of some databases, and if you're lucky you will pick the database that just happens to be the database the supplier uses for their major development work. If not, you may find that database independence is an unpleasant overhead.

Database developers put a lot of effort into making their technology efficient, and basically assume that if they design a good feature into their systems you will be prepared to pay a small performance penalty in one part of their code in order to win a big performance gain elsewhere. Database-independent code doesn't use features, it uses vanilla-flavored, lowest common denominator elements—so you pay every possible penalty, but never pick up the benefits.

In fact, the Holy Grail of database independence is unlikely to be achieved. Users of the Internet Oracle newsgroups, list servers, and forums will know that one of the commonest types of problem is the one that fits in the framework of "I can do xyz using {insert name of database}, but it doesn't work with Oracle." Unless your supplier started as a real expert in all the database technologies that they had planned to design for, they won't achieve database independence. They may start with good intentions, and have a reasonable idea of where the major differences are, but there will be numerous details that they take for granted that simply don't apply to the next database down the line. (I was amazed when I first discovered many years ago that DB2 simply didn't provide read consistency; it had never occurred to me that any major database vendor would fail to supply such an obviously important requirement.)

Strangely, a little expertise can be worse than total ignorance. Imagine you start developing against database X and manage to work out some smart workarounds for the problems that particular database causes. When you move on to the next database, the problems don't exist—so do you rewrite the code because the workarounds aren't needed? Probably not—if the code still works, why change it? But what if the resulting code is very inefficient on the second database? Alas, the answer is likely to be the same; stick with what you've got, or you'll have to rewrite it for both databases.

So where did database independence have the most impact on my pet project? There were lots of funny little details and various oddities that I may mention, but the points that seemed to have the most significant impact in this case were probably the vendor's comments that

- We don't need to know anything about Oracle, except for tables and indexes.

- We don't do referential integrity in the database.

- We don't use Oracle sequences—although our surrogate keys are generated as sequence numbers.

- We don't use database-dependent types (like dates).

- We just need to add indexes to address performance issues.

It's Just Tables and Indexes?

There are many things that automatically go wrong if you don't know anything about the technology that you are using. (Imagine the effect of getting into a car with a manual gearbox if the only thing you've ever driven is an automatic—hey, it's just four wheels and an engine.) It doesn't matter which database you use, the optimistic belief that you can survive if you do nothing but fire simple SQL at simple tables with simple indexes is going to land you in trouble. If you're lucky, no one will attempt to use your code for a large-scale system, and you'll never discover how bad it really is. But if you want to succeed with big customers (where big may refer to the volume of data, the rate of data change, or the number of concurrent users), you need to know the foibles of the database engine.

Oracle puts a lot of work into doing some things extremely well, but it won't come as a surprise that for every benefit you get there is a price you have to pay. Oracle's strategies for avoiding the contention issues that normally occur at high concurrency or high load are fantastic, but they do have a cost; and if you aren't aware of that cost and make it appear unnecessarily without taking advantage of the corresponding benefits, you will have problems.

In the case of Oracle, you could probably summarize the key features that need special recognition and some understanding under just four headings: redo, undo, read consistency, and sharable SQL.

Redo

Every change you make to a database block is made only after a description of that change has been written into the redo log buffer. The redo log buffer is being continuously dribbled out to disk in order to protect those changes, but there are critical moments (when any session issues a *commit*) where the redo buffer *must* be written to disk and sessions can start to queue up for that write to complete.

You can reap enormous benefits from this strategy. Firstly, you do not have to write changed data blocks to disk to protect them; the redo log is the final arbiter of what has changed, and can be used to reconstruct data block changes if necessary, so the number of random writes to disk is dramatically reduced. Secondly, the redo log can be used to recover the database in the event of a catastrophic failure of the database. Thirdly, the redo log can be replayed (in real, near-real, or lagged time) into a spare running copy of the database to allow for rapid switchover and minimal downtime in the event of a catastrophic system failure. A final, relatively recent, benefit is the option for reviewing the log file long after the event for such things as auditing, troubleshooting, and activity analysis.

The downside is that the redo log buffer serializes database changes, and issuing a *commit* is a particularly critical serializing event. So if you are not aware of this, and issue extremely frequent but redundant commits, then you are paying a penalty that need not be paid, and has no justification. Unfortunately, some database engines encourage, or even require, excessive commits to avoid locking issues—so a strategy of designing to the lowest common denominator will penalize Oracle; and a design that started life on a different database engine may need restructuring before it will scale on Oracle.

Undo

Before a user-visible data block is changed, Oracle records the prior version of the data in a globally available location, and builds a complex chain of pointers so that currently running queries can locate and reconstruct older versions of the data block if needed. The benefit of this is that readers don't need to block writers, and writers don't need to block readers—which is a massive advantage in a highly concurrent system.

The downside is the cost of generating these prior copies, which requires fairly complex linked lists (see "An Aside on Linked Lists") to be constructed in a variety of ways. In particular, there is a "per-transaction" linked list that has to be initiated and terminated with the transaction—so if you are committing too frequently, you've just hit another part of Oracle that introduces an unexpected overhead.

An Aside on Linked Lists

Oracle makes a lot of use of the "linked list" concept, not only for laying down trails through the data, but also for handling dynamic memory allocation.

There are several variations on a general theme, and the first schematic shows a very simple linked list. In this case, it starts with an *anchor point*, which is in a known location (such as the Undo Block Address portion of an Interested Transaction List (ITL) entry in a data block) that points to the first item in the list (in this case an undo record). But the first item in the list contains (implicitly or explicitly) a pointer to the next item in the list, and so on. The end of the list is identified by the appearance of a null pointer for the next item.

For memory manipulation, such as cache buffer chain handling, Oracle is particularly keen on the *doubly-linked list*, in which each item points both forward to the next item and backward to the previous item. These concepts are described in the following illustration:

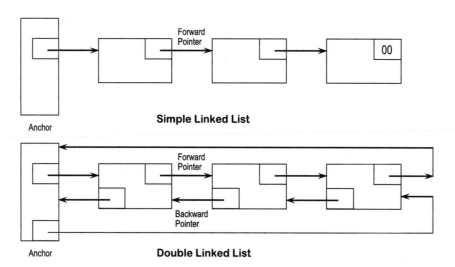

Simple Linked List

Anchor

Double Linked List

Anchor

Typically, Oracle also uses a strategy whereby the final item in the list connects back to the anchor point, so you have two closed loops of pointers built into each list. This strategy is particularly useful for memory management as it allows a better chance of the code being able to clean up shared memory after a process crash, but it takes more work to insert and delete items from such lists.

You also have the problem that undo is stored in database blocks, so it is protected by redo; the more redundant *undo* you generate, the harder you hit the *redo* log. Our application was a classic example of using a code generator for update screens: every screen used a single update statement that was a simple "update every column." But Oracle doesn't check if a column "update" really changes it, so when a user changed a single character flag field on screen, the code was generating a statement that told Oracle that every single column in the entire row had changed—and Oracle believed it. A full row update means the full row gets copied into the undo, and then gets copied into the redo twice (once because the user data changed, and once because the undo record was created). You can produce massive extra I/O if you don't know how Oracle works. There's also the unfortunate detail that if you do a no-change update to a row with an enabled foreign key constraint, the constraint is checked. So if you've got 15 foreign key constraints on a table, you are going to do 15 probes of primary key indexes, even though you didn't change the values.

Read Consistency

If a running query hits a block that has changed since the query started, Oracle follows a linked list of undo records to rebuild the version of the block as it was when the update started. This is tremendously useful for improved concurrency: reports don't block updates, updates don't block reports; moreover, updates don't result in inconsistent reports that show some old data and some new data.

The downside is that it costs in CPU consumption and stress on the data buffer as Oracle clones current data blocks and works its way backwards through the undo to rebuild older versions of the data. For long-running reports, this may even cost in excess I/O as very old undo information is reloaded from disk. It's also possible, of course, that Oracle will eventually discover that some elderly undo records have been overwritten because the report has been running too long, and the database has not been configured to protect the undo for long enough. Oracle error 1555 is a number that most DBA's can translate into the text without the aid of a manual: "snapshot too old." It isn't necessarily an issue, of course, so long as you are aware of the possibility and deliberately code for it.

But apart from the extra cost of building read-consistent versions of data, there is also the trap that Oracle returns a result immediately in situations where developers expect other database engines to wait to return the correct result. If all your experience is with a non-Oracle database engine, you may have written code that implicity joins a queue and waits if another user has made an uncommitted change to the data you are querying. Under Oracle, your code won't wait; it will return the data as it was when your query (or your transaction) started. In Oracle, the choice to wait, to be consistent at the query level, or to be consistent at the transaction level is one that has to be made explicitly, and the default is query-level consistency. You will see what nasty surprises this can cause when you get to the section on referential integrity ("Don't Trust Oracle, We'll Check It Ourselves").

Sharable SQL

Sharing is a wonderful concept: instead of analyzing and optimizing every SQL statement as it arrives, Oracle asks the questions, "Have I seen this text before?", "Does it mean the same as last time?", and "Is this user allowed to execute it?" This takes time and resources (latching and CPU), of course, but the saving is enormous if the answer to all three questions comes out positive very frequently. But if the answer to the first question is always no, then the feature is all cost and no benefit.

But why would the answer always be no? Because the application code has been written (or generated) the easiest way—quoting literal strings for all the input values, rather than using placeholders in the SQL and passing in the actual values separately. (There is a third, more sophisticated and even more efficient, option. This involves writing code to declare cursor variables as global variables, explicitly parsing text for each variable, and then calling Oracle to reexecute against the preparsed variable. This technique is usually only needed for highly concurrent systems, and it is relatively easy for a developer to produce code that leaks memory by accident if the whole thing has to be coded by hand. Fortunately, various tools and precompilers have compiler flags that allow the technique to be handled behind the scenes.)

Of course, I have made the claim that the saving is "enormous" if sharing occurs "very frequently." There are circumstances in which "enormous" is not big enough, and "very frequently" doesn't happen.

In an OLTP system, a perfectly reasonable 5-table join may take 0.02 seconds to optimize from cold, and 0.01 seconds to execute. That 0.02 seconds is enormous if you execute 2,500,000 virtually identical statements per day.

In a DSS system, a totally repellent 13-table join may take 5 seconds to optimize and 10 minutes to run. That 5 seconds is totally insignificant, even if you run 1,000 virtually identical statements per day. (And if you do, you should probably have taken time to learn about materialized views and query rewrite.)

The downside to sharable SQL in OLTP systems is nonexistent . . . unless you don't do any sharing, in which case it is all cost and no benefit. Because of this, Oracle has introduced a couple of dirty tricks (`cursor_sharing=force` or `cursor_sharing=similar`) to allow the database to impose an imitation of sharable SQL even when the application doesn't use it. If you enable either of these options, Oracle takes the incoming SQL, copies out any literal values, and rewrites the text with system-generated bind variables—then it can check to see if the text has been used before.

An Aside on Bind Variables, Histograms, and cursor_sharing

It is common knowledge that bind variables reduce (but don't entirely eliminate) the benefit of histograms. Sometimes, however, Oracle needs the full benefit of histograms to find the optimum execution path for a query, and there are usually a few bits of SQL in OLTP systems that need to use literal values. If you have control of the SQL, you can use the hint /*+ cursor_sharing_exact */ to override the cursor_sharing directive and stop the bind variable substitution. If you don't have control of the SQL, the option cursor_sharing = similar will activate bind variable substitution, but then reoptimize with the actual values if any histograms exist on any columns in the query that could make a difference to the execution path. Be careful with cursor_sharing = similar—it could make things worse, especially if you have far more histograms than you really need.

Unfortunately, dirty tricks tend to have limitations, and a few bugs. In the case of cursor_sharing, you will find that it simply doesn't work with the older form of calls to anonymous PL/SQL blocks. You may also find that it crashes your session if you use the newer form of calls to anonymous PL/SQL blocks but build your blocks with a mixture of literal strings and bind variables.

The Awful Truth

After that review of the four key features of Oracle, what do you say when you see that this application

- Commits on every statement sent to the database.

- Generates literal string SQL for every query and update from the user screens—and there are lots of them—and uses as a standard for parent/child screens the approach of selecting every related rowid for a child table, then fetching each child row by (literally quoted) rowid.

- Uses surrogate keys everywhere that have been generated as sequence numbers but padded out to very long character columns, and then has lots of (undeclared) foreign key columns so that all the rows are unnecessarily long, adding significant volume to the undo and redo. (This specific implementation of surrogate keys also happens to wreck the optimizer's ability to work out good execution paths, as we shall see later.)

- Updates every column in the table for every tiny update to the on-screen data. Luckily, the developers didn't believe in referential integrity, so the cost of checking all the (undeclared) foreign key constraints didn't take place at the database. Unfortunately, the generator had coded the screens to do a round-trip check against the database for every known foreign key, even if it hadn't changed.

The only cost-effective options are damage limitation. No one is going to rewrite the application; no one is going to rewrite their pet code generator (unless the change is really straightforward) without an overwhelmingly powerful argument—such as their most lucrative client dumping the project.

So the only option is to set `cursor_sharing = force` / `similar` in a login trigger for the screen users, and hope that you don't hit any of the related bugs, and that the side effects on the optimizer don't do any damage. And you suggest that the code generator, or standards document, be rewritten to generate code that understands bind variables—but that's probably not going to be considered a cost-effective thing to do (at least in the short term).

You suggest that the database should be used to deal with foreign key constraints. You also suggest that the most heavily used screens are modified by hand (as a short-term measure) so that they include code to perform the foreign key check only if the screen value has changed—but you have to be very lucky for that to be possible.

You suggest that when a screen is sending multiple update statements to the database, only one commit request is sent at the end of the proper business transaction. That might be impossible to implement, but perhaps a couple of the most heavily used screens could be fixed by hand.

You make the number of undo segments large, make the size of the redo log buffer large, and increase the number of CPUs, possibly hacking some of the undocumented parameters to increase the various latches to their legal maximum values.

But basically, short of buying extreme hardware and keeping your fingers crossed, there really isn't a lot you can do if an application has been written without any consideration of the costs and benefits of the Oracle database engine.

Don't Trust Oracle, We'll Check It Ourselves

One of the tremendous benefits of Oracle is the way that *declarative referential integrity constraints* are built into the database engine. If you insist that an order can exist only if there is a customer who has placed it, then it is not possible for an orphaned order to come into existence on your system.

The application vendor believed that it was important to make sure that the data was correct, so the designers and coders approved of referential integrity. Of course, the best way to implement referential integrity *might* be open to argument, and it *might* be database specific rather than database independent, and surely (they said) it would be more efficient for the application code to handle it than for the database to carry the overheads.

However, it is very dangerous to ignore the inefficiencies—and risks—inherent in coding the same constraint in many places in the application rather than just once in the database. Ultimately, you could try to write code outside the database to make sure that referential integrity is enforced—but you may be surprised to find that either it doesn't work properly or it turns your OLTP system into a single-user, or at best low-concurrency, system.

Consider the following actions:

Session 1	Session 2	Time
	delete from customers where customer_id = 999;	t0
select null from customers where customer_id = 999; -- one row returned, so proceed.		t1
	commit;	t2
insert into orders (customer_id, ...) values (999,...)		t3
commit; -- oops		t4

Unless you have strict rules to ensure that no one can delete primary key data (or change the key values), Oracle's read consistency will guarantee that eventually something will go wrong and you will insert orphan data. At time t1, session 1 can see customer 999, because the delete has not been committed. Remember that Oracle does not see uncommitted changes, and reads are not blocked by writes.

If you are not going to use Oracle's built-in referential integrity, your code has to do a select for update to lock the customer row for the duration of the insert (this is effectively what some other database engines do—by acquiring read locks implicitly). So the sequence would look more like this:

Session 1	Session 2	Time
	Delete from customers where customer_id = 999;	t0
select null from customers where customer_id = 999 for update; -- process now waits on session 2		t1
	commit;	t2
No rows returned Front end reports error		t3

But there is a drawback; you've just started to serialize the order entry process—only one session can insert an order for that customer at a time because only one session can hold that lock on that specific customer row. (In fact, unless you enforce strict controls that the customer_id on an order cannot be changed, you've affected both inserts and updates.) For example:

Session 1	Session 2	Time
select null from customers where customer_id = 999 for update; -- one row returned - so proceed.		t0
	Select null from customers where customer_id = 999 for update; - process waits on session 1	t1
Insert into orders (customer_id, ...) Values (999,...)	-- still waiting on session 1	t2
insert into order_lines(...);	-- still waiting on session 1	t3
insert into order_lines(...);	-- still waiting on session 1	t4
commit;		t5
	-- one row returned - so proceed insert into orders (customer_id, ...) values (999,...)	t6

Of course, as a damage-limitation exercise, you could decide that session 1 should commit the order insert at t3, releasing the customer row as soon as possible before inserting the order lines. And this is exactly what some applications do because that's what some underlying database engines need; but it's not good practice to break a "business transaction" into multiple database transactions. At best, this soon requires you to add further, potentially complex, code to clean up the messes that can be left behind when sessions crash in the middle of a business transaction after committing some incomplete data.

You may point out that my example of locking customers isn't going to be a realistic concurrency threat. True, the same customer is (probably) not going to be creating several orders at the same time. On the other hand, the same issue will be relevant to the products table. And since you may get multiple lines per order, with different products on each line, the locking requirement can lead to deadlocks:

Session 1	Session 2	Time

`select null`
`from products`
`where product_id = 111`
`for update;`
		t0

	`select null`
	`from products`
	`where product_id = 222`
	`for update;`
		t1

`-- one row returned - so proceed.`
`insert into order_lines (prod_id, )`
`values (111, )`
		t2

	`-- one row returned - so proceed.`
	`insert into order_lines (prod_id, )`
	`values (222, )`
		t3

`select null`
`from products`
`where product_id = 222`
`for update;`
`-- process waits on session 2`
		t4

	`select null`
	`from products`
	`where product_id = 111`
	`for update;`
	`-- process waits on session 1`
		t5

`-- deadlock detected (ora-00060)`
`-- rollback to t3`
`-- product 111 still locked`
		t6

	`-- still waiting on session 1`	t7

So now you have code that crashes out with startling regularity for no apparent reason. But it works perfectly in development when just one developer tests it! The only (quick, but bad) workaround to this problem is to commit on every single row—perhaps updating the order again on each line to keep running totals of value before the commit. And now you really do have a nasty data consistency problem—some other user could be running reports about the value of outstanding orders, and can see a partial order that shouldn't really exist yet.

Referential integrity in the database is important. If you don't put it there, the steps you have to take to make it work in the code are horrendously inefficient and will cause endless problems.

You've probably noticed that I haven't bothered to address the argument about referential integrity in the code being "more efficient" because it is pretty irrelevant when you realize that you have much more important details to worry about than simply how fast things go.

However, my opinion (which is not the same as fact) is that speed doesn't come into it anyway. You probably want to put existence tests into the user-facing code because users are happier with field-by-field error reporting, and don't want to be told at the end of the page that the customer code they've entered doesn't exist. But existence tests (or "probably will exist by the time we get to insert" tests) are not the same as referential integrity.

Watch Out, There's an Auditor About!

Accountants, auditors, and tax inspectors love sequence numbers—but only if no gaps exist in the sequence.

OO developers (particularly, but not exclusively) also like sequences but aren't so fussy about gaps because what they want is meaningless numbers that are guaranteed to be unique; and a noncyclic sequence will do the job perfectly well.

Nothing can scale well under the demands of accountants and tax inspectors (though it is possible to fake your way around the demands for no-gap sequential numbers), but Oracle can at least cope with OO developers very efficiently—provided the developers are allowed to use Oracle features and aren't trapped in the world of database independence.

Oracle supplies a *sequence* type, for example:

```
create sequence fast_seq cache 1000;
```

When all the defaults are expanded, this is short for the following:

```
create sequence fast_seq
   minvalue 1
   maxvalue 1E+27
   increment by 1
   start with 1
   cache 1000
   noorder
   nocycle;
```

Internally, Oracle stores this sequence as a row in a sys-owned table called seq$, recording various details in that row such as the cache size, and the latest high-water value (see the following note). When the sequence is in use its state, including the high-water value and the current value, is cached in memory (in the SGA) so that a session calling for the next value can get it quickly. When a session calls for a new value, the current value in memory is incremented and handed off. If the result matches the current high-water value, then a brief hiatus occurs as the high-water value is incremented by the cache size and the new high-water value is written back to the seq$ table. The average time that it takes a session to get a sequence number from Oracle is affected most significantly by the setting for the cache size.

 NOTE *There is a common belief that Oracle caches a sequence in the SGA by holding an actual list of outstanding values. In fact, Oracle needs to hold just two critical values—the next value to be issued, and a target value (or high-water value) that will trigger a write to disk. These details, and the rest of the infrastructure for a sequence, can be seen in the SYS-owned view* v$_sequences. *When the next value reaches the target value, the target value is increased by the cache size, and the new target value is written to disk in the* seq$ *table.*

Traditional Oracle-aware code for using sequences would be something like the following:

```
select fast_seq.nextval
into :bind_var
from dual;

insert into orders (order_id, ...)
values (:bind_var,...);
```

A better quality of Oracle-aware code would more likely do this:

```
insert into orders (order_id, ...)
values (fast_seq.nextval,...)
returning order_id into :bind_var;
```

The first version requires an SQL statement execution and a round-trip to get a value into a local variable for reuse. The second version with the `returning` clause (available from an early version of 8.1, or possibly even 8.0) is a nearly free acquisition of the sequence number, which is passed back on a preexisting message.

The primary purpose of Oracle sequences is to supply unique numbers rapidly; but as you can see from the description, the numbers are not subject to normal transaction control, so numbers can easily be lost. It is possible to reduce the *probability* of losing numbers by setting the cache size to zero—but then the time it takes to get the next sequence number is increased, and your application becomes serialized on the seq$ table, because every increment of the sequence number requires an update to a row in that table. (The time lost is relatively small, as the sequence operates outside your transaction, using an autonomous transaction to update the seq$ table.) However, even if you set the cache size to zero, your application can still "lose" sequence numbers if a session crashes, rolls back, or simply fails to use a sequence number that it has requested.

But sequences are an Oracle thing, and our application was database independent. So what do you do if you don't want to use Oracle sequences? Typically, something like this:

```
select seq_value
into :local_variable
from seq_table
where seq_name = 'SLOW_SEQ'
for update;

update seq_table
set seq_value = seq_value + 1
where seq_name = 'SLOW_SEQ';

commit;
```

The commit is necessary to reduce the time that other sessions sit waiting for you to get out of the way. Note, by the way, that even if you adopt this approach, your session may crash before you've used and committed the sequence number you've acquired, so you haven't addressed the accountants' and tax inspectors' requirements.

More significantly, you have reduced your scalability quite dramatically. Sessions will be queueing, and you've now achieved in three round-trips, three redo records, and six block changes, something that Oracle could do in one (or zero) round-trip, no redo records, and no block changes.

But our application didn't have just one home-grown sequence generator, it had a couple of hundred; and every single sequence had its own row in the sequences table, and every row was in the same block. Not only did the system suffer collisions on concurrent updates to an individual sequence, it spent a lot of time on *buffer busy waits* or *ITL waits* (see the following sidebar "Buffer Busy Waits and the ITL") even when different sessions were using different sequence generators. You can limit the damage, of course, by re-creating your sequences table with one row per block. You could decide that this is one of those rare cases where using a tablespace with a 2KB block size could be beneficial because it moves the problem into a segregated buffer cache. You could set pctfree to 99, set pctused to 1, and include a space-wasting column to make sure that only one row gets into a block. (An alternative is to create the first row, and then use the command to *minimize* records_per_block *before creating any more, but this still seems to let you get two rows per block, even in version 10g.*) In the following example, you can see that the rows are the first rows in four separate blocks:

```
create table seq_table (
    seq_name        varchar2(32),
    seq_value       number(38),
    padding         varchar2(1000),
    constraint sqt_pk primary key(seq_name)
)
pctfree 99 pctused 1
tablespace test_2K
;

insert into seq_table values('SLOW_SEQ_1', 0, rpad('x',1000));
insert into seq_table values('SLOW_SEQ_2', 0, rpad('x',1000));
insert into seq_table values('SLOW_SEQ_3', 0, rpad('x',1000));
insert into seq_table values('SLOW_SEQ_4', 0, rpad('x',1000));

commit;

select
    dbms_rowid.rowid_relative_fno(rowid)     file_no,
    dbms_rowid.rowid_block_number(rowid)     blk_no,
    dbms_rowid.rowid_row_number(rowid)       row_no,
    seq_name
from seq_table
;
```

FILE_NO	BLK_NO	ROW_NO	SEQ_NAME
9	058	0	SLOW_SEQ_1
9	1059	0	SLOW_SEQ_2
9	1060	0	SLOW_SEQ_3
9	1061	0	SLOW_SEQ_4

In fact, if you're using Real Application Clusters (RAC), you may want to consider rigging the value of `pctfree` on Oracle's internal `seq$` table when you build the database for a similar reason—provided you can get approval from Oracle support.

Buffer Busy Waits and the ITL

Despite the enormous degree of concurrency that Oracle allows, there are some operations, typically memory-related, that have to be serialized. Changing the contents of a buffer in the database block buffer is one such activity. When a process wants to change the contents of a buffered block, it has to acquire an exclusive pin on that buffer for a very short period of time. If another process wants to change the block at the same time, it will have to wait for that pin to be downgraded and effectively released. This type of collision is one of the more common reasons for the wait known as the *buffer busy wait*.

When a process wants to update a row in a block, it has to register an active transaction in a section of the block known as the *interested transaction list* (ITL). The initial size of the ITL is set by the `INITRANS` parameter when the table is created, but the ITL can grow dynamically. If too many concurrent processes want to update a block though, it is possible that there are not enough slots in the ITL for all of them, and no free space for the ITL to grow into. At this point a process can end up waiting. Unfortunately, it reports itself as waiting for an *enqueue*, rather than waiting for an ITL.

In Oracle 9.2, you can use the view `v$segstat` to check (among other statistics) the number of buffer busy waits and ITL waits that a segment has suffered.

Talking of RAC—home-grown sequences will not be rescued by RAC. In fact, home-grown sequences are one of the features that the writers of the *RAC Concepts Manual* (Release 2 (9.2) Part A96597-01) must have had in mind when they said on page 4-2

Poorly designed systems do not scale well on either single-instance Oracle databases or on Real Application Clusters databases—poorly designed applications will likely experience performance degradation as demand increases.

Think of all those nodes queuing for and updating the one block that holds the one row that represents your sequence. That one block is going to be endlessly flying back and forth across the interconnect, causing huge numbers of messages, lock upgrades and downgrades, and RAC-specific buffer activity all over the place.

In a live demonstration to the UKOUG, I showed how the effect of this design flaw caused 100% serialization in a pair of scripts running on different nodes in a 2-node RAC setup. (It should be no surprise that the same thing happened with a NOCACHE Oracle sequence, too.)

Gap-Free Sequences—How to Bodge It

If you aren't worried about gaps, use cached Oracle sequences; and if you want to get maximum benefit from Oracle sequences, set the cache to a suitable size and take advantage of the returning clause.

If you really can't have any gaps, you have a real scalability problem. If you can't use Oracle sequences, you have to implement some variation of getting your sequence numbers from an application table; and unless you have a low-throughput system, you will suffer the same unpleasant serialization problem as our application did, though with proper attention to design, you can minimize the damage.

The only way to avoid gaps (or at least to keep an audit trail of the numbers that have been acquired but not used) is to prepare and store a list of numbers so that you can use a number and then delete it from the list *in the same Oracle transaction*. If that one transaction fails, the number is still available for another session to use (or at least left in a state that identifies it as "acquired by user X at time Y but not applied"); if the transaction succeeds the number is not available.

For example, you could create a table to hold a list of numbers, and a function to acquire, conceal, mark, and return one of the numbers. The function would have to use something like the built-in (but undocumented and therefore unsupported) SKIP LOCKED feature used by advanced queuing. Something similar to the following pseudo-code can work (but still introduces a lot of overhead):

```
for r1 in (
    select /*+ index */ apparently free sequence numbers
    ordered by sequence number
) loop
    begin
        m_seq := autonomous_lock_attempt (r1.sequence_number);
    exception
        when busy then null;          -- it was already locked
        when no_data_found then null; -- it has been grabbed
        when others then raise;       -- unexpected error
    end;
```

```
  if m_seq is not null then        -- we've already marked it
     update seq_table
     set          status = 'used',
                  date_acquired = sysdate,
                  user_holding = sys_context('userenv','session_user')
     where        sequence_number  = m_seq;
     exit;
  end if;
end loop;
return m_seq;
```

The autonomous_lock_attempt() function should simply do a select for update nowait on the target row, using the incoming sequence number and a status of free to identify it. If the row has been grabbed by another session and is still in the middle of an update, Oracle will raise error ORA-00054 (translated here as an exception called busy). If the row has been grabbed by another session, changed to requested, and committed, the select process will fail with the well-known exception no data found.

If the routine can lock the row, it should immediately update its status to requested and record some audit information on the row in an autonomous transaction, and commit. The next step in the main loop updates the row status and audit information (again) with a normal transaction, terminates the loop, and returns the sequence number to the caller.

At this point, the caller now has a sequence number that has been logged in the sequence table. If the user does something with this sequence number and commits, the sequence table has a full audit; if the user's session terminates, or rolls back, the sequence number still has an audit record of "requested" in the sequences table.

It's not elegant, but it gets the job done (almost—as the sequence numbers are not likely to be used in strictly ascending order). Moreover, if you are running under RAC, you can add a column for the available instances, and use a table that is list-partitioned by instance to avoid cross-instance collisions in the search for available sequence numbers. And in Oracle 10g, you can even make it a list-partitioned Index Organized Table (IOT), to maximize efficiency (or, more truthfully, minimize the damage).

As far as our application was concerned, this was a viable solution—although the preceding pseudo-code had to be implemented in the front end, because PL/SQL procedures were database dependent and therefore banned.

What Did You Say This Was?

To avoid database independence, our application refused to recognize any special data types—even the ones that might have been coerced silently by the database engine. So dates and Oracle's more recent `timestamp with time zone` were not allowed. The application also denied the existence of `null` because handling nulls can be awkward and different databases may handle them differently. Instead, it used special values to represent missing data, for example, `'31-Dec-9999'` instead of a null date. Unfortunately both these decisions hit the cost-based optimizer at its weakest point—it doesn't actually know what you're trying to do, so it assumes you are using the database properly. Let's examine how this can affect the optimizer's ability to produce the appropriate execution path.

The application had to hold the classic seven years' worth of data demanded by the hypothetical tax man. To keep the numbers clean while getting a feel for how we approached this task, pretend you have data starting at January 1, 1995, and ending on December 31, 2001, for a total of (approximately) 2,500 days, and the table contains 10,000 rows per day. To avoid any dependency on Oracle dates, the application stores the date as an 8-digit number in the form YYYYMMDD, which allows the numbers and dates to sort correctly.

Run a report that summarizes data for the previous week. Since this covers a total of seven days out of 2,500 on a table where the data is tightly clustered (the data for any one day is all packed into a small set of blocks), Oracle would probably want to choose an indexed access path.

The go-live date is December 7, 2001, and all through December the report runs perfectly. On January 2, 2002, the report runs, and Oracle decides to use a tablescan on this table, and picks a terrible execution plan. What's gone wrong?

What you want to say is

```
select   *
from     orders
where    sale_date_d between '26-Dec-2001' and '01-Jan-2002';
```

What you've said is

```
select   *
from     orders
where    sale_date_n between 20011226 and 20020101;
```

The range of the report is seven days, so the query is supposed to cover December 26 to January 1 inclusive, seven days out of roughly 2,500 just as usual. But Oracle doesn't know it's looking at dates, it thinks it's looking at numbers, and you've just asked for the numbers between 20011226 to 20020101, a range of 8,875.

And Oracle doesn't know about 2,500 days, it's looking at a low-high range from 19950101 to 20020101, a total range of 70,000. Oracle thinks you want about 12.5% of the data, and even with a good clustering factor, that's quite likely to swing the optimizer from an indexed access path to a tablescan.

Whenever there is something funny about the data values, such as gaps in the range of available values, or dramatic variations in the number of occurrences of particular values, the optimizer can make the wrong decision about the execution path. Using the wrong data types can make this happen extremely frequently.

The unexpected switch between tablescans and indexes also appears (often the other way around) with null values, or special values, even in the cases where the data types are correct. You can see this with a different query on the seven-year table. Say you have a report that summarizes the last year. Assume you have some rows where the date stamp is technically supposed to be blank, but because the application is database independent the blanks are actually represented by the unrealistic data December 31, 9999. (In this case, it doesn't really matter whether you pretend the column is defined as a real date type or a numeric or character representation, the arithmetic works out about the same.)

Assume you're running a query for the whole of the year 2001. You know that you want about one seventh of the data. If nulls are used in the datestamp column, Oracle will also work this out for itself and act accordingly. But if you put in your silly value to get rid of nulls, Oracle will infer that the data ranges from 1995 to 9999, a total of about 8,000 years—which suggests your query wants slightly less than 0.125% of the total data. The execution path will probably be unsuitable.

Any time you see incorrect data types, or nulls being represented by special values, or even extreme values being used for special cases ("our accounting year has periods 1 to 13, but we use period 999 for adjustments"), you can assume that Oracle will eventually pick some very poor execution paths.

Of course, if our application had been using bind variables rather than literal strings, Oracle would have used a hard-coded value for the selectivity of bind variables with a between clause, and this hard-coded value happens to be 1 row in 400. By a lucky coincidence, this would have been a nearly perfect assumption for our first example (where we requested 7 days out of 2,500). On the other hand, Oracle would have used exactly the same value for our second query (where we requested one year out of seven), with appalling performance consequences—bind variables can produce surprising side effects on queries that are supposed to handle a large volume of data.

But when you upgrade from Oracle 8 to Oracle 9, things can go wrong—some lucky accidents will disappear because Oracle starts to do *bind variable peeking*. On the first parse of a new SQL statement (or on a reload if information about the execution path has been flushed), Oracle will check the actual values of the bind variables, and create a path that appears to be appropriate for the values it finds. There are numerous ways in which this can produce surprises, so check your data typing, null handling, and special values before upgrading.

You could, of course, create histograms on the data, and if you do you may give Oracle enough information to cope gracefully with these problems. In the seven-year table, there are about 84 holes in the data—the gaps in the numbers between the end of one month and the start of the next. If you create a histogram on the critical column with at least 84 buckets in it, the resulting statistics might be enough to allow Oracle to spot the gaps, and allow for them (to some degree) in its calculations. Similarly, in the year 9999 example, a histogram with nine buckets might be sufficient to tell Oracle about the enormous gap between the real data and the special value. (It would be better to work out what percentage of the data had the spurious value and, if possible, set the number of buckets to at least 100 / {calculated percentage}, as this would allow Oracle to push all the spurious data into a single bucket.)

The problems with data types that I've covered so far relate to Oracle calculation of selectivity for a range scan—the sample queries were using a between predicate. But it is possible to confuse the optimizer on equalities as well—which our application managed to do with a two-pronged approach. I have already described how the application used sequence numbers for surrogate keys, but I haven't yet mentioned that the code didn't store these numbers as numeric data, it converted them into character strings and padded them on the left with zeros to a fixed length of 35 characters.

Try this little experiment on 8.1.7.4 or 9.2.0.4. This emulates the way the application stored its surrogate keys and generated statistics on the key column. Before you run the code, have a guess at what the answer is likely to be for the closing query, which is supposed to report the number of distinct values stored. (As a starting point, you might count the number of rows in all_objects, which is what you might expect to see as the result.)

```
create table t1 as
select
      lpad(rownum, 35, '0') id
from
      all_objects
;

analyze table t1 compute statistics;

select
      num_distinct
from
      user_tab_columns
where
      table_name = 'T1'
and   column_name = 'ID'
;
```

You probably discovered that the actual result was roughly one thousand times smaller than you were expecting. What's gone wrong?

Oracle examines the first 32 bytes of a character field when analyzing statistics so `lpad(rownum,35,'0')` means the last three digits of the `rownum` have been lost by the analyze command. For my copy of Oracle 8, the number of distinct values (`num_distinct`) was 22.

To highlight how critical this error can be, set `autotrace` on, run the following query, and check the *cardinality* you get back from the execution plan:

```
select * from t1 where id = '00000000000000000000000000000000001';
```

The reported cardinality will be close to 1,000, despite the fact that we know that the number of rows returned will be one! But the estimated cardinality of each step of an execution plan has a dramatic impact on the table order and access paths used for the full plan—and we've managed to confuse the optimizer on a simple equality by using a totally pointless conversion and padding.

Don't forget that this simple little trick has turned a 5-digit number (internal representation about 4 bytes) into a 35-character string (internal representation 35 bytes) that will appear in the table, the primary key index (sorry, unique index—referential integrity isn't used in this database), and probably a (not-declared) foreign key that probably has an index on it. Not only are the indexes larger than they need to be, the number of entries in each branch block will be reduced because of the large number of leading zeros on every entry. Branch blocks are usually well packed because each entry is truncated to the first byte that distinguishes it from the next entry. But every entry in this case starts with 30 or more zeros, so an 8KB branch block that could hold around 550 entries comprised of 10-digit integers is reduced to holding 180 entries of zero-padded strings. If you wreck the packing on every branch block, you are likely to increase the height of the index on even relatively small tables by one or two levels. It's not a lot, but when every single-row access needs one or two extra logical I/Os, the latch and CPU costs start to climb.

Imagine, next, a table with just half a dozen (not-declared) foreign keys, and you have rows that start at 240 bytes before you put any other information into them.

A quick fix for the silly result on `num_distinct`—don't use the `analyze` command. Oracle Corp. has been telling its customers for some time that they should be using the `dbms_stats` package. As you migrate to the `dbms_stats` package, though, you may want to run some careful tests to make sure you know which statistics are produced by which options. Things to check for (by building a small test case) are whether you get index statistics, or not; whether you get simple column statistics, or not; whether you get histograms, or not. I've never noticed `dbms_stats` missing out statistics that I was expecting to see—but I have heard reports from time to time that some people have "lost" some statistics as they made the change. Some of the "lost" statistics may be deliberate—dbms_stats originally collected only the numbers of interest to the CBO; some of the statistics may go missing because the chosen method_opt is not an exact match for the options chosen with the analyze command.

Indexing

We don't have to worry about performance, we'll just add a few more indexes when we need to tune the important queries.

There are two drawbacks to this strategy. The first is that you can end up with an awful lot of indexes—some of which are redundant—and every index adds an overhead on inserts and deletes, and may add an overhead on updates. (Fortunately, a no-change update on an indexed column doesn't cause Oracle to descend the index and do a no-change update on the index.) The second is that the existence of an index doesn't mean Oracle will use it, so attempting to fix a performance issue by throwing indexes at the problem in a fairly arbitrary fashion could make matters worse.

There is, however, a directive that causes even more problems than the random introduction of magic indexes. It's the application for which the supplier says, "Don't mess with the indexes, or you're not supported." It's really bizarre to consider that a generic application could support all possible clients without some variation in data appearing; but that's exactly what the supplier is claiming with this demand.

Consider, for example, a basic stockbroker package installed at two different companies. One company has 100,000 clients who average about one trade per year and own an average of three different stocks, the other has 100 (very wealthy) clients who average one trade per day and own an average of 300 different stocks, bonds, and so on. How likely is it that the two implementations need exactly the same indexing strategy to perform well?

So what do you do when you discover one table with 23 different indexes on it (many of them related to the undeclared foreign keys, but there are others)? A quick scan of the index definitions shows you four indexes with the following definitions:

```
create index i0001647 on t0001143(c0021575, c0021578, c0021563, c0021571, c0021589)
create index i0001649 on t0001143(c0021575, c0021578, c0021563, c0021571)
create index i0001653 on t0001143(c0021575, c0021578, c0021571, c0021563)
create index i0001657 on t0001143(c0021575, c0021563, c0021571, c0021578, c0021589)
```

Because of the meaningless numbers (and yes, this really is a genuine sample), it's not all that easy to spot the severe degree of overlap between these indexes. The first thing you have to do is to translate the numeric columns into meaningful names as that may give you some clue about the function. Then you collect details about ranges, number of distinct values, number of nulls, and types of use (in other words, all the stuff the cost-based optimizer collects when deciding whether or not to use the indexes).

In this example, it is highly likely that one of the first two indexes can be dropped—the first four columns match, and it seems unlikely that the fifth column of the first index can be adding much value, and if it is, perhaps the second index is the one to drop. (You may have to find out why the second index was created—perhaps the developers created the second index because the optimizer was ignoring the first index. Perhaps the optimizer was ignoring the first index because of an anomaly with the `clustering_factor` that could have been fixed by calling the packaged procedure `dbms_stats.set_index_stats`.)

Index i0001657 looks redundant given that index i0001647 exists; if all five columns are specified, only one of the indexes would be useful; if only the first four columns are specified, again only one of the indexes should be necessary (although the same comment about the clustering factor applies). If only three or two columns were scanned, then perhaps one of the indexes should be only three columns long, rather than five columns.

Looking at the column names that appear in the last three indexes, it seems reasonably likely that all three could be replaced by a single, shorter index—although it may be necessary to change the column order of the first index to achieve this—but without information about the application, at least to the extent of knowing what those silly column names represent, it's impossible to be certain what to do for the best.

Always be suspicious about excessive indexing—in an OLTP system, indexes are very expensive to maintain: they cost in undo volume, hence undo segment header gets (a possible contention point), and they cost in redo records, hence redo allocation latch gets (another possible contention point) and volume of redo log generated.

Fortunately, this system didn't believe in referential integrity in the database. Some systems go overboard with indexes because they do believe in referential integrity in the database. There is a well-known issue relating to foreign keys and child tables being locked if you don't create indexes supporting the foreign keys. Oracle 9 introduced a small change that reduces the scale of the problem slightly, but doesn't make it go away.

Remember that this is only an issue if parent rows are deleted, or parent key values are updated. (Actually, there is an oddity that if the primary key is enforced by an index that contains extra columns, then the problem appears even if it is the non-key, indexed column that is updated.) So don't create indexes to support foreign keys unless you have to, or unless they are inherently useful indexes anyway.

Unfortunately, having said you don't need the foreign key index if you don't modify or delete the primary key, you may have one of those systems that updates every column in the table with no-change updates. If so, you will find that a no-change update counts as a primary key update, and the foreign key indexes are needed after all.

Data Extract to Warehouse

Having survived the rigors of the new application, next I'll discuss the analytic and warehousing systems—the existing in-house databases that needed to extract data from the new application. How were they going to get their data? It can be very difficult to connect existing systems to new systems, and I often get the impression that most of the cost and agony of a new system comes from tying it to existing systems.

Apart from the fact that the documentation is never up to date, it is almost always the case that the OLTP application that your data warehouse wants to raid wasn't originally designed with auditing or changed data capture (CDC) in mind.

Luckily, the OLTP application had implemented four audit columns on every single table.

```
dttm_cr    number(17)     Date and time created (yyyymmddhhmissccc)
user_cr    varchar2(35)   User creating - yes, it was a standard meaningless ID
dttm_upd   number(14)     Date and time of last update
user_upd   varchar2(35)   User updating
```

Fortunately, there were (nearly) readable names for these columns (the only other column with that privilege was the ubiquitous ID column).

In passing, these four columns were always the last four columns in the table but were always populated, the update values being the same as the creation values to start with. It's worth bearing in mind that there may be a little space benefit in arranging table columns so that the columns that are most likely to stay blank are at the end of the row—Oracle doesn't use any space to store trailing nulls. Mind you, just to put forward a perfectly valid, but contrary, piece of advice: it takes CPU to skip along a row to find a column, so you ought to put columns that are frequently in the select list or where clause near the start of the row if they will only be checked after the table has been reached by an indexed access.

Anyway, the proposed extract strategy was very straightforward: on each run of the extract, copy all rows that had a dttm_upd greater than the date of the previous extract.

There were three problems that I felt constrained to point out. The first was a simple business decision: what should occur when a row in the new OLTP system is deleted? Unless the new OLTP system did logical deletes rather physical deletes, there would be nothing in the OLTP system to tell the data warehouse extract program that a row that it found some time in the past had been deleted. Were rows like this supposed to remain in the data warehouse forever?

The second problem was nearly funny. Remember that the new OLTP system was a database-independent system, and that's why it could record the date/time stamp to the centisecond, it wasn't relying on Oracle's SYSDATE (which is only accurate to the second). The date/time stamp was coming from the front-end code—specifically, from each PC's clock. What's the probability that 500 PCs around the world all have the same time accurate to the hour, let alone the centisecond?

But the third problem was the classic database-independent problem—Oracle does that nonblocking read consistency thing. Consider the following steps:

User Program	Extract Program	Time
update tablex set dttm_upd = 17:01:01		17:01:01
	Store 17:01:02 as last run time. select * from tablex where dttm_upd > {previous run}	17:01:02
Commit;		17:01:03

The extract starts before the commit of the user program, so it doesn't see the (dirty) row with a timestamp of 17:01:01, nor does the extract wait for a read lock (Oracle is non-blocking, remember); it sees the row in its earlier version.

So it doesn't pick up the change on this run, and it won't pick up the change on the next run because the committed timestamp will be 17:01:01, and the extract will be looking for data with a timestamp newer than 17:01:02.

In theory, the business may have been happy with a few errors and omissions—it isn't unreasonable to say that the warehouse will be close to accurate, and will generally catch up within a few days on the odd rows that go wrong. In practice, that depends on your carefully specified requirements.

At last, the database independence swung in our favor. The new OLTP application was not allowed to use triggers, so we could. Essentially we could solve all three problems by creating row-level triggers on inserts, updates, and deletes that copied (non-declared) primary keys into a log table with an Insert/Update/Delete flag and a (database) timestamp. Since the application wasn't too worried about changing primary keys (notwithstanding the meaningless key concept), we had to make the update triggers record a delete/insert pair if the primary key changed.

The extract process was then able to (outer) join each trigger table to the base table on the primary key, and walk through the result set (one row at a time, PL/SQL loop, unfortunately) working out what had to be done at the data warehouse to bring it up to date. It wasn't efficient, but at least it was correct, and relatively easy to code as a short-term fix. (And it does sound just a little bit like Oracle's own replication, doesn't it?)

Even so, it's not easy to handle correct transfer of data, and the simple description omits some critical details.

Some of the problems are business related: what do you want to see on the warehouse, every change in state, or just the most recent state? And if you want to see every change in state (which means a simple primary key copy tracking mechanism won't do the job), what do you want to do about deletions?

Some of the problems are about correct implementation in Oracle. There are plenty of traps in Oracle's read consistency mechanisms that will eventually catch the unwary. As the extract program transfers data to the warehouse, what does it do to ensure that it does a proper job of cleaning up the log table behind itself? In general, the only safe strategy is to mark all the rows that you are going to delete, apply the marked rows, and then delete them. Any other strategy tends to result in deleting rows you haven't applied, or having processes crash with ORA-01555: snapshot too old errors.

The other main variation on the theme is to maintain two copies of your logging table, and use either a synonym switch or a partition exchange trick to make one copy current and the other copy static. This can work, but you have to remember that any procedures dependent on the target object will become invalid as you make the switch. (Oracle 10g has a little feature that should solve this problem—a synonym can be pointed to a new object without invalidating dependent procedures provided the new object is sufficiently similar in structure to the original.)

Perhaps the newest and nicest solution, though, is to take advantage of flashback queries. The concept is quite simple. At the start of each run to transfer data, you check the current SCN, and then do a transfer and cleanup *as at that SCN*. Using the 9.2 syntax, you could do something like

```
declare
    m_scn       number(38);
begin

    select dbms_flashback.get_system_change_number
    into m_scn
    from dual;

    insert into tableX@remote_database
    select    *
    from      log_table    as of scn m_scn
    where       {critical condition};
```

```
    delete from log_table
    where rowid in (
            select    rowid
            from      log_table as of scn m_scn
            where     {critical condition}
        );

    commit;
end;
/
```

There are only a limited number of scenarios that would allow you to use this mechanism. For example, your logging triggers should only be allowed to insert rows into the log table—if the triggers are allowed to update or delete log rows, then there is a chance that you will lose some data changes. But if you do have a situation in which you can use the flashback feature safely, you can avoid the problems caused by read consistency and eliminate the undo and redo that would otherwise go into marking the set of rows that is about to be processed.

Data Feeds

At the opposite end of the application, it was necessary to get some data into the database from automatic systems. In fact, a significant fraction of the volume was from automatic feeds—end users in front of screens were supplying transactions at the rate of thousands per day; external machines (or the customers using them) were supplying transactions in the region of tens to hundreds of thousands per day.

There was also the issue of getting data into the new OLTP system from the legacy system that it was replacing. Loading from legacy systems can be very difficult, especially when the new system has a very complicated data structure and surrogate keys all over the place.

The only safe way to get data into the system was through the standard APIs (the bits of code called by the screens themselves). So the external feeds had to pretend to be end users, and the code that was written to transfer data from the legacy system to the new system had to pretend to be a batch of end users. So every single item of data was loaded using single-row commits.

The bulk transfer of data from an old system to a new system is always a problem (unless the new system has a prewritten migration component, and the old system has a standard dump option generating CSV files or something similar). How do you make the transfer efficient, and still be sure that you've done all the correct data manipulations to meet the structural requirements of the new system? Sometimes the only way to do the transfer safely is to turn the old database (or at least the transactional part of it) into a massive script to replay all the old transactions.

If you are trapped in this situation, then there are only a few things you can do to make things work more smoothly. The first, and absolutely most important, is to make sure you get to do at least three full-scale test runs before you have to do a live run. After that, it's down to squeezing as much out of Oracle as you can for the load, and possibly living dangerously.

Drop as many indexes as you can for the load; and don't forget to time how long it takes you to rebuild them in nologging mode at the end of the run. Your first test run is probably going to highlight a couple of indexes that you shouldn't have dropped, and may give you hints (use SQL_TRACE and V$SQL) about indexes that could be created just for the load. You may also spot a couple of indexes and possibly reference tables that need to be pushed into the KEEP buffer pool, or converted to IOT's or single-table hash clusters (at least for the duration of the load).

If you can get enough RAM disk in place for objects that suffer extreme numbers of updates, then do it—when data blocks have to go to disk as rapidly as possible, try to help the ones that are going to cause most writes. On the other hand, you may get more mileage from putting temporary space on RAM disk rather than real data. Online redo logs and control files are another obvious candidate to consider. Think about running with just one or two control files rather than the statutory three that appear with the default install from DBCA, even running with just one copy of the online redo logs if things are really desperate. When you are trying to work out the cost/risk/benefit trade-off, check the wait events (v$session_event) to make sure that the more risky mechanisms really are going to give you the payoff you need.

Remember that you are (probably) going to have just a few processes running, and tweak the init.ora (spfile) accordingly—a very large db_block_buffer should help; an unusually large log_buffer may help, and a relatively small shared_pool may be sufficient. Try cursor_sharing=force / similar if the application is all literal string SQL; if you don't hit any of the listed bugs, it's almost certain to reduce CPU costs and latch contention. Make sure you set session_cached_cursors to a reasonable size—hardly anybody writes code to hold cursors (although I've been told that JDBC programmers have to be reminded to close cursors explicitly), and this parameter is another little push to reduce CPU costs and latch contention. Setting the parameter cursor_space_for_time = true can also help a batch process that has also been written as very large number of small SQL statements instead of a small number of large SQL statements.

Look for all the parameters that indicate avoidable use of resources—such as fast_start_mttr_target in Oracle 9, which may have been set to 300 (seconds) and makes dbwr work to keep writing dirty blocks to disk to minimize recovery time; or timed_statistics, which may only use a small amount of CPU and is invaluable in a test environment, but may waste CPU in the production migration.

You could go for broke—set the log files to something enormous (to reduce the number of checkpoints that take place) and set _disable_logging to true (and make sure that you're not running in *archivelog* mode); then you don't even need to consider putting your online log files on RAM disk. If the database crashes during migration, you've wrecked your database and have to start all over again some other time, but if you don't have to write the log file, you might just be able to complete the migration within the time window. Make sure you do a shutdown normal as soon as the migration is complete, and then reset this parameter. In passing, the effect of this parameter is to stop the actual writing of the redo log file blocks—all the other actions, such as allocating space in the buffer, calling lgwr to write, and so on, still take place. This is why you still need to make the log files large—checkpoints still happen when the (unwritten) log file would have been full.

Watch out in the first run for execution paths that seem to be quick for the first few thousand rows, and then turn out to be very slow. Be prepared to stop the (practice) migration from time to time to analyze the tables and restart. Make sure you export the statistics to a holding table each time you analyze—this gives you the option of importing the "right" statistics as part of your startup on the next test migration. As an alternative strategy, you should also consider capturing outlines when the migration is well on its way and is performing well, so that you can enable outlines for the duration of the next test run—as with statistics, it is possible to export outlines into private outline tables so that you can pick and choose the best outlines to apply.

Ideally, though, you should ensure that you have a sane and viable migration path from your old system before you commit to taking a new system on board. A proof of concept for bulk transfer of data should be one of the primary requirements before you sign on the dotted line.

Testing, Tuning, and Troubleshooting

It's too easy to criticize things you don't like; and you always have to think carefully when reviewing the way people do things to decide whether your criticisms are based on a balanced argument or on simple prejudice. This section contains just two examples of problems, one which you might decide is simple prejudice based on personal opinion, the other you will agree (I hope) is a definite case of an error.

Naming Conventions

Standards are good, and a naming convention is a good standard to have. But can you spot the error in the following SQL statement?

```
select
      {list of columns}
from
      t0001354,
      t0001368,
      t0001413
where
      ...
and       t0001413.c0015646 < t0001413.c0015612 + 60
;
```

Yes, there really are systems in which the naming convention dictates an 8-character limit on tables, indexes, and columns in order to be database independent and the names are a single character followed by a 7-digit number (I suspect this convention dates back to a system in which each object was a different file on a PCDOS file system.)

When I get absolutely no clues from the SQL, spotting errors becomes much more time consuming. Think how much time you would have saved (and perhaps how the error would not have occurred) if the preceding text actually looked like the following:

```
select
      {list of columns}
from
      orders,
      order_lines,
      deliveries
where
      ...
and       orders.date_invoiced < orders.date_ordered + 60
;
```

Most businesses like to deliver and invoice fairly promptly, so it makes sense to have a report highlighting any orders that weren't invoiced within 60 days. How long would it take you to spot that the query with useful names *isn't* querying orders that were invoiced more than 60 days after the order?

The problem doesn't just stop at the code level, of course. If you have an index defined on the columns (c0001532, c0001534, c0001529, c0001528), is it a sensible index or a silly index, and how many of the columns should be compressed? And how much extra time is it going to take working out the answers to those questions?

Personally, I find that I can tune SQL statements much more quickly if I recognize the meaning of the words used for the tables and columns—to the extent that it takes me longer to tune SQL statements written in foreign languages than it does to tune SQL statements written in English. Moreover, even with no prior knowledge of the business, it is possible to look at predicates and make intelligent guesses about whether they are likely to return many rows or a few rows. This may highlight a logic error in the code (as shown previously) or a problem that the optimizer is having with selectivity.

Obscure names encourage silly mistakes, and then make those mistakes hard to spot.

How do you deal with this problem? Essentially you can't, if it involves a third-party application with supplied code. But if you are writing extra reports for it, and making data structures visible to end users, you can create views to translate meaningless names into useful names—it's a fairly safe bet that the supplier won't redefine the columns in an upgrade, as there would probably be too much code in existence that needed checking and fixing.

Realistic Tests

As a trivial example of testing with realistic data, let's reconsider the query from the previous section ("Naming Conventions," where we refer to column `t0001413.c0015646` rather than column `orders.invoice_date`) that did its test the wrong way. In its incorrect form, it will probably return almost all the order data in your system; when corrected, it will return very little. The performance of the incorrect query will be dire—but if you don't test with a realistic data set, you won't notice the obvious error until the report goes into production and hammers the system to death.

Of course, my example had a fairly obvious error, and a lightweight test would have identified the mistake very quickly. After all, if you are testing against specification, all you need to do is create a sample data set with (say)

- One order without an invoice date

- One order with an invoice date comfortably inside the 60-day limit

- One order with an invoice date comfortably outside the 60-day limit

- One order with `date_invoiced` = `date_ordered` + 60 (to check the boundary condition)

The first item is interesting—as soon as you create a data set for testing, you may find that you've raised a question that the original specification didn't consider. What should you do for orders that do not have an invoice date yet? What if the order date on that order was more than 60 days in the past? And how do you work around the issue that there are no null dates, only dates set to December 31, 9999? A good tester may end up sending specifications back for review.

But let's consider a more serious test case. After loading the database with a month's worth of data, the company started to tune the "statement of account" run. After two or three iterations of reindexing, disk balancing, and parameter tweaking (it's third-party code, and they can't even see the source), the code ran in two and a half hours—comfortably inside the three-hour window for the batch run.

Unfortunately, it had been tested while nothing else was happening on the system—so when the report goes into production, the CPU might not be 100% available, and there might be other processes contending for the disks. One of the commonest problems with testing is that very few people test using the correct degree of concurrency. When you have ten concurrent users, you suddenly find the points where you have locking (enqueue) problems. When you have 100 concurrent users, you suddenly find the points where you have excess CPU usage and (more importantly because it may be harder to correct) low-level contention problems such as latch collisions and buffer collisions. But the failure to do any concurrency test wasn't the most important failure of this test. The code wasn't available for review—so nobody in the test team knew whether the entire code set had been exercised. For example, what would the code do if it found some bad data (the data generated for the test was perfect in every way—no missing customers, no late payments of previous bills, and so on).

No one had even run the test with `sql_trace` enabled to see what code had been tested, although they had checked `v$sql` with one of the popular "top ten" queries to work out which bits were the resource-intensive bits. Of course, this had not caught all the different, slightly expensive, literal string statements that summed to unreasonable amounts of work.

When we ran the test, just one more time, with `sql_trace` enabled, and ran `tkprof` against it, I found the following class of statements tucked away in the middle of a very long file (lots of literal string SQL, remember), looking totally harmless because its resource consumption had been close to zero.

```
select    sum(expenditure)
from      history_table
where     customer_id = '00000000000000000000000010293512345'
and       ref_date <= 20010601;
```

(Actually the table name and column names followed the convention of one character followed by seven digits—but after a few hours of mind-numbing tedium, we had some scripts that used sed to convert meaningless table and column names into something more readable.)

This translates into "For this customer, work out their cumulative expenditure since the account opened." On the test data, with one month's worth of data, there was no history in the history_table. On the production system, the intention was to hold the traditional seven-year history—which we estimated would result in an extra 50 real disk reads per customer *per year*.

The (predicted) solution in this case was to restructure the history_table as a *range partitioned, index-organized table,* with partitions of one year each. The estimated extra impact for this was less than one real disk read per customer per year (helped enormously by the fact that the statement program worked in customer_id order).

```
create table pt_iot (
    customer_id    number(12),
    ref_date       number(8),
    expenditure    number(6,2),
    constraint iot_pk primary key (customer_id, ref_date)
)
organization index
partition by range (ref_date)
(
    partition pt_1995 values less than (19950101),
    partition pt_1996 values less than (19960101),
    partition pt_1997 values less than (19970101),
    partition pt_1998 values less than (19980101),
    partition pt_1999 values less than (19990101),
    partition pt_2000 values less than (20010101),
    partition pt_2001 values less than (20020101),
    partition pt_2002 values less than (20030101)
)
;
```

From a good statement of requirements, you can often guess where the most resource-intensive bits of, say, a report are going to be, and can ask questions about how the code will cope with them, and build test data to exercise the points where the problems are most likely to be.

Even if you never get to see the source code, you can get a lot of information about what it is doing from a trace file (if you can survive the tedium of reading it all), and work out precise points where the code is going to come under stress. The more stress points you can find, the better your chances of producing a strategy of damage limitation, even if you can't really fix the underlying problem.

Postscript

So we have a system that started life

- Not doing referential integrity (properly)

- Generating unique IDs in the least scalable fashion possible

- Maximizing the cost and contention of parsing and optimizing

- Confusing the optimizer hugely

- Maximizing the cost of updates

- Doing its batch loads one row at a time

- Losing data on its data warehouse transfers

You'd probably like to know the name of the company that built this system, either to make sure that you never buy anything off them or get a job with them—if they're still in business, of course.

I'm afraid I have to admit to a cop-out. The company doesn't exist.

The errors I've described are ones that I have seen, individually and severally, at many sites. Some sites have committed all of them (and more) and survived the experience. Some sites have committed only a few and struggled for a long time to work around them.

There is no "worst" site; there are only sites that haven't found the time to learn the critical features of Oracle before committing themselves to producing a system. Some sites are luckier than others, and the errors they make don't matter. So remember, all the errors I have described are unpleasant errors, but they're only important if they make a difference to your business.

As a final example of what I mean by this, consider a business I visited a few years ago that had to complete a monthly bill run in six hours. They couldn't hit the deadline primarily because the code did single-row processing with a commit on every row. With two weeks to go live, there wasn't time to fix the job properly, but it turned out that it didn't need fixing, because the business requirement could be adjusted. Instead of running the process once per month on the 28th of the month (as per the original statement of requirements), they ran it three times per month (on the 7th, 14th, and 21st), billing one-third of the customers on each run. The critical code change took place outside the main report program, and was little more than a secured mechanism for pre-creating a view for each run:

```
create or replace view cust_view as
select * from customers
where mod(customer_id,3) = {0, 1 or 2, depending on date};
```

The problem is still there (I assume), but it's not important. The situation has been isolated, the issue has been identified, and in the longer term someone might rewrite the entire process to be much more efficient and cost-effective. But that rewrite can be budgeted and scheduled with a known cost/benefit analysis to justify it. Switching to three billing days per month didn't affect the profit line—so there was no (current) business justification for fixing badly written, badly performing, nonscalable code.

So remember, just because something is technically bad, or obviously wrong, that doesn't make it *the thing* that has to be fixed. As with all things, there's important and there's urgent—and only a few things are both at once.

Dear Reader,

I have met Tim twice: many years ago in Denver, and this year (2004) in Denver. With some luck I think I get to meet him a third time for the Database Forum 2004, where he has promised to show up with his family. Oh, the chance to pay him (them, really) back some of the hospitality and joy they heap upon others . . .

The first time I met Tim, I was travelling around the globe doing technical seminars for Lex de Haan. One of the seminars was my own, and it was about performance. I would burn the notes if I found them today, but back in those days a collection of tips and tricks was the way to go. (I did talk, of course, about the wait stuff.) In between talking about the optimal number of extents for rollback segments (thanks, Cary), and how to handle the 4031 error (thanks, Juan), that is.

I was busy. I had another seminar the following day somewhere else in the US, so it was agreed that the famous Oracle employee Tim Gorman—from the Oracle office in Denver—could do the last day (on performance) instead of me, for the audience in Denver. The handover should take place over dinner at a nice restaurant.

So Tim brought along his old friend Gary Dodge (who's still within Oracle). Together they would, a year or two later, write a very, very good book on data warehousing (it was green and fat). I bought it and found in there a few things that we had discussed that evening in a restaurant in Denver. Tim never misses a beat.

Back to the restaurant: Gary and Tim were both being their usual kind selves, and ordered a plate of "Rocky Mountain Oysters" for me. I ate them happily, and was then informed that they were, in fact, sliced buffalo testicles. One of my mottoes is that "You will sometimes have to wait a very, very long time—but eventually you will always get your revenge if you want it." I shall truly look forward to serving some Danish specialties for Tim. Liquorice with ammonium chloride, raw pickled herrings, and blood sausage are but a few.

While inside Oracle, Tim was incredibly active, helpful, and inventive on the various lists (HelpKern, for instance). The width and depth of his knowledge about Oracle products (and various OS'es) and other related stuff is really astounding. These days he'll post on the Oracle-L and OakTable lists in the same style, and he still amazes me (and a lot of others!) with the sheer amount of knowledge he is carrying around in his head, and his ability to always have tried it out himself.

The second time I met Tim was during the Rocky Mountain Oracle User Group (RMOUG) spring conference titled Training Days. He's president of RMOUG, and as such kindly invited me (and other OakTable members) to stay in his house at 8,000 feet altitude, and it was one of my better experiences in life.

Tim's family makes you wonder what you did wrong in your life. Open, unassuming, and always with a wonderful sense of humor (inherited from Tim, I'm sure), they made you feel right at home among the pines, the snow, and their two goats.

Since I'm from the cold North, I should of course be able to stand incredibly low temperatures wearing nothing. After all, Greenland is still Danish. Turns out that I can't. So I left it to Tim's teenage kid to do the barbecue boogie in T-shirt and shorts in temperatures of minus 30 degrees Celcius—I think I lasted about five minutes out there, but he just kept barbecuing. As an added benefit, there is no oxygen at that altitude. But instead of breathing through diving apparatus, these 8,000 feet'ers apparently hold their breath until they can get down the hill to Denver again.

The nearest (small) town is called Evergreen, and Tim has taken his company name from that (http://www.evdbt.com). Everwhite would have been more appropriate in my opinion. You will find some very fine papers on this website, and that's only to be expected from one of the biggest contributors to the collective body of Oracle knowledge available out there.

Tim—you're a very fortunate man, but fortune only comes to the well prepared. And that's what you always are.

—Mogens Nørgaard

CHAPTER 11

Bad CaRMa

By Tim Gorman

IN MY UNDERGRADUATE CAREER, I took a single course in philosophy, which was a requirement for my liberal arts degree in economics. Up to that point, my only exposure to philosophy was Monty Python, and the lyrics of overwrought 1960s folk songs and overblown 1970s rock songs. The course was entitled "Introduction to Ethics" and in the first session, the professor asked the class, "How many people are here just to fulfill a prerequisite?" It was apparent that the only hands that weren't raised belonged to those who didn't know the meaning of the word "prerequisite." The classroom was not quite a football stadium, but it probably should have been, as there were hundreds of people, and the majority of them appeared to be on athletic scholarships. Resignedly, the professor nodded and continued.

I immediately fell asleep but was soon roused when the professor asked, "What is *good*? In other words, what constitutes what is *good* and *right* and *decent*? How is *good* defined?" Despite a relatively spirited discussion, it became clear to all that nobody could really answer the question adequately. Finally, the professor, no doubt through long experience in teaching "Introduction to Ethics," posed the best answer of all the bad answers. He called it the "Schlitz Ethic." This was named after a well-known brand of fantastically bad American beer, whose advertising at the time always concluded with the jingle, "When it's right, you know it!"

When it's right, you know it. Implying that, although it is difficult to describe the meaning of *good*, you know *good* when you see it.

Warily, the entire class of 250 or so agreed that this worked as well as any of the other answers. The professor grinned sadly, correctly assuming that few of us appreciated the irony of beer advertising in relation to a discussion of ethics, and assigned Plato for homework.

When it's right, you know it. And stating the converse, *when it's not right, you know that too ...*

Obligatory Disclaimers

I will fictionalize names to protect the identities of those involved, because almost all of the people who were involved are still active in the IT world, although the corporations involved have long ago bitten the dust, gone to meet their makers, joined the choir invisible, and are now pushing up daisies.

If you think you recognize any person or corporation in this account, then you are most certainly mistaken. Just have two stiff whisky drinks and that feeling of recognition should pass ...

Introducing Vision

Those of us who work in *Information Technology* (IT) have all been on a project where something important is just not right. We know it, most everyone knows it, but nobody is quite able to put his or her finger on the problem in a convincing way. Why I was not able to muster a convincing argument at the time I can only attribute to lack of experience. As an old adage states: *Experience is what you get immediately after you need it.*

This story is about such an IT project, the most spectacular failure I have ever experienced. It resulted in the complete dismissal of a medium-sized IT department, and eventually led to the destruction of a growing company in a growing industry. The company, which we'll call "Upstart," was a successful and profitable subscription television business. Upstart at this time was a wholly owned subsidiary of a giant media conglomerate, which we'll call "BigMedia, Inc."

The project occurred in the early 1990s, and it was a custom-built order-entry and customer-service application, closely resembling what is now referred to as *Customer-Relationship Management* or *CRM*. The core functionality of the system included

- Order entry and inventory

- Customer service, help desk

- General ledger, accounts receivable, billing, and accounts payable

The application was called "Vision," and the name was both its officially stated promise for Upstart as well as a self-aggrandizing nod to its architect. The application was innovative, in that it was built to be flexible enough to accommodate any future changes to the business. Not just any *foreseeable* future changes to the business, but *absolutely any* changes to the business, in any form. It was quite a remarkable claim, but Vision was intended to be the last application ever built. It achieved this utter flexibility by being completely data-driven, providing limitless abstraction, and using object-oriented programming techniques that were cutting-edge at the time. The tools used to create Vision were

- Oracle7 RDBMS, versions 7.0.12 through 7.0.16

- Oracle SQL*Form version 3.0 with user exits written in C

- Oracle SQL*ReportWriter version 1.1

- Oracle PRO*C version 1.3

- C programming language

Like many such projects that set out to create a mission-critical application, the development effort spanned two years, about a year longer than originally projected. But that was acceptable, because this was the application that would last forever, adapting to any future requirements, providing unlimited Return On Investment (ROI). When the application finally went "live," almost everybody in the company had invested so much in it that literally the fate of the company hinged on its success.

However, in the event of total project malfunction, mission-critical applications running the core business of multinational corporations are not permitted the luxury of the type of fast flameout demonstrated by thousands of "dot-com" companies in the era of the Internet bubble a few years. Within a month of Vision going "live," it was apparent to all but those most heavily vested in its construction that it was a failure. The timeline went as follows:

- *Autumn 1991*: Development begins—the "build versus buy" decision is settled in favor of "build" (not "buy") as Upstart decides to build a custom CRM application.

- *September 1993:* "Go Live" launch—hope and euphoria.

- *October 1993:* Frustration at poor performance and inability to produce reports.

- *November 1993:* Desperation.

- *December 1993:* Despair, IT director resigns.

- *January 1994:* Firings, IT department decimated.

- *February 1994:* New faces.

- *March 1994:* New replacement system chosen, the "build versus buy" decision is settled in favor of "buy (then customize)."

- *November 1994:* Replacement system launched, "Vision" retired.

- *March 1995:* BigMedia, Inc. sells Upstart to another company.

So, the entire debacle lasted three years, from inception to grave, generating an estimated ROI of minus $10 million. Such implosions remained rare until the spectacular supernovas when the Internet "bubble" burst in 2001.

Seeing and Vision

Vision was designed and implemented by a person whom we'll call "Randy." Randy originally came to Upstart as a consultant working for Oracle Corporation. Before joining the consulting arm of Oracle, Randy worked in product development, where he was a lead developer of Oracle's proprietary PL/SQL programming language and a vigorous proponent of object-oriented programming and modular programming languages such as Ada. From product development, he moved into consulting where he was regarded as brilliant but controlling, sarcastic, and impatient, according to those who worked with him. Apparently, there were no openings in marketing at the time.

Oracle placed Randy on an engagement at Upstart in 1991 during the initial strategy phase of the Vision project. It wasn't long before Upstart realized that they had a systems architect with all of the answers. For each of their requirements, Randy had a solution:

Build an order-entry and customer-service application that integrates all of the elements of customer interaction

Upstart wanted a better end-user interface for their reservation agents. They also wanted that system to be capable of retrieving every bit of information about a customer while the reservation agent was interacting with the customer. Such systems now come shrink-wrapped, but in the early 1990s the "build-versus-buy" decision still came down firmly on the "build" side for this kind of functionality. Randy promised to build an application that could do absolutely anything.

Make it reliable

Upstart spent a lot of money on its IT infrastructure. They bought the most reliable servers at the time, Sequent, and they bought the best relational database technology, Oracle. They also had a very capable IT infrastructure team who utilized these components effectively. Despite all that went wrong with Vision during its brief lifetime, reliability was not one of its problems.

Make it fast

Interaction between customers and company representatives could not pause indefinitely while the system retrieved and posted information. Although Sequent servers were not the cheapest machines available, Upstart made sure to obtain the largest machines that Sequent could provide. Not just one, but two of them. Upstart also employed the newest version of Oracle7, which had just become generally available. Oracle7 was a vast improvement over Oracle version 6.0, because it had actual stored procedures and triggers compiled into the database itself.

As far as Upstart was concerned, Vision would be fast, *ipso facto*, because it had the best server hardware and the best database software.

Build an application that is flexible enough to be adapted to meet any new requirements

This was the toughest requirement, and this was where Randy really impressed everyone.

In computing, there is often a three-way trade-off between *speed*, *reliability*, and *flexibility*. This is truly the devil's triangle of IT, where the conventional wisdom is that you can pick any two out of the three.

Vendor after vendor promised Upstart that their product could meet all of their present requirements, speedily and reliably. But changes? Future requirements? This is where the hemming and hawing started. The vendors would admit, with varying degrees of enthusiasm, to the presence of an *application programming interface* or API, allowing modifications and customizations to the application. How easy is it to change? Well, that's what our professional services organizations are for!

It was not until Upstart talked to Randy that they heard a story that they liked, which was that all those existing products are built on the wrong technology.

Randy proposed building, from scratch, a completely *data-driven* application. Most conventional database applications are written in *code* using programming languages that access and manipulate *data*. Code is very difficult to change once it is written, but code controls data.

Randy's idea was that all of the forms, all of the reports, all of the functionality of the system would be stored as *metadata*, or *data about data*, and the only thing coded in a programming language would be an *engine* to process both metadata and data. For example, instead of defining a table just to store order-line information, why not also store the basic business logic about inserting, updating, and deleting order-lines in the table, as well as details about the structure of an order-line. Once an engine was built, then that would be the end of all coding, forever and ever, amen. After that, the engine would process data about data then the data itself, and in this fashion any form, report, or program could be built. When new functionality or modifications were needed to the system, you only had to change the metadata, not the code.

Theoretically, this allowed rapid implementation of changes and new applications, because while changes to programming code required recompilation and relinking, changes to metadata had no such requirements.

And Randy delivered on these promises—*most* of them ...

The Data-Driven Application

One of Randy's inspirations for this design was early *Computer-Aided Software Engineering* (CASE), in particular Oracle's own CASE*Tools product. In its early incarnations, this product included a table named SDD_ELEMENTS that contained both *data* and *metadata* indistinguishably—it was all just grist for the processing logic within the CASE product. The metadata was initialized as "seed data" by the product installation software, and then the "engine" used this as the basis for recursive queries back into itself when new data or metadata was being added. Randy commented that this recursive design was a "eureka" moment, an epiphany, for him and it came to fruition in the Vision system.

The idea was that nothing about the application logic was declared or coded. Not the business logic, and not the data structures for storage.

The pity is that Randy did not temper that epiphany with some real-world practicality. For example, what works very well for a CASE application supporting 1–5 developers who think a lot and type only a little may not work well at all for a mission-critical order-entry application supporting 300–400 reservation agents who think very little and type very rapidly. The database workload generated by a small number of users generating transactions intermittently has little in common with the database workload generated by an order-entry application. Just considering the growth in the volume of data between the two situations reveals striking differences.

Recalling the three-way design trade-off between *speed*, *reliability*, and *flexibility*, a CASE application needs *flexibility* the most in order to capture the most complex ideas and designs. It needs *reliability* and robustness as well in order for the application developer to trust it enough to use it. It does need to perform well, but with such a small user community, *speed* is probably the least important side of the triangle.

For an order-entry, inventory, customer-service, and financial application, *reliability* and high availability might be the most important characteristic of all, as the mission-critical application that is not available or which loses data is worth nothing. Next, such a system has to perform well, as the lack of *speed* for the dozens or hundreds of concurrent users can also render the application unfit to fulfill business requirements. Of the three qualities, *flexibility* may well be the least important attribute as far as business users are concerned.

The Vision systems best quality, *flexibility*, was least important to Upstart as a company, despite its attractiveness to Upstart's IT division. It was *reliable* enough, but it did not have the *speed* to fulfill its business requirements.

This is a classic example of what can happen when the priorities of the IT "department" do not match, and are not appropriately aligned with, the priorities of the "business." Often what appears desirable to the propeller heads and what is seen as a high priority (e.g., using cutting-edge technology, flexible, database independence, etc.) may implicitly conflict with the priorities and business requirements of the company. When IT decisions are made in a vacuum from the business rather than considering the wishes of the business foremost, these sad cases become an unfortunate reality.

When It's Not Right, You Know It . . . or Not?

In addition to mixing metadata with data, the Vision system had another peculiarity that made it truly memorable, at least to those with any experiences building databases.

The Vision system was comprised of a single table, named DATA appropriately enough (see Figure 11-1). When you consider the overriding goal of complete flexibility where all rules are interpreted at run time, it seems inevitable that every involving "structure" would also be made as generic and undistinguished as possible. Why have multiple tables when there is no differentiation of data structure? Instead, just pile all of the 150 or so different logical entities into the same table. Plunk the various items of data into generically defined columns—the application data itself contains the metadata identifying each item of data and how it should be stored and displayed.

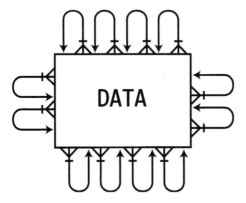

Figure 11-1. Single table DATA encapsulating 150+ logical entities

The basic premise was that just about all of the features of the relational database were eschewed, and instead it was used like a filing system for great big plastic bags of data. Why bother with other containers for the data—just jam it into a generic black plastic garbage bag. If all of those bags full of different types of data all look the same and are heaped into the same pile, don't worry! We'll be able to differentiate the data after we pull it off the big pile and look inside.

Incredibly, Randy and his crew thought this was incredibly clever. Database engineer after database engineer were struck dumb by the realization of what Vision was doing, but the builders of the one-table database were blissfully aware that they were ushering in a new dawn in database design.

Here are some facts about the Vision system:

- The data model comprised a single table named DATA.

- The DATA table had 240+ columns.

- The primary key column was a numeric named SYSNO.

- Columns existed for attributes, such as TYPE, SUBTYPE, CATEGORY, SUBCATEGORY, STATUS, SUBSTATUS, GROUP, and OWNER, which were intended to fully describe what type, category, or grouping to which the row belonged. Each of these columns were themselves SYSNOs, joining back to other rows in DATA for more detail.

- The majority of columns in DATA provided sequencing, descriptive text, names, values, amounts, dates entered and modified, and so on. Some of these columns would be named and data-typed appropriately, while others were "generic spare" columns, several for each datatype.

- When the Vision system was finally decommissioned, a year after it went into production, the DATA table consumed 50GB of space.

- 40+ associated indexes consumed another 250GB of space.

Suppose you wanted to find a Customer record. To find that information, you first needed to retrieve metadata describing the structure of a customer entity from the DATA table. This might involve first a query on DATA to retrieve a row describing one of about 150 different logical "entities," then a row describing another specific entity of Customer. Then, it would be necessary to use the information retrieved so far to query DATA for rows related to "entity" to describe "columns," so that we know in what column on the DATA table the COMPANY_NAME and address information is stored within.

Once all of this metadata has been retrieved, we are ready to start querying the DATA table for a specific row for a specific customer. Using all of the metadata previously retrieved, we know how many of the 240 columns in data are populated with customer data, what type of data they should be, what the acceptable ranges of values are, how the numeric or date data should be displayed, and so forth.

A SQL query for a customer record in a conventional database application might look like this:

```
Select name,
       mailing_street_addr1,
       mailing_street_addr2,
       mailing_city,
       mailing_state_province,
       mailing_postal_zip,
       ...
from company
where company_id = <company-ID>
```

In the Vision system, a similar SQL query might look like this:

```
Select cn.description,
       ma.string82,
       ma.string83,
       mc.string44,
       mc.string63,
       mz.numeric31,
       ...
from      data c,
       data cc,
       data cn,
       data ma,
       data mc,
       data mz,
       data ...
where     c.description = 'CUSTOMER'
and       cc.entity_id = c.sysno
and       cc.description = 'COLUMN'
and       ma.column_id = cc.sysno
and       ...
```

It was not unusual for such a simple query, intended only to retrieve information for one customer, to perform 6–10 recursive "self-joins" back to the DATA table, over and over again. More demanding queries, for instance those retrieving several customer records, or order details, required at least 12–15 recursive "self-joins." Every operation had first to retrieve the metadata about the structure of the data before retrieving or modifying the data itself.

Analogy

In real life, when a fire department receives an alarm about a fire in progress, the nearest fire station is notified and a crew is dispatched to handle the situation. The advantage of this situation is that both the dispatcher and crew handle the situation automatically and quickly. The disadvantage of this situation is that if there is a change in procedure, it may take some time to retrain the personnel to make them accustomed to the new procedure.

If this were instead handled the way the Vision system operated, each alarm would cause the fire dispatcher to check his or her training manuals on what to do when an alarm is received. Then, upon receipt of a dispatch, each fire crew member would have to check his or her training manuals to determine what to do when handling a fire call. Then, the crew would go handle the situation, carrying training manuals with them for any eventuality. The advantage of this approach is that each alarm would be handled the way the training manuals dictate, so that changes in procedures can be instantly implemented. The disadvantage, of course, is that you have dispatchers reading manuals when they should be dispatching, and fire crew members reading manuals when they should be fighting fires. Chaos in the streets, as trucks careen wildly while their drivers consult manuals instead of keeping their eyes on the road. Ah, I feel a Hollywood screenplay coming on ...

To illustrate its remarkable flexibility, the entire Vision application consisted of a single form written in SQL*Forms version 3.0. This single form utilized code extensions called "user exits" written in C which called the Vision "engine." This single form was therefore able to display and accept user input for any of the 150+ data entities that comprised all of the modules of the Vision system.

So, the Vision engine was able to generate these SQL statements very easily, because it was coded to piece together metadata to retrieve the data. However, each invocation of the form required that the relevant form be generated afresh. If 300 data-entry operators invoked a form, the logic to build the form was generated 300 times. If operators hopped back and forth between screens, then all of this form-generation logic occurred again and again and again. Please note that changes to order-entry forms tend to occur rather infrequently, so you have to wonder if this incredible flexibility was a solution in search of a problem.

For human beings, the situation was dire. What the Vision application's object-oriented "engine" did very rapidly and easily did not come quickly to the carbon-based meat-processors in the skulls of developers. For example, developers would be asked to compose a report about customer orders or summarize monthly sales. Sounds straightforward enough, but before retrieving the data, we have to retrieve the instructions on how to retrieve the data. Once we retrieve that logic, then we have to retrieve the structure in which data is stored, for each individual item of data we want. Using Oracle's SQL*Plus *ad-hoc* query tool or reporting tools such as Oracle's SQL*ReportWriter or Crystal Reports became unbelievable drudgery, bordering on the impossible. Reporting tools that generated their own SQL, based upon expectations of a standard normalized data model, were completely out of the question. In order to shorten the number of levels of recursive logic, developers ended up hard-coding as much of the metadata as they could, in an effort to query only the data. This expediency drove Randy out of his mind, as he rightly perceived that all of Vision's flexibility was slowly and surely leaking out in each instance of hard-coded metadata.

Expanding Vision

The DATA table eventually grew to 50GB in size. Remember that Oracle7 did not have any partitioning, so as the table grew larger, every access became correspondingly slower. Using the 2,048 byte database blocks which were common at the time, most of the indexes on DATA grew to 5–6 branch levels, which made navigation of the branch levels expensive, even for UNIQUE scans into the index. Moreover, the clustering of data values in the table with regard to their value in the 40+ indexes was almost uniformly poor. The ordering in which rows were inserted into the table only matched the ordering of the data values on the SYSNO column, so that was the only index which had a good clustering factor of values in the index compared to the rows in the table. This meant that the index on the SYSNO column was the only index that was well suited to RANGE scans across the leaf blocks of the index. Unfortunately, since SYSNO was the primary key of the DATA table, a UNIQUE probe for individual rows from that index was the most common operation. So, the only index suited for RANGE scans was also the index that was hardly ever used for RANGE scans. All of the other columns against which RANGE scans might be performed were huge, with many branch levels from the "root" node to the "leaf" nodes, and they were poorly suited to scanning for multiple rows.

Moreover, because the DATA table contained over 150 logical data entities, and some of those entities were frequently updated and deleted from, all of the 40+ indexes had an enormous number of deleted entries. These "holes" in the index entries are due to the fact that Oracle does not remove an index entry, but rather enables its possible future reuse by simply nullifying the pointer to the table row and keeping the data value portion in its slot. Thus, as rows were deleted and updated in the DATA table, most of the indexes were becoming more and more sparsely populated over time.

Because the entire application was encapsulated inside that table, and because much of the data-driven logic contained within DATA was recursive, we noted that the growth rate of DATA was exponential. The phenomenon seemed to resemble the growth of the human population of the earth: as more people procreate, more people are added more rapidly, which causes more people to procreate, which causes more people to be added even more rapidly, which causes even more people to procreate, (and so on) ...

So, DATA itself was growing exponentially. Its indexes were mirroring that growth, but growing even faster as deleted entries compounded the problem. The Sequent server on which the database resided was among the largest in the United States at the time, but it was quickly being gobbled by this fast-expanding database.

My first recommendation, upon being consulted by Upstart to help improve performance, was to break all 150+ logical entities into separate tables, similar to any other conventional database application built on hierarchical or relational databases. This consultation occurred about a month prior to Vision going live, and the Upstart project managers smiled indulgently and commented, "Every database consultant who comes in here says that." The implication was, "Tell us something new, because that's not going to happen." They went on to explain that this application was something new, and that the way it stored data and metadata in the database would revolutionize computing. I listened carefully, because the customer is always right, but in the end, I had nothing else to offer, and the interview was ended. Randy was not present at that initial meeting, as his faithful were well able to deal with the infidel.

Four months later, after Vision had been in production for three months, I was called back in to help improve performance, which was crippling all areas of business within Upstart. Again, I looked at what the application was doing and how the DATA table was growing, and repeated the same conclusion: this application needs a more conventional data model, with each logical entity stored in its own relational table.

This time, the reception was a little different. Randy was present at this meeting and repeated what had been said by his minions on my previous visit: it was impossible to break up DATA. Vision's design was revolutionary, so be clever and think of something else. Change some database initialization parameters, or something. After all, the poor performance was Oracle's problem, as the Vision application "engine" was operating flawlessly, so the problem had to be Oracle.

I noticed that the IT director who had been present at the last meeting four months earlier was missing, and found that he had resigned only two weeks prior. The new IT director was present, and she was obviously not one of Randy's faithful. In fact, I couldn't help noticing that even the faithful were not presenting a solid front anymore, and that Randy seemed isolated. So, I pressed on with my litany of the problems with Vision.

Too many indexes

The DATA table had over 40 indexes, so each INSERT statement had to insert over 40 index entries for each table row inserted and each DELETE statement had to delete over 40 index entries for each table row deleted.

When modifications were made to existing data using Oracle's SQL*Forms v3.0, the program had a nasty habit of including all of the columns in the table in the resulting UPDATE statement. So, even when just one column was modified in the form, the resulting update would still attempt to change all of the columns maintained by the form. As a result, each UPDATE statement performed modifications on all 40 related index entries for each table row updated

Each UPDATE and DELETE made each of the 40 indexes more sparsely populated, making them less efficient for just about every type of index access method.

Too many branch levels

With the 2,048 byte database block size that was the norm at the time, each of these 40 indexes had four, five, and sometimes six levels of B*Tree branches. Thus, the simplest use of any of the indexes was several times more "expensive" than they needed to be, as all branch levels had to be traversed from the index's "root" node to one of the "leaf" nodes on each access.

Breaking the DATA table up into 150 smaller tables would allow the indexes on the smaller tables to have fewer branch levels, making each access more efficient.

Index access contention

One of the 40+ indexes, the unique index supporting the primary key column SYSNO, was populated with numeric values generated by a sequence generator. Likewise, a column named TIMESTAMP was populated with the current system DATETIME value. Both sequence values and datetimestamps are monotonically ascending data values which present special problems for indexes

Therefore, the index "leaf" block containing the highest values was always being fought over by all of the sessions inserting new rows, representing a knot of contention within the application that is difficult to resolve.

 NOTE *In Oracle8,* REVERSE *indexes became available to resolve this problem.*

Could not exploit new CACHE feature

Oracle7 had introduced a new CACHE command for caching individual tables into memory. With only one table in the application, it would be impossible to cache frequently used logical entities into memory.

Users could not write queries against DATA

It was too difficult and complex for humans to write queries on the DATA table, with the need to join back to DATA again and again in order to retrieve structural meta-data before getting around to the actual purpose of the query itself.

All developers were now short-circuiting these recursive self-joins by memorizing specific SYSNO values and hard-coding specific SYSNO values into their queries. This had the effect of reducing the number of recursive self-joins in the query, allowing them to run and complete, but it also had the side effect of eliminating all of the flexibility designed into the Vision application.

As I described these shortcomings, Randy kept shaking his head, muttering about what a piece of junk the Oracle database was, what kind of fools complained about the complexity of a revolutionary data model when writing queries, and so on. Finally, he simply stood up and walked out of the meeting.

It was the last point, the least technical point, which resonated with everyone. Each of the previous points were technical mumbo-jumbo, but the point about humans not being able to write queries struck a nerve.

Death of a Vision

Also present in the meeting was a sales representative from a market research company, whom we'll call "Joe," who had been trying to sell his market-research software to Upstart. Joe knew that he would have to extract data from Vision, as his application was an *Executive Information System* (EIS), which is more commonly referred to as a *data mart* today.

Joe mostly sat and listened throughout the meeting. After I finished my laundry list of problems with Vision, and after Randy stormed out of the room, he finally spoke. He asked one of the Vision project team leads, one of Randy's faithful, whom we'll call "Rick," whether Vision was indeed as complicated as I was making it out to be. Rick proudly answered, "Yes, it is." Joe then asked how long it took to train an application developer to implement changes in functionality, and Rick frowned, thought a moment, and then answered, "Six months." Joe looked thunderstruck and slowly repeated, "Six months?" Rick explained that they had just finished bringing a new application developer up to speed on Vision, and it took six months. "He was really bright, too!" Rick said pensively. Joe nodded and then turned to the new IT director.

He stated, "You are in a world of hurt. It takes six months to train a new maintenance person and a database consultant," waving at me, "says that the simplest of reports can only be created with the greatest difficulty using the most low-level reporting tools." He stood up, walked to the white board, picked up a pen, and wrote, "RUN LIKE HELL!"

Joe said, "You people," waving at the accounting director, "have been operating in the dark for over four months, unable to get real financial data from Vision. You haven't done a valid month-end closing since this new system started." The new IT director looked quickly at the accounting director, who looked a little sheepish as he explained, "We've never been able to get our reconciliation data." Rick quickly interjected, "It is pretty difficult to get that report out." Joe smiled and continued, "It would be a waste of your money and my time to have you buy my market-research application, because you would not be able to feed it any data either." At this, the marketing director straightened up, looking alarmed. I didn't realize it at the time, but this was the decisive blow that killed Vision.

That night, I took Joe out for drinks and we had a great time as he filled me in on all the undercurrents I had missed or failed to understand. Techies can be pretty pathetic at that stuff, but occasionally folks take pity on us, and I realized what I wanted to be when I grew up.

Private Vision

Another thing that the good folks at Upstart didn't fully realize was that Randy had his own vision. Although he had been introduced to Upstart as an employee of Oracle Consulting, he quickly cut Oracle out of the picture by forming his own company and taking the entire engagement for himself. This is considered extremely bad form in any contracting business, where the basic ethic is "*you dance with whom what brung ya!*" Customer contacts are the life-blood of the IT contracting business, and contracting companies consider it a capital offense to steal a customer contact, and rightly so. As soon as it appeared that Upstart was leaning toward his ideas for the new application, Randy bailed from Oracle and formed his own business, which we'll call "MetaVision."

MetaVision and its founder signed a contract with Upstart to develop the Vision system for Upstart, but MetaVision managed to reserve for itself the source-code rights to resell Vision as it saw fit. This was an extraordinary concession made by Upstart, as works for hire are usually owned by the paying customer. How Randy managed this sweetheart deal is another mystery, but undoubtedly he felt that his design for a completely flexible design for Vision was innovative enough that he could not part with all rights to it. Additionally, since Vision was billed as the "last application ever to be built," Randy could have argued that he was putting himself out of business with this development effort, so he needed to retain rights.

Over the course of the two-year project to develop Vision, Randy charged Upstart $200/hour as the application architect, grossing an estimated $800,000 or so in billings. In addition, he hired two junior programmers and billed them to Upstart for $100/hour, grossing another $800,000 or so in billings over two years and then some. Since the two junior programmers were being paid around $60,000/year apiece (good money in those days!), Randy was doing quite well for himself, making over $500,000/year. For the few months that Vision was in production before the entire development team was fired, Randy continued to bill Upstart at the same pace, and even attempted to sue for breach of contract after he was fired.

All in all, Randy had found a lucrative gravy train, allowing him to bill well over $1.5 million over two years, while he got to experiment with his new ideas, and then keep the fruits of his labors to resell to other customers to boot. After the Vision project was cancelled, Randy dissolved MetaVision and went trekking in the Himalayas for several months. In the ten years that have elapsed since, I have not seen or heard anything about him, although I have been watching. I recently found the slides from a presentation from someone with his name, dated in 1998, on the practical aspects and technical challenges of operating a porn website. It seemed to fit, and the author was quite adamant about the advantages of copyrighting images even if they were stolen. He also recommended strongly that content management be as automated and flexible as possible, touting the software he developed for his own website. I'm sure that he's making as much money as ever.

Looking Back at Vision

After the decision was made to replace Vision in January 1994, Upstart conducted a search for a replacement application. Analysis was initiated to rewrite Vision into a more conventional data model, but Upstart executives squashed "Vision II" before it ever got off the ground.

The software selection process was a repetition of the original selection process that had occurred two-and-a-half years earlier, which had resulted in the decision to develop Vision. Instead, this time the runner-up, a tried-but-true yet aged application based on Digital VAX-VMS and RMS (instead of Oracle) was selected. It was the complete antithesis of Vision and I was sure that Randy was aware of it.

While the "new" application was being deployed, I had imagined that I would disengage from Upstart and find a new engagement, but a fitting punishment was being devised for me also. Upstart and BigMedia, Inc. arranged to have me manage Vision as its new database administrator until it was retired, even though I had no prior experience as a DBA. Thus, my career swerved into database administration, away from application development, a detour I have yet to correct.

In November 1994, the new application finally went "live" and Vision was decommissioned. During those nine months, I learned hard lessons in 24×7 production support, managing "hot" backups and archived redo log files, managing space in the database as well as file systems and logical volumes, working with Oracle Support and applying patches, and database recovery at 4:00 a.m. I worked 20-hour days, 120-hour weeks, slept under desks to avoid direct lighting, ate the worst that vending machines could offer, and picked up all kinds of other bad habits that persist to this day.

The main lesson that I took away from this fiasco was that sometimes the cleverest people made the most fundamental errors, losing sight of the ultimate goal. The ultimate goal for the Vision system was to create an integrated order-entry and customer-service application to meet the needs of a fast-growing company, not to change the world of IT and usher in a brave new world of programming.

I sometimes wish that I too had heeded Joe's admonition to "RUN LIKE HELL," but at other times I realize that this job really does beat working for a living.

Join the BAARF Party (or Not)

By James Morle and Mogens Nørgaard

As Monty Python would have said: and now for something completely different:

Origins of BAARF

The millenium year of 2000 was used, among other things, by Oracle Marketing to attempt to finish off various international user group events. The plan really was rather simple: Oracle stopped supporting the events such as the Oracle Applications User Group (OAUG), the International Oracle User Group (IOUG), the European Oracle User Group (EOUG), and several others.

One particular harsh treatment fell on the OAUG, when Oracle withdrew all support, and all speakers bar one or two panel participants, two weeks before the event in Honolulu. Take that.

The idea, which the then-CMO of Oracle Mark Jarvis didn't try to hide from anyone, was to create Oracle-directed, marketing-oriented events instead of the more technical, "nerdy" events that the user groups were setting up. (Mark started his career in Oracle Europe, by the way, as a SQL*Net programmer, and did rather well.)

It worked in most places. OAUG, IOUG, EOUG ... they all shrank to just about nothing in the following years. And attendance at Oracle World in the US and Oracle World conferences in Europe and elsewhere soared.

It worked for a while. But then attendance dropped dramatically at Oracle World events, perhaps because most people came there for technical content, and didn't find much. That's when it became possible to attend for free if you just wanted to be in the Exhibition Hall or view Larry's keynote change from criticizing Microsoft to criticizing IBM.

This all led to a revival of the smallish, local user groups. The New York Oracle User Group, the Northern California Oracle User Group, the Rocky Mountain Oracle User Group, and many more, sprang to life and provided the technical information and networking that the true, long-time supporters of Oracle craved.

Mark Jarvis's strategy didn't work at all in the United Kingdom, his own homeland. The UKOUG just kept going as if nothing had ever happened, and Oracle didn't dare question it, and just kept supporting it as if nothing had happened. Stiff upper lip, if ever there was one.

The annual UKOUG conference in Birmingham in November took place as always that year, and as always between 2000 and 3000 attendees came. The speakers were as usual a very impressive bunch, and the contents were as technical as ever.

They are still going very strong.

The UKOUG currently has about 15 full-time employees, runs at least one event per week all year round somewhere in the UK, has numerous Special Interest Groups (SIGs), and a number of directors (not employed or paid) and chairmen to coordinate activities.

Where are we heading with all this? Well, the UKOUG UNIX SIG chairman is currently David Kurtz, who is blessed with a terrific sense of humour and a very sharp and analytical mind.

David started inviting OakTable members to present at his SIG meetings, and thus, suddenly, we—James and Mogens—found ourselves in Birmingham one summer night in 2003, and so we had a beer.

Then we had another beer, and we started talking about yet another episode in the never-ending soap opera of RAID-5 systems. Yet another case of a customer being persuaded to buy something which really wasn't the best thing for him, nor the cheapest.

Mogens suggested, because he had just had lunch with a psychologist friend of his a few days earlier, that we should lower our blood pressure and stop complaining about this RAID-5 nonsense. So we joked for a while about how we should stop telling people the same, old truths that we'd been telling them for fifteen years, and instead tell them that we were not discussing it anymore. Period.

We probably both had one cognac more before we decided to go to bed. That's when James wrote on a piece of paper the four letters B-A-R-F—Battle Against Raid Five. After a few minutes we decided it ought to be B-A-A-R-F—Battle Against Any Raid Five. And then we decided that the F should stand not only for Five, but also for Four and, err, Free. And so the BAARF Party was born, among much laughter. The former Iraqi Information Minister was still fresh in our minds back then, and it was easy to imagine him explaining the virtues of RAID-5 to IT managers. "There is NO write penalty in our system. Lies, and more lies." "Performance of RAID-10 is far worse than RAID-5. I have the proof here in my hand." And so on.

Battle Lines Are Drawn

The following day we asked David Kurtz if we could present the BAARF Party to the SIG, and thus about 100 participants in the UKOUG UNIX SIG meeting that day became the first to know about the party. Both announcers were careful to sport the "Enough is Enough" look (including arms folded across the chest) while delivering the message to about 80 delegates.

The reception was positive. Since then, several people have joined the party, and they can all be viewed on http://www.baarf.com. Membership is free, and one day we will have the BAARF Party convention we always dreamed about. Following is an extract from the text that appeared on the website the next day:

The reason for BAARF is that we've had it. Enough is Enough. For 15 years a lot of the world's best database experts have been arguing back and forth with people (vendors and others) about the pros and cons of RAID-3, -4 and -5.

Cary Millsap has written excellent articles on RAID technologies that should have stopped the use- and pointless discussions many years ago. Many others have written splendid articles about it as well. James Morle and others have written books where they discussed the uselessness of RAID-F stuff.

It has been the same arguments, the same mistakes, the same misunderstandings that have guided the discussions for all those years. The same frustrations from people that knew RAID-F is not a good choice.

The laws of Nature are still solidly in place and are not going to be changed by RAID-F vendors anytime soon.

So we've decided to stop arguing and debating with people about it. We will lower our blood pressure permanently by refusing to have any more arguments about it.

We're done. It's done. Everything has been said. It's time for action—and making up your mind.

You can join BAARF. Or not. You're either in. Or not.

We will of course form the BAARF Party, and we'll arrange various BAARF Party Conventions where we'll proudly display our logo, which says "I'm NOT talking anymore about RAID-5. Join us. Or not."—or something to that effect.

We will collect the usual horror stories about RAID-F stuff and customers being cheated first, and surprised later.

The BAARF party will have its own equivalent of the Iraqi Information Minister to deliver key notes at their conventions.

But no more discussions.

Birmingham, 6th of June, 2003-06-06

James Morle & Mogens Nørgaard

Also on BAARF.com, you can find links to several excellent articles about why RAID-10 is the right choice, including the original RAID paper, which seems to be forgotten by vendors who claim to have revolutionized the RAID-5 concepts. In addition, there are articles by Art S. Kagel (a well-known Informix specialist), Juan Loaiza, along with those mentioned in the preceding text by Cary and James.

Also, you can view a membership list along with quotes from each of the members. And there's the RAID-F simulator which can be run in SQL*Plus, created by

Jesper Haure Nørrevang from the Copenhagen Business School. Finally, anyone can apply for membership by sending an email to us via the "Join BAARF" button. Use of the BAARF logo (created by James) is also welcome.

BAARF. The Musical

For the Miracle Database Forum 2003, we created "BAARF. The musical," heavily inspired by the Queen musical "We Will Rock You." Our old friend Gaja Vahatney-hatneyhatney (who has his own chapter in this book, Chapter 7) played himself as a lost and confused young man who couldn't really believe that RAID-F wasn't the solution to anything.

The songs included "I want to RAID Free," "Raid-IO Gaja," and "We will Frock You," and included 15 or more OakTable members playing air guitar in front of an ecstatic audience. The DVD/CD is available upon request. It lasts almost 42 minutes.

Is the Enemy in Retreat?

Before we turn to the more technical and serious side of this, we would like to ask ourselves this question: Has the creation of the BAARF Party made any difference? Has it had any impact?

No, not at all.

Since we started the BAARF Party, sales of RAID-5 systems have exploded. Most big SAN systems sold today are indeed RAID-5, and they have the performance to prove it ...

We are constantly amazed at the fact that the SAN vendors are able to sell RAID-5 systems MIRRORED ... instead of the much better RAID-10 setups. But it's a fact: RAID-5 (and RAID-4 for Hitachi systems and some IBM Shark systems, for example) sales are higher than ever.

We're also seeing a very interesting trend: the price of these SAN systems can be so high that it is not permitted to criticize or question the performance of them. Really. We have visited sites where we are told that the SAN is NOT the problem, and that we should NOT look for the problem there. Maybe the Oracle Wait Interface shows that IO is the main bottleneck, but that is NOT correct.

It's not just us. Several other OakTable members (we are, after all, talking about the World's best Oracle scientists here) have reported similar work constraints, even if they worked for Oracle. SAN's are now so expensive that they have to be a success. Period.

So the former Iraqi Information Minister might actually have his place in this story. Only he could argue forcefully, and consistently, against the evil forces of RAID-10.

BAARF. The Interview

The Northern California Oracle User Group were kindly pointed towards the BAARF initiative by Gaja, and so we ended up doing an interview about BAARF for the NcOUG magazine. Here's the interview in its entire length, with me asking the questions and James responding:

Q1: James, what is your opinion today, 1st of April 2004, of RAID-5?
My opinion has not changed since I first came across RAID-5 in the early 90s. I think that RAID-5 was devised at a time when disk technology was relatively expensive, and is an interesting concept in CS terms. However, I think that the street logic about where to apply RAID-5 technology is not adequately reflecting the needs of many enterprises.

Q2: Why do you think vendors like IBM (with Shark), HP (EVA), and Hitachi are selling RAID-5 systems as their default, or indeed sometimes as the only, option?
I think this issue highlights the source of much of this erroneous logic. Ultimately, this is a sales-led option, not a requirements-led option. The whole storage industry seems to have become obsessed with dollars-per-GB metric, effectively ignoring the IOs-per-second metric.

This is the equivalent of expanding all the highways to 50 lanes and ignoring the issue of how cars get on and off the road. The highway can now hold many more cars, but getting them on and off takes the same amount of time. In driving down the $/GB, the vendors have been forced to line up behind RAID-5 as the only way to keep the price down.

Q3: Has the price of disks actually fallen? If yes, then why does RAID-1+0 or -0+1 end up looking more expensive than a RAID-5 solution?
First of all, let's stop even referring to 0+1. It is a solution that requires the same hardware as 1+0, at the same cost, but has a significantly worse failure profile. The performance is comparable between them, so why should we even think about using 0+1?

Now that's off my chest, we can return to the original question. Yes, the price of disks has fallen, both in terms of $/GB AND the unit price (and thus the $/IO). This statement includes ATA drives AND SCSI and Fibre Channel drives. In fact, the differential between the consumer ATA format and the "Pro" SCSI and FC drives is now in the region of 2-3:1, a big improvement over previous years.

RAID-1+0 will always be more expensive compared to RAID-5, when comparing simple storage capacity. RAID-1+0 requires twice as much physical storage as logically required, whereas RAID-5 requires only one additional drive to cater for the storage of the parity information (but the actual location of the parity is distributed among all the drives).

Therefore RAID-5 actually looks even more attractive if you implement very wide ranks of RAID-5. Nothing in life is free, however, and the write penalty and failure landscape deteriorate in direct proportion to the number of disks in the RAID-5 rank.

Q4: Do you also (like me) see mirrored RAID-5 systems being sold? What is the logic behind this?

The logic is simple. RAID-5 is not as resilient as RAID-1+0, and the mirroring is there to protect against the failures. Of course, the cost of doing this takes mirrored RAID-5 beyond that of RAID-1+0, and the write penalty remains. The mirroring protects against running in degraded mode when a failure occurs, and provides protection against a secondary failure.

Q5: Has the famous RAID-5 write penalty for small writes (traditionally 4 IO's versus 1 for non-RAID-5 systems) been improved as claimed by some storage vendors?

No, not from my observations. The logic used by the vendors is that the cache provides enough buffering of these small writes to allow the physical writes to occur as "full-stripe writes." Full-stripe writes should not occur the write penalty, because the whole stripe can be written without being preceded by the reads required to recalculate the parity information.

In actual fact, I can think of at least one situation where the cache could make the writes worse, instead of better. Consider the case where a small write is issued to a RAID-5 array. This write must be cached to avoid the write penalty, but depending on how the cache is implemented, this could result in many reads being issued just in order to refresh the cache lines for each device. If there are seven drives in the array, this could equate to 7×32KB reads in order to satisfy a 4KB write. This is not for reasons of parity calculation, but rather for reasons of cache coherency. The parity must then be calculated for this larger quantity of data!

In the case of small sequential writes, this overhead does not lead to a great deal of additional reads for cache coherency, as the cache information can be reused by subsequent writes. For scattered writes, there is a good chance each one will require this full set of larger reads each time.

Finally, this raises a good point about write cache efficiency. If many cache lines of a minimum size are needed to be retained to satisfy a single write, this means that the cache size needs to be relatively that much larger in order to provide the same benefit as RAID-1+0.

Q6: In my mind, I see a cache being good at handling spikes and handling repetitions. Are there other reasons for having cache? Repetitions mean waste, don't they? If yes, are spikes then the only reason for having cache?

There are two reasons for maintaining a cache, whether it is in a SAN or anywhere else: reading and writing. The two cases are different. In the write case, nonvolatile cache is an effective way to handle spikes, and to combine small writes into more efficient larger writes.

Like any kind of buffering, it is ultimately providing a time-based protection against waiting for the physical device. If the underlying disk can only deliver 50MB per second, and you are writing at a sustained rate of 100MB per second, your cache will simply fill, slowing the system down to the physical disk speed once more.

In the case of reads, cache is not providing much protection against spikes, mostly providing repetition benefit. I have fairly strong opinions in this area when using a SAN in conjunction with an enterprise database (such as Oracle) over the top.

Due to the fact that Oracle, for example, is already operating an MRU-based cache before the I/Os are sent to the SAN, the physical I/Os that are eventually requested after a miss in the Oracle cache are almost devoid of any easily cached pattern.

This white-noise of I/O requests makes it very difficult for the SAN cache to pick up any kind of spatial locality of reference, leaving mostly just the temporal locality hits based upon the cycling time of the Oracle cache.

For this cache to be effective, it needs to be orders of magnitude larger than the Oracle cache would need to be for the same effect! This phenomena is very well documented in CS circles as the impact of a multi-stage hierarchical cache. It's the reason why the L1 cache of a CPU is small (like 16KB), and L2 and L3 caches are in the region of megabytes. It's also the reason that the cache in your SAN is many gigabytes before it is very effective.

Q7: Have you been able to persuade customers to switch from an installed RAID-5 system to a RAID-1+0 or -0+1? If yes: And what arguments did you use? Did the solution become more expensive?

Most of the time, this is only possible as part of an initial implementation, or a platform migration. It is normally relatively easy to persuade customers of the negative aspects of RAID-5 if they are already running that solution!

My arguments normally start from the basis of theory, but very quickly turn into scientific tests that return real data. In real terms, when the number of I/O's per second AND the storage requirements are taken into account, RAID-1+0 need not be a great deal more expensive than RAID-5.

When the write throughput is taken into account, RAID-1+0 can very quickly become a cheaper solution than RAID-5! And when the costs to the business are taken into account for the failure scenarios, RAID-5 has real problems looking like the best solution.

Q8: How many reads can you perform with a RAID-1+0 or -0+1 system with, say, four mirrored disks (total of eight disks) that can each handle, say, 100 IO's per second—400 or 800 or somewhere in between? And how many writes?

The theoretical read rate of this array is 800 reads per second. The reality is that it could be a greater or lesser number than this, depending upon the actual read requests issued. For example, using the preferential read policies found in most RAID-1 implementations, the number of seeks could be substantially reduced, thus increasing the number of I/O's per second the array can support way beyond the nominal 100 quoted.

Writes are a different story, because the writes must go to the same location on both drives. The number in this case is close to 400, depending on the implementation.

Q9: Has anything regarding RAID technology changed since you wrote your book *Scaling Oracle8i,* perhaps even to the point where you'd like to rewrite or add to the 20 pages on storage systems?

Not really from the technology perspective. I have been consulting with a wide spectrum of clients since the publication of the book, however, and I think there would be a slightly different spin if I were to rework this chapter. I tried to write that chapter in an objective, mostly non-opinionated way; I think I would approach it in a more strongly opinionated way on a second run.

This reflects the thought process behind BAARF—I think the message needs to get out there so that people stop making the same mistakes over and over again!

Q10: Do you have a SAN yourself in your home office?

There are many valid reasons for choosing RAID-5, but not very many for a busy production database! For example, it might be very valid to use RAID-5 for file storage, near-line storage, or archiving. It might also make sense to use RAID-5 for smaller databases that are not used aggressively, where the cache in the RAID device has a good chance of helping.

A traditional argument for using RAID-5 is for read-mostly tablespaces, but I dispute this in most cases, as I will explain. With a read-mostly tablespace, or even a read-only tablespace in a data warehouse, it is very tempting to create very wide RAID-5 arrays (in other words, many component disks), and to put the data on those. The logic is that this data will only be read, and much space is required, so a least-loss redundancy that provides good striped read performance is perfect. To counter this, it is important to determine whether or not this data is in any way performance critical. The reason for this is in a failure scenario, where one of the component drives of the RAID-5 array has failed and the array is running in the infamous "degraded mode." In this mode, the data that resided on the failed drive must be reconstructed by reading ALL the other drives in the array in order to compute the missing values. It should be fairly self-evident that this will significantly slow down the reads and writes to this array while operating in this state. The array will remain in this state until the drive is replaced and a full rebuild is completed, slowing down the performance of the array even more significantly. When this is combined with the statistically higher chance of a drive failure when more drives make up the array, it makes a fairly powerful argument against this type of deployment, even in data warehouse environments.

Q11: It seems that the total price of a SAN is much, much, much bigger than the price of the disks put into it. Are there any SAN/NAS solutions available that actually reflect e.g. the very low price of ATA disks?

The problem is that the cost of entry of these systems is very high, and once all the cache memory is applied, there is very little left in the pot for the drives. The sales pitch will assert that the cache will save your life—don't EVER believe this philosophy.

For a scientific life of certainty, configure the SAN from the disks upwards, leaving the cache spend until last ... ATA disk solutions are starting to get to market, and can represent good value for money. However, they are not generally aligned with performance systems, rather with high-capacity near-line storage.

Subsequently, they often contain relatively slow (sometimes 5400 rpm), high-density drives, such as 250GB drives. I am hoping that once Serial Attached SCSI becomes a reality, with the flexibility this affords of using SATA or SAS drives, the price of storage systems could drop significantly depending on the configuration.

Q12: Is it true that ATA disks are both cheap, good, and can be part of a SAN? If yes, why are they cheap and good at the same time?

Parallel ATA is not very suited to a SAN, because of both electrical and implementation deficiencies. The Serial ATA (SATA) technology addresses most of these deficiencies, and could provide a strong solution. Also, ATA drives have historically not been manufactured to the tolerances and life-cycle requirements of SCSI or FC drives, thus making them theoretically less reliable.

Again, this is a trend that has now started to change, in the most part because of blade servers adopting ATA technology.

Q13: Do you have a SAN yourself in your home office?

Err, yes. It is part of my three (soon to be four to five) node RAC cluster ...

Ed: Don't listen to these guys. RAID-F isn't all bad you know. It's pretty good, really, if your look at it in the right way.

Index

forums.apress.com

FOR PROFESSIONALS BY PROFESSIONALS™

JOIN THE APRESS FORUMS AND BE PART OF OUR COMMUNITY. You'll find discussions that cover topics of interest to IT professionals, programmers, and enthusiasts just like you. If you post a query to one of our forums, you can expect that some of the best minds in the business—especially Apress authors, who all write with *The Expert's Voice*™—will chime in to help you. Why not aim to become one of our most valuable participants (MVPs) and win cool stuff? Here's a sampling of what you'll find:

DATABASES

Data drives everything.

Share information, exchange ideas, and discuss any database programming or administration issues.

PROGRAMMING/BUSINESS

Unfortunately, it is.

Talk about the Apress line of books that cover software methodology, best practices, and how programmers interact with the "suits."

INTERNET TECHNOLOGIES AND NETWORKING

Try living without plumbing (and eventually IPv6).

Talk about networking topics including protocols, design, administration, wireless, wired, storage, backup, certifications, trends, and new technologies.

WEB DEVELOPMENT/DESIGN

Ugly doesn't cut it anymore, and CGI is absurd.

Help is in sight for your site. Find design solutions for your projects and get ideas for building an interactive Web site.

JAVA

We've come a long way from the old Oak tree.

Hang out and discuss Java in whatever flavor you choose: J2SE, J2EE, J2ME, Jakarta, and so on.

SECURITY

Lots of bad guys out there—the good guys need help.

Discuss computer and network security issues here. Just don't let anyone else know the answers!

MAC OS X

All about the Zen of OS X.

OS X is both the present and the future for Mac apps. Make suggestions, offer up ideas, or boast about your new hardware.

TECHNOLOGY IN ACTION

Cool things. Fun things.

It's after hours. It's time to play. Whether you're into LEGO® MINDSTORMS™ or turning an old PC into a DVR, this is where technology turns into fun.

OPEN SOURCE

Source code is good; understanding (open) source is better.

Discuss open source technologies and related topics such as PHP, MySQL, Linux, Perl, Apache, Python, and more.

WINDOWS

No defenestration here.

Ask questions about all aspects of Windows programming, get help on Microsoft technologies covered in Apress books, or provide feedback on any Apress Windows book.

HOW TO PARTICIPATE:

Go to the Apress Forums site at **http://forums.apress.com/**.

Click the New User link.